Seventh Edition

I Never K

Exploration

DATE DUE

Res Fall 02	1		
Res Winter 03	8		
Res Spr 03	0		
Res Summer 03	0		
ILL UFO			
9455008			
10/26/03			
ILL GTA 3782465			
4/30/04			
JAN 07 05			
MAY 24 06			

DEMCO 38-297

Seventh Edition

I Never Knew I Had a Choice
Explorations in Personal Growth

GERALD COREY
California State University, Fullerton
Diplomate in Counseling Psychology,
American Board of Professional Psychology

MARIANNE SCHNEIDER COREY
Private Practice/Consultant

BROOKS/COLE

™
THOMSON LEARNING

Australia • Canada • Mexico • Singapore • Spain • United Kingdom • United States

Sponsoring Editor: *Julie Martinez*
Editorial Assistant: *Cat Broz*
Marketing: *Caroline Concilla/Megan Hansen*
Developmental Editor: *Sherry Symington*
Project Editor: *Tessa Avila*
Production Service: *The Cooper Company*
Manuscript Editor: *Kay Mikel*
Permissions Editor: *Lillian Campobasso*
Photograph credits are on page 476.

Interior and Cover Design: *Delgado Design*
Cover Photo: *Masterfile*
Photo Researcher: *Judy Mason*
Indexer: *Rosemary Kane*
Print Buyer: *Vena Dyer*
Typesetting: *ColorType, San Diego*
Cover Printing: *Phoenix Color Corp.*
Printing and Binding: *R. R. Donnelley/Crawfordsville*

For more information about this or any other Brooks/Cole product, contact:
BROOKS/COLE
511 Forest Lodge Road
Pacific Grove, CA 93950 USA
www.brookscole.com
1-800-423-0563 (Thomson Learning Academic Resource Center)

Printed in the United States of America

10   9   8   7   6   5   4   3   2   1

Library of Congress Cataloging-in-Publication Data

Corey, Gerald.
    I never knew I had a choice: explorations in personal growth / Gerald Corey, Marianne
    Schneider Corey.—7th ed.
        p.   cm.
    Includes bibliographical references and index.
    ISBN 0-534-34790-8
    1. Self-perception. 2. Choice (Psychology) I. Corey, Marianne Schneider.
    Title.
    BF697.5.S43 C67 2001
    158—dc21

                                                        00-046845

In memory of our friend Jim Morelock,
a searcher who lived and died with dignity and
self-respect, who struggled and questioned,
who made the choice to live his days fully
until time ran out on him at age 25.

ABOUT THE AUTHORS

 **GERALD COREY** is Professor Emeritus of Human Services at California State University at Fullerton and also Adjunct Professor in the Counseling and Family Sciences Department at Loma Linda University. He teaches both undergraduate and graduate courses in group counseling, as well as courses in experiential and therapeutic groups, the theory and practice of counseling, and ethics in counseling practice. He received his doctorate in counseling from the University of Southern California. He is a California licensed psychologist; a Diplomate in Counseling Psychology, American Board of Professional Psychology; a National Certified Counselor; a Fellow of the American Psychological Association (Counseling Psychology); a member of the Western Psychological Association; and a Fellow of the Association for Specialists in Group Work.

Jerry received the Outstanding Professor of the Year Award from California State University at Fullerton in 1991. With his colleagues he has conducted workshops in the United States, Germany, Ireland, Belgium, Scotland, Mexico, and China, with a special focus on training in group counseling. He often presents workshops for professional organizations, special intensive courses at various universities, and residential training and supervision workshops for group leaders. In his leisure time, Jerry likes to travel, hike, and bicycle in the mountains and drive his 1931 Model A Ford.

Recent publications by Jerry Corey, all with Brooks/Cole, include:

> *Theory and Practice of Counseling and Psychotherapy,* Sixth Edition (and *Manual*) (2001)

> *Case Approach to Counseling and Psychotherapy,* Fifth Edition (2001)

> *The Art of Integrative Counseling* (2001)

> *Theory and Practice of Group Counseling,* Fifth Edition (and *Manual*) (2000)

Jerry is coauthor, with his daughters Cindy Corey and Heidi Jo Corey, of an orientation-to-college book entitled *Living and Learning* (1997), published by Wadsworth. He is also coauthor (with Barbara Herlihy) of *Boundary Issues in Counseling: Multiple Roles and Responsibilities* (1997) and *ACA Ethical Standards Casebook,* Fifth Edition (1996), both published by the American Counseling Association.

He has also made three videos on various aspects of counseling practice: (1) *Student Video and Workbook for the Art of Integrative Counseling* (2001, with Robert Haynes); (2) *The Evolution of a Group: Student Video and Workbook* (2000, with Marianne Schneider Corey and Robert Haynes); and (3) *Ethics in Action: Student Video and Workbook* (1998, with Marianne Schneider Corey and Robert Haynes). All of these student videos and workbooks are available through Brooks/Cole.

 **MARIANNE SCHNEIDER COREY** is a licensed marriage and family therapist in California and is a National Certified Counselor. She received her master's degree in marriage, family, and child counseling from Chapman College. She is a Fellow of the Association for Specialists in Group Work and a clinical member of the American Association for Marriage and Family Therapy. She also holds memberships in the California Association of Marriage and Family Therapists, the American Counseling Association, the Association for Spiritual, Ethical, and Religious Values in Counseling, the Association for Counselor Education and Supervision (both national and regional), the Western Psychological Association, and the Association for Specialists in Group Work.

Marianne has been actively involved in leading groups for different populations, providing training and supervision workshops in group process, facilitating self-exploration groups for graduate students in counseling, and cofacilitating training groups for group counselors and weeklong residential workshops in personal growth. She sees groups as the most effective format in which to work with clients and finds it the most rewarding for her personally. With her husband, Jerry, Marianne has conducted training workshops, continuing-education seminars, and personal-growth groups in Germany, Ireland, Belgium, Mexico, and China, as well as regularly doing these workshops in the United States. In her free time Marianne enjoys traveling, reading, visiting with friends, and hiking.

Marianne and Jerry have been married since 1964. They have two adult daughters, Heidi and Cindy. Marianne grew up in Germany and has kept in close contact with her family there.

Coauthored books by Marianne Schneider Corey and Jerry Corey include:

> *Groups: Process and Practice,* Sixth Edition (2002)

> *Becoming a Helper,* Third Edition (1998)

> *Issues and Ethics in the Helping Professions,* Fifth Edition (1998, with Patrick Callanan)

> *Group Techniques,* Second Edition (1992, with Patrick Callanan and J. Michael Russell)

Preface

I Never Knew I Had a Choice is intended for college students of any age and for all others who wish to expand their self-awareness and explore the choices available to them in significant areas of their lives. It is also used by counselors in private practice settings and in public and private mental health organizations for workshops and groups. The topics discussed include choosing a personal style of learning; reviewing childhood and adolescence and the effects of these experiences on current behavior and choices; meeting the challenges of adulthood and autonomy; maintaining a healthy body and wellness; managing stress; appreciating the significance of love, intimate relationships, gender roles and sexuality; work and recreation; dealing creatively with loneliness and solitude; understanding and accepting death and loss; choosing one's values and meaning in life; and pathways to growth.

This is a personal book because we encourage readers to examine the choices they have made and how these choices affect their present level of satisfaction. It is also a personal book in another sense, inasmuch as we describe our own concerns, struggles, decisions, and values with regard to many of the issues we raise. Each chapter begins with a self-inventory (Where Am I Now?) that gives readers the opportunity to focus on their present beliefs and attitudes. Within the chapters, Take Time to Reflect exercises offer an opportunity to pause and reflect on the issues raised. Additional activities and exercises (Where Can I Go From Here?) are suggested at the end of each chapter for use in the classroom or outside of class. We wish to stress that this is an unfinished book; readers are encouraged to become coauthors by writing about their personal reactions in the book and in their journals.

Although the themes underlying the book are basically the same, whenever possible we have updated material to reflect current thinking. The introductory chapter continues to emphasize the importance of self-exploration and invites students to consider the values and excitement, as well as the commitment and work, involved in learning about oneself, others, and personal growth. Social concerns must balance self-interests, however, and although we still emphasize self-actualization, we also maintain that self-fulfillment can occur only if individuals have a sense of social consciousness. To improve the book and to keep current with developments in the field, we have added new topics, expanded and revised current topics, curtailed discussion of certain topics, and updated the references.

In Chapter 1 we have added a detailed description of Maya Angelou, a well-known writer and poet, as an example of a self-actualizing person. New also is a discussion of the concept of emotional intelligence and its implications for learning styles. We have also expanded the discussion of active learning and creating personal goals for college, and streamlined the discussion of how to get the most from this book and the course.

We made some major alterations in Chapter 2 in the treatment of development during childhood and adolescence. We dropped the Freudian perspective of development, retained Erikson's psychosocial model, and added the self-in-context theories as they deal with development throughout the life span. There is a new section on pubescence and an updated section on adolescence, with a greater emphasis on connections with others and interdependence.

In Chapter 3 we continue the discussion of the life-span perspective by focusing on the psychosocial theory and the self-in-context perspective. Our treatment of autonomy has been broadened to include self-in-relation and self-in-context. The stages of adulthood have been revised to reflect individual variation at each of these stages, and there is new material on emerging adulthood, late middle age, and the aging process.

Chapter 4 has been streamlined to focus on body image and wellness. We have updated the coverage on wellness and life choices and made some minor changes in the section dealing with bodily identity. There is new material on maintaining sound health practices, spirituality as a key factor in health and wellness, a holistic approach to health, and diet and developing sensible eating habits.

Chapter 5 examines the impact of stress on the body, causes of stress, destructive and constructive reactions to stress, and stress and the healthy personality. This chapter now contains expanded discussions of meditation, yoga, mindfulness, deep relaxation, massage therapy, time management, and money management.

Chapter 6 deals with the many facets of love and the meaning of love, and Chapter 7 contains guidelines for meaningful interpersonal relationships, including friendships, couple relationships (including gay and lesbian relationships), and family relationships. There is a new section on recognizing and dealing effectively with anger and conflict in relationships and a discussion of the role of forgiveness in relationships.

Although the organization of topics in Chapter 8 is much the same as in the previous edition, there has been considerable updating. This chapter continues with a developmental theme but focuses on how life experiences influence beliefs about gender identity. There is new material on current trends in the psychology of women and men, gender role strain, and life cycle roles.

Chapter 9 contains an updated section on the HIV/AIDS crisis and its effects on sexual behavior along with practical guidelines to reduce the risks of infection. There is an expanded section on sexual abuse and harassment, and incest, date and acquaintance rape, and sexual harassment on the campus and in the workplace are also discussed.

Chapter 10 benefits from some of the newer sources on the role of work and recreation in our lives and contains updated discussion of key topics.

Chapter 11 discusses the creative dimensions of solitude, with a revised and expanded section on shyness. There is also new material on loneliness.

Chapter 12 deals with fears of death, the interdependence of life and death, the importance of grieving, and suicide. The expanded discussion of suicide includes more of the myths and misconceptions surrounding suicide along with coverage on physician-assisted suicide. The information on hospice, grief work, and the stages of dying has also been updated.

The meaning of life is the central subject of Chapter 13, and the section on diversity has been expanded.

Chapter 14, which is new to this edition, encourages students to think about where they will choose to go from here. Readers are reminded that their journey toward personal growth is only beginning. This chapter offers a variety of avenues for growth that readers may wish to pursue now and in the future. Included in this chapter are new discussions of counseling as a pathway to growth and understanding the meaning of one's dreams.

Fundamentally, our approach in *I Never Knew I Had a Choice* is humanistic and personal; that is, we stress the healthy and effective personality and the common struggles most of us experience in becoming autonomous. We especially emphasize accepting personal responsibility for the choices we make and consciously deciding whether and how we want to change our lives.

Although our own approach can be broadly characterized as humanistic and existential, our aim has been to challenge readers to recognize and assess their own choices, beliefs, and values rather than to convert them to a particular point of view. Our basic premise is that a commitment to self-exploration can create new potentials for choice. Many of the college students and counseling clients with whom we work are relatively well-functioning people who desire more from life and who want to recognize and remove blocks to their personal creativity and freedom. Most of them are looking for a practical course, one that deals with real issues in everyday living and that will provide an impetus for their own personal growth. It is for people like these that we have written this book.

The experiences of those who have read and used the earlier editions of *I Never Knew I Had a Choice* reveal that the themes explored have application to a diversity of ages and backgrounds. Readers who have taken the time to write us about their reactions say that the book encouraged them to take an honest look at their lives and challenge themselves to make certain changes. Many readers who have used this book for a college course have told us that they have shared it with friends and relatives.

I Never Knew I Had a Choice was developed for a variety of self-exploration courses, including Introduction to Counseling, Therapeutic Group, Psychology of Personal Growth, Personal Development, Personal Growth and Development, Personality and Adjustment, Introduction to Human Behavior, Life Processes, Personal and Interpersonal Effectiveness, Character and Conflict, Values of the

Helping Professions, Human Potential Seminar, Psychology of Personal Well-Being and Adjustment, and Applied Psychology. *Choice* has also been adopted in courses ranging from the psychology of personal growth on the undergraduate level to graduate courses for training teachers and counselors. It is also used in group counseling courses as a catalyst for small group interaction and for workshops in training group leaders. Courses that make use of an interactive approach will find *Choice* a useful tool for discussion.

We have written this book to facilitate interaction—between student and instructor, among the students within a class, between students and significant people in their lives, between the reader and us as authors—but most important of all, our aim is to provide the reader with an avenue for reflection. This is not a book that can be read passively; it is designed to provoke thoughtful reflection. Readers are encouraged to look at the direction of their lives to see if they like where they are heading. Our experience has been that active, open, and personal participation in these courses can lead to expanded self-awareness and greater autonomy in living.

An updated and expanded *Instructor's Resource Manual* accompanies this textbook. It includes about 40 test items, both multiple-choice and essay, for each chapter; a student study guide covering all chapters; suggested reading; questions for thought and discussion; numerous activities and exercises for classroom participation; guidelines for using the book and teaching the course; examples of various formats of personal-growth classes; guidelines for maximizing personal learning and for reviewing and integrating the course; transparency masters; additional Web sites and InfoTrac suggestions; and a student evaluation instrument to assess the impact of the course on readers.

Acknowledgments

We would like to express our deep appreciation for the insightful suggestions given to us by friends, associates, reviewers, students, and readers. The following people, many of whom had used *I Never Knew I Had a Choice* in earlier editions, reviewed the entire manuscript and provided useful suggestions that were incorporated into this edition: Eva Glahn-Atkinson of Brescia University, Owensboro, Kentucky; Howard Ingle of Salt Lake Community College, Utah; John Johnson of Pennsylvania State University, DuBois, Pennsylvania; Patrick Johnson of Montana State University, Bozeman, Montana; Richard Kandus of Mt. San Jacinto College, San Jacinto, California; Zelda Powell-Spalding of Jefferson Community College, Louisville, Kentucky.

The following people reviewed selected chapters: Randy Alle-Corliss of California State University at Fullerton (Chapter 8); Carolyn Zerbe Enns of Cornell College (Chapters 2, 3, and 8); Robert Lock of Jackson Community College (Chapter 10); Barbara McDowell of California State University at Fullerton (Chapter 8); Michael Moulton of Northwestern State University (Chapter 9); Phillip Rice of Minnesota State University, Moorhead, Minnesota (Chapters 4 and 5); and David Shepard, California State University at Fullerton (Chapter 8).

We appreciate our student reviewers from California State University at Fullerton who provided insightful comments and constructive suggestions: Jamie Bludworth, Patti Gantz, Mimi Lawson, and John Perry. Special thanks are extended to our students who contributed personal stories for this edition.

We want to recognize the following people who offered ideas for revision of this edition: Patrick Callanan, Cindy Corey, J. Michael Russell, and Veronika Tracy-Smith. We also appreciate the photographs and art suggestions contributed by Heidi Jo Corey.

Finally, as is true of all our books, *I Never Knew I Had a Choice* continues to develop as a result of a team effort, which includes the combined talents of a number of people. Special recognition is due to those individuals with whom we worked closely on the production of this book. These people include Julie Martinez, editor of counseling and human services, who works closely with us on all our projects; Tessa Avila, the production manager on the project; Cecile Joyner, the production editor; and Kay Mikel, the manuscript editor, whose insight and creative editorial skills kept this book reader-friendly. Recognition goes to those who worked on the appearance of this book: Lisa Delgado, the designer, and Judy Mason, the photo researcher. We are grateful to all of these people who continue to devote extra time and effort to ensure the quality of our books. Our thanks go to John Perry for his work on compiling a list of Web site links and InfoTrac key words that appear at the end of each chapter, and we appreciate Rosemary Matuz Kane's work in compiling the index.

Gerald Corey
Marianne Schneider Corey

Contents

CHAPTER 4   YOUR BODY AND WELLNESS   117

CHAPTER 5   MANAGING STRESS   151

CHAPTER 6   LOVE   187

CHAPTER 7   RELATIONSHIPS   213

CHAPTER 8   BECOMING THE WOMAN OR MAN YOU WANT TO BE   253

CHAPTER 9   SEXUALITY   283

CHAPTER 10 WORK AND RECREATION 323

CHAPTER 11 LONELINESS AND SOLITUDE 363

CHAPTER 12 DEATH AND LOSS 389

CHAPTER 13   MEANING AND VALUES   423

CHAPTER 14   PATHWAYS TO PERSONAL GROWTH   451

Seventh Edition

I Never Knew I Had a Choice
Explorations in Personal Growth

The unexamined life is
not worth living—*Socrates*

Galen Rowell/Corbis

INVITATION TO PERSONAL LEARNING AND GROWTH

Each chapter begins with a self-inventory designed to assess your attitudes and beliefs regarding a particular topic. Think carefully about each question. By answering these questions as honestly as you can, you will increase your awareness and clarify your personal views on a range of subjects.

Use this scale to respond to these statements:

4 = This statement is true of me *most* of the time.

3 = This statement is true of me *much* of the time.

2 = This statement is true of me *some* of the time.

1 = This statement is true of me *almost none* of the time.

_____ 1. I believe I can influence the course of my life through my choices.

_____ 2. I have a good sense of the areas in my life that I can change and those aspects that I cannot change.

_____ 3. Generally, I have been willing to pay the price for taking personal risks involved in choosing for myself.

_____ 4. It is within my power to change even if others around me do not change.

_____ 5. Happiness and success are largely related to a sense of belonging and to social connectedness.

_____ 6. Our present personality is determined both by who and what we have been and by the person we hope to become.

_____ 7. At their deepest core people are good and can be trusted to move forward in a positive way.

_____ 8. I am an active learner.

> ## Where Am I Now? *(continued)*

_____ 9. I am looking forward to getting fully involved in this course.

_____ 10. I am willing to challenge myself to examine my life in an honest way.

Here are a few suggestions for using this self-inventory:

- Retake the inventory after reading the chapter and again at the end of the course and compare your answers.

- Have someone who knows you well take the inventory for you, giving the responses he or she thinks actually describe you. Discuss any discrepancies between your sets of responses.

- Compare your responses with those of other class members and discuss the similarities and differences between your attitudes and theirs.

If you are interested in examining your life and living by choice, this book is for you. Is your life fully satisfying? If not, you may want to learn more about yourself. You may decide to make some changes. Some of you may feel powerless right now and think that external circumstances prevent you from making any real change. You may say: "If my parents weren't so critical of me, I'd feel much better." "When my partner becomes more affectionate toward me, I'll feel worthwhile." "I'd like to say what I feel, but I'm afraid I'll lose my friends if I do." "I know I'm shy, but it's too late for me to change. I've been this way since I was a kid." "I would be fine if the people around me were different." It is true that you cannot change others, but you are a powerful person—you can examine your own life and choose another path.

CHOICE AND CHANGE

We Do Have Choices!

It is exciting for us when our students and clients discover that they can be in charge of their own lives to a greater degree than they ever dreamed possible. As one counseling client put it: "One thing I can see now that I didn't see before is that I can change my life if I want to. *I never knew I had a choice!*" This remark captures the central message of this book: We can make choices, and we do have the power to reinvent ourselves through our choices. Are you living the way you want to live? If not, what is keeping you from doing so? This book will teach you how to become proactive rather than reactive.

Reflect on the quality of your life and decide for yourself how you want to change. We encourage you to challenge your fears rather than being stopped by them. Socrates, in his wisdom, said, "The unexamined life is not worth living." Examine your values and your behavior. Recall a crisis you have faced in your life. Did that crisis represent a significant turning point for you? The Chinese symbol for crisis represents both *danger* and *opportunity*. As you engage yourself in this book, consider ways to use critical life situations as opportunities for personal growth.

Are You Ready to Change?

Deciding to change is not a simple matter. You may wonder if you need to change or if it is worth the price to change. You may have entertained some of these thoughts when you contemplated making a change in your life.

> I don't know if I want to rock the boat.
> Things aren't all that bad in my life.
> I'm fairly secure, and I don't want to take the chance of losing this security.
> I'm afraid that if I start probing around I may uncover things that will be tough for me to handle.

It is not a sign of cowardice to have doubts and fears about making changes. In fact, it is a mark of courage to acknowledge your resistance to change and your anxiety over taking increased control of your life.

It is a challenge and a struggle to take an honest look at your life and begin to live differently. Those who are close to you may not approve of or like your changes, and they may put up barriers to your designing a new life. Your cultural background may make it more difficult for you to assume a new role and to modify certain values. These factors are likely to increase your anxiety as you contemplate making your own choices rather than allowing others to choose for you.

If you desire change in a certain area of your life, what is the best way to bring about this change? The process of change begins when you are able to recognize and accept a certain side of yourself, even though you may have a tendency to want to deny a given characteristic. Sometimes it is not possible to make a desired change, but even in these cases you have a great deal of choice about the way you perceive and interpret your situation. The Serenity Prayer* outlines the sphere of our responsibility: "God, grant me the serenity to accept the things I cannot change, courage to change the things I can, and wisdom to

---

*Attributed to Friedrich Oetinger (1702–1782) and Reinhold Niebuhr, "The Serenity Prayer" (1934).

know the difference." Even in those circumstances that you cannot change, you do have power over your attitude.

The paradoxical theory of change holds that personal change tends to occur when we become aware of *what we are* as opposed to trying to become *what we are not* (Beisser, 1970). The more we attempt to deny some aspect of our being, the more we remain the same. Thus, if you desire change in some area of your personal life, you must first accept who and what you are rather than striving to become what you "should be." Recognizing who you are at the present time is the starting point for the path you might take.

Change is not facilitated by beating yourself or guilting yourself over all that you are not. Change occurs when you are able to view yourself as you are and treat yourself kindly. Once you are able to identify certain disowned parts of yourself, these facets of your self will have less power in your life, and you open yourself to rich possibilities for changing. Take small steps in the direction you want to move. It may help to remember that perfection is a direction—not a goal that you arrive at once and for all. Wanting to be different is the beginning of a new direction.

Self-exploration, being honest with yourself and others, thinking for yourself, and making a commitment to live by your choices require diligent effort. Taking charge of your life exacts a price. A degree of discomfort and even fear are associated with discovering more about yourself. Ask yourself if you are willing to pay the price in choosing for yourself. Change is a proactive process, and only you can decide what you are willing to risk and how much change is right for you.

What About Other People?

Making choices for yourself and being in control of your life is important, but you cannot ignore the reality that you are a social being and that many of your decisions will be influenced by your relationships with significant people in your life. Philip Hwang (2000) asserts that happiness entails possessing a healthy balance of both *self-esteem* and *other-esteem.* Rather than searching for ways to enhance self-esteem, Hwang makes a strong case for promoting personal and social responsibility. *Other-esteem* involves respect, acceptance, caring, valuing, and promoting others, without reservation. We need to strive to understand others who may think, feel, and act differently from us. American culture stresses the self, independence, and self-sufficiency. Hwang suggests that our challenge is to learn to see the world anew by reexamining our attitudes, values, and beliefs and developing a balance of caring for self and yet at the same time showing high esteem for others.

The authors of *Habits of the Heart* assert that the goal of most Americans is to "become one's own person, almost to give birth to oneself" (Bellah, Madsen, Sullivan, Swidler, & Tipton, 1985, p. 84). But in their many interviews they also found as a common theme the notion that the good life cannot be lived alone, that we do not find ourselves in isolation, and that connectedness to others in love, work, and community is absolutely essential to our self-esteem and happiness.

> WE FIND OURSELVES not independently of other people and institutions but through them. We never get to the bottom of ourselves on our own. We discover who we are face to face and side by side with others in work, love, and learning. (p. 84)

Making a commitment to examine your life does not mean becoming wrapped up in yourself to the exclusion of everyone else. Unless you know and care about yourself, however, you will not be able to develop caring relationships with others.

A MODEL FOR PERSONAL GROWTH

One of the obvious benefits of choosing to change your life is that you will grow by exposing yourself to new experiences. But just what does personal growth entail? In this section we contrast the idea of growth with that of adjustment and offer a humanistic model of what ideal growth can be. We also deal with divergent perspectives on what constitutes the ideal standard of personal growth.

Adjustment or Growth?

Although this book deals with topics in what is often called "the psychology of adjustment," we have an uneasy feeling about this common phrase. The term *adjustment* is frequently taken to mean that some ideal norm exists by which people should be measured. This notion raises many questions: What is the desired norm of adjustment? Who determines the standards of "good" adjustment? Is it possible that the same person could be considered well adjusted in our culture and poorly adjusted in some other culture? Do we expect people who live in chaotic and destructive worlds to adjust to their life situations?

One reason we resist "adjustment" as a goal of human behavior is that those who claim to be well adjusted have often settled for a complacent existence, with neither challenge nor excitement. Within the limits imposed by genetic and environmental factors, we have many possibilities for creating our own definitions of ourselves as persons. No single standard of measurement exists for identifying universal qualities of the well-adjusted or psychologically healthy person. The concept of adjustment cannot be understood apart from the person-in-the-environment, for cultural values and norms play a crucial role. For example, if you are in your 20s and still live with your parents, some would view this as dependent behavior on your part and think that you should be living apart from your family of origin. From another cultural perspective, however, it might be inappropriate for you to be living on your own.

Instead of talking about adjustment, we tend to talk about growth. A psychology of growth rests on the assumption that growth is a lifelong adventure, not some fixed point at which we arrive. Personal growth is best viewed as a process rather than as a goal or an end. We will face numerous crises at various stages of our lives. These crises can be seen as challenges to change, giving our lives new meaning. Growth also encompasses our relationship with significant others, our community, and our world. We do not grow in a vacuum but through our engagement with other people. To continue to grow, we have to be willing to let go of some of our old ways of thinking and acting so new dimensions can develop. During your reading and studying, think about the ways you have stopped growing and the degree to which you are willing to invest in personal growth. Ask yourself these questions:

> What do I want for myself, for others, and from others?

> What do I like about my life?

> What about my life am I having difficulty with?
> How would I like to be different?
> What are possible consequences if I do or do not change?
> How will my changes affect others in my life?
> What range of choices is open to me at this time in my life?
> How has my culture influenced the choices I have made? How might my cultural values either enhance or inhibit my ability to make changes?

A Humanistic Approach to Personal Growth

I Never Knew I Had a Choice is based on a humanistic view of people. A central concept of this approach to personal growth is self-actualization. Striving for self-actualization means working toward fulfilling our potential, toward becoming all that we are capable of becoming. Humanistic psychology is based on the premise that this striving for growth exists but is not an automatic process. Because growth often involves some pain and considerable turmoil, many of us experience a constant struggle between our desire for security, or dependence, and our desire to experience the delights of growth.

Although other people have made significant contributions to humanistic psychology, we have chosen to focus on four key people who devoted much of their professional careers to the promotion of psychological growth and the self-actualization process: Alfred Adler, Carl Jung, Carl Rogers, and especially Abraham Maslow, who did extensive research on the process of self-actualizing individuals. It is particularly interesting to note the close parallels between the struggles of these men in early childhood and the focus of their theories. Based on a set of life experiences, each of these men made a choice that influenced the development of his theory.

Alfred Adler (1958, 1964, 1969) made major contributions during Sigmund Freud's era and was a forerunner of the humanistic movement in psychology. In opposition to Freud's deterministic views of the person, Adler's theory stresses self-determination. Adler's early childhood experiences were characterized by a struggle to overcome weaknesses and feelings of inferiority, and the basic concepts of his theory grew out of his willingness to deal with his personal problems. Adler is a good example of a person who shaped his own life as opposed to having it determined by fate.

Adlerian psychologists contend that we are not the victims of fate but are creative, active, choice-making beings whose every action has purpose and meaning. Adler's approach is basically a growth model that rejects the idea that some individuals are psychologically sick. Instead of sickness, Adlerians talk of people being discouraged. Adlerian therapists view their work as providing encouragement so people can grow to become what they were meant to be. They teach people better ways to meet the challenges of life tasks, provide direction, help people change unrealistic assumptions and beliefs, and offer encouragement to those who are discouraged.

One of Adler's basic concepts is social interest, an individual's attitudes in dealing with other people in the world, which includes striving for a better future. Adler equates social interest with identification and empathy with others. For him, our happiness and success are largely related to a sense of belonging and a social connectedness. As social beings, we need to be of use to others and to establish meaningful relationships in a community. Adler asserted that only when we feel united with others can we act with courage in facing and dealing with life's problems. Because we are embedded in a society, we cannot be understood in isolation from our social context. Self-actualization is thus not an individual matter; it is only within the group that we can actualize our potential. Adler maintained that the degree to which we successfully share with others and are concerned with their welfare is a measure of our maturity. Social interest becomes the standard by which to judge psychological health. M. Scott Peck (1987) captures this idea of social interest: "It is true that we are created to be individually unique. Yet the reality is that we are inevitably social creatures who desperately need each other not merely for sustenance, not merely for company, but for any meaning to our lives whatsoever" (p. 55).

The Western concept of social interest is grounded in individualism, which affirms the uniqueness, autonomy, freedom, and intrinsic worth of the individual and emphasizes personal responsibility for our behavior and well-being. The ultimate aim of this orientation is the self-actualization of the individual—becoming all that you can be. By contrast, the Eastern concept of social interest rests on collectivism, which affirms the value of preserving and enhancing the well-being of the group as the main principle guiding social action. This collective orientation emphasizes unity, unification, integration, and fusion. It does not view self-actualization as the ultimate good. Instead, it emphasizes cooperation, harmony, interdependence, achievement of socially oriented and group goals, and collective responsibility.

Carl Jung (1961), who was a contemporary of Adler, made a monumental contribution to the depth of understanding of the human personality. His pioneering work sheds light on human development, particularly during middle age. Jung's personal life paved the way for the expansion of his theoretical notions. His loneliness as a child is reflected in his personality theory, which focuses on the inner world of the individual. Jung's emotional distance from his parents contributed to his feeling of being cut off from the external world of conscious reality. Largely as a way of escaping the difficulties of his childhood, Jung turned inward and became preoccupied with pursuing his unconscious experiences as reflected in his dreams, visions, and fantasies. At age 81 he wrote about his recollections in his autobiography *Memories, Dreams, Reflections* (1961). He made a choice to focus on the unconscious realm in his personal life, which also influenced the development of his theory of personality.

According to Jung, humans are not merely shaped by past events but strive for growth as well. Part of the nature of humans is to be constantly developing, growing, and moving toward a balanced and complete level of development. For Jung, our present personality is determined both by who and what we have been

According to Carl Jung, humans are not merely shaped by past events, but they strive for growth as well.

and also by the person we hope to become. The process of self-actualization is oriented toward the future. Jung's theory is based on the assumption that humans tend to move toward the fulfillment or realization of all their capabilities. Achieving individuation—a fully harmonious and integrated personality—is a primary goal. To reach this goal, we must become aware of and accept the full range of our being. The public self we present is only a small part of who and what we are. For Jung, both constructive and destructive forces coexist in the human psyche, and to become integrated we must accept the dark side of our nature with our primitive impulses such as selfishness and greed. Acceptance of our dark side (or shadow) does not mean being dominated by this dimension of our being but simply recognizing that this is a part of our nature.

Carl Rogers (1980), a major figure in the development of humanistic psychology, focused on the importance of nonjudgmental listening and acceptance as a condition for people to feel free enough to change. Rogers's emphasis on the value of autonomy seems to have grown, in part, out of his own struggles to become independent from his parents. Rogers grew up fearing his mother's critical judgment. In an interview Rogers mentioned that he could not imagine talking to his mother about anything of significance because he was sure she would have some negative judgment. He also grew up in a home where strict religious standards governed behavior. In his early years, while at a seminary studying to be a minister, Rogers made a critical choice that influenced his personal life and the focus of his theory. Realizing that he could no longer go along with the religious thinking of his parents, Rogers questioned the religious dogma he was being taught, which led to his emancipation and his psychological independence. As a college student, he took the risk of writing a letter to his parents telling them that his views were changing from fundamentalist to liberal and that he was developing his own philosophy of life. Even though he knew that his departure from the values of his parents would be difficult for them, he felt that such a move was necessary for his own intellectual and psychological freedom.

Rogers built his entire theory and practice of psychotherapy on the concept of the "fully functioning person." Fully functioning people tend to reflect and ask basic questions such as "Who am I?" "How can I discover my real self?" "How can I become what I deeply wish to become?" "How can I get out from behind my facade and become myself?" Rogers maintained that when people give up their facade and accept themselves they move in the direction of being open to experience (that is, they begin to see reality without distorting it). They trust themselves and look to themselves for the answers to their problems, and they no longer attempt to become fixed entities or products, realizing instead that growth is a continual process. Such fully functioning people, Rogers wrote, are in a fluid process of challenging and revisiting their perceptions and beliefs as they open themselves to new experiences.

In contrast to those who assume that we are by nature irrational and destructive unless we are socialized, Rogers exhibited a deep faith in human beings. In his view people are naturally social and forward-moving, strive to function fully, and have at their deepest core a positive goodness. In short, people are to be trusted, and because they are basically cooperative and constructive, there is no need to control their aggressive impulses.

Abraham Maslow was one of the most influential psychologists contributing to our understanding of self-actualizing individuals. He built on Adler's and Jung's works in some significant ways, yet he distinguished himself in discovering a psychology of health. Maslow was concerned with taking care of basic survival needs, and his theory stresses a hierarchy of needs, with satisfaction of physiological and safety needs prerequisite to being concerned about actualizing one's potentials. Self-actualization became the central theme of the work of Abraham Maslow (1968, 1970, 1971). Maslow uses the phrase "the psychopathology of the average" to highlight his contention that merely "normal" people may never extend themselves to become what they are capable of becoming. Further, he criticized Freudian psychology for what he saw as its preoccupation with the sick and crippled side of human nature. If our findings are based on observations of a sick population, Maslow reasoned, a sick psychology will emerge. Maslow believed that too much research was being conducted into anxiety, hostility, and neuroses and too little into joy, creativity, and self-fulfillment.

In his quest to create a humanistic psychology that would focus on our potential, Maslow studied what he called self-actualizing people and found that they differed in important ways from so-called normals. Some of the characteristics Maslow found in these people included a capacity to tolerate and even welcome uncertainty in their lives, acceptance of themselves and others, spontaneity and creativity, a need for privacy and solitude, autonomy, a capacity for deep and intense interpersonal relationships, a genuine caring for others, a sense of humor, an inner-directedness (as opposed to the tendency to live by others' expectations), and the absence of artificial dichotomies within themselves (such as work/play, love/hate, and weak/strong). Maslow's theory of self-actualization, along with the implications for the humanistic approach to psychology, is presented next.

Overview of Maslow's Self-Actualization Theory

Maslow postulated a hierarchy of needs as a source of motivation. The most basic are the physiological needs. If we are hungry and thirsty, our attention is riveted on meeting these basic needs. Next are the safety needs, which include a sense of security and stability. Once our physical and safety needs are fulfilled, we become concerned with meeting our needs for belonging and love, followed by working on our need for esteem, both from self and others. We are able to strive toward self-actualization only after these four basic needs are met: physiological, safety, love, and esteem. Maslow emphasized that people are not motivated by all five needs at the same time. The key factor determining which need is dominant at a given time is the degree to which those below it are satisfied. Some people come to the erroneous conclusion that if they were "bright" enough or "good" enough they would be further down the road of self-actualization. The truth may be that in their particular cultural, environmental, and societal circumstances these people are motivated to work toward physical and psychological survival, which keeps them functioning at the lower end of the hierarchy. Keep in mind that an individual is not much concerned with actualization, nor is a society focused on the development of culture, if the basic needs are not met.

We can summarize some of the basic ideas of the humanistic approach by means of Maslow's model of the self-actualizing person (Figure 1.1). He describes self-actualization in his book *Motivation and Personality* (1970), and he also treats this concept in his other books (1968, 1971). Some core characteristics of self-actualizing people are self-awareness, freedom, basic honesty and caring, and trust and autonomy.

Self-Awareness Self-actualizing people are more aware of themselves, of others, and of reality than are nonactualizing people. Specifically, they demonstrate the following behavior and traits:

1. *Efficient perception of reality*
   a. Self-actualizing people see reality as it is.
   b. They have an ability to detect phoniness.
   c. They avoid seeing things in preconceived categories.

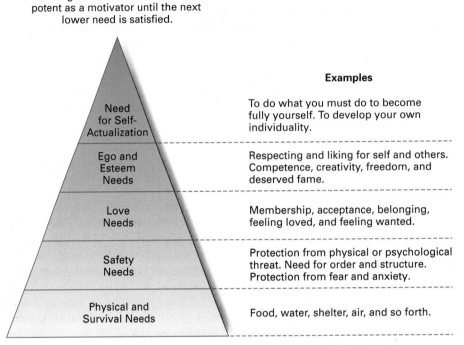

Figure 1.1
Maslow's Hierarchy of Needs

Each higher need does not become potent as a motivator until the next lower need is satisfied.

Examples

Need for Self-Actualization — To do what you must do to become fully yourself. To develop your own individuality.

Ego and Esteem Needs — Respecting and liking for self and others. Competence, creativity, freedom, and deserved fame.

Love Needs — Membership, acceptance, belonging, feeling loved, and feeling wanted.

Safety Needs — Protection from physical or psychological threat. Need for order and structure. Protection from fear and anxiety.

Physical and Survival Needs — Food, water, shelter, air, and so forth.

From *Motivation and Personality* by Abraham H. Maslow. Copyright © 1987. Reprinted by permission of Prentice-Hall, Inc., Upper Saddle River, N.J.

2. *Ethical awareness*
   a. Self-actualizing people display a knowledge of what is right and wrong for them.
   b. They have a sense of inner direction.
   c. They avoid being pressured by others and living by others' standards.

3. *Freshness of appreciation.* Like children, self-actualizing people have an ability to perceive life in a fresh way.

4. *Peak moments*
   a. Self-actualizing people experience times of being one with the universe; they experience moments of joy.
   b. They have the ability to be changed by such moments.

Freedom Self-actualizing people are willing to make choices for themselves, and they are free to reach their potential. This freedom entails a sense of detachment and a need for privacy, creativity and spontaneity, and an ability to accept responsibility for choices.

1. *Detachment*
   a. For self-actualizing people, the need for privacy is crucial.
   b. They have a need for solitude to put things in perspective.

2. *Creativity*
   a. Creativity is a universal characteristic of self-actualizing people.
   b. Creativity may be expressed in any area of life; it shows itself as inventiveness.

3. *Spontaneity*
   a. Self-actualizing people do not need to show off.
   b. They display a naturalness and lack of pretentiousness.
   c. They act with ease and grace.

Basic Honesty and Caring Self-actualizing people show a deep caring for and honesty with themselves and others. These qualities are reflected in their interest in humankind and in their interpersonal relationships.

1. *Sense of social interest*
   a. Self-actualizing people have a concern for the welfare of others.
   b. They have a sense of communality with all other people.
   c. They have an interest in bettering the world.

2. *Interpersonal relationships*
   a. Self-actualizing people have a capacity for real love and fusion with another.
   b. They are able to love and respect themselves.
   c. They are able to go outside themselves in a mature love.
   d. They are motivated by the urge to grow in their relationships.

3. *Sense of humor*
   a. Self-actualizing people can laugh at themselves.
   b. They can laugh at the human condition.
   c. Their humor is not hostile.

Trust and Autonomy Self-actualizing people exhibit faith in themselves and others; they are independent; they accept themselves as valuable persons; and their lives have meaning.

1. *Search for purpose and meaning*
   a. Self-actualizing people have a sense of mission, of a calling in which their potential can be fulfilled.
   b. They are engaged in a search for identity, often through work that is a deeply significant part of their lives.

2. *Autonomy and independence*
   a. Self-actualizing people have the ability to be independent.
   b. They resist blind conformity.
   c. They are not tradition-bound in making decisions.

3. *Acceptance of self and others*
   a. Self-actualizing people avoid fighting reality.
   b. They accept nature as it is.
   c. They are comfortable with the world.*

This profile is best thought of as an ideal rather than a final state that we reach once and for all. Thus, it is more appropriate to speak about the self-actualizing process rather than becoming a self-actualized person.

---

*From *Motivation and Personality* by Abraham H. Maslow. Copyright © 1987. Reprinted by permission of Prentice-Hall, Inc., Upper Saddle River, N.J.

MAYA ANGELOU:
An Example of a Self-Actualizing Person

A person we consider to be on the path of self-actualizing is Maya Angelou, a well-known writer and poet. She has written many books that continue to have an impact on her readers, and she is a frequent speaker to various groups. You may recall that she delivered one of her poems at the second inaugural ceremony for President Clinton. Angelou embodies many of the characteristics Maslow describes. In *Maya Angelou: The Poetry of Living*, Margaret Courtney-Clarke (1999) uses ten words to describe Maya Angelou—joy, giving, learning, perseverance, creativity, courage, self-respect, spirituality, love, and taking risks. Various contributors expanded on these themes and gave brief personal reactions to this woman whom they view as very special.

JOY: "Maya's message to young children is: Laugh as much as you can! Take every opportunity to rejoice. Find the humor in life at every opportunity." (Defoy Glenn, p. 19)

GIVING: "You cannot give what you don't have. Maya has this reservoir of love for people and that's why they love her, because it's like a mirror image." (Louise Meriwether, p. 28)

LEARNING: "She has an absolute rapacious desire to know; she really wants to know about everything. . . ." (Connie Sutton, p. 40)

PERSEVERANCE: "Maya has come to believe that troubles are a blessing. They force you to change, to believe." (Andrew Young, p. 62)

CREATIVITY: "The human brain is capable of more things than we can imagine, and if one dreams it—and believes it—one certainly should try it. As Maya says, 'The human mind is a vast storehouse, there is no limit to it.'" (Defoy Glenn, p. 69)

COURAGE: "Maya speaks with courage all the time. She talks about courage as a virtue. In most of her presentations she uses this. She has the courage to say, 'We are more alike than we are unalike.'" (Velma Gibson Watts, p. 76)

SELF-RESPECT: "Maya often says, 'I am a human being and nothing human can be alien to me, and if a human did it, I can do it. I possess the capacity to do it.'" (Defoy Glenn, p. 90)

SPIRITUALITY: "A phenomenal woman! She embraces us with her great love, informs us with her profound wisdom, and inspires us with her poetic and artistic genius. A person of uncommon dignity, rare courage, undaunted faith, dogged determination, grace, integrity, and finally, matchless generosity—Maya Angelou is an international treasure." (Coretta Scott King, p. 108)

LOVE: "If you want to see a miracle in the twentieth century look at Maya Angelou. The spirit is always moving. It moves to far ends of the earth. A spirit of love, of care, of liberation. . . . Maya Angelou's spirit liberates." (Rev. Cecil Williams, p. 110)

TAKING RISKS: "The process of decay starts the moment things are created. So, to hold on too tightly prevents one from getting things, because one's hands are so full one cannot take on anything else." (Defoy Glenn, p. 126)

What are some ways you can engage yourself in the self-actualizing process? The activities at the end of each chapter and the Take Time to Reflect sections scattered throughout the book can help you begin this lifelong quest. As you read about the struggles you are likely to encounter in trying to become all you are capable of becoming, we hope you will begin to see some options for living a fuller life.

Take Time to Reflect   The Take Time to Reflect sections in this book are an opportunity for you to pause and reflect on your own experiences as they relate to the topic being discussed. Unlike most quizzes and tests you have taken, these inventories do not emphasize "right" and "wrong" answers but rather answers that make sense to you and have personal meaning. Taking these inventories will probably be a different experience for you, and you may have to make a conscious effort to look within yourself for the response or answer that makes sense to you rather than searching for the expected response that is external to you.

1. To what degree do you have a healthy and positive view of yourself? Are you able to appreciate yourself, or do you discount your own worth? Respond to these statements using the following code:

    4 = This statement is true of me *most* of the time.

    3 = This statement is true of me *much* of the time.

    2 = This statement is true of me *some* of the time.

    1 = This statement is true of me *almost none* of the time.

    _____ I generally think and choose for myself.
    _____ I usually like myself.
    _____ I know what I want.
    _____ I am able to ask for what I want.

(continued)

_____ I feel a sense of personal power.

_____ I am open to change.

_____ I feel equal to others.

_____ I am sensitive to the needs of others.

_____ I care about others.

_____ I can act in accordance with my own judgment without feeling guilty if others disapprove of me.

_____ I do not expect others to make me feel good about myself.

_____ I can accept responsibility for my own actions.

_____ I am able to accept compliments.

_____ I can give affection.

_____ I can receive affection.

_____ I do not live by a long list of "shoulds" and "oughts."

_____ I am not so security-bound that I will not explore new things.

_____ I am generally accepted by others.

_____ I can give myself credit for what I do well.

_____ I am able to enjoy my own company.

_____ I am capable of forming intimate and meaningful relationships.

_____ I live in the here and now and do not get stuck dwelling on the past or the future.

_____ I feel a sense of significance.

_____ I am not diminished when I am with those I respect.

_____ I believe in my ability to succeed in projects that are meaningful to me.

Now go back over this inventory and identify not more than five areas that keep you from being as self-accepting as you might be. What can you do to increase your awareness of situations in which you do not fully accept yourself? For example, if you have trouble giving yourself credit for things you do well, how can you become aware of times when you discount yourself? When you do become conscious of situations in which you put yourself down, think of alternatives.

2. Take a few minutes to review Maslow's theory of self-actualization and then consider these questions as they apply to you:

> Which of these qualities do you find most appealing? Why?

> Which would you like to cultivate in yourself?

> Which of Maslow's ideal qualities do you most associate with living a full and meaningful life?

> Who in your life comes closest to meeting Maslow's criteria for self-actualizing people?

3. We recommend that later in the course you review your answers to this exercise and take this inventory again. Compare your answers and note any changes that you may have made in your thinking or behavior.

ARE YOU AN ACTIVE LEARNER?

The self-actualization process of growth implies that you will be an active learner: that is, you will assume responsibility for your education, you will question what is presented to you, and you will apply what you learn in a personally meaningful way. Your schooling experiences may not have encouraged you to learn actively. Instead of questioning and learning to think for yourself, you can easily assume a passive stance by doing what is expected, memorizing facts, and giving back information on tests. Review your school experiences and assess whether you are an active learner.

What do you want out of college or out of life in general? Identifying, clarifying, and reaching goals must be an active process related to your values. Getting a clear sense of your values is no easy task. Many people have trouble deciding what they really want. If this is true for you, a first step you can take in sorting out what you want from college is to ask yourself these questions:

> Is what I am doing now what I want to be doing?

> Does it reflect my values?

> Do I believe I have the right to make my own choices?

> Am I finding meaning in what I am doing?

> What would I rather be doing?

Use the idea of what you would rather be doing as a catalyst for changing. What will it take for you to say "I am doing what I really want to be doing right now"? Many of your values may be redefined at various points in your college career and in life. But your goals will be much more meaningful if you define them for yourself rather than allowing others to set goals for you. It is unrealistic to expect all of your time in college to be exciting, but there is a lot you can do to create interest, especially when you have a goal.

Take Time to Reflect

1. How would you evaluate your experience in elementary school?

_____

_____

(continued)

2. How would you evaluate your high school experience?

_____

_____

3. How do you evaluate your present college experience up to this point?

_____

_____

4. To what degree have you been a questioner?

_____

_____

5. To what degree have you been motivated externally or internally?

_____

_____

6. To what degree are you a confident learner?

_____

_____

7. To what degree has your learning been real and meaningful?

_____

_____

8. What effects do you think your schooling has had on you as a person?

_____

_____

9. What important things (both positive and negative) did you learn about yourself as a result of your schooling?

_____

_____

10. If you do not like the kind of learner you have been up until now, what can you do about it? What changes would you like to make?

_____

_____

11. As you review your responses to these questions, what are you learning about yourself?

_____

_____

MULTIPLE INTELLIGENCES AND MULTIPLE LEARNING STYLES

To get the most out of your education, you need to know where your talents lie and how you learn. People differ in how they learn best and in what kinds of knowledge they tend to learn most easily. For example, auditory learners tend to understand and retain ideas better from hearing them spoken, whereas visual learners tend to learn more effectively when they can literally see what they are learning. Some students learn best by listening to lectures and reading, others by hands-on experience. By learning as much as you can about your own learning style, you can maximize your success in college regardless of your field of study.

There are multiple
intelligences and
multiple learning styles.

Peter Southwick/Stock, Boston

Behind differences in learning styles may lie basic differences in intelligence. Intelligence itself is not one single, easily measured ability but a group of abilities. Howard Gardner (1983), a professor of education at Harvard University, has discovered that we are capable of at least seven different types of intelligence and learning:

> Verbal-linguistic
> Musical-rhythmic
> Logical-mathematical
> Visual-spatial
> Bodily-kinesthetic
> Intrapersonal
> Interpersonal

To this list, Daniel Goleman (1995) adds *emotional intelligence* as a critical aspect intelligence with definite implications for personal learning. Emotional intelligence pertains to the ability to control impulses, empathize with others, form responsible interpersonal relationships, and develop intimate relationships.

Traditional approaches to schooling—teaching methods, class assignments, and tests—have been geared to and measure the growth of verbal-linguistic and logical-mathematical abilities, what we generally refer to as IQ. Yet several, if not all, of the other forms of intelligence and learning are equally vital to success in life. Emotional intelligence is certainly basic to learning interpersonal skills, yet this domain tends not to be emphasized in the educational programs of our schools and colleges.

The implications of learning in a different combination of ways are enormous, for both teaching and learning. For example, if you have trouble learning in the logical-mathematical sense, you should not assume that you are not "intelligent." You may well have strengths in one or several other areas. Moreover, if you have difficulty learning in one form of intelligence, you can probably compensate by using the forms of intelligence in which you are stronger to learn similar material.

Let's examine the specific characteristics of each of these kinds of intellectual abilities and then consider the implications for college learning.

❯ If you are a *verbal-linguistic* learner, you have highly developed auditory skills, enjoy reading and writing, like to play word games, and have a good memory for names, dates, and places; you like to tell stories; and you are good at getting your point across. You learn best by saying and hearing words. People whose dominant intelligence is in the verbal-linguistic area include poets, authors, speakers, attorneys, politicians, lecturers, and teachers.

❯ If you are a *musical-rhythmic* learner, you are sensitive to the sounds in your environment, enjoy music, and prefer listening to music when you study or read. You appreciate pitch and rhythm. You probably like singing to yourself. You learn best through melody and music. Musical intelligence is obviously demonstrated by singers, conductors, and composers, but it is also found in those who enjoy, understand, and use various elements of music.

❯ If you are more *logical-mathematical,* you probably like to explore patterns and relationships, and you enjoy doing activities in sequential order. You are likely to enjoy mathematics, and you like to experiment with things you do not understand. You like to work with numbers, ask questions, and explore patterns and relationships. You may find it challenging to solve problems and to use logical reasoning. You learn best by classifying information, engaging in abstract thinking, and looking for common basic principles. People with well-developed logical-mathematical abilities include mathematicians, biologists, medical technologists, geologists, engineers, physicists, researchers, and other scientists.

❯ If your intellectual orientation is primarily *visual-spatial,* you probably feel at home with the visual arts, maps, charts, and diagrams. You tend to think in images and pictures. You are able to visualize clear images when you think about things, and you can complete jigsaw puzzles easily. You are likely to engage in imagining things and daydreaming. You probably like to design and create things. You learn best by looking at pictures and slides, watching videos or movies, and visualizing. People with well-developed visual-spatial abilities are found in professions such as sculpting, painting, surgery, and engineering.

❯ If you are a *bodily-kinesthetic* learner, you process knowledge through bodily sensations and use your body in skilled ways. You have good balance and coordination; you are good with your hands. You need opportunities to move and act things out. You tend to respond best in classrooms that provide physical activities and hands-on learning experiences, and you are able to manipulate objects with finesse. You learn best by touching, moving around, and processing knowledge through bodily sensations. People who have highly developed bodily-kinesthetic abilities include carpenters, television and stereo repairpersons, mechanics, dancers, gymnasts, swimmers, and jugglers.

❯ If you are an *intrapersonal* learner, you prefer your own inner world, you like to be alone, and you are aware of your own strengths, weaknesses, and feelings. You tend to be a creative and independent thinker; you like to reflect on ideas. You probably possess independence, self-confidence, determination, and are highly motivated. You may respond with strong opinions when controversial topics are discussed. You learn best by engaging in independent study projects rather than working on group projects. Pacing your own instruction is important to you. People with intrapersonal abilities include entrepreneurs, philosophers, and psychologists.

❯ If you are an *interpersonal* learner, you enjoy being around people, like talking to people, have many friends, and engage in social activities. You learn best by relating, sharing, and participating in cooperative group environments. People with strong interpersonal abilities are found in sales, consulting, community organizing, counseling, teaching, or one of the helping professions.

❯ If you are an *emotional* learner, you have competence in the emotional realm: empathy, concern for others, curiosity, self-control, cooperation, the ability to resolve conflicts, the ability to listen well, communication skills, and relatedness to others. According to Goleman (1995), academic performance is related to the emotional and social area as much as it hinges on other facets of intelligence.

Intelligence is not a singular entity. It is complex and multidimensional, and you may find that you have strengths in several different areas. The model of multiple intelligences is best used as a tool to help you identify areas you may want to pursue. As you will see in Chapter 10, other factors besides ability (or intelligence) need to be considered in deciding on a field of study or a career. The more you can view college as a place to use all your talents and improve your learning abilities in all respects, the more meaningful and successful your college journey will be.

Choices in Learning

You can use the knowledge of your own learning strengths to improve your college learning. In addition to different kinds of intelligences and the learning styles that flow from them, consider four different kinds of learners: auditory, visual, kinesthetic, and emotional. As you read the following descriptions, consider how you can best learn—and reflect on the choices you have open to you as a learner.

❯ If you are an *auditory learner,* it is important that you hear the message. Your learning is facilitated by opportunities to listen and to speak. You prefer to learn by listening to lectures or audiotapes, and by discussing what you have heard. You will probably profit more from reading after you have heard about the material you are to read. You may learn best by taping lectures and listening to them again or by listening to your textbook on audiotape. Reciting information and teaching others what you know are useful ways for you to learn.

❯ If you are a *visual learner,* you prefer to learn by reading, watching video-tapes, and observing demonstrations. You will learn better by seeing pictures and graphically mapping out material to learn rather than relying mainly on listening to lectures. It is important that you envision the big picture. You are likely to get more from a lecture *after* you have read the material. Besides the printed word, you may learn well by seeing pictures and forming images of what is to be learned. You learn by looking at pictures, watching movies, and seeing slides. You may rely on word processors, books, and other visual devices for learning and recall.

❯ If you are a *kinesthetic learner,* you prefer to learn by doing, by getting physically involved through movement and action. It is a good idea to figure out ways to participate in movement exercises while learning or to use body language in learning. You tend to learn best by experimenting and figuring out ways of solving a problem. As a kinesthetic learner, if you had a problem with your computer, car, or videocassette recorder, you might lack the patience to plow through a manual. Instead, you would probably manipulate gadgets until you figured out for yourself what was wrong with the equipment. You acquire and remember information best through movement, hands-on experience, role playing, working with materials, dramatic improvisation, games, and participatory workshops.

❯ If you are an *emotional learner,* you are as interested in cultivating matters of your heart as much as you are your head, and you are interested in the interdependence of people at least as much as you are in developing your own independence. You are able to express and control a range of your emotions; you are accepting of the emotions of others; you strive for connections with others; and you have an interest in increasing both your self- and other-esteem (Hwang, 2000). When emotional competencies are lacking, Goleman (1995) believes this results in disconnection, which, in turn, leads to prejudice, self-involvement, aggressive behavior, depression, addictive behavior, and an inability to manage emotions. Emotional learners promote cooperative and collaborative learning, reach out to others, and apply what they know to making the world a better place to live.

Although you may have a preference for one of these ways of learning, remain open to incorporating elements from the other styles as well. In a course such as this, we particularly hope that you will find ways to blend the emotional domain with the other forms of intelligence and learning styles. You are likely to find that you learn best by integrating many pathways rather than by depending exclusively on one avenue in your educational journey.

Different Ways of Thinking and Approaching Learning

Some of you may have a high need for structure and little tolerance for ambiguity. You may have been conditioned to find the "one correct answer" to a problem and to support whatever statements you make with some authoritative source. Our experience with university students repeatedly shows us how hesitant students are when it comes to formulating and expressing a position on an issue. Yet many of you are disenchanted with mechanical and impersonal learning and truly want to learn how to think through issues and find meaning in the courses you take. One of the ways to do this involves employing what is known as divergent thinking.

In approaching a problem you can use either convergent thinking or divergent thinking. In *convergent thinking* the task is to sort out alternatives and arrive at the best solution to the problem. A multiple-choice test taps convergent thinking; you must select the one best answer from a list of alternatives given. Certainly, there is a place for convergent thinking, especially in the sciences. However, in all fields of learning there are not singular best answers. In many subjects there are many possible ways to deal with a particular problem. *Divergent thinking* involves coming up with many acceptable answers to the problem. Essay tests have the potential to tap divergent thinking. Divergent thinking is an important skill to master if you choose to be an active learner. Part of being an active learner is having the capacity to raise questions, to brainstorm, and to generate multiple answers to your questions. This process implies a personal involvement with the material to be learned. This book is based on divergent thinking; the themes it addresses do not have simple solutions. It is designed to engage you in exploring how these themes apply to you and to help you find your own answers.

Taking Responsibility for Learning

At the beginning of a new semester some college students are overwhelmed by how much they are expected to do in all their courses while maintaining a life outside of school. One reaction to this feeling of being swamped is to put things off, which results in getting behind with your assignments, which typically leads to discouragement.

If you take responsibility for your own learning, you are much more likely to succeed. Students who fail to see their own role in the learning process often blame others for their failures. If you are dissatisfied with your education, first take a look at yourself and see how much you are willing to invest in making it more vital.

We think you will get a great deal more from your college education if you spend time now reflecting on your past experiences. Think about how your present values and beliefs are related to your experiences in school. Recall a particularly positive school experience. How might it be affecting you today? Consider your educational experiences up to this point and think about your attitudes and behaviors as a student. What kinds of experiences have you had as a student so far, and how might these experiences influence the kind of learner you are today? If you like the kind of learner you are now, or if you have had mostly good experiences with school, you can build on that positive framework as you approach this course. You can continue to find ways to involve yourself with the material you will read, study, and discuss. If you feel cheated by a negative educational experience, you can begin to change it now. In what ways do you want to become a different learner now than you have been in the past? We challenge you to find ways to bring meaning to your learning by being active in the process. You can get the most out of your courses if you develop a style of learning in which you raise questions and search for answers within yourself.

You can make the choice to be actively engaged or only marginally involved in applying the themes in this book in your life. You can make this class different by applying some of the ideas discussed in this chapter. Once you become aware of those aspects of your education that you do not like, you can decide to change your style of learning.

It is also essential that you develop effective study habits and learn basic time management skills. Although acquiring these skills alone does not guarantee successful learning, knowing how to organize your time and how to study can contribute significantly to assuming an active and effective style of learning. One aid to learning, found in the Where Can I Go From Here? section at the end of this chapter, is the five-step SQ3R technique for studying, reading, and reviewing. We have also included the Rogers Indicator of Multiple Intelligence self-evaluation, which can help you understand how you learn best.

One way to begin to become an active learner is to think about your reasons for taking this course and your expectations concerning what you will learn. This Take Time to Reflect exercise will help you focus on these issues.

Take Time to Reflect

1. What are your main reasons for taking this course? _____

_____

2. What do you expect this course to be like? Check all the comments that fit you.

_____ I expect to talk openly about issues that matter to me.
_____ I expect to get answers to certain problems in my life.
_____ I hope I will become a more fulfilled person.
_____ I hope I will have less fear of expressing my feelings and ideas.
_____ I expect to be challenged on why I am the way I am.
_____ I expect to learn more about how other people function.
_____ I expect to understand myself more fully by the end of the course.

3. What do you most want to accomplish in this course? _____

_____

4. What are you willing to do to become actively involved in your learning? Check the appropriate comments.

_____ I am willing to participate in class discussions.

(continued)

_____ I am willing to read the material and think about how it applies to me.

_____ I am willing to question my assumptions and look at my values.

_____ I am willing to spend some time most days reflecting on the issues raised in this course.

_____ I am willing to keep a journal and to record my reactions to what I read and experience, and to also assess my progress on meeting my goals and commitments.

Other commitments to become an active learner include: _____

_____

GETTING THE MOST FROM THIS BOOK: SUGGESTIONS FOR PERSONAL LEARNING

Throughout this book both of us write in a personal style and openly share with you how we arrived at our beliefs and values. We hope that knowing our assumptions, biases, and struggles will help you evaluate your own position more clearly. We are not suggesting that you adopt our philosophy of life but that you use the material in this book as a catalyst for your own reflection. There are no simple answers to complex life issues, and each person's life is unique. Although self-help books provide insights and useful information for many people, we have concerns about the kinds of books that give an abundance of advice or attempt to offer easy answers. The same can be said of television talk shows or therapists who offer counsel on the radio to callers with personal problems. Information and even suggestions can be useful at the right time, but rarely can an individual's problems be resolved by uncritically accepting others' advice or directives.

In the chapters that follow we will offer a great deal of information that we hope you will reflect on and use as a basis for making better choices. Our aim is to raise questions that lead to thoughtful reflection on your part and to meaningful dialogue with others. We encourage you to develop the practice of examining questions that engage you and have meaning in your life. Instead of looking for simple solutions to your problems, we hope you will increasingly make time for personal reflection and consider the direction of your life. Listen to others and consider what they say, but even more important, learn to look inside yourself for direction. Listen to your inner voice. This book can become a personal companion; use it to enhance your reflection on questions that are personally significant to you.

This course is likely to be different from many of the courses you have taken. Few courses deal primarily with you as the subject matter. Most college courses challenge you intellectually, but this book is geared toward integrating intellectual and personal learning. To a large degree, what you get from this course will depend on what you are willing to invest of yourself. It is important that you clarify your goals and the steps you can take to reach them. The following guidelines will help you become active and involved in personal learning as you read the book and participate in your class.

1. **Preparing.** Reading and writing are excellent devices for getting the most from this class. Read this book for your personal benefit, and make use of the Take Time to Reflect sections and the Where Can I Go From Here? exercises at the end of each chapter, which can help you apply the material to your own life. Many of the exercises, questions, and suggested activities will appeal differently to different readers. Considerations such as your age, life experiences, and cultural background will have a bearing on the meaning and importance of certain topics to you. We have written this book from our own cultural framework, but the topics we address are common to all of us. In our work with people from various cultures, we continue to find that these human themes transcend culture and unite us in our life struggles. Before you reject these ideas too quickly, reflect on ways you might be able to adapt them to your own cultural background.

2. **Dealing with fears.** It is natural to experience some fear about participating personally and actively in the class. Participation may involve taking risks you do not usually take in your courses. How you deal with your fears is more important than trying to eliminate your anxieties about getting involved in a personal way. You have the choice of remaining a passive observer or acknowledging your fears and dealing with them openly, even though you will likely experience some degree of discomfort. Facing your fears takes courage and a genuine desire to increase your self-awareness, but by doing so you take a first big step toward expanding the range of your choices.

3. **Establishing trust.** You can choose to take the initiative in establishing the trust necessary for you to participate in this course in a meaningful way, or you can wait for others to create a climate of trust. Students often have feelings of mistrust or other negative feelings toward an instructor, yet avoid doing anything. One way to establish trust is to talk with your instructor outside of class.

4. **Practicing self-disclosure.** Disclosing yourself to others is one way to come to know yourself more fully. Sometimes participants in self-awareness courses or experiential groups fear that they must give up their privacy to be active participants. However, you can be open and at the same time retain your privacy by deciding how much you will disclose and when it is appropriate to do so. Although it may be new and uncomfortable for you to talk in personal ways to people you do not know that well, you can say more than you typically would in most social situations. You will need patience in learning this new communication skill, and you will need to challenge yourself to reveal yourself in meaningful ways.

5. **Being direct.** Adopt a direct style in your communication. Make "I" statements. For example, instead of saying "You can't trust people with what you

feel, because they will let you down if you make yourself vulnerable," try instead, "I can't trust people with what I feel because they will let me down if I make myself vulnerable." Make eye contact and speak directly to a person rather than at or about the person. Of course, directness may not be part of your cultural repertoire. You may have been taught that being direct is rude and that indirect communication is highly valued. You will need to adapt these guidelines to fit your cultural context.

6. **Listening.** Work on developing the skill of really listening to what others are saying without thinking of what you will say in reply. Active listening (really hearing the full message another is sending) requires remaining open and carefully considering what others say instead of too quickly giving reasons and explanations.

7. **Avoiding self-fulfilling prophecies.** You can increase your ability to change by letting go of ways you have categorized yourself or been categorized by others. If you start off with the assumption that you are stupid, helpless, or boring, you will probably convince others as well. Your negative beliefs about yourself will certainly get in the way of being the person you would like to be. If you see yourself as boring, you will probably present yourself in such a way that others will respond to you as a boring person. If you like the idea of changing some of the ways in which you see yourself and present yourself to others, you can experiment with going beyond some of your self-limiting labels. Once you experience yourself differently, others might experience you differently too.

8. **Practicing outside of class.** One important way to get the maximum benefit from a class dealing with personal learning is to think about ways of applying what you learn in class to your everyday life. You can make specific contracts with yourself (or with others) detailing what you are willing to do to experiment with new behavior and to work toward desired changes.

   At this point, pause and assess your readiness for taking an honest look at yourself. You may feel some hesitation in exploring these personal topics. If so, leave the door open and give yourself and the course a chance. If you open yourself to change and try the techniques we have suggested, you may well experience a sense of excitement and promise.

9. **Keeping a journal.** In one sense this is an *unfinished* book. You are invited to become a coauthor by completing the writing of this book in ways that are meaningful to you. Throughout the book we make suggestions for keeping a journal, but the important thing is for you to decide what to put in and how to use it. Reviewing your journal will help you identify some of your critical choices and areas of conflict. Consider writing about some of these topics:

   > What I learned about others and myself through today's class session

   > The topics that were of most interest to me (and why)

   > The topics that held the least interest for me (and why)

   > The topics I wanted to talk about

> The topics I avoided talking about
> Particular sections (or issues) in the chapter that had the greatest impact on me (and why)
> Some things I am learning about myself by reading the book
> Some specific things I am doing in everyday life as a result of this class
> Some concrete changes in my attitudes, values, and behavior that I find myself most wanting to make
> What I am willing to do to make these changes
> Some barriers I encounter in making the changes I want to make

It is best to write what first comes to mind. Spontaneous reactions tend to tell you more about yourself than well-thought-out comments.

10. **Organizing your reading.** There is no perfect organization or sequencing of chapters in this kind of book. Generally, we had some rationale for the order of the chapters, but each of the 14 chapters can be read separately, as each was written to stand alone. We do have some suggestions, however, about reading parts of certain chapters early during the course. Chapter 14 contains a list of specific suggestions of how to continue the self-exploration process once you complete the course. It would be a good idea to read this early in the course to determine whether specific ideas mentioned there can be incorporated in your daily practice. Chapter 13 contains a detailed discussion of formulating your philosophy of life, and some instructors assign some type of philosophy of life paper as a course project. If this is the case, you would do well to read parts of this chapter early in the semester. Regardless of which chapters are assigned, certain chapters will be more compelling to some students than to others due to the nature of the subject matter. We encourage you to focus on the content that you find personally most meaningful, but remain open to exploring topics that you may be inclined to ignore.

SUMMARY

We do not have to passively live out the plans that others have designed for us. With awareness we can begin to make significant choices. Taking a stand in life by making choices can result in both gains and losses. Changing long-standing patterns is not easy, and there are many obstacles to overcome. Yet a free life has many rewards.

One of these benefits is personal growth. Growth is a lifelong process of expanding self-awareness and accepting new challenges. It does not mean disregard for others but rather implies fulfilling more of our potentials, including our ability to care for others. Four scholars who have made significant contributions to the concept of personal growth in a framework of humanistic psychology are Alfred Adler, Carl Jung, Carl Rogers, and Abraham Maslow. Perhaps the best way to conceptualize personal growth is by considering Maslow's ideal of self-actualization. Keep in mind that until our basic needs have been met we are not really much concerned about becoming fully functioning persons. If you are hungry or are living on the streets, you are not likely to reflect on the meaning of becoming an actualized individual. Remember also that self-actualization is not something that we do in isolation; rather, it is through meaningful relationships with others and through social interest that we discover and become the person we are capable of becoming. Paradoxically, we find ourselves when we are secure enough to go beyond a preoccupation with our self-interests and become involved in the world with selected people.

Striving for self-actualization does not cease at a particular age but is an ongoing process. Rather than speaking of self-actualization as a product we attain, it is best to consider the process of becoming a self-actualizing person. Four basic characteristics of self-actualizing people are self-awareness, freedom, basic honesty and caring, and trust and autonomy. This course can be a first step on the journey toward achieving your personal goals and living a self-actualizing existence while at the same time contributing to making the world a better place.

People differ in how they learn best and the kind of knowledge they tend to learn most easily. Understanding the various learning styles will enable you to approach learning in a personal and meaningful way. Intelligence is not a singular entity; rather, it is complex and multidimensional. Discovering your dominant forms of intelligence can help you identify areas for study or career options.

A major purpose of this chapter is to encourage you to examine your responsibility for making your learning meaningful. It is easy to criticize impersonal institutions if you feel apathetic about your learning. It is more difficult but more honest to look at yourself and ask these questions: "When I find myself in an exciting class, do I get fully involved and take advantage of the opportunity for learning?" "Do I expect instructors to entertain and teach me while I sit back passively?" "If I'm bored, what am I doing about it?"

Even if your earlier educational experiences have taught you to be a passive learner and to avoid risks in your classes, being aware of this influence gives you the power to change your learning style. We invite you to decide how personal you want your learning to be in the course you are about to experience.

❯ Where Can I Go From Here?

At the end of each chapter are additional activities and exercises that we suggest you practice, both in class and out of class. Ultimately you will be the one to decide which activities you are willing to do. You may find some of the suggested exercises too threatening to do in a class, yet exploring the same activities in a small group in your class could be easier. If

❭ Where Can I Go From Here? *(continued)*

small discussion groups are not part of the structure of your class, consider doing the exercises alone or sharing them with a friend. Do not feel compelled to complete all the activities; select those that have the most meaning for you at this time in your life.

1. These are exercises you can do at home. They are intended to help you focus on specific ways in which you behave. We have drawn the examples from typical fears and concerns often expressed by college students. Study the situations by putting yourself in each one and deciding how you might typically respond. Then keep an account in your journal of actual instances you encounter in your classes.

   Situation A: You would like to ask a question in class, but you are afraid that your question will sound dumb and that others will laugh.

   ❭ Issues: Will you simply refrain from asking questions? If so, is this a pattern you care to continue? Are you willing to practice asking questions, even though you might experience some anxiety? What do you imagine will happen if you ask questions? What would you like to have happen?

   Situation B: You feel that you have a problem concerning authority figures. You feel intimidated, afraid to venture your opinions, and even more afraid to register a point of view opposed to your instructor's.

   ❭ Issues: Does this description fit you? If it does, do you want to change? Do you ever examine where you picked up your attitudes toward yourself in relation to authority? Do you think they are still appropriate for you?

   Situation C: Your instructor seems genuinely interested in the students and the course, and she has extended herself by inviting you to come to her office if you have any problems with the course. You are having real difficulty grasping the material, and you are falling behind and doing poorly on the tests and assignments. Nevertheless, you keep putting off going to see the instructor to talk about your problems in the class.

   ❭ Issues: Have you been in this situation before? If so, what kept you from talking with your instructor? If you find yourself in this kind of situation, are you willing to seek help before it is too late?

2. Review Maslow's characteristics of self-actualizing people, and consider the following questions:

   a. To what degree are these characteristics a part of your personality?

   b. Do you think Maslow's ideal of self-actualization fits for individuals of all cultural and ethnic groups? Are any characteristics inappropriate for certain cultures?

(continued)

Where Can I Go From Here? *(continued)*

3. In keeping with the spirit of developing active learning habits, we suggest that you tackle your reading assignments systematically. A useful approach is Robinson's (1970) SQ3R technique (*survey, question, read, recite, review*). It is intended to get you actively involved with what you are reading. The technique does not have to be applied rigidly; in fact, you can develop your own way of carrying it out. This five-step method involves breaking a reading assignment down into manageable units and checking your understanding of what you are reading. The steps are as follows:

Step 1: Survey. Rather than simply reading a chapter, begin by skimming it to get a general overview of the material. Look for the ways topics are interrelated, strive to understand the organization of the chapter, and give some preliminary thought to the information you are about to read.

Step 2: Question. Once you get the general plan of the chapter, look at the main chapter headings. What questions do they raise that your reading of the chapter should answer? Formulate in your own words the questions that you would like to explore as you read.

Step 3: Read. After skimming the chapter and raising key questions, proceed to read one section at a time with the goal of answering your questions. After you have finished a section, pause for a few moments and reflect on what you have read to determine if you can clearly address the questions you raised.

Step 4: Recite. In your own words, recite (preferably out loud) the answers to your questions. Avoid rote memorization. Attempt to give meaning to factual material. Make sure you understand the basic ideas in a section before you go on to the next section. Writing down a few key notes is a good way to have a record for your review later. Then go on to the next section of the chapter, repeating Steps 3 and 4.

Step 5: Review. After you finish reading the chapter, spend some time reviewing the main points. Test your understanding of the material by putting the major ideas into your own words. Repeat the questions, and attempt to answer them without looking at the book. If there is a chapter summary or listing of key terms, be sure to study this carefully. A good summary will help you put the chapter into context. Attempt to add to the summary by listing some of the points that seem particularly important or interesting to you.

4. The *Rogers Indicator of Multiple Intelligences* (RIMI) is a self-inventory created by Dr. Keith Rogers, a professor at Brigham Young University. By taking this inventory you can pinpoint your dominate intelligences. It should take you approximately 15 minutes to complete the inventory. Use the grid at the end of the RIMI to interpret each of your scores on the seven kinds of intelligences, indicating low intensity, moderate intensity, and high intensity areas.

The Rogers Indicator of Multiple Intelligences

DIRECTIONS: For each statement, mark a box for your most accurate response according to descriptors above the boxes. Think carefully about your knowledge, beliefs, preferences, behavior, and experience. Decide quickly and move on. There is no right or wrong, no good or bad, no expected or desirable response. Use your heart as well as your head. Focus on the way you really are, not on the way you "ought to be" for someone else.

	Rarely 1	Occasionally 2	Sometimes 3	Usually 4	Almost always 5
1. I am careful about the direct and implied meanings of the words I choose.	❏	❏	❏	❏	❏
2. I appreciate a wide variety of music.	❏	❏	❏	❏	❏
3. People come to me when they need help with math problems or any calculations.	❏	❏	❏	❏	❏
4. In my mind, I can visualize clear, precise, sharp images.	❏	❏	❏	❏	❏
5. I am physically well-coordinated.	❏	❏	❏	❏	❏
6. I understand why I believe and behave the way I do.	❏	❏	❏	❏	❏
7. I understand the moods, temperaments, values, and intentions of others.	❏	❏	❏	❏	❏
8. I confidently express myself well in words, written or spoken.	❏	❏	❏	❏	❏
9. I understand the basic precepts of music such as harmony, chords, and keys.	❏	❏	❏	❏	❏
10. When I have a problem, I use a logical, analytical, step-by-step process to arrive at a solution.	❏	❏	❏	❏	❏
11. I have a good sense of direction.	❏	❏	❏	❏	❏
12. I have skill in handling objects such as scissors, balls, hammers, scalpels, paint-brushes, knitting needles, pliers, etc.	❏	❏	❏	❏	❏
13. My self-understanding helps me to make wise decisions for my life.	❏	❏	❏	❏	❏
14. I am able to influence other individuals to believe and/or behave in response to my own beliefs, preferences, and desires.	❏	❏	❏	❏	❏
15. I am grammatically accurate.	❏	❏	❏	❏	❏
16. I like to compose or create music.	❏	❏	❏	❏	❏

Reprinted by permission from the Rogers Indicator of Multiple Intelligences © 1995 by J. Keith Rogers, Ph. D.

(continued)

The Rogers Indicator of Multiple Intelligences *(continued)*

	Rarely 1	Occasionally 2	Sometimes 3	Usually 4	Almost always 5
17. I am rigorous and skeptical in accepting facts, reasons, and principles.	❏	❏	❏	❏	❏
18. I am good at putting together jigsaw puzzles, and reading instructions, patterns, or blueprints.	❏	❏	❏	❏	❏
19. I excel in physical activities such as dance, sports, or games.	❏	❏	❏	❏	❏
20. My ability to understand my own emotions helps me to decide whether or how to be involved in certain situations.	❏	❏	❏	❏	❏
21. I would like to be involved in "helping" professions such as teaching, therapy, or counseling, or to do work such as political or religious leadership.	❏	❏	❏	❏	❏
22. I am able to use spoken or written words to influence or persuade others.	❏	❏	❏	❏	❏
23. I enjoy performing music, such as singing or playing a musical instrument for an audience.	❏	❏	❏	❏	❏
24. I require scientific explanations of physical realities.	❏	❏	❏	❏	❏
25. I can read maps easily and accurately.	❏	❏	❏	❏	❏
26. I work well with my hands as would an electrician, seamstress, plumber, tailor, mechanic, carpenter, assembler, etc.	❏	❏	❏	❏	❏
27. I am aware of the complexity of my own feelings, emotions, and beliefs in various circumstances.	❏	❏	❏	❏	❏
28. I am able to work as an effective intermediary in helping other individuals and groups to solve their problems.	❏	❏	❏	❏	❏
29. I am sensitive to the sounds, rhythms, inflections, and meters of words, especially as found in poetry.	❏	❏	❏	❏	❏
30. I have a good sense of musical rhythm.	❏	❏	❏	❏	❏
31. I would like to do the work of people such as chemists, engineers, physicists, astronomers, or mathematicians.	❏	❏	❏	❏	❏

The Rogers Indicator of Multiple Intelligences (continued)

	Rarely 1	Occasionally 2	Sometimes 3	Usually 4	Almost always 5
32. I am able to produce graphic depictions of the spatial world as in drawing, painting, sculpting, drafting, or map-making.	❑	❑	❑	❑	❑
33. I relieve stress or find fulfillment in physical activities.	❑	❑	❑	❑	❑
34. My inner self is my ultimate source of strength and renewal.	❑	❑	❑	❑	❑
35. I understand what motivates others even when they are trying to hide their motivations.	❑	❑	❑	❑	❑
36. I enjoy reading frequently and widely.	❑	❑	❑	❑	❑
37. I have a good sense of musical pitch.	❑	❑	❑	❑	❑
38. I find satisfaction in dealing with numbers.	❑	❑	❑	❑	❑
39. I like the hands-on approach to learning when I can experience personally the objects that I'm learning about.	❑	❑	❑	❑	❑
40. I have quick and accurate physical reflexes and responses.	❑	❑	❑	❑	❑
41. I am confident in my own opinions and am not easily swayed by others.	❑	❑	❑	❑	❑
42. I am comfortable and confident with groups of people.	❑	❑	❑	❑	❑
43. I use writing as a vital method of communication.	❑	❑	❑	❑	❑
44. I am affected both emotionally and intellectually by music.	❑	❑	❑	❑	❑
45. I prefer questions that have definite "right" and "wrong" answers.	❑	❑	❑	❑	❑
46. I can accurately estimate distances and other measurements.	❑	❑	❑	❑	❑
47. I have accurate aim when throwing balls or in archery, shooting, golf, etc.	❑	❑	❑	❑	❑
48. My feelings, beliefs, attitudes, and emotions are my own responsibility.	❑	❑	❑	❑	❑
49. I have a large circle of close associates.	❑	❑	❑	❑	❑

(continued)

The Rogers Indicator of Multiple Intelligences *(continued)*

DIRECTIONS: In the chart below, the box numbers are the same as the statement numbers in the survey. You made a rating judgment for each statement. Now, place the numbers that correspond to your ratings in the numbered boxes below. Then add down the columns and write the totals at the bottom to determine your score in each of the seven intelligence categories. Then, for the meanings of the scores, consult the interpretations that follow the chart.

Verbal/ Linguistic	Musical/ Rhythmic	Logical/ Mathematical	Visual/ Spatial	Bodily/ Kinesthetic	Intrapersonal	Interpersonal
1	2	3	4	5	6	7
8	9	10	11	12	13	14
15	16	17	18	19	20	21
22	23	24	25	26	27	28
29	30	31	32	33	34	35
36	37	38	39	40	41	42
43	44	45	46	47	48	49
Totals						
Interpretations of knowledge, belief, behavior						

The Rogers Indicator of Multiple Intelligences (continued)

To some degree we possess all of these intelligences, and all can be enhanced. We are each a unique blend of all seven; however, we all differ in the degree to which we prefer and have the competence to use each of the intelligences. Here are interpretations for the scores in the three ranges of low, moderate, and high.

Score	Intensity of Preference and/or Competence
7–15 (3)	Low Intensity: You tend to "avoid" it, and are probably uncomfortable when required to use it. Tertiary preference (3). This intelligence probably is not one of your favorites. In most circumstances, you lack confidence and will go out of your way to avoid situations involving intensive exercise of this intelligence. Your competence is probably relatively low. Unless you are unusually motivated, gaining expertise might be frustrating and likely would require great effort. All intelligences, including this one, can be enhanced throughout your lifetime.
16–26 (2)	Moderate Intensity: You tend to "accept" it, or use it with some comfort and ease. Secondary preference (2). You could take or leave the application or use of this intelligence. Though you accept it, you do not necessarily prefer to employ it. But, on the other hand, you would not necessarily avoid using it. This may be because you have not developed your ability, or because you have a moderate preference for this intelligence. Your competence is probably moderate also. Gaining expertise would be satisfying, but probably would require considerable effort.
27–35 (1)	High Intensity: You tend to "prefer" it, and use it often with comfort and facility. Primary preference (1). You enjoy using this intelligence. Applying it is fun. You are excited and challenged by it, perhaps even fascinated. You prefer this intelligence. Given the opportunity, you will usually select it. Everyone knows you love it. Your competence is probably relatively high if you have had opportunities to develop it. Becoming an expert should be rewarding and fulfilling, and will probably require little effort compared to a moderate or low preference.

NOTE: After you have scored the RIMI, ask yourself: Do the scores I received on the RIMI correspond to what I know about myself? Based on this inventory, what are the implications of my style of learning? How might I want to change the way I approach learning? How can I best learn?

Resources for Future Study

Web Site Resources

WADSWORTH, THE COMPLETE PSYCHOLOGY PUBLISHER
http://psychology.wadsworth.com/

This is a resource for both students and faculty alike that provides numerous resources in the field of psychology. It offers a continuously updated professional association conference calendar, links to current research through journal sites and professional associations, and a Faculty Lounge (password required) with resources for instructors.

MENTAL HELP NET
http://www.mentalhelp.net/

Mental Help Net is an excellent site that explores all aspects of mental health. It "has become the most comprehensive source of online mental health information, news, and resources available today." This site includes items such as HealthScout, which offers daily updated news articles, online support forums, books, and so on. There are links to more than 8,000 resources, so whatever you are looking for about mental health, it is probably here.

AMERICAN SELF-HELP CLEARINGHOUSE SOURCE BOOK
http://www.cmhc.com/selfhelp/

This site provides contact information for more than 800 self-help groups and organizations across the United States.

AMERICAN COUNSELING ASSOCIATION (ACA)
http://www.counseling.org

ACA is a major organization of counselors that puts out a resource catalog that provides information on the various aspects of the counseling profession. The site provides information about membership, journals, books, home-study programs, videotapes, and audiotapes.

AMERICAN PSYCHOLOGICAL ASSOCIATION (APA)
http://www.apa.org/

This is the major professional organization of psychologists. This resource give leads for current research and literature on many of the topics in this book.

InfoTrac College Edition Resources

For additional readings, explore InfoTrac College Edition, our online library.

Go to **http://www.infotrac.college.com/wadsworth**

Hint: Enter the search terms:

personal growth
active learning
multiple intelligence
learning style
personal adjustment
humanistic psychology
Adlerian psychology
Jungian psychology
self-actualization
self-awareness

Print Resources

Goleman, D. (1995). *Emotional intelligence.* New York: Bantam Books.

Hwang, P. O. (2000). *Other-esteem: Meaningful life in a multicultural society.* Philadelphia, PA: Accelerated Development (Taylor & Francis).

Miller, T. (1995). *How to want what you have: Discovering the magic and grandeur of ordinary existence.* New York: Avon.

Peck, M. S. (1987). *The different drum: Community making and peace.* New York: Simon & Schuster (Touchstone).

Seligman, M. E. P. (1993). *What you can change and what you can't.* New York: Fawcett Columbine.

What we resist persists

R. Hutchings/PhotoEdit

REVIEWING YOUR CHILDHOOD AND ADOLESCENCE

Use this scale to respond to these statements:

4 = This statement is true of me *most* of the time.
3 = This statement is true of me *much* of the time.
2 = This statement is true of me *some* of the time.
1 = This statement is true of me *almost none* of the time.

_____ 1. I am capable of looking at my past decisions and then making new decisions that will significantly change the course of my life.

_____ 2. "Shoulds" and "oughts" often get in the way of my living my life the way I want.

_____ 3. To a large degree I have been shaped by the events of my childhood and adolescent years.

_____ 4. When I think of my early childhood years, I remember feeling secure, accepted, and loved.

_____ 5. As a child, I was taught not to express feelings such as rage, anger, hatred, jealousy, and aggression.

_____ 6. I had desirable models to pattern my behavior after when I was growing up.

_____ 7. In looking back at my early school-age years, I had a positive self-concept and experienced more successes than failures.

_____ 8. I went through a stage of rebellion during my adolescent years.

_____ 9. My adolescent years were lonely ones.

_____ 10. I was greatly influenced by peer group pressure during my adolescence.

This chapter and the next one lay the groundwork for much of the rest of the book by focusing on our lifelong struggle to achieve psychological emancipation, or autonomy. The term *autonomy* refers to mature independence and interdependence. As you will recall from the previous chapter, becoming a fully functioning person occurs in the context of relationships with others and with concern for the welfare of others. If you are an autonomous person, you are able to function without constant approval and reassurance, are sensitive to the needs of others, can effectively meet the demands of daily living, are willing to ask for help when it is needed, and can provide support to others. In essence, you have the ability both to stand alone and to stand by another person. You are at home with both your inner world and your outer world. Although you are concerned with meeting your needs, you do not do so at the expense of those around you. You are aware of the impact your behavior may have on others, and you consider the welfare of others as well as your own self-development. Self-development that occurs at the expense of others will almost inevitably backfire because harm you bring to others will generally result in harm being returned to you. Concern for others is not simply an obligation that requires self-sacrifice. Healthy relationships involve self-enhancement and attention to the welfare of others.

Achieving personal autonomy is a continuing process of growth and learning. Your attitudes toward gender-role identity, work, your body, love, sexuality, intimacy, loneliness, death, and meaning—themes we discuss in later chapters— were originally influenced by your family of origin and your cultural context and by the decisions you made during your early years. Each stage of life has its own challenges and meanings, and you continue to develop and change throughout your life. In this chapter we describe the stages from infancy through adolescence; in Chapter 3 we take up early, middle, and late adulthood.

STAGES OF PERSONALITY DEVELOPMENT: A PREVIEW

Each of the developmental theorists have a somewhat different conceptualization of the stages from infancy to old age. By getting a picture of the challenges at each period of life, you will be able to understand how earlier stages of personality development influence the choices you make later in life. These stages are not precise categories that people fall into neatly, and different theories have slightly different conceptualizations of how long people remain in a given stage of life. In reality there is great variability among individuals within a given developmental phase. Your family of origin, culture, race, gender, and socioeconomic status all have a great deal to do with the manner in which you experience the developmental process. Some people at age 70 are truly old in their appearance, way of thinking, and general health. Yet others at 70 may still retain a great deal of vitality and truly be young. Chronological age is not the only index in considering emotional, physical, and social age.

There are many theoretical approaches to understanding human growth and development. These theories provide a road map to understanding how people develop in all areas of personal functioning. We cannot address all of these models in this book, but we can establish a foundation from which you will be able to reflect on turning points in your childhood and adolescent years. As you read the detailed descriptions of the life cycle, think about how what is written either fits or does not fit for you. Although the cognitive presentation is important, reflecting on your life experiences will bring enhanced meaning to the discussion of these life stages.

In much of this chapter we describe a model that draws on Erik Erikson's (1963, 1982) theory of human development. We also highlight some major ideas about development from the self-in-context approach, which emphasizes the individual life cycle in a systemic perspective (see McGoldrick & Carter, 1999, for more on this). The systemic perspective is grounded on the assumption that how we develop can best be understood through learning about our role and place in our family of origin. The systemic view is that individuals cannot really be understood apart from the family system of which they are a part. We also draw on some basic concepts of Freudian psychoanalytic theory of personality.

Sigmund Freud, the father of psychoanalysis, developed one of the most comprehensive theories of personality in the early 1900s. He pioneered new techniques for understanding human behavior, and his efforts resulted in the most comprehensive theory of personality and psychotherapy ever developed. Freud emphasized unconscious psychological processes and stressed the importance of early childhood experiences. According to his viewpoint, our sexual and social development is largely based on the first 6 years of life. During this time, Freud maintained, we go through distinct stages of development. Our later personality development hinges on how well we resolve the demands and conflicts of each stage. Most of the problems people wrestle with in adulthood have some connection with unresolved conflicts dating from early childhood.

Erikson built on and extended Freud's ideas, stressing the psychosocial aspects of development and carrying his own developmental theory beyond childhood. Erikson is often credited with bringing an emphasis on social factors to contemporary psychoanalysis. Although intellectually indebted to Freud, Erikson suggested that we should view human development in a more positive light, focusing on health and growth. Erikson's theory focuses on the emergence of the self and the ways in which the self develops through our interactions with our social and cultural environment. Later in this chapter we will return to a more detailed discussion about development and protection of the self.

Erikson believes that we face the task of establishing an equilibrium between ourselves and our social world at each stage of life. Psychosocial theory stresses integration of the biological, psychological, and social aspects of development. It provides a conceptual framework for understanding trends in development; major developmental tasks at each stage of life; critical needs and their satisfaction or frustration; potentials for choice at each stage of life; critical turning points or developmental crises; and the origins of faulty personality development, which lead to later personality conflicts.

Erikson described human development over the entire life span in terms of eight stages, each marked by a particular crisis to be resolved. For Erikson, crisis implies a turning point in life, a moment of transition characterized by the potential to go either forward or backward in development. Levinson and Levinson (1996) write that a developmental crisis occurs when individuals have great difficulty meeting the tasks of the current period and that people often experience moderate to severe crises during transitional periods. The crisis revolves around being caught between the ending of one phase of life and the beginning of another era in one's development. Individuals may not know which way to turn. They can move neither forward nor backward, and there is a sense of imminent danger of the loss of a future. Indeed, as was mentioned in Chapter 1, crisis offers both dangers and opportunities. At these critical turning points we can achieve successful resolution of our conflicts and move ahead, or we can fail to resolve the conflicts and regress. To a large extent, our lives are the result of the choices we make at each stage.

McGoldrick and Carter (1999) have criticized Erikson's theory of individual development for underplaying the importance of the interpersonal realm and connection to others. Contextual factors have a critical bearing on our ability to formulate a clear identity as an individual and also to be able to connect to others. The self-in-context perspective, as described by McGoldrick and Carter (1999), takes into account race, socioeconomic class, gender, ethnicity, and culture as central factors that influence the course of development throughout the individual's life cycle.

The feminist perspective is also critical of the Freudian psychoanalytic approach and Erikson's focus on the individual. During the late 1960s and the early 1970s, feminist writers began to focus on the limitations of traditional psychoanalytic theories and techniques that neglected or misunderstood many aspects of women's experiencing. Feminists began to develop conceptual models and ways of practicing that emphasized human connections (Miller & Stiver, 1997). Feminist thought provides a unique perspective on developmental concerns of both women and men and broadens the psychodynamic approach and the psychosocial model of Erikson. Not limited to individual development and autonomy, the focus is on going beyond the self and establishing connections with others. In their excellent book, *The Healing Connection: How Women Form Relationships in Therapy and in Life*, Jean Baker Miller and Irene Pierce Stiver (1997) develop this theme, explaining how we create connections with others and how disconnections derail us throughout our lives.

Our approach has been to combine Erikson's psychosocial theory, the self-in-context theory, and the feminist model, integrating their separate strengths to provide a meaningful framework for understanding key factors influencing our development throughout the life cycle. The life-span perspective presented in these two chapters relies heavily on concepts borrowed from Erikson's model and the self-in-context theories (especially McGoldrick & Carter, 1999). We have also drawn from significant parts of Miller and Stiver's (1997) book as it applies to the various life stages. In addition, we are indebted to a number of other writers, including Berne (1975), Borysenko (1996), Elkind (1984), Gould (1978), Goleman (1995), Mary and Robert Goulding (1978, 1979), Hamachek (1988, 1990), Jordan, Kaplan, Miller, Stiver, and Surrey (1991), Levinson and Levinson (1996), Sheehy (1976, 1981, 1995), and Steiner (1975). Table 2.1 provides an overview of the major turning points in the life-span perspective of human development.

Table 2.1   Overview of Developmental Stages

Life stage	Self-in-context view	Erikson's psychosocial view	Potential problems
Infancy (birth to age 2)	This is a time for the development of empathy and emotional attunement. Some specific tasks include learning to talk, making needs known, developing coordination, recognizing self as a separate person, and trusting others. Infants learn how to sit, stand, walk, run, manipulate objects, and feed themselves. They communicate both frustration and happiness.	*Infancy.* Basic task is to develop a sense of trust in self, others, and the environment. Infants need a sense of being cared for and loved. Absence of a sense of security may lead to suspiciousness and a general sense of mistrust toward human relationships. Core struggle: *trust* versus *mistrust.* Theme: hope.	Later personality problems that stem from infancy can include greediness and acquisitiveness, the development of a view of the world based on mistrust, fear of reaching out to others, rejection of affection, fear of loving and trusting, low self-esteem, isolation and withdrawal, and inability to form or maintain intimate relationships.
Early childhood (ages 2–6)	The theme of this phase is a growing understanding of interdependence. Great strides in language and motor development are made. A key task is to develop emotional competence, which involves being able to delay gratification. This stage ushers in the awareness of "otherness" in terms of gender, race, and disability. Other tasks include learning cooperative play, being able to share, developing peer relationships, becoming aware of self in relation to the world around us, and increasing our ability to trust others.	*Early childhood.* A time for developing autonomy. Failure to master self-control tasks may lead to shame and doubt about oneself and one's adequacy. Core struggle: *self-reliance* versus *self-doubt.* Theme: will. *Preschool age.* Characterized by play and by anticipation of roles; a time to establish a sense of competence and initiative. Children who are not allowed to make decisions tend to develop a sense of guilt. Core struggle: *initiative* versus *guilt.* Theme: purpose.	Children experience many negative feelings such as hostility, rage, destructiveness, anger, and hatred. If these feelings are not accepted, individuals may not be able to accept their feelings later on. Parental attitudes can be communicated verbally and nonverbally. Negative learning experiences tend to lead to feelings of guilt about natural impulses. Strict parental indoctrination can lead to rigidity, severe conflicts, remorse, and self-condemnation.

(continued)

Table 2.1 **Overview of Developmental Stages** (continued)

Life stage	Self-in-context view	Erikson's psychosocial view	Potential problems
Middle childhood (ages 6–12)	This is a time when children learn to read, write, and do math. They increase their understanding of self in terms of gender, race, culture, and abilities. There is an increased understanding of self in relation to family, peers, and community. A key task is developing empathy, or being able to take the perspective of others.	*School age.* Central task is to achieve a sense of industry; failure to do so results in a sense of inadequacy. Child needs to expand understanding of the world and continue to develop appropriate gender-role identity. Learning basic skills is essential for school success. Core struggle: *industry* versus *inferiority*. Theme: competence.	Problems that can originate during middle childhood include negative self-concept, feelings of inferiority in establishing social relationships, conflicts over values, confused gender-role identity, dependency, fear of new challenges, and lack of initiative.
Pubescence (ages 11–13 for girls) (ages 12–14 for boys)	A time of finding one's own voice and the beginning of developing a sense of autonomy. Some specific developmental tasks include asserting oneself, developing emotional competence, increasing capacity for moral understanding, coping with dramatic bodily changes, increasing ability to deal with social relationships and work collaboratively, and developing awareness of own and others' sexuality. This is a time of expanded sense of self in relation to peers, family, and community.		
Adolescence (ages 13–20)	The theme of this period is searching for an identity, continuing to find one's voice, and balancing caring of self with caring about others. Key developmental themes include dealing with rapid body changes and body image issues, learning self-management, developing one's sexual identity, developing a philosophy of life and a spiritual identity, learning to deal with intimate relationships, and an expanded understanding of self in relation to others.	*Adolescence.* A critical time for forming a personal identity. Major conflicts center on clarification of self-identity, life goals, and life's meaning. Struggle is over integrating physical and social changes. Pressures include succeeding in school, choosing a job, forming relationships, and preparing for future. Core struggle: *identity* versus *role confusion*. Theme: fidelity.	A time when individual may anticipate an *identity crisis*. Caught in the midst of pressures, demands, and turmoil, adolescents often lose a sense of self. If *role confusion* results, individual may lack sense of purpose in later years. Absence of a stable set of values can prevent mature development of a philosophy to guide one's life.

Table 2.1   Overview of Developmental Stages (continued)

Life stage	Self-in-context view	Erikson's psychosocial view	Potential problems
Early adulthood (ages 21–35)	The major aim of this period of life is being able to engage in intimate relationships and find satisfying work. Some developmental issues include caring for self and others, focusing on long-range goals, nurturing others physically and emotionally, finding a meaning in life, and developing a tolerance for delayed gratification to meet long-range goals.	*Young adulthood.* Sense of identity is again tested by the challenge of achieving intimacy. Ability to form close relationships depends on having a clear sense of self. Core struggle: *intimacy* versus *isolation.* Theme: love.	The challenge of this period is to maintain one's separateness while becoming attached to others. Failing to strike a balance leads to self-centeredness or to exclusive focus on needs of others. Failure to achieve intimacy can lead to alienation and isolation.
Middle adulthood (ages 35–55)	A time for "going outside oneself." This period sees the reassessment of one's work satisfactions, of involvement in the community, and of accepting choices made in life. A time for solidifying one's philosophy of life. Tasks include nurturing and supporting one's children, partner, and older family members. One challenge is to recognize accomplishments and accept limitations.	*Middle age.* Individuals become more aware of their eventual death and begin to question whether they are living well. The crossroads of life; a time for reevaluation. Core struggle: *generativity* versus *stagnation.* Theme: care.	Failure to achieve a sense of productivity can lead to stagnation. Pain can result when individuals recognize the gap between their dreams and what they have achieved.
Late middle age (ages 55–70)	This is the beginning of the wisdom years, in which key themes are helping others, serving the community, and passing along one's values and experiences. A few critical tasks of this period include dealing with declining physical and intellectual abilities, coming to terms with the choices one has made in life, planning for work transitions and retirement, defining one's senior roles in work and community, and dealing with the death of parents.		

(continued)

Table 2.1   **Overview of Developmental Stages** *(continued)*

Life stage	Self-in-context view	Erikson's psychosocial view	Potential problems
Late adulthood (age 70 onward)	Themes of this final stage of life are grief, loss, resiliency, retrospection, and growth. This is a time to find new levels of meaning in life and to appreciate what one has accomplished. Some tasks of this period are responding to loss and change, remaining connected to others, coming to terms with death, focusing on what else one can do for others and oneself, engaging in a life review, accepting increased dependence on others, accepting death of a spouse or loved ones, and dealing with diminished control of one's life.	*Later life.* Ego integrity is achieved by those who have few regrets, who see themselves as living a productive life, and who have coped with both successes and failures. Key tasks are to adjust to losses, death of others, maintaining outside interests, and adjusting to retirement. Core struggle: *integrity* versus *despair.* Theme: wisdom.	Failure to achieve ego integrity often leads to feelings of hopelessness, guilt, resentment, and self-rejection. Unfinished business from earlier years can lead to fears of death stemming from sense that life has been wasted.

INFANCY

From birth to age 2 infants are becoming acquainted with their world. Developmental psychologists contend that a child's basic task in the first year of life is to develop a sense of trust in self, others, and the environment. Infants need to count on others; they need to sense that they are cared for and that the world is a secure place. They learn this sense of trust by being held, caressed, and loved.

Infants form a basic conception of the social world during this time, and Erikson saw their core struggle as *trust* versus *mistrust.* If the significant other persons in an infant's life provide the needed warmth, cuddling, and attention, the child develops a sense of trust. When these conditions are not present, the child becomes suspicious about interacting with others and acquires a general sense of mistrust toward human relationships. Although neither orientation is fixed in an infant's personality for life, it is clear that well-nurtured infants are in a more favorable position with respect to future personal growth than are their more neglected peers.

Daniel Goleman (1995) believes infancy is the beginning point for establishing emotional intelligence. He identifies the most crucial factor in teaching emo-

Joe Polillio/Stone

A sense of being loved during infancy is the best safeguard against fear, insecurity, and inadequacy.

tional competence as timing, especially in our family of origin and in our culture of origin during infancy. He adds that childhood and adolescence expand on the foundation for learning a range of human competencies. Later development offers critical *windows of opportunity* for acquiring the basic emotional patterns that will govern the rest of our lives.

A sense of being loved during infancy is the best safeguard against fear, insecurity, and inadequacy. Children who receive love from parents or parental substitutes generally have little difficulty accepting themselves, whereas children who feel unloved and unwanted may find it very difficult to accept themselves. In addition, rejected children learn to mistrust the world and to view it primarily in terms of its ability to do them harm. Some of the effects of rejection in infancy include tendencies in later childhood to be fearful, insecure, jealous, aggressive, hostile, or isolated. This disconnection with self and others inhibits learning the essential emotional habits that will enable them to care about others, to be compassionate, and to form meaningful connections with others.

At times parents may be unduly anxious about wanting to be the perfect mother and father. They spend time worrying about "doing the right thing at the right time," and they hope to have the "perfectly well-adjusted child." This chronic anxiety can be the very thing that causes difficulties, as their sons and daughters will soon sense that they must be "perfect children." Children can and do survive the "mistakes" that all parents make, but chronic neglect or over-protection can have negative long-term effects. Sally's story illustrates the possible effects of severe deprivation during the early developmental years.

SALLY'S STORY

I was released for adoption by my biological parents and spent the first decade of my life in orphanages and foster homes. I pleaded to stay with one set of foster parents who had kept me for over a year and then said I had to go. I spent many years thinking that something was wrong with me. If my own parents didn't want me, who could? I tried to figure out what I had done wrong and why so many people sent me away.

As an adult, I still yearn for what I missed during infancy and childhood. I don't get close to anyone now because if I do they might leave me. I had to isolate myself emotionally to survive when I was a child, and I still operate on the assumptions I had as a child. I am so fearful of being deserted that I won't venture out and take even minimal risks. I am 40 years old now, but I still feel like a child.

Sally is not unusual. We have worked with a number of individuals who suffer from the effects of early psychological deprivation, and we have observed that in most cases such deprivation has lingering adverse effects on a person's level of self-love and the ability to form meaningful relationships later in life. Many people, of all ages, struggle with the issue of trusting others in a loving relationship. They are unable to trust that another can or will love them, they fear being rejected, and they fear even more the possibility of closeness and being accepted and loved. Many of these people do not trust themselves or others sufficiently to make themselves vulnerable enough to experience love. We have all heard about children who were adopted, perhaps as infants, who are now striving to find their natural parents. Even if they love their adopted parents and view them as having done a splendid parenting job, these adult children often feel a void and wonder about the circumstances of their adoption. These adult children may feel that their biological mother and father did not want them or that in some way they were at fault for what happened. Many people reexperience their childhood feelings of hurt and rejection during the process of counseling; in this way they come to understand that even though they did not feel loved by their parents this does not mean that others find them unlovable now.

At this point, pause and ask yourself these questions:

❭ Am I able to trust others? Myself?

❭ Am I willing to make myself known to a few selected people in my life?

❭ Do I basically accept myself as being OK, or do I seek confirmation outside of myself?

❭ How far will I go in my attempt to be liked? Do I need to be liked and approved of by everyone?

❭ Am I in any way like Sally? Do I know of anyone who has had experiences similar to hers?

❭ How much do I really know about my early years? What have I heard from my parents and extended family about my infancy and early childhood?

EARLY CHILDHOOD

The tasks children must master in early childhood (ages 2–6) include learning independence, accepting personal power, and learning to cope with impulsive and aggressive reactions and behavior. The critical task is to begin the journey toward autonomy by progressing from being taken care of by others to meeting some of their own physical needs.

Erikson identified the core struggle of early childhood, which for him ranges from ages 1 to 3, as the conflict of *autonomy* versus *shame and doubt*. Children who fail to master the task of establishing some control over themselves and coping with the world around them develop a sense of shame, and they doubt their capabilities. Erikson emphasized that during this time children become aware of their emerging skills and have a drive to try them out. To illustrate this point, I (Marianne) remember when I was feeding one of our daughters during her infancy. Heidi had been a very agreeable child who swallowed all of the food I put into her mouth. One day, much to my surprise, she spit it right back at me! No matter how much I wanted her to continue eating, she refused. This was one way in which Heidi began asserting herself with me. As my children were growing up, I strove to establish a good balance between allowing them to develop their own identity and at the same time providing them with guidance and appropriate limits.

During early childhood, great strides in language and motor development are made. This is a time for the beginning of a growing understanding of what it means to be interdependent. Goleman (1995) points to the importance of developing emotional competence, especially learning to regulate and control emotions and impulses, and also to delay gratification. Peer relationships are particularly critical at this time, and children need to acquire a cooperative spirit

Heidi Jo Corey

A child's basic task in the first year of life is to develop a sense of trust in self, others, and the environment.

and the ability to share. This is a time when children begin to become aware of themselves in relation to the world around them. They also become aware of "otherness" in terms of gender, race, and disability (McGoldrick & Carter, 1999).

Erikson identified the preschool years (ages 3–6) as being characterized by play and by anticipation of roles. During this time, children try to find out how much they can do. They imitate others; they begin to develop a sense of right and wrong; they widen their circle of significant persons; they take more initiative; they learn to give and receive love and affection; they identify with their own gender; they begin to learn more complex social skills; they learn basic attitudes regarding sexuality; and they increase their capacity to understand and use language.

According to Erikson, the basic task of these preschool years is to establish a sense of competence and initiative. The core struggle is between *initiative* and *guilt*. Preschool children begin to initiate many of their own activities as they become physically and psychologically ready to engage in pursuits of their own choosing. If they are allowed realistic freedom to make some of their own decisions, they tend to develop a positive orientation characterized by confidence in their ability to initiate and follow through. If they are unduly restricted or if their choices are ridiculed, however, they tend to experience a sense of guilt and ultimately to withdraw from taking an active stance. One middle-aged woman we talked with still finds herself extremely vulnerable to being seen as foolish. She recalls that during her childhood family members laughed at her attempts to perform certain tasks. Even now she very vividly carries these pictures in her head and allows them to have some control of her life.

Preschool children begin to pay attention to their genitals and experience pleasure from genital stimulation. They typically engage in both masturbatory and sex-play activities. They begin to show considerable curiosity about the differences between the sexes and the differences between adults and children. This is the time for questions such as "Where do babies come from?" and "Why are boys and girls different?" Parental attitudes toward these questions, which can be communicated nonverbally as well as verbally, are critical in helping children form a positive attitude toward their own sexuality. This is a time of conscience formation, and parents must refrain from instilling rigid and unrealistic moral standards, which can lead to an overdeveloped conscience. Children who learn that their bodies and their impulses are evil soon begin to feel guilty about them. Carried into adult life, these attitudes can prevent people from appreciating and enjoying sexual intimacy. Another danger is that strict parental indoctrination, which can be accomplished in subtle, nonverbal ways, will lead to an infantile conscience. Children may develop a fear of questioning and thinking for themselves and blindly accept the dictates of their parents. Other effects of such indoctrination include rigidity, severe conflicts, guilt, remorse, and self-condemnation.

Pause and reflect on some of your own current struggles with these issues:

❭ What did you learn from your culture about the way to behave as a woman or a man?

❭ Are you comfortable with your own sexuality? With your body?

❭ Are there any unresolved conflicts from your childhood that get in the way of your enjoyment?

❭ Does your present behavior, or current conflicts, indicate areas of unfinished business?

Parents who squelch any emerging individuality and who do too much for their children hamper their development. They are saying, however indirectly, "Let us do this for you, because you're too clumsy, too slow, or too inept to do things for yourself." Young children need to experiment; they need to be allowed to make mistakes and still feel that they are basically worthwhile. If parents insist on keeping their children dependent on them, the children will begin to doubt their own abilities. If parents do not appreciate their children's efforts, the children may feel ashamed of themselves or become insecure and fearful.

Sometimes children may want to do more than they are capable of doing. For example, the 5-year-old son of a friend of ours went on a hike with his father. At one point the boy asked his father to let him carry a heavy backpack the way the "big people" do. Without saying a word, the father took his backpack off and handed it to his son, who immediately discovered that it was too heavy for him to carry. The boy simply exclaimed, "Dad, it's too heavy for me." He then went happily on his way up the trail. In a safe way the father had allowed his son to discover experientially that he was, indeed, too small. He had also avoided a potential argument with his son.

In the preschool years, children widen their circle of significant persons and learn more complex social skills.

Barbara Rios/Photo Researchers, Inc.

Young children also must learn to accept the full range of their feelings. They will surely experience anger, and it is important that they know and feel that anger is permissible. They need to feel loved and accepted with all of their feelings, otherwise they will tend to stifle their anger so as not to lose the love of their parents. When anger cannot be acknowledged or expressed, it becomes toxic and finds expression in indirect ways. One of the results of denying anger is that children begin to numb all of their feelings, including joy.

As adults, many of us have difficulty acknowledging our anger, even when it is fully justified. We may swallow our anger and rationalize away other feelings because we learned when we were 2 or 3 years old that we were unacceptable when we had such feelings. As children we might have shouted at our parents: "I hate you! I never want to see you again!" Then we may have heard an equally enraged parent reply: "How dare you say such a thing—after all I've done for you! I don't ever want to hear that from you again!" We soon take these messages to mean "Don't be angry! Never be angry with those you love! Keep control of yourself!" And we do just that, keeping many of our feelings to ourselves, stuffing them in the pit of our stomach and pretending we do not experience them. It is not surprising that so many of us suffer from migraine headaches, peptic ulcers, hypertension, and heart disease.

Again, take time out to reflect in a personal way on some of your current struggles toward autonomy and self-worth. Ask yourself these questions:

❭ Am I able to recognize my own feelings, particularly if they are "unacceptable" to others?

❭ How do I express my anger to those I love?

❭ Have I established a good balance between depending on others and relying on myself?

❭ Am I able to let others know what I want? Can I be assertive without being aggressive?

IMPACT OF THE FIRST 6 YEARS OF LIFE

You may be asking yourself why we are emphasizing the events of this period. In working with clients we continue to realize the influence of these early years on their levels of integration and functioning as adults. Sometimes people ask, "Why look back into my past? I don't see any point in dredging up that painful period, especially since I've worked so hard to get that part of my life under control."

Many of these childhood experiences have a profound impact on both the present and the future. If you reached faulty conclusions based on your early life experience, you are likely to still be operating on the basis of them. If you told yourself as a child that "I can never do enough for my father," as an adult you may feel today that you can never do enough (or be enough) to meet the expectations of those who are significant in your life. Not only is our current functioning influenced by early interpretations, but our future is too. Our goals and purposes have some connection with the way we dealt with emerging issues during the first 6 years of life.

In working in counseling groups with relatively well-functioning adults who have "normal" developmental issues, we find that a new understanding of their early years often entails a certain degree of emotional pain. Yet by understanding these painful events, they have a basis for transcending them and not being stuck replaying old self-defeating themes throughout their lifetime. We do not think healthy people are ever really "cured" of their vulnerabilities or their shadow. For example, during your preschool years, if you felt abandoned by the divorce of your parents, you are still likely to have vestiges of fears and hesitations when forming close relationships. Yet you do not have to surrender to these traces of mistrust. Instead, you can gain control of your fears of loving and trusting.

In reviewing your childhood, you may well find some aspects that you like and do not want to change. You may also find a certain continuity in your life that gives you meaning. At the same time, if you are honest with yourself, you are likely to become aware of certain revisions you would like to make. This awareness is the first critical step toward changing.

Typical problems and conflicts we confront among people in our personal-growth groups include an inability to trust oneself and others; an inability to freely accept and give love; difficulty recognizing and expressing the full range of one's feelings; guilt over feelings of anger or hatred toward those one loves; an inability or unwillingness to control one's own life; difficulties in fully accepting one's sexuality or in finding meaning in sexual intimacy; difficulty in accepting oneself as a woman or a man; and problems concerning a lack of meaning or purpose in life or a clear sense of personal identity and aspirations. Notice that most of these adult problems are directly related to the turning points and tasks of the early developmental years. The effects of early learning are reversible in most cases, but these experiences, whether favorable or unfavorable, clearly influence how we interpret future critical periods in our lives.

Some people learn new values, come to accept new feelings and attitudes, and overcome much of their past negative conditioning. Other people steadfastly hang on to the past as an excuse for not taking any action to change in the present. We cannot change in a positive direction unless we stop blaming others for the way we are now. Statements that begin "If it hadn't been for . . ." are too often used to justify an immobile position. Blaming others for our present struggles ultimately keeps us trapped, waiting for "them out there" to change before we can change. Whenever you catch yourself pointing an accusing finger at someone else, it is a good idea to look at your other fingers—pointing back at you. Once we are able to see in ourselves the very traits that we accuse others of, and once we quit blaming others, we make it possible to take charge of our own lives.

You may experience anger and hurt for having been cheated in the past. However, it is imperative that you eventually reclaim the power you have given away to the people who were once significant in your life. Unless you recognize and exercise the power you now have to take care of yourself, you close the door to new choices and new growth.

Take Time to Reflect

1. Close your eyes and reflect for a moment on your memories of your first 6 years. Attempt to identify your earliest concrete single memory—something you actually remember that happened to you, not something you were told about. Spend a few minutes recalling the details and reexperiencing the feelings associated with this early event.

   a. Write down your earliest recollection: _____

   _____

b. What is your main memory of your father? Mother? Siblings? _____

_____

2. Reflect on the events that most stand out for you during your first 6 years of life. In particular, think about your place in your family, your family's reaction to you, and your reactions to each person in your family. What connections do you see between how it felt to be in your family as a child and how you now feel in various social situations? What speculations do you have concerning the impact your family had then and the effect that these experiences continue to have on your current personality?

_____

_____

3. Take the following self-inventory. Respond quickly, marking "T" if you believe the statement is more true than false for you as a young child and "F" if it tends not to fit your early childhood experiences.

_____ As a young child, I felt loved and accepted.
_____ I basically trusted the world.
_____ I felt that I was an acceptable and valuable person.
_____ I felt I needed to work for others' approval.
_____ I experienced a great deal of shame and self-doubt as a child.
_____ I felt that it was not OK for me to express anger.
_____ My parents trusted my ability to do things for myself.
_____ I believe I developed a natural and healthy concept of my body and my gender-role identity.
_____ I had very few friends as a young child.
_____ I felt that I could talk to my parents about my problems.

Look over your responses. What do they tell you about the person you now are? If you could live your childhood over again, how would you like it to be? Record some of your impressions in your journal.

MIDDLE CHILDHOOD

During middle childhood (ages 6–12), children face these key developmental tasks: engage in social activities; expand their knowledge and understanding of the physical and social worlds; continue to learn and expand their concepts of an appropriate feminine or masculine role; develop a sense of values; learn new communication skills; learn how to read, write, and calculate; learn to give and take; learn how to accept people who are culturally different; learn to tolerate ambiguity; and learn physical skills. McGoldrick and Carter (1999) point out that during middle childhood there is an increased understanding of self in terms of gender, race, culture, and abilities; of self in relationship to family, peers, and community; and an increase in the capacity for empathy. These authors add that by ages 9 to 12 children begin to form an identification with causes, aspirations, and privileges of groups they belong to, which provides the motivation for them to think and act in certain ways. A key social ability in children is empathy, which involves understanding the feelings of others, being able to take others' perspective, and respecting differences in how people feel about things (Goleman, 1995). This empathy includes being able to understand distress beyond an immediate situation and to feel for the plight of an entire group such as those who are oppressed or live in poverty. Goleman gives a clearer picture of the role relationships play in the development of children:

> RELATIONSHIPS ARE A MAJOR FOCUS, including learning to be a good listener and question-asker; distinguishing between what someone says or does and your own reactions and judgments; being assertive rather than angry or passive; and learning the arts of cooperation, conflict resolution, and negotiating compromise. (p. 268)

According to Erikson, the major struggle of middle childhood is between *industry* and *inferiority*. The central task of this period is to achieve a sense of industry; failure to do so results in a sense of inadequacy and inferiority. Development of a sense of industry includes focusing on creating and producing and on attaining goals. Of course, starting school is a critical event of this time. The first 4 years of school are vital to successful completion of a healthy outcome of this stage. The child's self-concept is especially fragile before the fourth grade; if teachers are critical of a child's performance, this could have a lasting impact. Children who encounter failure during the early grades may experience severe handicaps later on. A child with early learning problems may begin to feel worthless as a person. Such a feeling may, in turn, drastically affect his or her relationships with peers, which are also vital at this time. Helen's story illustrates some of the common conflicts of the elementary school years.

HELEN'S STORY

I started kindergarten a bit too early and was smaller than most of the other children. I had looked forward to beginning school, but I soon felt overwhelmed. I began to fail at many of the tasks other children were enjoying and mastering. Gradually, I began to avoid even simple tasks and to find excuses for my failures. I became increasingly afraid of making mistakes, and I thought that everything I did had to be perfect. If a picture I was drawing didn't come out right, I would soon become frustrated and rip up the piece of paper.

My teachers thought I was sensitive and needed a lot of encouragement and direction, but I continued to quit too soon because I didn't think my work was "good enough." Some of my teachers did not demand much of me because they didn't want to push me, but then I felt even more different from the other children and I became angry with my teachers. When I was in the third grade, I was at least a grade level behind in reading, despite having repeated kindergarten. I began to feel stupid and embarrassed because I couldn't read as well as the other children, and I did not want to read aloud. Eventually, I received instruction in remedial reading. I liked this attention, but then they gave me some reading tests and I didn't do well. I hate taking tests, and I always think I will fail.

I might have given up on school a long time ago, but many people helped me continue in spite of my fears. I am in college now, and I am still anxious about taking tests. I am learning to control my feelings of inadequacy and self-doubt, and I am arguing back to those old voices that say I am basically inadequate.

Helen's case indicates that the first few years of school can have a powerful impact on a child's life and future adjustment to school. Her school experiences colored her view of her self-worth and affected her relationships with other children. At this point ask yourself these questions:

> Can I identify in any ways with Helen's feelings?

> What struggles did I experience in forming my self-concept?

> Does Helen remind me of anyone I know?

Forming a self-concept is a major task of middle childhood. Let's take a closer look at what this entails.

Developing a Self-Concept

The term *self-concept* refers to your cognitive awareness about yourself. It is your private mental image of yourself and a collection of beliefs about the kind of person you are (Hamachek, 1988, 1990). This picture includes your view of your worth, value, and possibilities; the way you see yourself in relation to others; the way you ideally would like to be; and the degree to which you accept yourself as you are. From ages 6 to 12 the view you have of yourself is influenced greatly by the quality of your school experiences, by contact with your peer group and with teachers, and by your interactions with your family. To a large extent, your self-concept is formed by what others tell you about yourself, especially during the formative years of childhood. Whether you develop a positive or negative outlook on yourself has a good deal to do with what people close to you have expected of you.

PhotoDisc

To a large extent, your self-concept is formed by what others tell you about yourself, especially during childhood.

This view of yourself influences how you present yourself to others and how you act and feel when you are with them. For example, you may feel inadequate around authority figures. Perhaps you tell yourself that you have nothing to say or that whatever you might say would be stupid. More often than not, others will see and respond to you in the way you "tell" them you are, both verbally and nonverbally. Monitor the messages you are sending to others about yourself, and become aware of the patterns you might be perpetuating. It is difficult for those who are close to you to treat you in a positive way when you consistently discount yourself. Why should others treat you better than you treat yourself? In contrast, people with a positive self-concept are likely to behave confidently, which causes others to react to them positively.

Once we have established our self-concept, there are a variety of strategies available to help us maintain and protect it from outside threats. We will explore these defense mechanisms next.

Protecting the Self: Ego-Defense Mechanisms

Ego-defense mechanisms are psychological strategies we use to protect our self-concept from unpleasant emotions. We use these protective devices at various stages of life to soften the blows of harsh reality. Ego defenses typically originate during our childhood years, and later experiences during adolescence and adulthood reinforce some of these self-defense styles. We often carry these habitual responses into adulthood—long after we have any need of them. We will use Helen's story to illustrate the nature and functioning of some of these ego defenses. For the most part Helen made poor adjustments to her school and social life during her childhood years. Other children stayed away from her because of her aggressive and unfriendly behavior. She did not like her elementary school experience, and her teachers were not overly fond of her. Helen's behavioral style in coping with the pressures of school included blaming the outside world for her difficulties. In the face of these failures in life, she might have made use of any one or a combination of the following ego-defense mechanisms.

Repression The mechanism of repression is one of the most important processes in psychoanalytic theory, and it is the basis of many other ego defenses. By pushing threatening or painful thoughts and feelings from awareness, we sometimes manage the anxiety that grows out of situations involving guilt and conflict. Repression may block out stressful experiences that could be met by realistically facing and working through a situation. Helen was unaware of her dependence/independence struggles with her parents; she was also unaware of how her painful experiences of failure were contributing to her feelings of inferiority and insecurity. Helen had unconsciously excluded most of her failures and had not allowed them to come to the surface of awareness.

Denial Denial plays a defensive role similar to that of repression, but it generally operates at a preconscious or conscious level. In denial there is a conscious effort to suppress unpleasant reality. It is a way of distorting what the individual thinks, feels, or perceives to be a stressful situation. Helen simply "closed her eyes" to her failures in school. Even though she had evidence that she was not performing well academically, she refused to acknowledge this reality.

Displacement Displacement involves redirecting emotional impulses (usually hostility) from the real object to a substitute person or object. In essence, anxiety is coped with by discharging impulses onto a "safer target." For example, Helen's sister Joan was baffled by the hostility she received from Helen. Joan did not understand why Helen was so critical of her every action. Helen used Joan as the target of her aggression because Joan did exceptionally well at school and was very popular with her peers.

Projection Another mechanism of self-deception is projection, which consists of attributing to others our own unacceptable desires and impulses. We are able to clearly see in others the very traits that we disown in ourselves, which serves the purpose of keeping a certain view of ourselves intact. Typically, projection involves seeing clearly in others actions that would lead to guilt feelings in ourselves. Helen tended to blame everyone but herself for her difficulties in school and in social relationships. She complained that her teachers were unfairly picking on her, that she could never do anything right for them, and that other children were mean to her.

Reaction Formation One defense against a threatening impulse is to actively express the opposite impulse. This involves behaving in a manner that is contrary to one's real feelings. A characteristic of this defense is the excessive quality of a particular attitude or behavior. For example, Helen bristled when her teachers or parents offered to give her help. She was convinced that she did not need anyone's help. Accepting their offers would have indicated that she really was stupid.

Rationalization Rationalization involves manufacturing a false but "good" excuse to justify unacceptable behavior and explain away failures or losses. Such excuses help restore a bruised ego. Helen was quick to find many reasons for the difficulties she encountered, a few of which included sickness, which caused her to fall behind in her classes; teachers who went over the lessons too fast; other children who did not let her play with them; and siblings who kept her awake at night.

Compensation Another defense reaction is compensation, which consists of masking perceived weaknesses or developing certain positive traits to make up for limitations. The adjustive value in this mechanism lies in keeping one's self-esteem intact by excelling in one area to distract attention from an area in which the person is inferior. The more Helen experienced difficulties at school and with her peers, the more she withdrew from others and became absorbed in artwork that she did by herself at home.

Regression Faced with stress, some people revert to a form of immature behavior that they have outgrown. In regression, they attempt to cope with their anxiety by clinging to such inappropriate behaviors. Faced with failure in both her social and school life, Helen had a tendency to engage in emotional tirades, crying a lot, storming into her room, and refusing to come out for hours.

Fantasy Fantasy involves gratifying frustrated desires by imaginary achievements. When achievement in the real world seems remote, some people resort to screening out unpleasant aspects of reality and living in their world of dreams. During her childhood, Helen developed a rich fantasy in which she imagined herself to be an actress. She played with her dolls for hours and talked to herself. In her daydreams she saw herself in the movies, surrounded by famous people.

Although ego-defense mechanisms have some adaptive value, their overuse can be problematic. Self-deception can soften harsh reality, but the fact is that reality does not change through the process of distorting those aspects of it that produce anxiety. When these defensive strategies do not work, the long-term result is an even greater degree of anxiety. Overreliance on these defenses leads to a vicious circle—as the defenses lose their value in holding anxiety in check, people step up the use of other defenses.

All defenses are not self-defeating, however, and there is a proper place for them, especially when stresses are great. In the face of certain crises, for example, defenses can enable people to cope at least temporarily until they can build up other resources, both from their environment and from within themselves.

Before moving on to the section on adolescence, spend some time reflecting on the defense mechanisms you used during your childhood years. Do you see any analogies between the defenses you employed as a child and those you sometimes use at this time in your life? Think about some of the defenses you use and how they might serve you. Imagine how your life might be different if you gave up all your defenses.

PUBESCENCE

The years from about 11 to 14 constitute a stage of transition between childhood and adolescence. During this phase, boys and girls experience major physical, psychological, and sexual changes. Most people find the pubescent period particularly difficult. It is a paradoxical time. Preadolescents are not treated as mature adults, yet they are often expected to act as though they had gained complete maturity. Continually testing the limits, young people have a strong urge to break away from dependent ties that restrict their freedom. It is not uncommon for preadolescents to be frightened and lonely, but they may mask their fears with rebellion and cover up their need to be dependent by exaggerating their independence. They are typically finding they have a voice and are willing to use it. Much of preadolescent rebellion is an attempt to declare their uniqueness and establish a separate identity. This is the time when individuals assert who and what they want to be.

As infants we must learn to trust ourselves and others; as preadolescents we need to find a meaning in life and adult role models in whom we believe. As toddlers we begin to assert our rights as independent people by struggling for autonomy; as preadolescents we make choices that will shape our future. As preschoolers we try to achieve a sense of competence; as preadolescents and as adolescents we explore choices about what we want from life, what we can succeed in, what kind of education we want, and what career may suit us.

ADOLESCENCE

Adolescence spans the period from about age 13 for girls and age 14 or 15 for boys until the late teens or to about age 20. Adolescence is a critical period in the development of personal identity. For Erikson, the major developmental conflicts of adolescence center on clarification of who they are, where they are going, and how they are going to get there. He sees the core struggle of adolescence as *identity* versus *role confusion.* Failure to achieve a sense of identity results in role confusion. Adolescents may feel overwhelmed by the pressures placed on them and find the development of a clear identity a difficult task. They may feel pressured to make an occupational choice, to compete in the job market or in college, to become financially independent, or to commit themselves to physically and emotionally intimate relationships. In addition, they may feel pressured to live up to the standards of their peer group. Peer group pressure is a potent force, and some adolescents lose their focus on their own identities and conform to the expectations of their friends and classmates. If the need to be accepted and liked is stronger than the need for self-respect, adolescents will most likely find themselves behaving in nongenuine ways and increasingly looking to others to tell them what and who they should be.

Adolescence is a time when young people evolve their sexual and gender identities, learn to form intimate relationships, and learn to function in an increasingly independent manner. Adolescents renegotiate their identity and relationship with their parents, acquire a range of new attitudes and skills, develop their ethical and spiritual identity, and begin the process of defining who they want to become as women or men.

A crucial part of the identity-formation process is *individuation,* separating from our family system and establishing an identity based on our own experiences. This process of psychological separation from parental ties is the most agonizing part of the adolescent struggle and lays the foundation for future development. Achieving psychological separation from one's family is a common theme in Western cultures, but in some other cultures the wishes of parents continue to have a major influence on the behavior of adult children. Furthermore, becoming psychologically separate from one's family may not be seen as a guiding value. Instead, the collective good is given far more weight than individual fulfillment. In many developing countries there is no adolescent phase. At puberty boys and girls are initiated into adult roles for which they have long been prepared. Adolescence is a luxury these cultures cannot afford. The cultural conflict can be enormous when such families emigrate to the West and their children want to become "teens."

Feminist therapists view the early adolescent period as one of expanding relationships with parents—not "getting rid" of parents (Miller & Stiver, 1997). More than needing "separation" from their parents, both preadolescents and adolescents need to *change* their relationship with their parents. If adolescents are able to maintain trustworthy connections with parents, they will be better able to undertake other changes they need to make.

Adolescents confront dilemmas similar to those faced by older people in our society. Both age groups must deal with finding a meaning in life and must cope with feelings of uselessness. Older people may be forced to retire and may encounter difficulty replacing work activities; young people have not completed their education or acquired the skills necessary for many occupations. Instead, they are in a constant process of preparation for the future. Even in their families adolescents may feel unneeded. Although they may be given chores to do, many adolescents do not experience much opportunity to be productive.

The question of options is made even more urgent by the myth that the choices we make during adolescence bind us for the rest of our lives. Adolescents who believe this myth will be hesitant to experiment and test out many options. Too many young people yield to pressures to decide too early what they will be and what serious commitments they will make. Thus, they may never realize the range of possibilities open to them. To deal with this problem, Erikson suggested a *psychological moratorium*—a period during which society would give permission to adolescents to experiment with different roles and values so they could sample life before making major commitments.

Forming a philosophy of life is a central task of adolescence. Sexual, religious, spiritual, and racial issues take on a new perspective and are subject to new understanding and revision (McGoldrick & Carter, 1999). Adolescents are faced with choosing the beliefs and values that will guide their actions as adults. In meeting this challenge young people need adequate models, for a sense of moral living is largely learned by example. Adolescents are especially sensitive to duplicity and are quick to spot phony people who tell them how they ought to live while themselves living in very different ways. They learn values by observing and interacting with adults who are positive examples rather than by being preached to. Of course, not all role models are positive. In some cases adolescents adopt drug dealers or other criminals as role models. Many adolescents look for an identity by affiliation with a gang, and they may find role models within this group.

Today's adolescents also have to cope with violence at school. It is not uncommon for adolescents, and even children, to bring guns or knives to school. News reports of an adolescent injuring fellow classmates or a teacher are all too common. Not only do today's teens have to contend with peer pressure, parental pressure, and the confusion and pain that accompanies finding their identities, they also have to worry about being shot by a schoolmate or being the victim of some other form of violence or intimidation.

Our childhood experiences have a direct influence on how we approach the adolescent years, and how well we master the tasks of adolescence has a bearing on our ability to cope with the critical turning points of adulthood. If we do not develop a clear sense of identity during adolescence, finding meaning in adult life becomes extremely difficult. As we progress from one stage of life to the next, we at times meet with roadblocks and detours and may experience anxiety, depression, or alienation. These barriers are often the result of having failed to master basic psychological competencies at an earlier period. When we encounter such obstacles, we can accept them as signposts and continue down the same path or use them as opportunities for growth. Miller and Stiver (1997) contend that these roadblocks can be turned to pathways of connection between people, which leads to the development of healthy individuals.

Adolescence is typically a turbulent and fast-moving period of life, often marked by feelings of powerlessness, confusion, and loneliness. It is a time for making critical choices, even the ultimate choice of living fully or bringing about one's own death. Decisions are being made in almost every area of life, and these decisions to a large extent define our identity. The following Take Time To Reflect is a chance for you to identify some of the choices you made during your adolescent years and to clarify the impact these experiences continue to exert on you today.

Take Time to Reflect Review the choices open to adolescents, and especially think of the choices you remember having made at this time in your life. How do you think those choices have influenced the person you are today?

1. What major choices did you struggle with during your adolescent years?

_____

_____

_____

2. How do you think your adolescence affected the person you are today?

_____

_____

_____

SUMMARY

A road map of the developmental tasks of the life span reveals that each stage presents certain dangers and offers particular opportunities. Crises can be seen as challenges to be met rather than as catastrophic events that happen to us. In normal development critical turning points and choices appear at each developmental stage. Our early experiences influence the choices we make at later stages in our development. Developmental stages are not discrete but blend into one another. We all experience each period of life in our own unique ways.

The struggle toward autonomy, or psychological independence, begins in early childhood, takes on major proportions during adolescence and young adulthood, and extends into later adulthood. The process of individuation, and the value attached to it, are greatly influenced by culture. Actualizing our full potential as a person and learning to stand alone in life, as well as to stand beside others, is a task that is never really finished. Although major life events during childhood and adolescence have an impact on the way that we think, feel, and behave in adult life, we are not helplessly molded and hopelessly determined by such events. Instead, we can choose to change our attitude toward these events, which in turn will affect how we behave today.

Critical turning points face us during each transition in our lives. At these points we can either successfully resolve the basic conflict or get stuck on the road to development. The basic task of infancy is to develop a sense of trust in others and our environment so we can trust ourselves. Later personality problems that can stem from a failure to develop trust include fearing intimate relationships, low self-esteem, and isolation. Early childhood presents the challenge of beginning to function independently and acquiring a sense of self-control. If we do not master this task, becoming autonomous is extremely difficult. During this phase of life, we are forming our gender-role identity, and ideally we experience a sense of competence that comes with making some decisions for ourselves. Parental attitudes during this period are very powerful, and these attitudes are communicated both verbally and nonverbally. Our school experiences during middle childhood play a significant role in our socialization. At this time the world is opening up to us, and we are expanding our interests outside of the home. Problems that typically begin at this phase include a negative self-concept, conflicts over values, confused gender-role identity, a fear of new challenges, and disturbed interpersonal relationships. Adolescence is the period when we are forming an identity as well as establishing goals and values that give our lives meaning. A danger of this time of life is that we can follow the crowd out of a fear of being rejected and fail to discover what it is that we want for ourselves.

Each of these developmental stages helps lay the foundation on which we build our adult personality. As you will see in the next chapter, mastery of these earlier challenges is essential if we are to cope with the problems of adult living.

> ## Where Can I Go From Here?

1. Write an account in your journal of the first 6 years of your life. Although you may think that you cannot remember much about this time, you can learn more by following these guidelines:
   a. Write down a few key questions that you would like answered about your early years.
   b. Seek out your relatives, and ask them some questions about your early years.
   c. Collect any reminders of your early years, particularly pictures.
   d. Visit the place or places where you lived and went to school.

2. From among the many exercises in this chapter, chose those that you are willing to integrate into a self-help program during your time in this course. What things are you willing to do to bring about some of the changes you want in your life?

3. Pictures often say more about you than words. What do your pictures tell about you? Look through any pictures of yourself as a child and as an adolescent, and see if there are any themes. What do most of your pictures reveal about the way you felt about yourself? Bring some of these pictures to class. Have other members look at them and tell you what they think you were like then. Pictures can also be used to tap forgotten memories.

Resources for Future Study

Web Site Resources

ADOLESCENT DIRECTORY ONLINE
http://education.indiana.edu/cas/adol/adol.html

This site offers resources about adolescents that cover a range of health, mental health, and parenting issues.

AMERICAN ACADEMY OF CHILD AND ADOLESCENT PSYCHIATRY (AACAP): FACTS FOR FAMILIES
http://www.aacap.org/web/aacap/factsFam/

The materials available from this site deal with a range of psychological concerns of children and adolescents.

 InfoTrac College Edition Resources

For additional readings, explore InfoTrac College Edition, our online library.

Go to **http://www.infotrac.college.com/wadsworth**

Hint: Enter the search terms:

> human development AND psychosocial
> life span AND development
> human development AND stages
> developmental crisis
> feminist AND development
> infancy
> early childhood
> middle childhood
> ego defense mechanism

Print Resources

Bloomfield, H. H., with Felder, L. (1985). *Making peace with yourself: Transforming your weaknesses into strengths.* New York: Ballantine.

Borysenko, J. (1996). *A woman's book of life: The biology, psychology and spirituality of the feminine life cycle.* New York: Riverhead Books.

Covey, S. R. (1990). *The seven habits of highly effective people.* New York: Simon & Schuster (Fireside Books).

Edelman, M. W. (1992). *The measure of our success: A letter to my children and yours.* Boston: Beacon Press.

Erikson, E. (1963). *Childhood and society* (2nd ed.). New York: Norton.

Erikson, E. (1982). *The life cycle completed.* New York: Norton.

Goleman, D. (1995). *Emotional intelligence.* New York: Bantam Books.

McGoldrick, M., & Carter, B. (1999). Self in context: The individual life cycle in systemic perspective. In B. Carter & M. McGoldrick (Eds.) *The expanded family life cycle: Individual, family, and social perspectives* (3rd ed.) (pp. 27–46).

Miller, J. B. & Stiver, I. P. (1997). *The healing connection: How women form relationships in therapy and in life.* Boston: Beacon Press.

Independence means not being lonely even when you are alone—*Bernie Siegel*

Corbis

3

ADULTHOOD AND AUTONOMY

❯ **Where Am I Now?**

Use this scale to respond to these statements:

4 = This statement is true of me *most* of the time.

3 = This statement is true of me *much* of the time.

2 = This statement is true of me *some* of the time.

1 = This statement is true of me *almost none* of the time.

_____ 1. My family of origin has greatly influenced my values and beliefs.

_____ 2. I'm an independent person more than I am a dependent person.

_____ 3. I think about early messages I received from my parents.

_____ 4. I am psychologically separated from my parents and have become my own parent.

_____ 5. As I get older, I feel an urgency about living.

_____ 6. Much of my life is spent doing things that I do not enjoy.

_____ 7. I look forward with optimism and enthusiasm to the challenges that lie ahead of me.

_____ 8. I expect to experience a meaningful and rich life when I reach old age.

_____ 9. There are many things I cannot do now that I expect to do when I retire.

_____ 10. I have fears of aging.

In this chapter we continue our discussion of the life-span perspective by focusing on the transitions and turning points in adulthood. Our childhood and adolescent experiences provide the foundation for our ability to meet the developmental challenges of the various phases of adulthood. But throughout adulthood many choices remain open to us. Before taking up early, middle, and late adulthood, we examine how you can become more autonomous. One facet of the struggle toward autonomy involves recognizing the early life decisions you made and realizing that you can change them if they are no longer appropriate or useful. This change entails questioning some of the messages you received and accepted during your early childhood. You can also learn to argue with your self-defeating thoughts and beliefs and acquire a more positive and constructive set of beliefs.

We describe some typical developmental patterns, but everybody does not go through these stages in the same way at the same time. We are not trying to box you in to categories of what is "normal" at each of the stages of development. There is a range of variability at each of these stages, and you will need to determine what meaning your experiences have for you and how you have dealt with the tasks of the various stages of life.

Your family and your culture influence the manner in which you confront developmental tasks. It is important that you understand the ways your culture and family-of-origin experiences have contributed to influencing the person you are. Your passage through adulthood is characterized by the choices you make in response to the demands made on you; look for a pattern of choices in your life. You may see that you are primarily adapting yourself to others, or you may discover a pattern of choosing the path of security rather than risking new adventures. You may be pleased with many of the decisions you have made, or you may wish you had decided differently. As you think about these choices at critical turning points in your adulthood, look for a unifying theme beginning in childhood. Once you become aware of patterns in your life, you can work to change those patterns that you determine are not serving you well. When you understand your earlier experiences and any self-defeating decisions that have influenced you, you can begin to revise these decisions and create a different future.

If you are a young adult, you may wonder why you should be concerned about middle age and later life. We invite you to look at the choices you are making now that will have a direct influence on the quality of your later adulthood. As you read this chapter, reflect on what you hope to be able to say about your life when you reach later adulthood.

THE STRUGGLE TOWARD AUTONOMY AND INTERDEPENDENCE

As we leave adolescence and enter young adulthood, our central task is to assume increased responsibility and independence. Although most of us have moved away physically from our parents, our extended family, and often our

Robert Brenner/PhotoEdit

It is important that you understand the ways your culture and family-of-origin experiences have contributed to influencing the person you are.

community, not all of us have done so psychologically. To a greater or lesser degree, the people who have been significant in your early years will have a continuing influence on your life. Be aware of how you are presently influenced and determine whether these forces are enhancing your life or restricting your development as mature adults. Many people may have had a significant influence during your childhood and adolescent years, but in this chapter we emphasize the role parents (or caretakers) had. In later chapters we discuss in detail relationships other than parental relationships.

Autonomy, or maturity, entails that you accept responsibility for the consequences of your choices rather than hold others accountable if you are not satisfied with the way your life is going. Furthermore, separating from your family and finding your own identity is not something you do at a given time once and for all. The struggle toward autonomy begins in early childhood and continues throughout life.

Maturity is not necessarily equal to independence and self-sufficiency. In writing about genuine maturity from the self-in-context perspective, McGoldrick and Carter (1999) remind us that the ultimate goal is to develop a mature, interdependent self. We must establish a solid sense of our unique self in the context of our connection to others. This systemic perspective is based on the assumption that maturity requires the ability to empathize, communicate, collaborate, connect, trust, and respect others. McGoldrick and Carter maintain that the degree to which we are able to form meaningful connections with people who differ from us in gender, class, race, and culture "will depend on how these differences and connections were dealt with within our family of origin, within our communities, within our culture of origin, and within our society as a whole" (p. 28).

The feminist approach to psychological development stresses connections and disconnections in relationships. Miller and Stiver (1997) use the word *connection* to mean "an interaction between two or more people that is mutually empathic and mutually empowering" (p. 26). They use the term *disconnection* to mean "an encounter that works against mutual empathy and mutual empowerment" (p. 26). Miller and Stiver believe the source of psychological problems is disconnection, or the "psychological experience of rupture that occurs whenever a child or adult is prevented from participating in a mutually empathic and mutually empowering interaction" (p. 65). The goal is to learn to be an authentic individual who finds meaningful connections or relationships with others. Those invested in relationships participate in ways that foster the development of one another. Optimum mental health involves creating relationships based on caring for others, or a sense of mutual empathy. Mutually empowering relationships are characterized by both parties in the relationship fulfilling their needs and feeling good about each other. In contrast, a relationship in which one person gains power at the expense of the other is characterized as a disconnection.

Cultural factors play a significant role in determining the kinds of relationships that govern our lives. For example, some cultures value cooperation and a spirit of interdependence over independence. In some cultures parents, extended family, and the community continue to have a significant influence on children even once they reach adulthood. Respect and honor for parents and extended family members may be values that are extolled above individual freedom by these adult children.

Regardless of your cultural background, your parents influenced your decisions and behavior throughout your childhood and adolescent years. In your struggle toward autonomy and connection with others, you need to evaluate these past decisions and work toward self-approval rather than living your life primarily by your parents' designs. You very well may share many of your parents' values, but in striving for maturity you must learn self-direction and self-determination. Rebellion against whatever your parents stand for is not a sign of being autonomous. The self-in-relation theory stresses the interdependence of people rather than independence, and Jordon and her colleagues (1991) put this matter nicely:

> THUS, THE SELF DEVELOPS IN THE CONTEXT OF RELATIONSHIPS, rather than as an isolated or separate autonomous individual. We are emphasizing the importance of a two-way interaction model, where it becomes as important to understand and to be understood, to empower as well as to be empowered. (p. 59)

Making decisions about the quality of life you want for yourself and affirming these choices is partly what autonomy is about. Another part of autonomy is the quality of relationships with people who are significant in your life. To be able to relate to others in a meaningful way—to form connections—you first need self-knowledge and a mature sense of yourself. Autonomy includes far more than being a separate self; our conception of autonomy includes *self-in-relation* and *self-in-context.*

Becoming your own person is not "doing your own thing" irrespective of your impact on those with whom you come in contact. Instead, being autonomous implies that you have questioned the values you live by and made them your own; part of this process includes concern for the welfare of those people you love and associate with. Consider these questions as a way of clarifying the meaning autonomy has for you:

> ❯ Is it important to you to feel that you are your own person?
> ❯ To what degree do you think you can live by your own standards and still be sensitive to the needs and wants of others?
> ❯ Are you satisfied with living by the expectations that others have for you?
> ❯ Do you want to become more autonomous, even though this involves some risk?

Recognizing Early Learning and Decisions

Transactional analysis (TA) offers a useful framework for understanding how our learning during childhood extends into adulthood. TA is a theory of personality and a method of counseling that was originally developed by Eric Berne (1975) and later extended by practitioners such as Claude Steiner (1975) and Mary and Robert Goulding (1978, 1979). The theory is built on the assumption that adults make decisions based on past premises, premises that were at one time appropriate to their survival needs but may no longer be valid. It stresses the capacity of the person to change early decisions and is oriented toward increasing awareness, with the goal of enabling people to alter the course of their lives. Through TA, people learn how their current behavior is affected by the rules and regulations they received and incorporated as children and how they can identify the "life script," and also the family script, that determines their actions. These scripts are almost like plots that unfold. Individuals are able to realize that they can now change what is not working while retaining that which serves them well.

The Life Script The concept of the life script is an important contribution of TA. A life script is made up of both parental teachings and the early decisions we make as a child. Often, we continue to follow our script as an adult.

Scripting begins in infancy with subtle, nonverbal messages from our parents. During our earliest years, we learn much about our worth as a person and our place in life. Later, scripting occurs in both subtle and direct ways. Some of the messages we might "hear" include: "Always listen to authority." "Don't act like a child." "We know you can perform well, and we expect the best from you, so be sure you don't let us down." "Never trust people; rely on yourself." "You're really stupid, and we're convinced that you'll never amount to much." These messages are often sent in disguised ways. For example, our parents may never have told us directly that sexual feelings are bad or that touching is inappropriate. However, their behavior with each other and with us may have taught us to think in this way. Moreover, what parents do not say or do is just as important as what they say directly. If no mention is ever made of sexuality, for instance, that very fact communicates significant attitudes.

On a broader level than the messages we receive from our parents are the life scripts that are part of our cultural context. Cultural values are transmitted in many ways in the family circle. Here are a few examples of cultural messages pertaining to the family:

❯ Older people are to be revered and respected.
❯ Don't bring shame to the family.
❯ Don't talk about family matters outside the family circle.
❯ Don't demonstrate affection in public.
❯ Always obey your parents and grandparents.
❯ The mother is the heart of the family.
❯ The father is the head of the family.
❯ Avoid conflict and strive for harmony within the family.
❯ Never get a divorce.

Our life script, including the messages from both our family of origin and our culture, forms the core of our personal identity. Our experiences may lead us to conclusions such as these: "I really don't have any right to exist." "I can only be loved if I'm productive and successful." "I'd better not trust my feelings, because they'll only get me in trouble." These basic themes running through our lives tend to determine our behavior, and very often they are difficult to unlearn. In many subtle ways these early decisions about ourselves can come back to haunt us in later life. Our beliefs about ourselves can even influence how long and how well we live. After his liver transplant, the late Mickey Mantle looked back on his life with a number of regrets. He thought he would die very young because both his father and grandfather died at an early age, leading to his famous line: "If I had known I was going to live so long, I'd have taken better care of myself."

A personal example may help clarify how early messages and the decisions we make about them influence us in day-to-day living. In my (Jerry's) own case, even though I now experience myself as successful, for many years I felt unsuccessful and unworthy. I have not erased my old script completely, and I still experience self-doubts and struggle with insecurities. I do not think I can change such long-lasting feelings by simply telling myself "OK, now that I'm meeting with success, I'm the person I was meant to be." I continue to deal with feelings of insecurity. My striving for success is one way of coping with feelings of inadequacy.

I am convinced that part of the dynamics motivating me toward success are linked to the acceptance I wanted from my parents, especially from my father. In many important ways my father did not feel successful, and I believe on some level that my own strivings to prove my worth are entangled with a desire to make up for some of the successes that could have been his. Even though my father died 30 years ago, on a psychological plane I am still making some attempt to win his acceptance and make him proud of my accomplishments. Although my external reality has certainly changed from the time I was a child to now, I continue to play out some of these underlying patterns. For me this does not mean that I need to put an end to my projects, but I do want to be aware of who I am in service to and not spend the rest of my life living up to probably imagined parental expectations.

In short, although I believe I can change some of my basic attitudes about myself, I cannot get rid of all vestiges of the effects of my early learning and decisions. We need not be determined by old decisions, but it is wise to be continually aware of manifestations of our old ways that interfere with our attempts to develop new ways of thinking and being.

Injunctions Let's look more closely at the nature of the early messages (often called injunctions) that we incorporate in our lives. First of all, these injunctions are not just planted in our heads while we sit by passively. By making decisions in response to real or imagined injunctions, we assume some of the responsibility for indoctrinating ourselves. Thus, if we hope to free ourselves, we must become aware of what these "oughts" and "shoulds" are and of how we allow them to operate in our lives. Here are some common injunctions and some possible decisions that could be made in response to them (Goulding & Goulding, 1978, 1979).

1. *"Don't make mistakes."* Children who hear and accept this message often fear taking risks that may make them look stupid. They tend to equate making mistakes with being a failure.
   > *Possible decisions:* "I'm scared of making the wrong decision, so I simply won't decide." "Because I made a dumb choice, I won't decide on anything important again!" "I'd better be perfect if I hope to be accepted."

2. *"Don't be."* This lethal message is often given nonverbally by the way parents hold (or do not hold) the child. The basic message is "I wish you hadn't been born."
   > *Possible decisions:* "I'll keep trying until I get you to love me."

3. *"Don't be close."* Related to this injunction are the messages "Don't trust" and "Don't love."
   > *Possible decisions:* "I let myself love once, and it backfired. Never again!" "Because it's scary to get close, I'll keep myself distant."

Childhood injunctions can affect our entire lives. This girl may have received the family message "don't belong" and could be a loner as an adult.

Myrleen Ferguson/PhotoEdit

4. *"Don't be important."* If you are constantly discounted when you speak, you are likely to believe you are unimportant.
   > *Possible decisions:* "If, by chance, I ever do become important, I'll play down my accomplishments."

5. *"Don't be a child."* This message says: "Always act adult!" "Don't be childish." "Keep control of yourself."
   > *Possible decisions:* "I'll take care of others and won't ask for much myself." "I won't let myself have fun."

6. *"Don't grow."* This message is given by the frightened parent who discourages the child from growing up in many ways.
   > *Possible decisions:* "I'll stay a child, and that way I'll get my parents to approve of me." "I won't be sexual, and that way my father won't push me away."

7. *"Don't succeed."* If children are positively reinforced for failing, they may accept the message not to seek success.
   > *Possible decisions:* "I'll never do anything perfect enough, so why try?" "I'll succeed, no matter what it takes." "If I don't succeed, then I'll not have to live up to high expectations others have of me."

8. *"Don't be you."* This involves suggesting to children that they are the wrong sex, shape, size, color, or have ideas or feelings that are unacceptable to parental figures.
   > *Possible decisions:* "They'd love me only if I were a boy (girl), so it's impossible to get their love." "I'll pretend I'm a boy (girl)."

9. *"Don't be sane"* and *"Don't be well."* Some children get attention only when they are physically sick or acting crazy.
   > *Possible decisions:* "I'll get sick, and then I'll be included." "I am crazy."

10. *"Don't belong."* This injunction may indicate that the family feels that the child does not belong anywhere.
    > *Possible decisions:* "I'll be a loner forever." "I'll never belong anywhere."

Injunctions in Alcoholic Families In our work with both undergraduate and graduate students in human services and counseling, we are surprised by the large number whose parents are alcoholics. Certain patterns of injunctions, roles that are learned, and decisions about life often characterize adult children from alcoholic families.

In *It Will Never Happen to Me*, Claudia Black (1987) vividly portrays the life histories of adult children of alcoholics (ACAs), and we have adapted much of the material in this section from her book. Black discusses three central injunctions that she detects over and over in her work with these clients:

> *"Don't talk."* The family injunction is not to discuss real issues in the family. Children are conditioned to ignore these issues in the hope that the hurt will go away. Children learn not to rock the boat. The key dynamic is denial of the family secret of alcoholism.

> *"Don't trust."* Adult children of alcoholics learn to always be on guard, to rely on themselves and not to trust others with their feelings. In alcoholic homes children learn that their parents are not consistently available and cannot be relied on for safety. Unfortunately, they carry this pattern of not trusting from their childhood into their adulthood.

> *"Don't feel."* Children develop a denial system to numb their feelings. They learn not to share what they feel because they are convinced that their feelings will not be validated within their family. Gradually, they build walls for self-protection as a way of coping with a feared world. They learn to deny and discount their feelings, they hide their pain, and they do not express what is inside of them. This process of denial interferes in their emotional life when they reach adulthood.

Children raised in alcoholic families enter adulthood with strategies for survival that worked to some degree in their childhood and adolescent years. Over the years they have refined behaviors such as being responsible, adjusting, or placating, as well as not talking, not trusting, and not feeling. On reaching adulthood, most ACAs continue to struggle with problems related to trust, dependency, control, identification, and expression of feelings.

Children tend to adopt certain roles for survival in alcoholic families. In her research and therapeutic work with ACAs, Black has found that later, as adults, they play out these same roles. She writes that the majority of ACAs adopt one or a combination of these three roles:

> *The responsible person.* Children who miss their childhood by having to mature very early often take on household and parenting responsibilities for other siblings. When structure and consistency are not provided, these children provide it for themselves. They rely completely on themselves, for they have learned many times over that they cannot count on their parents.

> *The adjuster.* Some children make an early decision that "since I can't do anything about the family situation, I'll adjust to it." As children, adjusters become detached; as adults they have no sense of self, they are not autonomous, and they typically feel that they have few choices.

> *The placater.* Some children become skilled at listening and providing empathy and tend to deny their own feelings in the hopes that adapting will bring peace to the family. Placaters have a difficult time dealing with their own feelings. For example, if they cry, they tend to cry alone.

These roles are often found in other people besides ACAs. Many students who read about these roles question why they find so many similarities to ACAs, even though they did not grow up in alcoholic homes. There are many other forms of dysfunctional behavior in families besides alcoholic patterns. For example, incest victims get the message that what is going on is secret, which can be reinforced with the threat of violence if the child informs. People who experienced incest frequently learn to deny what is taking place, both outside of them and in their inner world as well. They are likely to incorporate shame, guilt, and feelings of self-blame. All of these are manifestations of accepting injunctions on either a verbal or a nonverbal level.

As you can see, these are not rigid categories that box people in but general patterns of learned behavior. The roles that children play in a dysfunctional family tend to evolve from childhood to adulthood. As children, individuals may busy themselves by taking care of others and pleasing others; as adults, they often become professional helpers and strive to please their clients. They become carriers of the pain of others. Yet if they do not attend to their own needs and feelings, eventually they burn out. These adults have a difficult time asking for what they need for themselves, and in their personal relationships they tend to seek out others who are takers.

Overcoming Injunctions I (Marianne) want to share some messages I heard growing up, as a personal example of a struggle with listening to injunctions from both parents and society. I was born and spent my childhood and adolescence in a farming village in Germany. Some of the messages I received, though they were not typically verbalized, were "You can't do anything about it." "Things could be worse, so don't talk so much about how bad things are." "Accept what you have, and don't complain about what you don't have." "Don't be different. Fit in with the community. Do what everybody else does." "Be satisfied with your life."

Although my childhood was very good in many respects and I was satisfied with part of my life, I still wanted more than I felt I could get by remaining in the village and becoming what was expected of me. It was a continuing struggle not to surrender to these expectations, but having some adult role models who themselves had challenged such injunctions inspired me to resist these messages. As early as age 8 I felt a sense of daring to be different and hoping someday to go to the United States. Although I doubted myself at times, I still began saving every penny I could lay my hands on. Finally, at the age of 19 I asked my father for permission to take a ship to the United States and surprised him when I told him that I had saved enough money to buy a ticket.

Even though there were many obstacles, I seemed to be driven to follow a dream and a decision that I made when I was only 8 years old. When I did come to the United States, I eventually fulfilled another dream, and consequently challenged another injunction, by furthering my education. The theme of my struggles during my earlier years is that I was not willing to surrender to obstacles. I argued with myself about simply accepting what seemed like limited choices for a life's design, and in doing so I began writing a new life script for myself. It was important to me not to feel like a victim of circumstances. I was willing to do what was necessary to challenge barriers to what I wanted and to pursue my dreams and goals. Although I fought against these injunctions at an early age, they have not gone away forever. I continue to have to be aware of them and not allow them to control me as an adult.

Think about some of the childhood decisions you made about yourself and about life. For example, you might have made any one of these early decisions:

> I will be loved only when I live up to what others expect of me.

> I had better listen to authorities outside of myself, because I cannot trust myself to make decent decisions.

> I will not let myself trust people, and that way they won't ever let me down again.

Themes like these that run through your life determine not only your self-image but also your behavior. It is a difficult matter to discard these self-defeating assumptions and to learn new and constructive ones in their place. This is one reason for learning how to critically evaluate these questions:

> What messages have I listened to and "bought"?

> How valid are the sources of these messages?

> In what ways do I now continue to say self-defeating sentences to myself?

> How can I challenge some of the decisions I made about myself and make new ones that will lead to a positive orientation?

Learning to Dispute Self-Defeating Thinking

As children and adolescents, we uncritically incorporate certain assumptions about life and about our worth as a person. Rational emotive behavior therapy and other cognitive-behavioral therapies are based on the premise that emotional and behavioral problems are originally learned from significant others during childhood. Others gave us faulty beliefs, which we accept unthinkingly. We actively keep alive false beliefs by the processes of self-suggestion and self-repetition (Ellis, 1999). It is largely our own repetition of early-indoctrinated faulty beliefs that keeps dysfunctional attitudes operational within us. Self-defeating beliefs are supported and maintained by negative and dysfunctional statements that we make to ourselves over and over again: "If I don't win universal love and approval, then I'll never be happy." "If I make a mistake, that would prove that I am an utter failure."

Albert Ellis (1999), who developed rational emotive behavior therapy (REBT), describes some of the most common ways people make themselves miserable by remaining wedded to their irrational beliefs. Ellis has devised an A-B-C theory of personality that explains how people develop negative evaluations of themselves. He holds that it is our faulty thinking, not actual life events, that creates emotional upsets and leads to our misery. He contends that we have the power to control our emotional destiny and suggests that when we are upset it is a good idea to look to our hidden dogmatic "musts," "oughts," and absolutistic "shoulds." For Ellis, practically all human misery and serious emotional turmoil is unnecessary.

An example will clarify this A-B-C concept. Assume that Sally's parents abandoned her when she was a child (A, the activating event). Sally's emotional reaction may be feelings of depression, worthlessness, rejection, and unlovability (C, the emotional consequence). However, Ellis asserts, it is not A (her parents' abandonment of her) that caused her feelings of rejection and unlovability; rather, it is her belief system (B) that is causing her low self-esteem. She made her mistake when she told herself that there must have been something terrible about herself for her parents not to want her. Her faulty beliefs are reflected through self-talk such as this: "I am to blame for what my parents did." "If I were more lovable, they would have wanted to keep me." The A-B-C theory of disturbance holds that when dysfunctional emotional reactions occur there are usually several core irrational beliefs, which include *absolutistic musts and shoulds, awfulizing, I-can't-stand-it-itis,* and *damning oneself and others.* This kind of thinking is what gets us into psychological trouble and results in much of our misery (Ellis, 1999).

According to Ellis (1988, p. 60), most of our irrational ideas can be reduced to three main forms of what he refers to as "musturbation." The three basic "musts" that create emotional problems are these:

> I *must* perform well and win the approval of important people, or else I am an inadequate person!

> Others *must* treat me fairly and considerately!

> My life *must* be easy and pleasant. I need and must have the things I want, or life is unbearable!

REBT is designed to teach people how to dispute faulty beliefs such as these. Let's apply REBT to our example. Sally does not need to continue believing she is basically unlovable. Instead of clinging to the belief that something must have been wrong with her for her parents to have rejected her, Sally can begin to dispute this self-defeating statement and think along different lines: "It hurts that my parents didn't want me, but perhaps they had problems that kept them from being good parents." "Maybe my parents didn't love me, but that doesn't mean that nobody could love me." "It's unfortunate that I didn't have parents in growing up, but it's not devastating, and I no longer have to be a little girl waiting for their protection."

One member of a therapeutic group of ours had major struggles in believing he was a worthwhile person. Joaquin learned how to pay attention to his internal dialogue and realized how his thoughts influenced what he did and how he felt about himself. Joaquin reported the following about how his self-talk got in his way.

JOAQUIN'S STORY

What I am noticing and changing are my internal dialogues that I carry on within myself. I see how I have always judged myself critically. I have somehow made a major breakthrough on giving myself a break from the negative chatter that has always gone on in my thoughts. It finally dawned on me that I am my own worst critic.

I seem to finally be in the process of forgiving myself and getting down to some more reasonable expectations for myself. I am attempting to allow myself the many small failures in my life. The part that is different is that I am asking myself what I could do different next time. I want to focus on the lesson that allows me to learn, not the mistakes.

Joaquin is a good example of a person who can change his life by challenging and changing his self-destructive beliefs about himself. Ellis stresses that your feelings about yourself are largely the result of the way you think. Thus, if you hope to change a negative self-image, it is essential to learn how to dispute the illogical sentences you now continue to feed yourself and to challenge faulty premises that you have accepted uncritically. Further, you also need to work and practice replacing these self-sabotaging beliefs with constructive ones. If you wish to learn how to combat the negative self-indoctrination process, we highly recommend *How to Make Yourself Happy and Remarkably Less Disturbable* (Ellis, 1999). Other useful books in this area are *Feeling Good: The New Mood Therapy* (Burns, 1981) and *How to Want What You Have: Discovering the Magic and Grandeur of Ordinary Existence* (Miller, 1995).

Learning to Challenge Your Inner Parents

We would like to expand a bit on the general concepts of transactional analysis and rational emotive behavior therapy and discuss some related ideas about challenging early messages and working toward autonomy. The term *inner parent* refers to the attitudes and beliefs we have about ourselves and others that are a direct result of things we learned from our parents or parental substitutes. The willingness to question and challenge this inner parent is one of the marks of autonomy.

Many of the qualities we incorporated from our parents may be healthy standards for guiding our behavior. No doubt our past has contributed in many respects to the good qualities we possess, and many of the things we like about ourselves may be largely due to the influence of the people who were important to us in our early years. But it is essential to look for the subtle ways we have incorporated our parents' values in our lives without making a deliberate choice.

How do we learn to recognize the influence our parents continue to have on us? One way to begin is by talking back to our inner parent. Begin to notice things you do and avoid doing, and ask yourself why. For instance, suppose you avoid enrolling in a college course because you long ago branded yourself as "stupid." You may tell yourself that you would never be able to pass the class, so why even try? In this case an early decision you made about your intellectual capabilities prevents you from branching out to new endeavors. Rather than stopping at this first obstacle, however, you could challenge yourself by asking, "Who says I'm too stupid? Even if my father or my teachers have told me that I'm slow, is it really true? Why have I accepted this view of myself uncritically? Let me check it out and see for myself."

In carrying out this kind of dialogue, we can talk to the different selves we have within us. You may be struggling to open yourself to people and to trust them, for example, while at the same time you hear the inner injunction "Never trust anybody." In this case you can carry on a two-way discussion between your trusting side and your suspicious side. The important point is that we do not have to passively accept as truth the messages we learned when we were children. As adults we can now put these messages to the test.

David Young-Wolff/PhotoEdit

If you become aware of negative self-talk, you may need help in challenging your inner parents.

Hal and Sidra Stone (1993) have developed a therapeutic process aimed at transforming this "inner critic" from a crippling adversary to a productive ally. The inner critic checks your thoughts, controls your behavior, kills your spontaneity and creativity, and leads to feelings of shame, anxiety, depression, exhaustion, and low self-esteem. Developed as a way to protect you from the pain and shame of being discovered as being less than you should be, this inner voice reflects the concerns of your parents, church, and significant others from your early years. You may recognize some of these characteristics of the inner critic:

> It constricts your ability to be creative.
> It prevents you from taking risks.
> It makes you particularly vulnerable to fearing mistakes and failure.
> It warns you never to look foolish.
> It takes the fun out of life.
> It makes you susceptible to the judgments of others.

The content of the inner critic may vary from culture to culture, according to the value system of each particular culture, but this critical voice is universal and seems to have the power to cripple people and render them less effective than they might be. The Stones explain how to minimize the negative impact of this self-destructive internal dialogue and how to transform this negative force by developing an internal source of support very much like an internal parent who protects you and your creative process.

In his excellent book *Making Peace With Your Parents,* psychiatrist Harold Bloomfield (1983) makes the point that many of us suffer from psychological wounds as a result of unfinished business with our parents. We often keep the past alive by insisting on blaming them for all our problems. Instead of pointing the blaming finger at our parents, as adults we can give ourselves some of the things we may still expect or hope for from our parents. If we do not get past the blaming, we end up wedded to resentment. As long as we cling to our resentments, expect our parents to be different than they are, or wait for their approval, we are keeping painful memories and experiences alive. If we harbor grudges against our parents and focus all our energies on changing them, we have little constructive energy left over to assume control of our own lives.

If you want a closer relationship with your father and insist that he talk to you more and approve of you, for example, you are likely to be disappointed. He may not behave the way you want him to, and if you make changing him your central goal, you are keeping yourself helpless in many respects. You do not have the power to control your father's attitudes or behavior, yet you do have choices with respect to how you will relate to your father. As long as you are stuck in a blaming mode, you will not be able to recognize the power you have within you to change the influence that you allow your father to have in your life. You can learn to ask yourself before you act, "Will doing or saying what I am about to do or say bring us closer together? If it won't, then I won't do or say it." If you make some significant changes in the way you talk to your father and in the way you treat him, you may be greatly surprised at how he might change. You will increase your chances of success if you do what you want him to do.

To be at peace with yourself, you need to let go of festering resentments, to work through unresolved anger, and to cease blaming others. These factors not only poison relationships but also take a toll on the way you feel about yourself. It is only when you find a sense of inner peace that you can ever hope to make peace with the significant people in your life. You do have a choice. Even though your family situation may have been far from ideal, you now can choose the attitude you take toward your past circumstances. If you choose to assume responsibility for the person you are now, you are moving in the direction of becoming your own parent.

Take Time to Reflect This self-inventory is designed to increase your awareness of the injunctions you have incorporated and to help you challenge the validity of messages you may not have critically examined.

1. Place a check (✔) in the space provided for each of these "don't" injunctions that you think applies to you.

———— Don't be you.
———— Don't think.
———— Don't feel.
———— Don't be close.
———— Don't trust.
———— Don't be sexy.
———— Don't fail.
———— Don't be foolish.
———— Don't be important.
———— Don't brag.
———— Don't let us down.
———— Don't change.

List any other injunctions you can think of that apply to you:

_____

2. Check the ways you sometimes badger yourself with "do" messages.

———— Be perfect.
———— Say only nice things.
———— Be more than you are.
———— Be obedient.
———— Work up to your potential.
———— Be practical at all times.
———— Listen to authority figures.
———— Always put your best foot forward.
———— Put others before yourself.
———— Be seen but not heard.

List any other injunctions you can think of that apply to you:

_____

3. What messages have you received concerning

your self-worth? _____

your ability to succeed? _____

your gender role? _____

your intelligence? _____

your trust in yourself? _____

trusting others? _____

making yourself vulnerable? _____

(continued)

your security? _____

your aliveness as a person? _____

your creativity? _____

your ability to be loved? _____

your capacity to give love? _____

4. Because your view of yourself has a great influence on the quality of your interpersonal relationships, we invite you to look carefully at some of the views you have of yourself and also to consider how you arrived at these views. To do this, reflect on these questions:

   a. How do you see yourself now? To what degree do you see yourself as confident? Secure? Worthwhile? Accomplished? Caring? Open? Accepting?

   _____

   b. Do others generally see you as you see yourself? What are some ways others view you differently from how you view yourself?

   _____

   c. Who in your life has been most influential in shaping your self-concept? How did this person do this?

   _____

5. Review your responses to these exercises and identify areas where you would like to change. Ask yourself, "Is this a person with whom I would like to have a relationship?" In your journal write some of your ideas about how you can begin the process of detecting the messages you now give yourself. Write about some of the areas you most want to change.

STAGES OF ADULTHOOD

Some developmental theorists reject the notion of well-defined stages of adulthood, contending that adult development is highly individualized. Other researchers conceptualize the life cycle in general periods of development. We will continue to discuss the developmental process from the point of view of Erikson's psychosocial stages and the self-in-context perspective, concentrating on the core struggles and choices from early adulthood through late adulthood. Levinson and Levinson (1996) conducted in-depth interviews with 45 women and found that women go through the same sequence of seasons as men, and at the same ages, making a case for the underlying order in the course of human development. However, they emphasize that although there is a single human life cycle there are myriad variations related to gender, class, race, culture, historical epoch, specific circumstances, and genetics. In short, there are wide variations between and within genders as well as in the specific ways individuals traverse each season of life. It is best to keep this variation in mind as we examine the stages of adulthood.

In *New Passages*, Gail Sheehy (1995) describes a new map for the stages of adult life. Contending that we need new markers for life transitions, she states that "the old demarcation points we may still carry around—an adulthood that begins at 21 and ends at 65—are hopelessly out of date" (p. 7). People who are today in their 20s, 30s, and early 40s are confronted with a different set of conditions than was the case 20 years ago. Middle age has been pushed ahead to the 50s. Today, people at 50 are dealing with transitions that were characteristic of people at 40 just a couple of decades ago. Sheehy's research, based on a collection of life histories of people facing the challenges of "second adulthood" (age 45 and beyond), leads her to one overriding conclusion: "There is no longer a standard life cycle. People are increasingly able to customize their life cycles" (p. 16). Sheehy's revised map of adult life includes these overarching periods: provisional adulthood (18 to 30), first adulthood (30 to 45), and second adulthood (45 to 85+).

EARLY ADULTHOOD

Early adulthood encompasses ages 21 through 35. There are many changes during this stage of adulthood, and the decisions made here will have far-reaching effects.

Provisional Adulthood

The period of provisional adulthood encompasses people ages 18 to 30. According to Sheehy (1995), contemporary young adults live at an accelerated pace, even though many of the responsibilities of full adulthood are delayed. This is a time when we begin detaching from the family and searching for a personal identity. Some of the tasks of this period involve locating ourselves in a peer group role, establishing a gender identity, finding an occupation, separating from our family of origin, and developing a personal worldview. From the perspective of the Levinsons (1996), this period of life is necessarily provisional in that it is an initial attempt to make a place for ourselves in a new world and a new generation. According to Erikson (1963, 1968), we enter adulthood after we master the adolescent conflicts over *identity* versus *role confusion*. Our sense of identity is tested anew in adulthood, however, by the challenge of *intimacy* versus *isolation*.

One characteristic of the psychologically mature person is the ability to form intimate relationships. Before we can form such relationships, we must be sure of our own identity. Intimacy involves sharing, giving of ourselves, and relating to another out of strength and a desire to grow with the other person. Failure to achieve intimacy can result in isolation from others and a sense of alienation. The fact that alienation is a problem for many people in our society is evidenced by the widespread use of drugs and by other ways in which we try to numb a sense of isolation. If we attempt to escape isolation by clinging to another person, however, we rarely find success in the relationship.

Erikson's concept of intimacy can be applied to any kind of close relationship between two adults. Relationships involving emotional commitments may be between close friends of the same or the opposite sex, and they may or may not have a sexual dimension. Some of the characteristics of people who have achieved a sense of intimacy include having a clear sense of personal identity; being tolerant of differences in others; trusting others and themselves in relationships; establishing cooperative, affiliative relationships with others; being willing to give in relationships; believing in the value of mutual interdependence as a way to work through difficulties; being willing to commit to relationships that demand some degree of sacrifice; and being able to form close emotional bonds without fearing the loss of personal identity (Hamachek, 1990).

The self-in-context theory of McGoldrick and Carter (1999) place the early adulthood period from ages 21 to 35. At this stage the major aim is development of the ability to engage in intense relationships committed to mutual growth and in satisfying work. McGoldrick and Carter acknowledge the differences in the pathways at this phase, depending on the person's culture, race, gender, class, and sexual orientation. In general, they view this phase as one of generativity in terms of partnering, working, and rearing children, but barriers to healthy development can derail potentially productive people. Racism and poverty can make it extremely difficult to escape from the underclass, especially as the life cycle continues. Gay and lesbian young adults also may have difficulties at this stage because of the stigma attached to their partnering and parenting or to the necessity of keeping their identity a secret at school or work.

Emerging Adulthood

The late teens and the early 20s can no longer be considered a brief period of transition from adolescence into adult roles. This distinct period in the life cycle is characterized by change and exploration of possible life directions. Arnett (2000) proposes a new theory of human development focusing on the period from roughly ages 18 to 25 that he calls the period of "emerging adulthood." The term *emerging* captures the dynamic, rich, complex, changeable, and fluid quality of this period of life.

HAVING LEFT THE DEPENDENCY OF CHILDHOOD AND ADOLESCENCE, and having not yet entered the enduring responsibilities that are normative in adulthood, emerging adults often explore a variety of possible life directions in

> love, work, and worldviews. Emerging adulthood is a time of life when many different directions remain possible, when little about the future has been decided for certain, when the scope of independent exploration of life's possibilities is greater for most people than it will be at any other period of the life course. (p. 469)

Arnett (2000) characterizes this time as a period of change and exploration for most young people in industrialized societies—a time when they examine life's choices regarding love, work, and worldviews. In his research studies of emerging adults, Arnett found that emerging adults do not rank highly some of the traditional notions of what it means to attain adulthood. Completing an education, establishing a career, getting married and becoming a parent, and moving out on one's own are ranked at the bottom in importance by these young adults. What matters most to emerging adults are three individualistic qualities: accepting responsibility for one's self, making independent decisions, and becoming financially independent. This notion of becoming a self-sufficient person is similar to the concept of autonomy described earlier in this chapter.

Three areas offer rich opportunities for exploring personal identity for emerging adults: love, work, and worldviews (Arnett, 2000).

> ❯ *Love.* Explorations in love during emerging adulthood generally involve a deeper level of intimacy than in adolescence. The emerging adult considers the kind of person he or she is and questions what kind of person he or she wishes to have as a partner through life.

> ❯ *Work.* Emerging adults consider how their work experiences are apt to set the foundation for the jobs they may have throughout adulthood. Identity issues are closely related to the exploration of work possibilities. Questions typically raised include "What kind of work will best fit the person that I am?" "What kind of work will be satisfying in the long term?" "What are the chances of securing a job in the field that seems to best suit me?"

> ❯ *Worldview.* Emerging adults often find themselves questioning the worldview they were exposed to during childhood and adolescence. Many young people go through a process of reexamining the religious beliefs and values they learned as children. This explanation sometimes results in forming a different value system, but oftentimes it leads to rejecting an earlier belief system without constructing a new set of values.

Emerging adulthood must be understood within a cultural context, for this period exists only in cultures that allow young people a prolonged period of independent exploration during their late teens and 20s. This is a time when personal freedom and exploration are higher for most people than at any other time in life. The nature of this period of emerging adulthood has changed considerably since the time of the writings of Erikson (1968) and Levinson (1978), and the current trend is toward postponing marriage and parenthood and increasing the time spent exploring a diversity of life directions.

Entering the 20s

During their 20s, young adults are faced with a variety of profound choices. They move away from the safe shelter of the family and confront insecurity about the future as they attempt to establish independence. This time is often characterized by considerable agitation and change.

If you are in this age group, you are no doubt facing decisions about how you will live. Your choices probably include questions such as "Will I choose the security of staying at home, or will I struggle financially and psychologically to live on my own?" "Will I stay single, or will I get involved in some committed relationship?" "Will I stay in college full time, or will I begin a career?" "If I choose a career, what will it be, and how will I go about deciding what I might do in the work world?" "If I marry, will I be a parent or not?" "What are some of my dreams, and how might I make them become reality?" "What do I most want to do with my life at this time, and how might I find meaning?"

Choices pertaining to work, education, marriage, family life, and lifestyle are complex and deeply personal, and it is common to struggle over what it is we really want. There is the temptation to let others decide for us or to be overly influenced by the standards of others. But if we choose that path, we remain psychological adolescents at best. We have the choice of living by parental rules or leaving home psychologically and deciding for ourselves what our future will be. Steve and Amanda are both struggling with issues common to this stage of growth. These struggles are typical of the concerns faced by emerging adults.

STEVE'S STORY

I want to live on my own, but it's very difficult to support myself and go to college at the same time. The support and approval of my parents is surely something I want, yet I am working hard at finding a balance between how much I am willing to do to get their approval and how much I will live by my values. I love my parents, yet at the same time I resent them for the hold they have on me.

AMANDA'S STORY

I want to be in a close relationship with a man, but I know that I am also afraid of getting involved. I wonder if I want to spend the rest of my life with the same person. At other times I'm afraid I'll never find someone I can love who really loves me. I don't want to give up my freedom, nor do I want to be dependent on someone.

Transition From the 20s to the 30s

The transition from the late 20s to the early 30s is a time of changing values and beliefs for most people. Inner turmoil often increases during this period, and commitments to relationships and careers are often made. Others may defer these responsibilities for various reasons, and couples may delay having children until their late 30s.

During this transition, people often take another look at their long-term dreams, and they may reevaluate their life plans and make significant shifts. Some become aware that their dreams may not materialize. This recognition often brings anxiety, but it can be the catalyst for making new plans and working hard to attain them. Consider Pam's evolution in her process of striving to make her dreams turn to reality.

PAM'S STORY

When I was growing up, a college education was not considered essential for a female. The belief in my family was that as a female I would grow up, get married, have children, live in a home with a white picket fence and be financially supported by my husband. The most I might have expected of myself was to become a part-time secretary.

When I turned 17 I attended college for a couple of years, but I did not take my studies seriously, which showed in my grades. I was just biding my time until Mr. Right came along to carry me away. I got married, and in the next few years reality set in. My husband and I had marital problems, the economy took a severe downturn, and I eventually ended up getting a divorce. Reality turned out to be very different from the dreams I had while growing up.

In my late 20s I began taking inventory of my life. I began to think about my life goals and what it was that I truly wanted for myself. I realized that I wanted a career that I found meaningful, one that I felt would make a difference. I wanted financial security and a nice home in which to raise my children. Although I had remarried by this time, I did not want to make the same mistake again of depending on someone else to fulfill my goals and secure my future. For me, education seemed to be the key to achieve these goals. At 30, I returned to college and completed my last 2 years with a 4.0 grade point average. What I learned and what I am continuing to learn is that you don't achieve goals by dreaming about them, wishing for them, or depending on someone else to fulfill them. Instead, dreams become reality by working hard. I did not understand the value of an education and how having a college education could change my life and help me achieve my goals. I see things very differently now. I see how life is not about meeting Prince Charming and being swept away, or about luck. Life is about choices, personal responsibility, and hard work.

Take Time to Reflect

1. Think about a few of the major turning points in your young adulthood. Write down two significant turning points, and then state how you think they were important in your life. What difference did your decision at these critical times make in your life?

Turning point: _____

Impact of the decision on my life:

_____

_____

_____

Turning point: _____

Impact of the decision on my life:

_____

_____

_____

2. Complete the following sentences by giving the first response that comes to mind:

   a. To me, being an independent person means _____

   b. The things I received from my parents that I most value are _____

   c. The things I received from my parents that I least like and most want to change are _____

   d. If I could change one thing about my past, it would be _____

   e. My fears of being independent are _____

   f. One thing I most want for my children is _____

   g. I find it difficult to be my own person when _____

   h. I feel the freest when _____

MIDDLE ADULTHOOD

The period of life between the ages of 35 to the early 50s is characterized by a "going outside of ourselves." This is a time when people are likely to engage in a philosophical reexamination of their lives and, based on this evaluation, may reinvent themselves in their work and their involvement in the community (McGoldrick & Carter, 1999). It is a time for learning how to live creatively with ourselves and with others, and it can be the time of greatest productivity in our lives. In middle age we reach the top of the mountain yet at the same time realize that we eventually will begin the downhill journey. In addition, we may painfully experience the discrepancy between the dreams of our 20s and 30s and the hard reality of what we have achieved.

Sheehy (1995) compares life to a three-act play: "It's as though when we are young, we have seen only the first act of the play. By our forties we have reached the climactic second-act curtain. Only as we approach fifty does the shape and meaning of the whole play become clear. We move into the third act with the intention of a resolution and tremendous curiosity about how it will all come out" (p. 150).

The Late 30s

People in their 30s often experience doubts and reevaluate significant aspects of their lives. Both Gould (1978) and Levinson (1978) found signs of increased turmoil during this stage, and it is not uncommon for people to experience a crisis at this time in their lives. These crises center on doubts about their earlier commitments and on concerns over getting locked into choices that make it difficult for them to move in new directions. During this period of unrest, disillusionment, and questioning, people often modify the rules and standards that govern their lives. They also realize that their dreams do not materialize if they simply wish for things to happen; that there is no magic in the world; that life is not simple but, in fact, is complicated and bewildering; and that we get what we want not by waiting and wishing passively but by working actively to attain our goals. As we open up in our 30s, a crisis can be precipitated when we discover that life is not as uncomplicated as we had envisioned it to be.

At this stage of life Sheehy (1976) contends that we become impatient with living a life based on "shoulds," and both men and women speak of feeling restricted and may complain that life is narrow and dull. Sheehy asserts that these restrictions are related to the outcomes of the choices we made during our 20s. Even if these personal and career choices have served us well to date, we are now ready for some changes. This is a time for making new choices and perhaps for modifying or deepening old commitments. We are likely to review our commitments to career, marriage, children, friends, and life's priorities. Because we realize that time is passing, we make a major reappraisal of how we are spending our time and energy. We begin to realize that we do not have forever to reach our goals.

This process of self-examination may involve considerable turmoil and crisis. We may find ourselves asking: "Is this all there is to life?" "What do I want for the rest of my life?" "What is missing from my life now?" A woman who has primarily been engaged in a career may now want to spend more time at home and with the children. A woman who has devoted most of her life to being a homemaker may want to begin a new career outside the home. Men may do a lot of questioning about their work and wonder how they can make it more meaningful. It is likely that they will struggle with defining the meaning of success. They may be exteriorly focused in measuring success, which puts the source of the meaning of life on quicksand. They are likely to begin to question the price of success. Single people may consider finding a partner, and those who are married may experience a real crisis in their marriage, which may be a sign that they cannot continue with old patterns.

Life During the 40s

Sheehy (1976) used to consider the mid-30s as the halfway mark and the prime of life. She referred to the period between 35 and 45 as the "Decline Decade," as if people had only until their mid-40s to resolve the crisis of midlife. Now Sheehy (1995) claims that it is a mistake to view the early 40s as a time when people drop off the edge of a cliff. Although many people believe their time is running out when they reach 40, more and more people are finding ways to avoid the restrictive identity that used to define middle age. In the 1990s Sheehy found a new theme of rebirths permeating the stories of people in middle life. She writes: "More and more people were beginning to see there was the possibility of a new life to live, one in which we could concentrate on becoming better, stronger, deeper, wiser, funnier, freer, sexier, and more attentive to living the privileged moments, even as we were getting older, lumpier, slower, and closer to the end" (p. xiii). Indeed, we are retaining some of our youth for a longer period of time. The second half of life enlarges the boundaries of vital living, and it offers new opportunities for growth and change.

Sheehy's views on middle life are supported by Erikson's psychosocial developmental theory. For Erikson, the stimulus for continued growth in middle age is the core struggle between *generativity* and *stagnation*. Generativity includes being productive in a broad sense—for example, through creative pursuits in a career, in leisure-time activities, in teaching or caring for others, or in some meaningful volunteer work. Two basic qualities of the productive adult are the ability to love well and the ability to work well. Adults who fail to achieve a sense of productivity begin to stagnate, a form of psychological death.

When we reach middle age, we come to a crossroads. During our late 30s and into our mid-40s, we are likely to question what we want to do with the rest of our lives. We face both dangers and opportunities—the danger of slipping into a deadening rut and the opportunity to choose to rework the narrow identity of the first half of our life.

Romilly Lockyear/Image Bank

What cultural "messages" do people get as they approach middle age?

During middle age we realize the uncertainty of life, and we discover more clearly that we are alone. We stumble on masculine and feminine aspects of ourselves that had been masked. We may also go through a grieving process, because many parts of our old self are dying, and we may reevaluate and reintegrate an emerging identity that is not the sum of others' expectations. Here are a few of the events that might contribute to a midlife transformation:

❯ We may come to realize that some of our youthful dreams will never materialize.

❯ We may begin to experience the pressure of time, realizing that now is the time to accomplish our goals.

❯ We recognize our accomplishments and accept our limitations.

❯ We may realize that life is not necessarily just and fair and that we often do not get what we had expected.

❯ There are marital crises and challenges to old patterns. A spouse may have an affair or seek a divorce.

❯ Coping with growing older is difficult for many; the loss of some of our youthful physical qualities can be hard to face.

❯ Our children grow up and leave home at this time. People who have lived largely for their children now may face emptiness.

❯ We may be confronted with taking care of our elderly parents when taking care of our children is just coming to an end.

❯ The death of our parents drives home a truth that is difficult for many to accept; ultimately, we are alone in this life.

❯ We may lose a job or be demoted, or we may grow increasingly disenchanted with our work.

❯ A woman may leave the home to enter the world of work and make this her primary interest.

❯ Women may be confronted with menopause, which can be a crisis for some.

Along with these factors that can precipitate a crisis, new choices are available to us at this time:

❯ We may decide to go back for further schooling and gear up for a new career.

❯ There may be a deepening of our friendships.

❯ We can choose to develop new talents and embark on novel hobbies, and we can even take steps to change our lifestyle.

❯ We may look increasingly inward to find out what we most want to do with the rest of our life and begin doing what we say we want to do.

❯ This is a time to make choices about solidifying our philosophy of life and deepening our spirituality.

Carl Jung was the first modern voice to address the possibility of adult personality development (see Schultz & Schultz, 2001, for an in-depth look at Jung's influence). He took the position that personality development simply cannot progress very far by the end of adolescence and young adulthood. According to Jung, we are confronted with major changes and possibilities for transformation when we begin the second half of life between 35 and 40. Jung's therapy clients consistently revealed signs of experiencing a pivotal middle-age life crisis. Although they may have achieved worldly success, they typically were challenged with finding meaning in projects that had lost meaning. Many of his clients struggled to overcome feelings of emptiness and flatness in life.

Jung believed major life transformations are an inevitable and universal part of the human condition at this juncture in life. He maintained that when the zest for living sags it can be a catalyst for necessary and beneficial changes. To undergo such a transformation requires the death of some aspect of our psychological being, so new growth can occur that will open us to far deeper and richer ranges of existence. To strive for what Jung called individuation—integration of the unconscious with the conscious and psychological balance—people during their middle-age years must be willing to let go of preconceived notions and patterns that have dominated the first part of their lives. Their task now is to be open to the unconscious forces that have influenced them and to deepen the meaning of their lives.

For Jung, people can bring unconscious material into awareness by paying attention to their dreams and fantasies and by expressing themselves through poetry, writing, music, and art. Individuals need to recognize that the rational thought patterns that drove them during the first half of life represent merely one way of being. At this time in life, you must be willing to be guided by the spontaneous flow of the unconscious if you hope to achieve an integration of all facets of your being, which is part of psychological health (Schultz & Schultz, 2001).

You may be some distance away from middle age right now, but you can reflect on the way your life is shaping up and think about the person you would like to be when you reach middle age. To help you in making this projection, consider the lives of people you know who are over 40. Do you have any models available in determining what direction you will pursue? Are there some ways you would not want to live?

Some of the issues facing middle-aged people are illustrated in the stories that follow. For example, Manuel says it is difficult to always be striving for success, and he shares some of his loneliness.

MANUEL'S STORY

*S*o much of my life has been bound up in becoming a success. While I am successful, I continually demand more of myself. I'm never quite satisfied with anything I accomplish, and I continually look ahead and see what has to be done. It's lonely when I think of always swimming against the tide, and I fear getting dragged into deep water that I can't get out of. At the same time, I don't seem to be able to slow down.

Noemi says that she has stayed in a miserable marriage for 23 years. She finally recognizes that she has run out of excuses for staying. She must decide whether to maintain a marriage that is not likely to change much or decide on ending it.

NOEMI'S STORY

I'm petrified by the idea that I have to support myself and that I'm responsible for my own happiness—totally. All these years I've told myself that if he were different I'd feel much more fulfilled than I do in life. I also had many reasons that prevented me from taking action, even when it became very clear to me that he wasn't even slightly interested in seeing things change. I'm not afraid to go out and meet people on a social basis,

(continued)

but I'm terrified of getting intimately involved with a man on a sexual or emotional basis. When I think of all those years in an oppressive marriage, I want to scream. I know I've kept most of these screams inside of me, for I feared that if I allowed myself to scream I'd never stop—that I might go crazy. Yet keeping my pain and tears inside of me has made my whole body ache, and I'm tired of hurting all the time. I want something else from life besides hurt!

A 49-year-old reentry student described going back to college as "a wonderful adventure that has opened new doors for me, and created a few obstacles." Although Linda had self-doubts and was intimidated over even the thought of becoming a student again, she cast her doubts aside and pursued her dream of attending a university. She challenged the expectations of remaining in old roles and made choices to do something different with her life.

LINDA'S STORY

*A*s a young woman I tried too hard to be superwife, mother, daughter, and friend. I had the role of peacemaker, was very quiet, stayed in the background, and desired to help a star to shine. I had always been there for others, sometimes to the neglect of my own needs and wants. I put too much effort into doing and little into just being. As a result of my personal therapy and other learning, I knew I wanted to change. I started to embrace being genuine and took more risks. I became more verbal and enjoyed participating in class. I began to notice where I could shine. I let go of the self-talk that kept me feeling stupid. I saw hope.

LATE MIDDLE AGE

The time between the ages of 50 or 55 and the early 70s can be considered late middle age blending into early aging. This is also a time when many adults are beginning to consider retirement, pursue new interests, and think more about what they want to do with the rest of their lives. This time in the life cycle is often characterized by the beginning of wisdom or the reclaiming of the wisdom of interdependence. This tends to be a time when serving others and passing along experiences becomes manifest.

The 50s

People begin the process of preparing for older age in their 50s. Many are at their peak in terms of status and personal power, and this can be a satisfying time of life. They do not have to work as hard as they did in the past, nor do they have to meet others' expectations. They can enjoy the benefits of their long struggle and dedication rather than striving to continually prove themselves. It is likely that rearing children and work are moving toward a culmination. Adults at this stage often do a lot of reflecting, contemplating, refocusing, and evaluating, so they can continue to discover new directions.

Rather than focusing on the 50s as a time of decline, we can enhance our lives by looking for what is going right for us. Instead of concentrating research on retirement, widowhood, meaninglessness, and impoverishment, Sheehy (1995) suggests that we look at the positive and creative dimensions of middle life—sources of love, meaning, fun, spiritual companionship, sexuality, and sustained well-being. Sheehy reports that this is an exciting time for women: "As family obligations fade away, many become motivated to stretch their independence, learn new skills, return to school, plunge into new careers, rediscover the creativity and adventurousness of their youth, and, at last, listen to their own needs" (p. 140). Although many women may experience this as an exciting time, they are often challenged to cope with both the physical and psychological adjustments surrounding menopause. Some women, fearing that menopause means losing their youthful looks, sink into depression. For many, menopause represents a crisis. In *The Silent Passage*, Gail Sheehy (1992) tells us that far from being a marker that signifies the beginning of the end menopause is better seen as a gateway to a second adulthood. Sheehy's book breaks the silence of menopause that is caused by shame, fear, misinformation, and the stigma of aging in a youth-obsessed society.

For men, the 50s can be a time to awaken their creative side. Instead of being consumed with achievement strivings, many men reveal human facets of themselves beyond rational thinking that can result in a richer existence. But men, too, are challenged to find new meaning in their lives. Projects that once were highly satisfying may now lack luster. Some men become depressed when they realize that they have been pursuing empty dreams. They may have met goals they set for themselves only to find that they are still longing for a different kind of life. For both women and men in their 50s, examining priorities often leads to new decisions about how they want to spend their time.

The 60s

During what Sheehy (1995) refers to as the "age of integrity," our central developmental tasks include adjusting to decreased physical and sensory capacities, adjusting to retirement, finding a meaning in life, being able to relate to the past without regrets, adjusting to the death of a spouse or friends, accepting inevitable losses, maintaining outside interests, and enjoying grandchildren. Moving into the aging phase brings a call for reflection and integration. Many physical and psychological changes occur as we approach old age. How we adapt to these changes is influenced by our past experiences, coping skills, beliefs about changing, and personality traits. At this time, work, leisure, and family relationships are major dimensions of life.

The vast majority of people in their 60s are quite able, both physically and mentally, to function independently. Most have reached a stage where maximum freedom coexists with a minimum of physical limitations. Indeed, only 10% of Americans 65 and over have a chronic health problem that interferes with their daily living (Sheehy, 1995, pp. 350–352).

A challenge during this phase of the life cycle is coming to terms with the reality that not everything could be done. People must let go of some of their dreams, accept their limitations, stop dwelling on what they cannot do, and focus on what they *can* do (McGoldrick & Carter, 1999).

Take Time to Reflect If you have reached middle age, write down your reactions to a few of these questions that have the most meaning for you. If you have not reached middle age, think about how you would like to be able to answer these questions when you reach that stage in your life. What do you need to do now to meet your expectations? Do you know a middle-aged person who serves as a role model for you?

> Is this a time of "generativity" or of "stagnation" for you? Think about some of the things you have done during this time of life that you feel the best about.

> Do you feel productive? If so, in what ways?

> Are there some things that you would definitely like to change in your life right now? What prevents you from making these changes?

> What questions have you raised about your life during this time?

> Have you experienced a midlife crisis? If so, how has it affected you?

> What losses have you experienced?

> What are some of the most important decisions you have made during this time of your life?

> What do you look forward to in your remaining years?

> If you were to review the major successes of your life to this point, what would they be?

LATE ADULTHOOD

In many countries those age 75 and older are the fastest growing portion of the population. America is aging, yet it is just one of many countries whose populations are growing older. As is the case for each of these developmental stages, there is a great deal of individual variation at this final stage of life. Many 70-year-old people have the energy of middle-aged people. How people look and feel during late adulthood is more than a matter of physical age; it is largely a matter of attitude. To a great degree, vitality is influenced by a state of mind more than by chronological years lived.

Themes During Late Adulthood

The death of parents and the loss of friends and relatives confront us with the reality of preparing ourselves for our own death. A basic task of late adulthood is to complete a life review in which we put our life in perspective and come to accept who we are and what we have done. This is also a time in life when spirituality may take on a new meaning and provide us with a sense of purpose, even as we face a growing dependence on others (McGoldrick & Carter, 1999). Borysenko (1996) put the challenge clearly: "This is the time to reflect and review one's life with appreciation of its successes and compassion for its failings, and with an effort to extract new levels of meaning that had previously been unappreciated" (p. 243).

Prevalent themes for people during late adulthood include loss; loneliness and social isolation; feelings of rejection; the struggle to find meaning in life; dependency; feelings of uselessness, hopelessness, and despair; fears of death and dying; grief over others' deaths; sadness over physical and mental deterioration; and regrets over past events. Today, many of these themes characterize people in their mid-80s more than people in their 60s and even 70s.

According to Erikson, the central issue of this age period is *integrity* versus *despair*. Those who succeed in achieving ego integrity feel that their lives have been productive and worthwhile and that they have managed to cope with failures as well as successes. They can accept the course of their lives and are not obsessed with thoughts of what might have been and what they could or should have done. They can look back without resentment and regret and can see their lives in a perspective of completeness and satisfaction. They accept themselves for who and what they are, and they also accept others as they are. They believe that who they are and what they have become are to a great extent the result of their choices. They approach the final stage of their lives with a sense of integration, balance, and wholeness. They can view death as natural, even while living rich and meaningful lives until the day they die.

Unfortunately, some elderly people fail to achieve ego integration. Typically, such people fear death. They may develop a sense of hopelessness and feelings of self-disgust. They approach the final stage of their lives with a sense of personal fragmentation. They often feel that they have little control over what happens to them. They cannot accept their life's cycle, for they see whatever they have done as "not enough" and feel that they have a lot of unfinished business. They yearn for another chance, even though they realize that they cannot have it. They feel inadequate and have a hard time accepting themselves, for they think that they have wasted their lives and let valuable time slip by. These are the people who die unhappy and unfulfilled.

Stereotypes of older people need to be challenged.

Ron Dahlquist/Stone

Stereotypes of Late Adulthood

It is truly a challenge for us to change the image of late adulthood and the assumptions often made about an aging society, which are based on myths and stereotypes (Deets, 2000). What gets in the way of understanding elderly people as individuals with this capacity for great variation are the common stereotypes many people hold about the elderly.

Ageism predisposes us to discriminate against old people by avoiding them or in some way victimizing them because of their age alone. Here are some of the stereotypes associated with older people that need to be challenged:

> All elderly eventually become senile.

> Old people are nonproductive and cannot contribute to society.

> Retirement is just a step away from death.
> It is disgraceful for an old person to remarry.
> Old people are not creative.
> Growing old always entails having a host of serious physical and emotional problems.
> Older people are set in their ways, stuck on following rigid patterns of thinking and behaving, and are not open to change.
> When people grow old, they are no longer capable of learning or contributing.
> Old people are no longer beautiful.
> An elderly person will die soon after his or her mate dies.
> Most elderly persons are lonely.
> Old people are no longer interested in sex.
> Most old people live in institutional settings.
> Depression is a natural consequence of aging.
> Preoccupation with death and dying is typical of older adults.

These negative perceptions and stereotypes of older people are common in our society. Older people can be rendered helpless if they accept them.

The attitudes older people have about aging are extremely important. Like adolescents, the aged may feel a sense of uselessness because of others' views of them. It is easy to accept the myths of others and turn them into self-fulfilling prophecies.

Challenging the Stereotypes

Old age does not have to be something we look toward with horror or resignation; nor must it be associated with bitterness. However, many elderly people in our society do feel resentment, and we have generally neglected this population, treating them as an undesirable minority that is merely tolerated. Their loss is doubly sad, because the elderly can make definite contributions to society.

Elderly people have a wealth of life experiences and coping skills, and they are likely to share this wisdom if they sense that others have a genuine interest in them. Many elderly persons are still very capable, yet the prejudice of younger adults often keeps us from acknowledging the value of the contributions the elderly offer us. Perhaps because we are afraid of aging and confronting our own mortality, we "put away" the elderly so they will not remind us of our future.

Do you know some older people who are living testimony that growing old does not mean that life is over? Do you know anyone in late adulthood who is blowing the stereotypes of aging? Here are some older people whose lives are evidence that aging is more than simply a chronological process. It has a lot to do with one's attitude and state of mind.

Aunt Mary We often imagine that people in their 80s and 90s live in rest homes and convalescent hospitals. We forget that many people of advanced age live by themselves and take care of themselves quite well. For instance, I (Marianne) occasionally visit with one of Jerry's aunts who is 99 years old. We always have good discussions about the past as well as the present. Aunt Mary has an incredible memory and shows interest in what is happening in the world. Until a few years ago, she was active through gardening, sewing, and taking care of her household. She is still able to knit, which she proudly displays during our visits. At times she resists fully accepting her limitations, but eventually she is willing to receive the help needed to make her life more comfortable. For example, at one time she fought her family when they wanted to give her a lifeline system (a system the elderly use to signal a need for help). Eventually she did accept the offer, and she recently enthusiastically explained how the system works as well as telling me with a smile that this gives her adult children peace of mind. She has a deep religious faith, which has given her the strength to cope with many of the hardships she has had to endure. Another source of vitality is her involvement with her children, grandchildren, and great grandchildren. Aunt Mary now has a caretaker staying at her house to help her during the week, and on the weekends her adult children take turns being with her. I always walk away from these visits feeling uplifted, positive about aging, and saying to myself "I hope I will feel as positive about life should I be fortunate enough to reach 99."

Billie Just turning 90, Billie was given a party in her honor by her friends, children, and grandchildren. Billie took care of her husband, who was paralyzed, for more than 25 years. She lived in another state, and she surprised her family by telling them that she was selling her home and moving to where her family lives. Billie recently made a number of new moves in her life. She bought a new home, joined a new church, enrolled in a swimming class, found herself a new hairdresser, bought herself a satellite dish so that she could watch sports events with her newfound friends, and plays bridge. She recently passed her driver's test and got her license renewed, and she still drives all over town. Billie manages fine living on her own, and she delights over the routine visits with family members. She recently had a bout with pneumonia, which she recovered from exceptionally well in her own home.

Art Art was widowed several years ago. No one would guess that he is 86 by looking at him. He recently moved 200 miles from the home he and his wife resided in for 30 years to make a new home with some of his family. His occupation was carpentry, and although he has been retired for many years, he is actively engaged in a number of building projects for others and for himself. Just recently he began to teach at-risk youth and ex-gang members the art of carpentry. In addition to learning carpentry from Art, one youth acknowledged that he also benefits from Art's wisdom on life. Art is still spry, is able to laugh and cry, retains his interest in the opposite sex, and recently remarried.

George Dawson At age 102 George Dawson became an author—4 years after learning to read (Kinosian, 2000). With the help of Seattle school teacher Richard Glaubman, Dawson wrote *Life Is So Good* (Dawson, 2000), a first-person narrative chronicling Dawson's journey as an African American man growing up and living in the South. Dawson explains his healthy and long life this way: "I never worry. Ever. What is there to worry about? That's just trying to control other people and things that happen to you" (Kinosian, 2000). This case is an excellent illustration of the point we made earlier that vitality is influenced by a state of mind more than by chronological years lived.

Bob and Betty A couple in their 80s who have been married for 60 years, Bob and Betty still enjoy each other's company. In addition to what they have as a couple, they are also blessed as individuals. They enjoy excellent health, live independently in their own home, are involved with a large extended family, enjoy many grandchildren and great grandchildren, and assume leadership roles in their church. They spend many hours doing volunteer work. Routinely, they make trips to Mexico where they serve as missionaries, providing assistance to an orphanage and a local church. Those who know them marvel at their ability to handle the strain connected with devoting countless hours to missionary work. What is most notable about them is their love for their family and their strong religious faith. Betty's quiet strength and gentleness blend nicely with Bob's incredible sharp wit and humor.

The Delany Sisters In their inspirational book, *Having Our Say* (Delany, Delany, with Hearth, 1993), Bessie and Sarah Delany show us, even at the ripe age of 102 and 104, that it is possible to maintain an interest in the world about them. The two women illustrate a wonderful example of aging with integrity. Both of them, of African American descent, were professional women, one a teacher and the other a dentist. The two sisters reflect on their long life and give us some insight about what led to their longevity. Although surprised at their longevity, they continued to live a healthy lifestyle that included exercise and a good diet. The sisters depended on each other as well as on family to care for them, yet they were able to retain a degree of independence. They gave a flavor of the challenge of growing old in their own words:

> BUT IT'S HARD BEING OLD, because you can't always do everything you want, exactly as *you* want it done. When you get as old as we are, you have to struggle to hang on to your freedom, your independence. We have a lot of family and friends keeping an eye on us, but we try not to be dependent on any one person. (p. 238)

Most people who have read their book or listened to their interviews are surprised by their incredible interest and definite opinions on a range of current affairs. The Delany sisters offer us a good illustration of remaining vital in spite of living more than 100 years.

Many octogenarians lead exemplary lives. Willard Scott, a national weatherman, often recognizes people on the morning news who have reached age 100 or above. Many of these individuals are described as living an active life, which shows us that aging is partially a state of mind. The Delany sisters, and others who have lived long and rich lives, frequently cite a host of elements that contributed to their advanced age:

> Being fortunate to have good genes
> Work that has provided meaning and fulfillment
> Involvement with family and friends
> An interest in doing good for others
> Staying involved in life and not retiring from life
> Having strong religious convictions
> A sense of humor
> The ability to grieve losses
> The willingness to forgive and not to be bitter
> Expressing rather than holding onto irritations
> A sense of pride in self
> Regular physical exercise
> Practicing good nutritional habits

Mary Cunningham On the KTLA 10 o'clock evening news (August 6, 2000), there was a report of a 93-year-old woman who certainly is challenging stereotypes about aging. She decided that it would be fun to sky dive, so she jumped from an airplane at 13,000 feet and soared through the air at a speed of over 100 miles per hour before her parachute opened. The report showed her jumping and landing. This was not her first experience with sky diving. Since she was 91 she has done this three times!

The people briefly described here do not fit the stereotypes of the elderly. They are living proof that one can age and at the same time live a full and rich life. There is no formula for growing old with grace and dignity. One of the ways to increase the chances of reaching an active old age is to make choices at earlier ages that will provide the foundation for these later years. Although you may not have reached old age, we hope you won't brush aside thinking about your eventual aging. Your observations of the old people you know can provide you with insights about what it is like to grow older. From these observations you can begin to formulate a picture of the life you would like to have as you get older.

Take Time to Reflect Imagine yourself being old. Think about your fears and about what you would like to be able to say about your life—your joys, your accomplishments, and your regrets. To facilitate this reflection, consider these questions:

> What do you most hope to accomplish by the time you reach old age?

> What are some of your greatest fears of growing old?

> What kind of old age do you expect? What are you doing now that might have an effect on the kind of person you will be as you grow older?

> Do you know some elderly person who is a role model for you?

> What are some things you hope to do during the later years of your life? How do you expect that you will adjust to retirement?

> How would you like to be able to respond to your body's aging? How do you think you will respond to failing health or to physical limitations on your lifestyle?

> Assume that you will have enough money to live comfortably and to do many of the things that you have not had time for earlier. What do you think you would most like to do and with whom?

> What would you most want to be able to say about yourself and your life when you are elderly?

In your journal write down some impressions of the kind of old age you hope for as well as the fears you have about growing older.

SUMMARY

Adulthood involves the struggle for autonomy, which means that we know ourselves and that we are able to form meaningful connections with others. Our quest for autonomy and maturity is truly a lifelong endeavor. Each stage of adulthood presents us with different tasks. Meeting the developmental tasks of later life hinges on successfully working through earlier issues. One part of this quest is learning to evaluate our early decisions and how these decisions currently influence us.

Transactional analysis can help us recognize early learning and decisions. Our life script is made up of both parental messages and decisions we make in response to these injunctions. The events of childhood and, to some extent, adolescence contribute to the formation of our life script, which we tend to follow into adulthood. By becoming increasingly aware of our life script, we are in a position to revise it. Instead of being hopelessly "scripted" by childhood influences, we can use our past to change our future. In short, we can shape our destiny rather than being passively shaped by earlier events.

During early adulthood, it is important to learn how to form intimate relationships. To develop intimacy, we must move beyond the self-preoccupation that is characteristic of adolescence. This is also a time when we are at our peak in terms of physical and psychological powers and can direct these resources to establish ourselves in all dimensions of life. Choices that we make pertaining to education, work, and lifestyle will have a profound impact later in life.

As we approach middle age, we come to a crossroads. Midlife is filled with a potential for danger and for new opportunities. At this phase we can assume a stance that "it's too late to change," or we can make significant revisions. There are opportunities to change careers, to find new ways to spend leisure time, and to find other ways of making a new life.

Later life can be a time of real enjoyment, or it can be a time of looking back in regret to all that we have not accomplished and experienced. It is important to recognize that the quality of life in later years often depends on the choices we made at earlier turning points in life.

To review the tasks and the choices of each period of the life span, we recommend that you review the developmental stages table presented in Chapter 2 and think about the continuity of the life cycle. Now that you have studied each stage of life, reflect on the meaning of these stages to you. If you have not yet arrived at a particular stage, think about what you can do at this time to assure the quality of life you would like in a future phase.

The experiences and events that occur during each developmental stage are crucial in helping to determine our attitudes, beliefs, values, and actions regarding the important areas of our lives that will be discussed in the chapters to come: gender-role identity, work, the body, love, sexuality, intimate relationships, loneliness and solitude, death and loss, and meaning and values. For this reason we have devoted considerable attention to the foundations of life choices. Understanding how we got where we are now is a critical first step in deciding where we want to go from here.

> Where Can I Go From Here?

1. Do you believe you are able to make new decisions? Do you think you are in control of your destiny? In your journal write down some examples of new decisions—or renewals of old decisions—that have made a significant difference in your life.

2. Mention some critical turning points in your life. Draw a chart in your journal showing the age periods you have experienced so far and indicate your key successes, failures, conflicts, and memories for each stage.

> ## Where Can I Go From Here? *(continued)*

3. After you have described some of the significant events in your life, list some of the decisions you have made in response to these events. How were you affected by these milestones in your life? Think about what you have learned about yourself from doing these exercises. What does all of this tell you about the person you are today?

4. Many students readily assert that they are psychologically independent. If this applies to you, think about some specific examples that show that you have questioned and challenged your parents' values and that you have modified your own value system.

5. To broaden your perspective on human development in various cultural or ethnic groups, talk to someone you know who grew up in a very different environment from the one you knew as a child. Find out how his or her life experiences have differed from yours by sharing some aspects of your own life. Try to discover whether there are significant differences in values that seem to be related to the differences in your life experiences. This could help you reassess many of your own values.

6. Talk with some people who are significantly older than you. For instance, if you are in your 20s, interview a middle-aged person and an elderly person. Try to get them to take the lead and tell you about their lives. What do they like about their lives? What have been some key turning points for them? What do they most remember of the past? You might even suggest that they read the section of the chapter that pertains to their present age group and react to the ideas presented there.

Resources for Future Study

Web Site Resources

Erikson Tutorial Home Page
http://snycorva.cortland.edu/~ANDERSMD/ERIK/WELCOME.HTML

This site provides handy information about Erik Erikson's eight stages of psychosocial development, including a summary chart of key facts for each stage, an introduction to each stage, and other links to information on Erikson and psychosocial development.

SeniorNet
http://www.seniornet.com/

SeniorNet seeks to provide access and education about computer technology and the Internet to those who are 50+ years old. The site offers links, information, and discussion groups on a wide variety of topics of interest to seniors. If you are interested in learning about computers and the Internet, you can look up their learning centers online here or call them at 415-495-4990 for the location nearest you.

ADULT DEVELOPMENT AND AGING: APA DIVISION 20
http://www.iog.wayne.edu/apadiv20/apadiv20.htm

Division 20 of the American Psychological Association is devoted to the study of the psychology of adult development and aging. Here you will find information on instructional resources for teachers, resources for students, and links for publications, conferences, and other related Web sites.

InfoTrac College Edition Resources

For additional readings, explore InfoTrac College Edition, our online library.

Go to **http://www.infotrac.college.com/wadsworth**

Hint: Enter the search terms:

    transactional analysis

    rational emotive behavior therapy (REBT)

    cognitive therapy

    early adulthood

    middle adulthood

    midlife crisis

    late adulthood

    multicultural aspects of development

Print Resources

Black, C. (1987). *It will never happen to me.* New York: Ballantine.

Bloomfield, H. H., with Felder, L. (1983). *Making peace with your parents.* New York: Ballantine.

Burns, D. D. (1981). *Feeling good: The new mood therapy.* New York: New American Library (Signet).

Ellis, A. (1999). *How to make yourself happy and remarkably less disturbable.* Atascadero, CA: Impact Publishers.

Goleman, D. (1995). *Emotional intelligence.* New York: Bantam Books.

Goulding, M., & Goulding, R. (1979). *Changing lives through redecision therapy.* New York: Brunner/Mazel.

Goulding, R., & Goulding, M. (1978). *The power is in the patient.* San Francisco: TA Press.

Levinson, D. J., in collaboration with Levinson, J. D. (1996). *The seasons of a woman's life.* New York: Ballantine Books.

McGoldrick, M., & Carter, B. (1999). Self in context: The individual life cycle in systemic perspective. In B. Carter & M. McGoldrick (Eds.) *The expanded family life cycle: Individual, family, and social perspectives* (3rd ed.) (pp. 27–46). Boston: Allyn & Bacon.

Miller, J. B., & Stiver, I. P. (1997). *The healing connection: How women form relationships in therapy and in life.* Boston: Beacon Press.

Miller, T. (1995). *How to want what you have: Discovering the magic and grandeur of ordinary existence.* New York: Avon.

Sheehy, G. (1995). *New passages: Mapping your life across time.* New York: Random House.

Sheehy, G. (1976). *Passages: Predictable crises of adult life.* New York: Dutton.

Stone, H., & Stone, S. (1993). *Embracing your inner critic: Turning self-criticism into a creative asset.* San Francisco: Harper.

Wellness stresses positive health rather than merely the absence of disabling symptoms

Merritt Vincent/PhotoEdit

YOUR BODY AND WELLNESS

Use this scale to respond to these statements:

4 = This statement is true of me *most* of the time.

3 = This statement is true of me *much* of the time.

2 = This statement is true of me *some* of the time.

1 = This statement is true of me *almost none* of the time.

_____ 1. Making basic changes in my lifestyle to improve my health is not something I often think about.

_____ 2. The way I take care of my body expresses the way I feel about myself.

_____ 3. When I look in the mirror, I feel comfortable with my physical appearance.

_____ 4. When something ails me, I tend to want to treat the symptom rather than looking for the cause.

_____ 5. I like to give hugs and get hugs.

_____ 6. My diet consists mainly of fast food.

_____ 7. Exercise is a priority in my life.

_____ 8. I am motivated to take better care of myself in all respects.

_____ 9. I get enough sleep.

_____ 10. I frequently do not take care of my physical and emotional needs.

Your body is the primary subject of this chapter, and emotional and interpersonal factors both play a role in maintaining physical well-being. Therefore, we take a holistic approach to wellness, which involves considering the physical, psychological, social, mental, and spiritual aspects of health.

We begin the chapter by exploring the topic of accepting responsibility for your general state of wellness. We look at the ways your self-image is influenced by your perception of your body. We explore how your bodily identity, which includes the way you experience yourself and express yourself through your body, affects your beliefs, decisions, and feelings about yourself. If you look at your body, you will see that it reflects some significant choices. Do you take care of the physical you? How comfortable are you with your body? How do your feelings and attitudes about your body affect your choices in areas such as self-worth, sexuality, and love? How aware are you of the impact your emotional state has on your physical state? How does the quality of your relationships affect your physical health?

Next, we explore the goal of wellness as a lifestyle choice that enhances body and mind. We take up subjects such as making decisions about diet, exercise, and rest and ultimately accepting responsibility for your body. Although you might readily say that you desire the state of wellness as a personal goal, many of us have experienced frustrations and discouragement in attaining this goal. Wellness is not something that merely happens to you. It is the result of being consciously aware of what your physical and psychological well-being entails and making a commitment to wellness. Wellness is more than the absence of illness. In many ways the medical model ignores wellness and focuses on the removal of symptoms, which results in a negative view of health. Relatively few physicians ask their patients questions about aspects of their lifestyles that may have contributed to their health problems.

An honest examination of the choices you are making about your body and your overall wellness can reveal a great deal about how you feel about your life. You are in charge of your general health, and the way you lead your life affects your physical and psychological well-being. This includes accepting responsibility for what you consume, how you exercise, and the stresses you put yourself under. (Stress and approaches to managing stress are the subjects of Chapter 5.)

If you listen to your body, you will be able to make life-enhancing choices. At this time in your life, how much priority do you place on your own wellness? How well are you taking care of yourself? In what ways are you practicing wellness principles in your life? If you are not taking care of your body, what beliefs may be getting in the way? What resources do you require to begin modifying those parts of your lifestyle that affect your bodily well-being?

Rest and sleep, exercise, diet and nutrition, and spirituality are all aspects of well-being. As you read this chapter, think about what you want for yourself in the long-term. What can you do to discontinue any habitual, unhealthy choices and replace them with new patterns of living? We invite you to look at the full range of choices available to you to help you stay healthy.

WELLNESS AND LIFE CHOICES

The concept of wellness fits into a holistic view of health. Traditional medicine focuses on identifying symptoms of illness and curing disease. By contrast, holistic health focuses on all facets of human functioning. The holistic approach is based on the assumption that the mind and the body are an integral unit and cannot be separated. It emphasizes the intimate relationship between our body and all the other aspects of ourselves—psychological, social, intellectual, and spiritual. Wellness is an active process consisting of conscious choices we make in fashioning a healthy lifestyle. It stresses positive health rather than merely the absence of disabling symptoms. Just as there are many degrees of being ill, there are degrees of wellness.

Donatelle, Snow-Harter, and Wilcox (1995) state that if you are living a wellness lifestyle you are moving toward more deliberate, conscious actions to create the best self possible within the limitations of your situation. Three aspects characterize this wellness lifestyle:

> Assume responsibility for your actions and the quality of your health.

> Have a concern for others and be tolerant of imperfections in others.

> Be willing to devote time and energy to developing a sound basis for making good decisions about health.

There are many rewards for adopting a wellness lifestyle. Donatelle and her colleagues (1995) list these important long-term benefits:

> Improved cardiovascular efficiency

> Increased muscular tone, strength, flexibility, and endurance

> Reduced risk for injuries

> Improved sense of self-control, self-efficacy, and self-esteem

> Improved management and control of stress

> Improved outlook on life

> Improved interpersonal relationships

> Decreased mortality (death) and morbidity (illness) from infections and chronic diseases

It is clear that wellness is a lifestyle choice rather than a one-time decision. Wellness is a process that involves identifying personal goals, prioritizing your goals and values, identifying any barriers that might prevent you from reaching your goals, making an action plan, and then committing yourself to following through on your plans to reach your goals. This may seem a rather simple pathway to wellness, but many people who desire general wellness are reluctant to put what they know into an action plan designed to bring about the changes they say they want.

In the *Wellness Workbook,* Travis and Ryan (1994) describe wellness as a bridge supported by two piers: self-responsibility and love. They write that self-responsibility and love flow from the appreciation that we are not merely separate individuals, nor are we simply the sum of separate parts. Instead, we are integrated beings, and we are united in one energy system with everything else in creation. For them, health is best conceived of on an illness–wellness continuum that ranges from premature death on one end to high-level wellness on the other end. The essence of wellness is captured in these brief statements:

> Wellness is a choice—a decision you make to move toward optimal health.

> Wellness is a way of life—a lifestyle you design to achieve your highest potential for well-being.

> Wellness is a process—a developing awareness that there is no end point but that health and happiness are possible in each moment, here and now.

> Wellness is an efficient channeling of energy—energy received from the environment, transformed within you, and sent on to impact the world outside.

> Wellness is the integration of body, mind, and spirit—the appreciation that everything you do and think and feel and believe has an impact on your state of health.

> Wellness is the loving acceptance of yourself. (p. xiv)

Wellness as an Active Choice

Wellness entails a lifelong process of taking care of our needs on all levels of functioning. Well people are committed to creating a lifestyle that contributes to taking care of their physical selves, challenging themselves intellectually, expressing the full range of their emotions, finding rewarding interpersonal relationships, and searching for a meaning that will give direction to their lives. Unfortunately, many of us know what to do, yet we do not want to accept the responsibility that is required to be well. Some of us would rather deny our part in our level of wellness. We may think of "getting sick" as something that is beyond our control. Although we have a great deal of information on wellness, many of us are hesitant in using this knowledge in living a healthy lifestyle. Most of us know what a healthy lifestyle entails; nevertheless, we continue to make unhealthy choices. Who does not know that smoking, excessive use of alcohol or drugs, poor diet, and lack of exercise is not conducive to good health? Yet, in spite of what we know, how many of us behave in ways that we know are not in our long-term best health interests? We need to learn to deny some short-term pleasures for longer term benefits if we hope to make changes in our health.

Part of the problem may be that we are accustomed to quick results and instant gratification. Achieving wellness is the process of conscious choice and takes effort, and the results are often slow. Self-discipline is required to consistently put forth the effort necessary to create a healthy lifestyle.

In a keynote address at the Evolution of Psychotherapy Conference, Dr. Herbert Benson (May 25, 2000) spoke to approximately 4,000 mental health professionals on his views of health and well-being. Benson contends that health and well-being are akin to a three-legged stool: one leg is pharmaceuticals, the second leg is surgery, and the third leg is self-care. Although the first two legs are awesome in their efficacy, they are not effective in treating 60% to 90% of the problems brought to health care professionals. According to Benson, visits to physicians are related to stress and other mind–body interactions, and the solutions to these problems lie in self-care. Learning the relaxation response (see Benson 1976, 1984), understanding our core beliefs, and spirituality are crucial to taking care of ourselves and fostering our sense of well-being. Benson also emphasizes the importance of the relationship between the doctor and the patient. Benson states that much of what cures people is due to the placebo effect, which is the patient's belief in the power of a relationship with a doctor or the interventions made by the doctor.

A combination of factors contributes to our sense of well-being. Thus, a holistic approach pays attention to specific aspects of our lifestyle, including how we work and play, how we relax, how and what we eat, how we think and feel, how we keep physically fit, our relationships with others, our values and beliefs, and our spiritual needs. One of our friends, Ron Coley, captures the essence of living a balanced life when he talks about the importance of REDS (rest, exercise, diet, and spirituality) as the keys to health. When something is amiss in our lives, we are generally failing to take proper care of one of these basic human dimensions. Maintaining a balanced life involves attending to our physical, emotional, social, mental, and spiritual needs. To the degree that we ignore or neglect one of these areas, we pay a price in terms of optimal functioning. We agree with Ron's assertion that if you pay attention to the balance among these four critical areas the general result is wellness.

Dr. Bernie Siegel, a psychologically and spiritually oriented physician, promotes a similar viewpoint. Siegel (1988) believes illness serves some function and makes sense if we look at what is going on with people who become physically sick. He investigates the quality of their psychological and spiritual lives as the key to understanding the mystery of illness and fostering health. From Siegel's perspective, when we are not meeting our emotional and spiritual needs, we are setting ourselves up for physical illness. In his work with cancer patients, Siegel finds that one of the most common precursors of cancer is a traumatic loss or a feeling of emptiness in one's life. He also finds that depressed people—those "going on strike from life"—are at much greater risk for contracting cancer than are nondepressed people. As a physician, Siegel views his role not simply as finding the right treatments for a disease but also as helping his patients resolve emotional conflicts, find an inner reason for living, and release the healing resources within.

The popularity of Siegel's works points to the power within us to keep ourselves well and heal ourselves. Scores of self-help books and home videos address the subjects of stress management, exercise, meditation, diet, nutrition, weight control, control of smoking and drinking, and wellness medicine. We are beginning to realize the value of preventive medicine, and wellness clinics, nutrition centers, and exercise clubs are becoming increasingly popular. We encourage you to think about the priority you are placing on physical and psychological well-being and invite you to consider whether you want to make any changes in your lifestyle to promote wellness.

One Man's Wellness Program

Kevin was in one of our therapeutic groups, and when we first met him, Kevin struck us as being closed off emotionally, rigid, stoic, and defensive. For many years he had thrown himself completely into his work as an attorney. Although his family life was marked by tension and bickering with his wife, he attempted to block out the stress at home by burying himself in his law cases and by excelling in his career. Here is his own account of his life.

KEVIN'S STORY

When I reached middle age, I began to question how I wanted to continue living. My father suffered a series of heart attacks. I watched my father decline physically, and this jolted me into the realization that both my father's time and my own time were limited. I finally went for a long-overdue physical examination and discovered that I had high blood pressure, that my cholesterol level was abnormally high, and that I was at relatively high risk of having a heart attack. I also learned that several of my relatives had died of heart attacks. I decided that I wanted to reverse what I saw as a self-destructive path. After talking with a physician, I decided to change my patterns of living in several ways. I was overeating, my diet was not balanced, I was consuming a great deal of alcohol to relax, I didn't get enough sleep, and I was "too busy" to do any physical exercise. My new decision involved making contacts with friends. I learned to enjoy playing tennis and racquetball on a regular basis. I took up jogging. If I didn't run in the morning, I felt somewhat sluggish during the day. I radically changed my diet in line with suggestions from my physician. As a result, I lowered both my cholesterol level and my blood pressure without the use of medication; I also lost 20 pounds and worked myself into excellent physical shape. Getting into personal counseling was extremely helpful, because my sessions with a counselor helped me make some basic changes in the way I approach life and also helped me put things into perspective.

Let's underscore a few key points in Kevin's case. First of all, he took the time to seriously reflect on the direction he was going in life. He did not engage in self-deception; rather, he admitted that the way he was living was not healthy. On finding out that heart disease was a part of his family history, he did not shrug his shoulders and assume an indifferent attitude. Instead, he made a decision to take an active part in changing his life on many levels. He cut down on drinking and relied less on alcohol as an escape. He changed his patterns of eating, sleeping, and exercise, which resulted in his feeling better physically and psychologically. Although he was still committed to his law practice, he pursued it less compulsively. He realized that he had missed play in his life, and he sought a better balance between work and play.

With the help of counseling, Kevin realized the high price he was paying for bottling up emotions of hurt, sadness, anger, guilt, and joy. Although he did not give up his logical and analytical dimensions, he added to his range as a person by allowing himself to express what he was feeling. He learned that unexpressed emotions would find expression in some form of physical illness or symptom. Kevin learned the value of taking his emotions seriously rather than denying them. He continued to question the value of living exclusively by logic and calculation, in both his professional and personal life. As a consequence, he cultivated friendships and let others who were significant to him know that he wanted to be closer to them. Kevin could have asked his physician for a prescription and could have assumed a passive stance toward curing his illness. Instead, he was challenged to review his life to determine what steps he could take to get more from the time he had to live. A person who knew him only casually commented one day that he seemed so much different than he had a year before. She remembered him as being uptight, unfriendly, uncommunicative, angry-looking, and detached. She was surprised at his changes, and she used adjectives such as warm, open, relaxed, talkative, and outgoing to describe him.

Accepting Responsibility for Your Body

The American public is becoming increasingly informed about exercise programs, dietary habits, and ways to manage stress. More health insurance companies are providing payment for preventive medicine as well as remediation; one does not need to look far to find a preventive health clinic. Many communities provide a wide variety of programs aimed at helping people improve the quality of their lives by finding a form of exercise that suits them.

Major health insurance companies take surveys of their clients' lifestyles to identify positive and negative habits that affect their overall health. One of our daughters signed up for health insurance with a major company. She was asked to fill out a series of surveys at regular intervals to monitor her health practices. This company also presented her with a book describing many common health problems and ways to prevent them. This move is certainly motivated by the company's desire to reduce payments to subscribers. However, another motivation might well be a desire to assist people in developing sound health habits that will lead to prevention of serious health problems.

Doctors often find that people they see are more interested in getting pills and in removing their symptoms than in changing a stressful lifestyle. Some of these patients see themselves as victims of their ailments rather than as being responsible for them. Some physicians resist prescribing pills to alleviate the symptoms of what they see as a problematic lifestyle. Psychologically oriented physicians emphasize the role of *choice* and *responsibility* as critical determinants of our physical and psychological well-being. In their practice these doctors challenge patients to look at what they are doing to their bodies through lack of exercise, the substances they take in, and other damaging behavior. Although they may prescribe medication to lower a person's extremely high blood pressure, they inform the patient that medications can do only so much and that what is needed is a radical change in lifestyle. The patient is encouraged to share with the physician the responsibility for maintaining wellness.

The many popular books on natural methods of healing on the market today reveal our interest in this area. Increasingly, people are showing concern over the possible side effects of drugs and medications, and they are taking steps to educate themselves about prescription drugs. These books offer information to consumers about the uses and potentially harmful side effects of medications and enable consumers to share with their physicians the responsibility for the proper use of medicine. Consumers are encouraged to question physicians about the medications they prescribe. Some people prefer to turn over complete

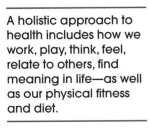

A holistic approach to health includes how we work, play, think, feel, relate to others, find meaning in life—as well as our physical fitness and diet.

Bob Torrez/Stone

authority for health care to their physicians, but many others are taking a more active role and assuming more responsibility in their health care.

"Natural" remedies are not necessarily superior to synthetic prescription drugs. Herbal remedies often share the same active ingredients as prescription drugs, but in unknown concentrations, and there may be side effects with herbal substances. These substances are not regulated by the FDA, so their effectiveness and contraindications are not well-documented. The natural remedy movement may extend your ability to heal yourself beyond what is currently provided by traditional medicine, but it is a mistake to conclude that anything "natural" is automatically good for you.

Whether you see yourself as a passive victim or an active agent in maintaining your health can make a world of difference. If you believe you simply catch colds or are ill-fated enough to get sick, and if you do not see what you can do to prevent bodily illnesses, your body is controlling you. But if you recognize that the way you lead your life (including accepting responsibility for what you consume, how you exercise, and the stresses you put yourself under) has a direct bearing on your physical and psychological well-being, you can be in control of your body. If you listen to yourself, you will be able to make choices about your health care that enhance the quality of your life. The following Take Time to Reflect exercise can help you answer the question, "Do I control my body, or does my body control me?"

Take Time to Reflect

1. Here are some common rationalizations people use for not changing patterns of behavior that affect their bodies. Look over these statements and decide what ones, if any, you use.

_____ I don't have time to exercise every day.

_____ No matter how I try to lose weight, nothing seems to work.

_____ I sabotage myself, and others sabotage me, in my attempts to lose weight.

_____ I'll stop smoking soon.

_____ When I have a vacation, I'll relax.

_____ Even though I drink a lot (or use drugs), it calms me down and has never interfered with my life.

_____ I need a drink (or marijuana) to relax.

_____ Food isn't important to me; I eat anything I can get fast.

_____ I simply don't have time to eat three balanced meals a day.

_____ Food has gotten so expensive, I just can't afford to eat decent meals anymore.

_____ If I stop smoking, I'll surely gain weight.

_____ I simply cannot function without several cups of coffee.

_____ If I don't stop smoking, I might get lung cancer or die a little sooner, but we all have to go sometime.

(continued)

What other statements do you sometimes use that you could you add to this list?

_____

_____

2. Complete the following sentences with the first word or phrase that comes to mind:

a. One way I abuse my body is _____

b. One way I neglect my body is _____

c. When people notice my physical appearance, I think that _____
_____

d. When I look at my body in the mirror, I _____

e. I could be healthier if only _____

f. One way I could cut down the stress in my life is _____
_____

g. If I could change one aspect of my body, it would be my _____

h. One way that I relax is _____

i. I'd describe my diet as _____

j. For me, exercising is _____

3. As you review your responses to this exercise, what changes, if any, do you want to make? Do you have any thoughts regarding initial steps you can take at this time to bring about these changes?

_____

_____

MAINTAINING SOUND HEALTH PRACTICES

Earlier we described REDS (rest, exercise, diet, and spirituality) as a formula for wellness. Developing sound habits pertaining to sleeping, eating, exercising, and cultivating our spirituality is basic to any wellness program. Getting adequate rest and sleep is a key element to overall health; if you are rested, you are

Dennis Degnan/Corbis

Developing sound habits pertaining to sleeping, eating, exercising, and cultivating our spirituality is basic to any wellness program.

less prone to the negative impact of stress. Exercise not only makes you look and feel better but is essential for cardiovascular fitness. Making healthy nutritional choices provides you with the necessary fuel to meet the challenges of life and is essential to physical well-being. Spiritual practices may be as important to your overall well-being as eating and exercising. A comprehensive view of health includes nourishing both your body and your spirit.

Rest and Sleep

Sleep is a fundamental aspect of being healthy. Rest is restorative. During sleep our physical body is regenerated, and dreaming enables us to explore our unconscious (George, 1998). Sleep helps you recover from the stresses you experienced during the day, and it provides you with energy to cope effectively with challenges you will face tomorrow. If you sleep between 6 and 9 hours each night, you are in the normal range. George (1998) reminds us that many of us disturb our sleeping cycle from taking its natural course by staying up longer to get more done and by jarring ourselves out of sleep with an alarm clock. George tells us that restful sleep is vital for relaxation and that we need to discover our personal sleeping cycle. He adds: "The key to quality sleep is being able to identify our natural sleeping pattern and then adhere to the required quota as much as possible" (p. 58).

Sleep deprivation leads to increased vulnerability to emotional upset and leaves you susceptible to the negative consequences of stress. Some of the signs that you may not be getting adequate sleep include moodiness, continuing tiredness, tiredness on waking up, difficulty concentrating, and falling asleep in class or when trying to study. Sleep disturbances or insufficient sleep tends to result in increased irritability, difficulty concentrating, memory loss, increased physical and emotional tension, and being overly sensitive to criticism. Insomnia can be caused by stress and is often the result of not being able to "turn off thinking" when you are trying to sleep. If you are interested in sleeping well, do what you can to take your mind off your problems. Ruminating about your difficulties is one of the key factors contributing to insomnia.

If you have problems sleeping, consider some of these tips for preventing and coping with insomnia and getting the best sleep possible:

❭ Establish a regular sleep routine, including going to bed at about the same time each night and getting up around the same time every morning. Although short naps during the day can be restorative, it is a good idea to avoid long naps.

❭ Unwind physically. Use relaxation methods such as deep muscular relaxation, breathing, and relaxing imagery.

❭ Consider meditating for at least 15 minutes before going to bed.

❭ Exercise regularly, especially earlier in the day to improve your sleep at night.

❭ Clear your mind of all your worries and thoughts of the day. Avoid feelings of anger or resentment, which often lead to wakefulness (Fontana, 1997).

❭ Minimize noise. Listening to the sound of your own breathing can help you relax and fall asleep or go back to sleep if you wake early.

❭ Avoid eating heavy meals close to bedtime, and avoid caffeine for several hours before sleep. Alcohol, even in small amounts, can make you sleep less soundly.

❭ Quit smoking; nicotine, like caffeine, is a stimulant.

❭ If you cannot sleep, get up and read or watch television or listen to soothing music.

> Maintain realistic self-talk about sleep. Avoid talking yourself into getting a poor sleep. Repeat a soothing formula such as, "I am going into deep sleep."

> Avoid taking your worries to bed with you at night. If you find yourself worrying, get up and write what you can do about it after you have had a good night of sleep.

> Avoid consistent use of sleeping pills, as some form of sleeping aids are addictive. Although they may help you fall asleep faster, they do not provide deep sleep.

> Do not ruminate about the amount you are sleeping. Worrying or annoyance because you cannot sleep is a guarantee of a sleepless night (Fontana, 1997).

Remember that the quality of sleep matters more than the quantity. The amount of sleep that is normal for different individuals can vary.

Not getting adequate sleep is one matter, but it is also possible to get more sleep than you need, which may have negative results. Sleeping more than 9 or 10 hours can have a number of side effects. Your overall metabolic rate may lower, making it difficult to maintain your ideal weight; muscle tone may drop, which can reduce the ease in which you can exercise; and mental performance may suffer due to lethargy (Rice, 1999).

It is a good idea to monitor how well and how often you get the sleep and rest you require to function optimally. Of course, most of us experience occasional insomnia, mild sleep disorders, and difficulty falling asleep. If this becomes a chronic problem, it certainly deserves attention. If you find that you have serious problems getting adequate sleep, we suggest that you consult your physician, your campus health center, or a sleep disorder specialist.

Exercise

A central component to maintaining wellness in any stress management program is regular exercise. Exercise is a natural means of reducing the negative effects of stress, and it can prolong and enhance your life. Exercise has a number of benefits; these are just a few of them:

> Releasing endorphins (which improve your mood and give you energy)
> Increasing respiratory capacity
> Slowing down the aging process
> Releasing anger, tension, and anxiety
> Releasing pent-up emotions
> Increasing feelings of well-being, self-esteem, and improved self-concept
> Preventing hypertension
> Improving work efficiency
> Alleviating and preventing depression

> Decreasing negative thinking
> Improving sleeping
> Reducing the risk of illnesses
> Reducing body weight
> Increasing physical strength and endurance
> Increasing muscle tone
> Providing you with a source of enjoyment

Weiten and Lloyd (2000) state that exercise is associated with greater longevity because it promotes an array of benefits, including these:

> Enhance cardiovascular fitness and reduce susceptibility to coronary heart disease.
> Reduce obesity-related health problems including diabetes, respiratory difficulties, arthritis, and back pain.
> Decrease risk for colon cancer in men and for breast and reproductive cancer in women.
> Reduce potentially damaging physical effects of stress.
> Produce desirable personality changes that may promote physical wellness.

Although there are many benefits to keeping physically fit, there are some risks involved with exercise. Some people approach exercise in a driven manner, which may undo some of its potential benefits. Bike riders may enjoy this form of exercise, but it takes only one car to spoil these benefits. There are some hazards to jogging, especially the risk of muscular and skeletal injuries. Moderation is a good course to follow. Before embarking on a rigorous physical fitness program, get a thorough physical examination and discuss your proposed exercise program with your physician. An exercise program needs to be planned with care to minimize the risks and maximize the gains to your overall wellness.

Our psychological fitness is every bit as important as physical fitness. George (1998) poetically captures this notion: "For true, holistic well-being, the health of the inner self must be given as much attention as our physical condition. If we neglect the mind's welfare, we become tense and pale, even seriously unwell. There is little point in maintaining the temple if the sanctuary inside is in ruins" (p. 63). George's words are a reminder to us to avoid thrashing our bodies to the limit to reap the rewards of fitness. Consider ways to exercise that bring the body and the mind together.

But how much exercise is enough? Allan Abbott, M.D. (personal communication, January 3, 2000) questions the advice of some physicians to exercise for 20 to 30 minutes, 3 times a week. Based on his review of experts in this field who assessed the scientific evidence, Abbott suggests that every adult should accumulate 30 minutes or more of moderate-intensity physical activity on most, preferably all, days of the week. For most people this moderate physical activity can be accomplished by brisk walking (about 3 to 4 miles an hour). Even short periods of intermittent activity accumulated over a day have value. The total amount of regularly performed physical activity seems to be more important than the manner in which the specific activity is performed. Although brisk walking for 30 minutes a day will provide many health benefits, intermittent activity can be beneficial. Try walking rather than driving short distances, walking up stairs instead of taking the elevator, or operating an exercise machine while watching television.

Designing an adequate program of physical activity is difficult for many people. Not only is exercise time consuming, but if you are not physically fit, your initial attempts can be painful and discouraging. Don't give up! If you are just starting out, exercise for 10 to 15 minutes and gradually increase the time. The secret to developing and maintaining a successful exercise program is to select a form of exercise that you enjoy. Create healthy goals for your exercise program. One of these goals might be the pure pleasure of moving your body in the way it was intended to move. It is a good idea to gradually increase your participation in your program. If you complete a goal that you set for yourself, reward yourself for sticking to your plan. Although it is important to engage in your exercise program regularly, be careful not to overdo it. More is not always better. If you approach exercise compulsively, it might become another demand on you, which may increase the stress in your life. Exercise, like rest, can be a break from the grind of work and can refresh you—and it can be fun!

Diet and Nutrition

There is a lot of truth in the axiom "You are what you eat." Your daily diet affects your long-term health more than any other factor within your control. If your primary diet is poor, you will not have the energy you need to meet the demands of everyday life. Irregular and inconsistent eating patterns are a key nutritional problem for many. We often hear students make the claim that eating healthy is too time consuming, and we typically invite them to look at the consequences of poor eating habits. Healthy eating does not have to take an abundance of time, especially when new patterns are developed and a varied diet becomes part of your daily life. Most nutritional experts suggest a varied diet, consisting of foods from each of these groups daily: fruits, vegetables, breads and other grain products, meat or poultry or fish, and milk products. Variety is a critical part of nutrition.

In *An Invitation to Health*, Dianne Hales (2001) makes the point that your health is basically up to you. By learning how to eat wisely and well, how to manage your weight, and how to become physically fit, you can begin a lifelong journey toward wellness. Making healthy choices about diet and nutrition entails having specific knowledge about what you eat, so it is well for you to become a smart nutrition consumer. Besides eating to live, eating can bring increased satisfaction to living. Hales (2001, p. 191) offers these guidelines for developing eating habits that will lead to physical and psychological wellness:

> Eat with people whom you like.

> Talk only of pleasant things while eating.

> Eat slowly and experience the taste of the food you are eating.

> When you eat, avoid reading, writing, working, or talking on the phone.

> Eat because you are hungry, not to change how you feel.

> After eating, take time to be quiet and rest.

Eating for health and eating for pleasure are not incompatible. From Dr. Andrew Weil's (2000) perspective, *eating well* means using food to influence health and well-being and, at the same time, to satisfy your senses and to provide pleasure and comfort. It is possible to eat in ways that best serve our body while also getting the enjoyment we expect from food. Weil believes *what* and *how* we eat are critical determinants of how we feel and how we age. He also believes food can function as medicine to influence a variety of common ailments.

At the University of Arizona's Program in Integrative Medicine, Weil teaches physicians and other health professionals lifestyle medicine, which is oriented toward prevention of diseases. He encourages people to change their lifestyle habits before disease appears. Eating well is one aspect of lifestyle, which is only one set of variables in the mix accounting for healthy living. Weil contends that there are multiple determinants of health, starting with genetics and including a great many environmental, psychosocial, and spiritual factors. But diet is one of the lifestyle factors over which we have a large degree of control. We cannot change our genes. We cannot always control the quality of air we breathe, and we cannot completely avoid the stresses of everyday life. But we can decide what to eat and what not to eat: "My conclusion is that diet is an important influence on health, one that you can control to a greater extent than other factors, and that eating a good diet does not excuse you from attending to other aspects of lifestyle if you want to enjoy optimum health" (Weil, 2000, p. 22).

Spirituality

Spirituality is another key ingredient in a balanced life. Spirituality has many meanings and plays greater or lesser roles in different people's lives. For us, spirituality encompasses our relationship to the universe and is an avenue for finding meaning and purpose in living. It is an experience beyond the merely physical realm that helps us discover unity in the universe. One definition of spirituality is the practice of letting go of external noise and connecting with your inner self. Religion may be a vital aspect of your spirituality, but many people perceive themselves as being deeply spiritual, but not religious, beings. Religion refers to a set of beliefs that connect us to a higher power or a God. For many people, affiliation with a church is an organized means by which they express their religion. In addition to formal prayer and religious practices, meditation, mindfulness, and living in the moment are some of the paths that can lead you to a greater sense of spirituality.

His Holiness the Dalai Lama is the spiritual leader of the Tibetan people. In his book, *Ethics for the New Millennium* (1999), he makes what he considers to be an important distinction between religion and spirituality. He views religion as being concerned with some form of faith tradition that involves acceptance of a supernatural reality, including perhaps the belief in a heaven or nirvana. A part of religion includes dogma, ritual, and prayer. The Dalai Lama sees spirituality as being concerned with qualities of the human spirit. These included love and compassion, patience, tolerance, forgiveness, contentment, a sense of responsibility, and a sense of harmony. Spiritual acts presume concern for others' well-being. At this point consider your definition of spirituality.

Feeding your soul may be as important as feeding your body for your overall health. There are many ways to nourish your spirit, among them, spending some time in quiet reflection, appreciating natural beauty in silence, lying on the ground and watching the clouds go by, visiting a sick person in the hospital, planting some seeds or flowers in a garden, engaging in volunteer work, attending a church service, kissing or hugging someone you love, writing a letter to someone you have not seen in a long time, reading something inspirational or spiritual, praying for yourself and others, writing in your journal, or watching an inspirational movie. Recall the last time you did something to nourish your spirit. What did you do? What was it like for you to participate in a spiritual experience? How important is spirituality for you? We will return to this topic in Chapter 13.

Reflect on the balance in your life. Are there some aspects of your daily living that you want to modify? The following Take Time to Reflect will help you identify how the REDS formula is functioning in your life.

Take Time to Reflect

1. How well do you sleep? Are you getting adequate rest and sleep? Are you willing to make any changes in this area?

_____

_____

_____

(continued)

2. Do you value regular physical exercise? What kind of physical activity do you enjoy most? What gets in your way of exercising? What patterns are you willing to change?

_____

_____

_____

3. Do you have a healthy diet? Are there any changes in your diet, nutrition, and eating habits you are willing to make?

_____

_____

_____

4. How do you define spirituality for yourself? Do you see a need within yourself right now for spiritual improvement?

_____

_____

_____

5. As you consider the balance involved in the REDS (rest, exercise, diet, and spirituality) formula, how do you see each dimension affecting the other aspects of your life? Identify one goal for each of these areas as a target for making changes in your life. What can you do today to increase the chances of committing yourself to a plan aimed at working on concrete changes in maintaining sound health practices?

_____

_____

_____

YOUR BODILY IDENTITY

We are limited in how much we can actually change our body, but there is much we can do to work with the material we have. First, however, we must pay attention to what we are expressing about ourselves through our body, so we can determine whether we *want* to change our bodily identity. This involves increasing our awareness of how we experience our body through touch and movement. As you read this section, reflect on how well you know your body and how comfortable you are with it. Then you can decide about changing your body image—for example, by losing or gaining weight.

Experiencing and Expressing Yourself Through Your Body

Some of us are divorced from our bodies; the body is simply a vehicle that carries us around. If someone asks you what you are thinking, you are likely to come up with a quick answer. If asked what you are experiencing and sensing in your body, however, you may be at a loss for words. Yet your body can be eloquent in its expression of who you are. Much of our life history is revealed through our bodies. We can see evidence of stress and strain in people's faces. Some people speak with a tight jaw and seem to literally choke off their feelings. Others typically walk with a slouch and shuffle their feet, expressing their hesitation in presenting themselves to the world. Their bodies may be communicating their low self-esteem and their fear of interacting with others. As you look at your body, what feelings do you have? What story does your body tell about you?

Here are some ways that your body can express your inner self:

> Your eyes can express life or emptiness.
> Your mouth can be too tight or too loose.
> Your neck can hold back expressions of anger or crying, as well as holding onto tensions.
> Your chest can develop armor that inhibits the free flow of crying, laughing, and breathing.
> Your diaphragm can restrict the expression of rage and pain.
> Your abdomen can develop armor that is related to fear of attack.

Unexpressed emotions do not simply disappear. The chronic practice of "swallowing" emotions can take a physical toll on your body and manifest itself in physical symptoms such as severe headaches, ulcers, digestive problems, and a range of other bodily dysfunctions. In counseling clients, we often see a direct relationship between a person's physical constipation and his or her emotional constipation. When people are successful in expressing feelings of hurt and anger, they often comment that they are finally no longer physically constipated.

If people seal off certain emotions, such as grief and anger, they also keep themselves from experiencing intense joy. Let's take a closer look at what it means to experience yourself through your body.

Experiencing Your Body One way of experiencing your own body is by paying attention to your senses of touch, taste, smell, seeing, and hearing. Simply pausing and taking a few moments to be aware of how your body is interacting with the environment is a helpful way of learning to make better contact. For example, how often do you allow yourself to really taste and smell your food? How often are you aware of the tension in your body? How many times do you pause to smell and touch a flower? How often do you listen to the chirping of birds or the other sounds of nature? We can increase our sensory experience by pausing more frequently to fully use all of our senses.

Enjoying our physical selves is something we often fail to make time for. Treating ourselves to a massage, for example, can be exhilarating and can give us clues to how alive we are physically. Singing and dancing are yet other avenues through which we can enjoy our physical selves and express ourselves spontaneously. Dance is a popular way to teach people through movement to "own" all parts of their bodies and to express themselves more harmoniously. Engaging in sports and other forms of physical exercise you enjoy can also be approached with the same playful attitude as dancing and singing. These are a few ways to become more of a friend and less of a stranger to your body. You can express your feelings through your body if you allow yourself to be in tune with your physical being.

The Importance of Touch Some people are very comfortable with touching themselves, with touching others, and with being touched by others. They require a degree of touching to maintain a sense of physical and emotional well-being. Other people show a great deal of discomfort in touching themselves or allowing others to be physical with them. They may bristle and quickly move away if they are touched accidentally. If such a person is embraced by another, he or she is likely to become rigid and unresponsive. For instance, in Jerry's family of origin there was very little touching among members. He found that he had to recondition himself to feel comfortable being touched by others and touching others. In contrast, Marianne grew up in a German family characterized by much more spontaneous touching.

Some time ago I (Marianne) was teaching in Hong Kong and became friends with a college counselor. One day while we were walking she spontaneously interlocked her arm with mine. Then she quickly pulled it back, looked embarrassed, and apologized profusely. Her apology went something like this: "I am very sorry. I know that you in America do not touch like this." I let her know that I, too, came from a culture where touching between females was acceptable and that I had felt very comfortable with her touching me. We discovered that we had had similar experiences of feeling rejected by American women who misunderstood our spontaneous touching.

In many cultures touching is a natural mode of expression; in others, touching is minimal and is regulated by clearly defined boundaries. Some cultures have taboos against touching strangers, against touching people of the same sex, against touching people of the opposite sex, or against touching in certain social situations. In spite of these individual and cultural differences, studies have demonstrated that physical contact is essential for healthy development of body and mind.

Harlow and Harlow (1966) studied the effects of maternal deprivation on monkeys. In these experiments the monkeys were separated from their mothers at birth and raised in isolation with artificial mothers. When young monkeys were raised under conditions of relatively complete social deprivation, they manifested a range of symptoms of disturbed behavior. Infant monkeys reared in isolation during the first 6 months after birth showed serious inadequacies in their social and sexual behavior later in life. There are critical periods in development when physical stimulation is essential for normal development. Touching is important for developing in healthy ways physically, psychologically, socially, and intellectually.

Your Body Image

Body image involves more than size. A healthy body and a positive image of your body gives you pleasure and helps you do what you want to physically. You might ask yourself if your body keeps you from doing what you would like to do. If you would like to be more agile and be able to do things that you are unable to do, it may help to assess what you can do to acquire the kind of body you want. One thing is for certain, self-hate and self-blaming are not effective routes to bring about change. Accepting the body you have and deciding what you can and will do to enhance that body can be the beginning of change.

We rarely come across people who are really satisfied with their physical appearance. Even when people receive compliments about the way they look, they may be quick to respond with "Thank you, but I need to lose some weight." Or, "I need to gain some weight." "I could be in better shape." "I need to exercise more." "I feel a little flabby right now." It seems as though everyone is striving for the "perfect body," yet few people achieve it.

Your view of your body and the decisions you have made about it have much to do with the choices we will study in the rest of this book. In our view people are affected in a very fundamental way by how they perceive their body and how they think others perceive it. If you feel basically unattractive, unappealing, or physically inferior, these self-perceptions are likely to have a powerful effect on other areas of your life.

Jeremy Horner/Stone

Young people are bombarded by unrealistic models of what constitutes an ideal body.

For example, you may be very critical of some of your physical characteristics; you may think your ears are too big, that you are too short, or that you are not muscular enough. Or you may have some of these common self-defeating thoughts:

> If I had a better body, then I'd be happy.
> If I were physically more attractive, people would like me.
> I never look good enough.
> It's too much work to change the things I dislike about my body.

Perhaps some part of you believes that others will not want to approach you because of your appearance. If you feel that you are basically unattractive, you may tell yourself that others will see your defects and will not want to be with you. In this way you contribute to the reactions others have toward you by the messages you send them. You may be perceived by others as aloof, distant, or judgmental. Even though you may want to get close to people, you may also be frightened of the possibility of meeting with their rejection.

You may say that there is little you can do to change certain aspects of your physical being such as your height or basic build. Yet you *can* look at the attitudes you have formed about these physical characteristics. How important are they to who you are? How has your culture influenced your beliefs about what constitutes the ideal body?

We are also prone to develop feelings of shame if we unquestioningly accept certain cultural messages about our bodies. Sometimes the sense of shame remains with people into adulthood. The following brief descriptions represent some typical difficulties:

> ❯ Donna painfully recalls that during her preadolescence she was much taller and more physically developed than her peers. She was often the butt of jokes by both boys and girls in her class. Although she is no longer taller than most people around her, she still walks stoop-shouldered, for she still feels self-conscious and embarrassed over her body.

> ❯ Herbert, a physically attractive young man, is highly self-conscious about his body, much to the surprise of those who know him. He seems to be in good physical condition, yet he gets very anxious when he gains even a pound. As a child he was overweight, and he developed a self-concept of being the "fat kid." Even though he changed his physique years ago, the fear of being considered fat still lurks around the corner.

Consider whether you, too, made some decisions about your body early in life or during adolescence that still affect you. Did you feel embarrassed about certain of your physical characteristics? Today you may still be stuck with some old perceptions and feelings. Even though others may think of you as an attractive person, you may react with suspicion and disbelief. If you continue to tell yourself that you are in some way inferior, your struggle to change your self-concept may be similar to that of Donna or Herbert.

Weight and Your Body Image

From years of experience reading student journals and counseling clients, we have concluded that many people are preoccupied with maintaining their "ideal weight." Although some people view themselves as too skinny and strive to gain weight, many more are looking for effective ways to lose weight. Young people are bombarded by unrealistic models of what constitutes an ideal body. In a recent television report, young college women were objecting to the unrealistic portrayal of ideal bodies by the use of models who did not look like them. These women took issue with the unrealistic standard of what it means to be physically fit and attractive. They refused to accept the image presented. They wanted models in advertisements to be more inclusive of the general population.

Unfortunately, you may be one of those people who struggle with societal standards of an attractive body. You may find that your weight significantly affects the way you feel about your body. Do these statements sound familiar?

> I've tried every diet program there is, and I just can't seem to stick to one.

> I'm too occupied with school to think about losing weight.

> I love to eat, and I hate to exercise.

In our travels to Germany and Norway we have noticed how the ideal weight differs from culture to culture. The same thin person who is viewed as attractive in the United States might well be seen as undernourished, skinny as a rail, and even somewhat sickly in Germany. A person with a certain amount of weight is generally considered attractive and healthy looking in Germany. One young American woman who struggled with her weight and body image told us that when she spent some time in Norway she did not think of herself as being physically unattractive. There many people commented about her vitality. However, when she returned to her home in the United States she was much more conscious of her appearance.

It may also help to examine how unrealistic societal standards regarding the ideal body can lead to the perpetual feeling that you are never physically adequate. For example, our society places tremendous pressure on women to be thin. Messages from the media reveal that thinness and beauty are often equated. For the many women who accept these cultural norms, the price they often pay is depression and loss of self-esteem.

Hirschmann and Munter (1995) describe a brief exercise on self-image in their book, *When Women Stop Hating Their Bodies: Freeing Yourself From Food and Weight Obsession.* Both men and women can benefit from these self-reflection questions. As you read, pause long enough to form your own answers to these questions. Did you have a bad body thought today? As you got up this morning and looked in the mirror, what did you see and what did you tell yourself? As you were choosing what you would wear today, what thoughts and feelings did you have? If you watched television and saw an advertisement or a model, did this leave you with the feeling that you are somehow deficient? Did you step on the scale to check your weight and use this scale as a barometer for how good you would feel about yourself for the rest of the day? Did you have an interaction with someone that left you feeling self-conscious about your body? If you do this, how much energy does it take from your life?

For the next few minutes, imagine that your body type somehow becomes the cultural ideal. Every magazine that you open has models in it who are built exactly like you rather than more than 20% thinner than the average person. How would you do things differently in your life? How would you dress? What would you eat? How would you feel when you looked in the mirror? What would you do with all the energy you used to expend on wishing you looked different?

Certainly, the topic of body image applies to both men and women. However, in this society women are subject to greater pressures to live up to ideal sizes, which results in their preoccupation with weight and body image. In some ways, keeping women focused on achieving a "perfect" body is a form of oppression. Many eating problems that women face have to do with their internalized hatred of not being thin. Consider the case of Kate, who writes about her personal experience with weight problems and her body image.

KATE'S STORY

*A*lthough I have overcome a large degree of my body hatred, I continue to struggle with accepting and living with my body as it is. My last relationship ended with my partner justifying his disinterest with a critique of my body size. His words will probably sting me as long as I live. However, I have begun to see that his verbal attacks, as well as those of many others throughout my life, are merely their attempts at making me a dumping ground for their own bad body thoughts and lack of self-acceptance.

Although part of me agrees with the negative comments people have made about my size, another part of me knows that their words are a form of oppression taught to them by our society. This does not excuse their behavior, but it helps me to understand that all of us are victims of our sexist standards. As a woman, I have worn my bad body image like a suit of armor. In many ways it protects me from having to examine other parts of my life.

The challenge in overcoming eating problems is multifold. Those of us who struggle with these issues need to continue to be brave and to ask ourselves if we can stand the thought of accepting ourselves for who we are. In recent months I have come to realize that my bad body image is not only a result of sociocultural factors but is also a form of self-preservation. I am used to being dismissed and rejected because of my body size. In an ironic way it has become a safe way to feel my pain. The challenge has been and continues to be for me to face those feelings within myself that have nothing to do with the size or shape of my legs, thighs, and stomach.

Kate's story illustrates a woman's struggle to accept her body, but other people are driven to meet societal standards of an attractive and "perfect" body. In its extreme form, this striving can lead to eating disorders. Anorexia and bulimia are frequently linked to the internalization of unrealistic standards that lead to negative self-perceptions and negative body images. Michelle's description of her struggle with anorexia nervosa illustrates how self-destructive striving for psychological and physical perfection can be.

MICHELLE'S STORY

*W*hen I was around 11 years old, I gradually began to lose weight for reasons that were a mystery even to me. I knew I was not slimming down to win the approval and acceptance of my peers at school, and I was not losing weight to feel fit and healthy. On the

(continued)

contrary, when my parents finally took me to the doctor to be examined for my weight loss, I was secretly hoping I would be diagnosed with some strange disease so I would receive everyone's attention and concern. I was consumed with guilt over the fact that I wanted my parents to worry about me, yet I continued to shed pounds. I vividly recall the moment my doctor explained that I had a disorder called anorexia nervosa. It was relatively unheard of at that time. I was sick, and just as a physical pain is the body's way of alerting one to a more serious problem, my anorexia was my psyche's way of alerting me to my deep emotional pain.

For most of my life I felt completely empty and emotionally dead inside. In retrospect I am certain that the loss of my birthmother (who gave me up for adoption when I was an infant) laid the foundation for subsequent losses in my life to be internalized very deeply. I must have justified my mother's departure with the excruciating message that "I was not enough." This theme of loss and abandonment in my life undoubtedly contributed to my emotional emptiness. I proceeded through life feeling grossly inadequate as a human being and attempted to remedy this by transforming myself into a "perfect" child—a parent's dream come true!

I strived to excel in virtually everything I attempted to ensure that I would be acceptable in the eyes of my parents. I couldn't risk losing my parent's affection and love, and my self-esteem was then so low that I believed I had to accomplish extraordinary feats to be deemed as worthy as the average child. So I did. At home, not only did I clean my own room but I thoroughly cleaned the entire house. In school I was just as tenacious to please! At that time my ego was so fragile that receiving a "B" would have probably pushed me over the edge. It is no wonder that I developed anorexia at such a young age. I was a time bomb, long overdue to explode.

At a very basic level I felt emotionally and spiritually bankrupt, and my starved, emaciated body was truly a reflection of my starved, malnourished soul. I had such a deflated sense of myself that my anorexia gave me an identity; it gave me someone to be. It gave me one more "label" to wear, which I misinterpreted as dimension.

I started to make the most progress in my recovery when I could finally let go of the false security of these labels I had clung to for so many years. After a great deal of work in therapy, I was able to let go of some control and allow myself to experience just being an ordinary person. I have accomplished a lot of things in my life that I am extremely proud of, but the one thing I am most proud of is that I have learned to be comfortable making mistakes and to simply be human.

It is easy to get trapped in self-destructive patterns of critical self-judgment. Being and feeling healthy—and choosing what that entails for you—are the real challenges to wellness.

Although weight is a significant health factor, nutritional and exercise habits are also crucial to your overall well-being. Rather than too quickly deciding that you need to either gain or lose weight or to change your nutritional habits, it is a good idea to consult your physician or one of the nutrition centers in your area. If you decide you want to change your weight, there are many excellent support groups and self-help programs designed for this purpose. The counseling centers at many colleges offer groups for weight control and for people with eating disorders.

A basic change in attitude and lifestyle is important in successfully dealing with a weight problem. People with weight problems do not eat simply because they are hungry. They are typically more responsive to external cues in their environment. One of these is the acquiescence of well-meaning friends, who may joke with them by saying, "Oh, don't worry about those extra pounds. What's life without the enjoyment of eating? Besides, there's more of you to love this way!" This kind of "friendship" can make it even more difficult to discipline ourselves and to watch what and how much we eat.

In our counseling groups we often encourage people who view themselves as having a weight problem to begin to pay more attention to their body and to increase their awareness about what their body communicates to them and to others. A useful exercise has been to ask them, "If your body had a voice, what would it be saying?" Here are some examples of what their bodies might communicate:

> I don't like myself.
> My weight will keep me at a distance.
> I'm making myself ill.
> I'm burdened.
> I don't get around much anymore!
> I'm basically lazy and self-indulging.
> I work very hard, and I don't have time to take care of myself.

If you do not like what your body is saying, it is up to you to decide what, if anything, you want to change. Should you decide that you do not want to change, you need not be defensive about it. There is no injunction that you must change.

If you have not liked your physical being for some time but have not been able to change it, there may be some genetic or physical reasons that make it extremely difficult for you to manage your weight. Some people's medical history prevents them from having a great deal of choice regarding their weight, in spite of exercise and healthy nutrition.

In *What You Can Change and What You Can't*, Seligman (1993) tells us that in 1990 Americans spent more than $30 billion on the weight-loss industry. Seligman believes dieting is a cruel hoax and that it does not work. In fact, he believes dieting might work against overweight people and that it may be bad for health. Furthermore, dieting may result in eating disorders such as bulimia and anorexia. He identifies several myths associated with being overweight:

> It is a good idea to diet down to one's ideal weight in order to live longer.
> Overweight people overeat.

❭ Overweight people have an overweight personality.

❭ Lack of physical activity is a major cause of obesity.

❭ Being overweight indicates a lack of willpower.

According to Seligman's findings, although there are some health risks to being overweight, there are also serious health risks from losing weight and regaining it. He suspects that the weight-fluctuation hazard may be greater than the risks of staying overweight. It is clear that Seligman does not view dieting as the answer to being overweight. Here are a few of the points he emphasizes:

❭ Weight is generally regained after dieting.

❭ There are some destructive side effects to dieting such as repeated failure, eating disorders, depression, and fatigue.

❭ Losing and regaining weight itself presents a health risk comparable to the risk of being overweight.

❭ Achieving fitness is a more sensible approach than fighting fatness.

Being overweight is a complex problem, and these thoughts on dieting are worth considering. Before you embark on any fitness or weight-loss program, consider your own situation carefully and talk with your doctor about alternatives.

Others may nag you to do something about your weight. They may be well intentioned, yet you may resist their efforts. Ultimately, it is you who must decide what you want to do about your body. Many of us get stuck because we focus on what society dictates should be the ideal weight and body image. We hope you are able to raise your awareness about the societal messages you have operated under, and we encourage you to challenge these cultural messages. The Take Time to Reflect exercise is designed to assist you in clarifying your attitudes about your perception of your body. Ask yourself: "How satisfied am I with the body I have? How can I move toward increased self-acceptance?"

Take Time to Reflect

1. What are your attitudes toward your body? Take some time to study your body and become aware of how you look to yourself and what your body feels like to you. Try standing naked in front of a full-length mirror, and reflect on some of these questions:

   ❭ Is your body generally tight or relaxed? Where do you feel your tension?

   ❭ What does your face tell you about yourself? What kind of expression do you convey through your eyes? Are there lines on your face? What parts are tight? Do you force a smile?

> Are there any parts of your body that you feel ashamed of or try to hide?

> What aspects of your body would you most like to change? What are the parts of your body that you like the best? The least?

2. After you have completed the exercise just described (perhaps several times over a period of a few days), record your impressions or keep an extended account of your reactions in your journal.

   a. How do you feel about your body?

   _____

   _____

   b. What messages do you convey through your body to yourself? To others?

   _____

   _____

   c. Are you willing to make any decisions about changing your body?

   _____

   _____

3. A helpful Gestalt therapy technique is to stand naked in front of a mirror and focus on each of your body parts in turn, "become each part" and let it "speak." For example, give your nose a personality and pretend that your nose could speak. What might it say? If your legs were to speak, what do you imagine they would say? (Do this for every part of your body, even if you find yourself wanting to bypass certain parts. In that case you might say, "I'm an ugly nose that doesn't want any recognition. I'd just like to hide, but I'm too big to be inconspicuous!")

4. If you are overweight, is your weight a barrier and a burden? For example, consider whether your weight is keeping you from doing what you want to do. Does it keep certain people away from you? Pick up an object that is equivalent to the extra pounds you carry with you. Let yourself hold this object, and then put it down and begin to experience the excess weight of your body.

5. Imagine yourself looking more the way you would like to. Let yourself think about how you might be different, as well as how your life would be different.

(continued)

6. As a result of reading this chapter and doing these exercises, what actions are you willing to take to become more invested in taking care of yourself? What themes stand out for you?

_____

_____

SUMMARY

The purpose of this chapter has been to encourage you to think about how you are treating your body and how you can take control of your physical and psychological well-being. Even if you are not presently concerned with health problems, you may have discovered that you hold some self-defeating attitudes about your body. A theme of this chapter has been to examine what might be keeping you from really caring about your body or acting on the caring that you say you have. It is not a matter of smoking or not smoking, of exercising or not exercising; the basic choice concerns how you feel about yourself and about your life. When you accept responsibility for the feelings and attitudes you have developed about your body, you begin to free yourself from feeling victimized by your body.

You can enhance your experience of the world around you by seeing, hearing, smelling, tasting, and touching. You can become less of a stranger to your body through relaxation, dance, and movement. Touch is particularly important. For healthy development, both physical and emotional, you need both physical and psychological contact.

Your body presents an image, both to you and to others, of how you view yourself. Your attitudes about your body are acquired in the context of your culture, and you can challenge these attitudes, especially if they are self-critical. Think about how your perceptions of your body affect other areas of your life. What are some of the changes you are most invested in making regarding self-care? Your ability to love others, to form nourishing sexual and emotional relationships with others, to work well, to play with joy, and to fully savor each day depends a great deal on both your physical and psychological health. You may be keeping yourself imprisoned if you are unwilling to initiate positive contact with other people simply because you assume they won't like the way you look. Allow your body to express your feelings of tenderness, anger, and enthusiasm. If you tend to be rigid and under control, imagine how it would feel to be free of these restraints.

Remember that you are a whole being, integrated in your physical, emotional, social, mental, and spiritual dimensions. If you neglect any one of these aspects of your self, you will feel the impact on the other dimensions of your being. Take a moment to think again about how well you are taking care of yourself physically. Ask yourself how committed you are to a wellness perspective. Consider the value you place on taking good care of yourself through practices such as meditation, relaxation exercises, paying attention to your spiritual life, participating in meaningful religious activities, maintaining good nutritional habits, getting adequate sleep and rest, and participating in a regular exercise program. Ask yourself whether your daily behavior shows that you value your physical and psychological health. Once you have made this assessment, decide on a few areas you would like to improve. Then begin working on a plan to change one aspect at a time.

❯ Where Can I Go From Here?

1. Wellness means different things to different people. When you think of wellness, what aspects of your life do you most think of? Look at what you are doing to maintain a general state of wellness. How much of a priority do you place on wellness?

2. If you sometimes have trouble sleeping, try some of the suggestions listed in this chapter to see if they might work for you. If you do not get adequate rest and sleep, what steps can you take to make changes?

3. Assess how exercise (or the lack of exercise) is affecting how you feel physically and psychologically and how it influences your ability to deal with stress. If you are interested in engaging in some form of regular physical activity, decide on some exercise that you would enjoy doing. Start small so you don't get overwhelmed, but stick with your physical activity for at least 2 to 4 weeks to see if you begin to feel a difference.

4. In your journal record for a week all of your activities that are healthy for your body as well as those that are unhealthy. You may want to list what you eat, whether you smoke or drink, your sleep patterns, and what you do for exercise and relaxation. Then look over your list and choose one or more areas that you would be willing to work on during the next few months.

Resources for Future Study

Web Site Resources

GO ASK ALICE!
http://www.goaskalice.columbia.edu/

Columbia University's Health Education Program has created a widely used Web site designed for undergraduate students. Alice! offers answers to questions about relationships, sexuality, sexual health, emotional health, fitness and nutrition, alcohol, nicotine and other drugs, and general health. If you cannot find an answer to what you are looking for, you can "Ask Alice!" yourself.

CENTERS FOR DISEASE CONTROL AND PREVENTION
http://www.cdc.gov/

The Centers for Disease Control and Prevention (CDC) offers news, fact sheets on disease information and health information, articles, statistics, and links regarding health and illness in the United States (also offered in Spanish).

MAYO CLINIC HEALTH OASIS
http://www.mayohealth.org/mayo/common/htm/index.htm

This site offers "reliable information for a healthier life" and provides news items, highlights, and specific health category centers for information and resources on various diseases, medications, and general health.

EATING DISORDERS SHARED AWARENESS
http://www.eating-disorder.com/

This site is dedicated to helping others through awareness, education, support, and friendship. It also provides links to other sites such as Mirror-Mirror (Canada) and Something Fishy (New York), which have a multitude of links and information on a wide variety of topics related to eating disorders.

InfoTrac College Edition Resources

For additional readings, explore InfoTrac College Edition, our online library.

Go to **http://www.infotrac.college.com/wadsworth**

Hint: Enter the search terms:

wellness
holistic health
holistic medicine
sleep deprivation
physical exercise
physical fitness
integrative medicine
spirituality
body image
eating disorder

Print Resources

Benson, H. (1976). *The relaxation response.* New York: Avon Books.

Benson, H. (1984). *Beyond the relaxation response.* New York: Berkeley Books.

Dalai Lama (1999). *Ethics for the new millennium.* New York: Riverhead Books.

Fontana, D. (1997). *Teach yourself to dream: A practical guide.* San Francisco: Chronicle Books.

Fontana, D. (1999). *Learn to meditate: A practical guide to self-discovery and fulfillment.* San Francisco: Chronicle Books.

George, M. (1998). *Learn to relax: A practical guide to easing tension and conquering stress.* San Francisco: Chronicle Books.

Hales, D. (1987). *How to sleep like a baby.* New York: Ballantine.

Hales, D. (2001). *An invitation to health* (9th ed.). Belmont, CA: Wadsworth/Thomson Learning.

Hales, D., with Zartman, Thomas C. (2001). *An invitation to fitness and wellness.* Belmont, CA: Wadsworth/Thomson Learning.

Hirshmann, J. R., & Munter, C. H. (1995). *When women stop hating their bodies: Freeing yourself from food and weight obsession.* New York: Fawcett Columbine.

Seligman, M. E. P. (1990). *Learned optimism: How to change your mind and your life.* New York: Pocket Books.

Seligman, M. E. P. (1993). *What you can change and what you can't.* New York: Fawcett Columbine.

Siegel, B. (1988). *Love, medicine, and miracles.* New York: Harper & Row (Perennial Library).

Siegel, B. (1989). *Peace, love, and healing. Bodymind communication and the path to self-healing: An exploration.* New York: Harper & Row.

Siegel, B. (1993). *How to live between office visits: A guide to life, love, and health.* New York: HarperCollins.

Travis, J. W., & Ryan, R. S. (1994). *Wellness workbook* (3rd ed.). Berkeley, CA: Ten Speed Press.

Weil, A. (2000). *Eating well for optimum health: The essential guide to food, diet, and nutrition.* New York: Alfred A. Knopf.

Either you control your stress,
or stress controls you

MANAGING STRESS

5

Use this scale to respond to these statements:

4 = This statement is true of me *most* of the time.

3 = This statement is true of me *much* of the time.

2 = This statement is true of me *some* of the time.

1 = This statement is true of me *almost none* of the time.

_____ 1. My lifestyle is generally stressful.

_____ 2. I have relied on drugs or alcohol to help me through difficult times, but I do not abuse these substances.

_____ 3. It is relatively easy for me to fully relax.

_____ 4. The way I live, I sometimes worry about having a heart attack.

_____ 5. I am able to recognize some of my thoughts and beliefs that contribute to my stress level.

_____ 6. Stress has sometimes made me physically ill.

_____ 7. If I do not control stress, I believe it will control me.

_____ 8. Meditation is a practice I use to deal with stress.

_____ 9. Burnout is a real concern of mine.

_____ 10. I feel a need to learn more stress management techniques.

Stress is an event or series of events that lead to strain, which often results in physical and psychological health problems. Everyday living involves dealing with frustrations, conflicts, pressures, and change. Moreover, at certain times in our lives most of us are confronted with severely stressful situations that are difficult to cope with—the death of a family member or a close friend, the loss of a job, a personal failure, or an injury. Even changes that we perceive to be positive, such as getting a promotion or moving to a new location, can be stressful and often require a period of adjustment. If stress is severe enough, it takes its toll on us physically and psychologically. Mike George (1998) introduces his book, *Learn to Relax,* with these words:

> OURS IS A WORLD OF EXPLOSIVE CHANGE, the breeding ground for uncertainty, insecurity and anxiety. While some believe that stress is necessary to reach peak performance, there are many more for whom stress is the cause of debilitating illness. (p. 8)

George identifies a range of physiological and psychological symptoms that serve as signs for us to reevaluate our priorities. Our body or state of mind may be telling us that something in our lives needs to change. Some of these signs include loneliness, insecurity, loss of concentration and memory, fatigue and sleeping difficulties, mood swings, impatience and irascibility, restlessness, obsessive working, loss of appetite, and fear of silence. These signs often serve as an invitation to examine what we are doing and to create better ways of dealing with life's demands. It is clear that learning to cope with stress is essential if we hope to maintain a sense of wellness. Managing stress is not something we do once and for all; it is a process of meeting challenges with calm and determination.

Siegel (1988) indicates that our level of stress is largely determined by cultural factors. Cultures that emphasize competition and individualism produce the most stress. Cultures that place a high value on cooperation and collectivism produce the least stress and also have the lowest rates of cancer. In collectivist cultures, supportive relationships are the norm, the elderly are respected and given an active role, and religious faith is valued. Siegel is convinced that chronic patterns of intense stress lower the efficiency of the body's disease-fighting cells. His work with cancer patients has taught him that stresses resulting from traumatic loss and major life changes are in the background of most of those who get cancer. He adds, however, that not everyone who suffers stressful changes in lifestyle develops an illness. The deciding factor seems to be how people cope with the problems and stresses they face. It seems to be particularly important to be able to express your feelings about situations rather than denying that your feelings exist or swallowing them.

Stress has both positive and negative effects. It is important to differentiate between eustress and distress. *Eustress,* or good stress (pronounced "you-stress"), provides us with the necessary motivation to strive for the best. A certain amount of stress can be a challenge and can help us draw attention to our reserves in meeting problems of everyday living. *Distress* refers to the kind of stress that leads to negative physical and psychological states. Distress can zap our energy and fragment us.

In most places in the modern world stress is an inevitable part of life. We cannot eliminate stress, but we can learn how to monitor its physical and psychological impact—we can manage stress. Recognizing ineffective or destructive reactions to stress is an essential step in dealing with stress. We do not have to allow ourselves to be victimized by the psychological and physiological effects of stress. Although many sources of stress are external, how we perceive and react to stress is subjective and internal. By interpreting the events in our lives, we define what is and is not stressful—we determine our level of stress. Therefore, the real challenge is learning how to recognize and respond constructively to the sources of stress rather than trying to eliminate them. Some constructive paths to stress management addressed in this chapter include learning time management and money management practices, challenging self-defeating thinking and negative self-talk, developing a sense of humor, acquiring mindfulness, practicing meditation and other centering activities, and learning how to relax.

SOURCES OF STRESS

Stress of one kind or another is present in each of the stages in the life cycle (Chapters 2 and 3). As we discovered in Chapter 4, wellness is a central buffer against stress, and stress frequently accelerates the development of illnesses. The topics addressed in the chapters to come provide both opportunities for a meaningful life and sources of stress. For example, relationships are certainly life enhancing, yet think of the stress many people experience when they are embroiled in a strained relationship or when they go through the breakup of a long-term relationship. Some of the things we most value in life also represent the biggest challenges—learning how to deal with stress.

Because how we perceive events influences our stress level, and because stress tends to be self-imposed, we have more control over stress than we typically realize. Before we can exert control, however, we must identify the source of our stress. Two major sources of stress are environmental and psychological factors.

Environmental Sources of Stress

Many of the stresses of daily life come from external sources. Consider some of the environmentally related stresses you face at the beginning of a semester. You are likely to encounter problems finding a parking place on campus. You may stand in long lines and have to cope with many other delays and frustrations. Some of the courses you need may be closed; simply putting together a decent

PhotoDisc

Stress levels are
influenced by how
we perceive stress.

schedule of classes may be next to impossible. You may have difficulty arranging your work schedule to fit your school schedule, and this can be compounded by the external demands of friends and family and other social
commitments. Loneliness can influence your psychological and physical well-
being, and extreme loneliness is often a stressor. Financial problems and the
pressure to work to support yourself (and perhaps your family too) make being
a student a demanding task. Test anxiety and attempting to fit too many things
into one day can add needless stress to the many new pressures college students
face. Typically, college is a time when many critical choices are made that will
shape an individual's career goals and professional identity (Rice, 1999).

Our minds and bodies are also profoundly affected by more direct physiological sources of stress. Illness, exposure to environmental pollutants, improper
diet, lack of exercise, poor sleeping habits, and abusing our bodies in any number of other ways all take a toll on us. Listening to news reports of violence on
the streets and in homes can also be stressful.

Psychological Sources of Stress

Any set of circumstances that we perceive as being threatening to our well-being puts a strain on our coping abilities. Stress is in the mind of the beholder, and our appraisals of stressful events are highly subjective. How we label, interpret, think about, and react to events in our lives has a lot to do with determining whether those events are stressful. Weiten and Lloyd (2000) identify frustration, conflict, change, and pressure as key elements of psychological stress. As we consider each of these sources of stress, think about how they apply to you and your situation.

Frustration results from something blocking attainment of your needs and goals. External sources of frustration (all of which have psychological components) include failures, losses, accidents, delays, traffic jams, hurtful interpersonal relationships, loneliness, and isolation. Additionally, internal factors can hinder you in attaining your goals. These include a lack of basic skills, physical handicaps, a lack of belief in yourself, and any self-imposed barriers you may create that block the pursuit of your goals. What are some of the major frustrations you experience, and how do you typically deal with them?

Conflict, another source of stress, occurs when two or more incompatible motivations or behavioral impulses compete for expression. Conflicts can be classified as approach/approach, avoidance/avoidance, and approach/avoidance (Weiten & Lloyd, 2000).

› *Approach/approach conflicts* occur when a choice must be made between two or more attractive or desirable alternatives. Such conflicts are inevitable because we have a limited time to do all the things we would like to do and be all the places we would like to be. An example of this type of conflict is being forced to choose between two job offers, both of which have attractive features.

› *Avoidance/avoidance conflicts* arise when a choice must be made between two or more unattractive or undesirable goals. At times you may feel caught "between a rock and a hard place." These conflicts are the most unpleasant and the most stressful. You may have to choose between being unemployed and accepting a job you do not like, neither of which appeals to you.

› *Approach/avoidance conflicts* are produced when a choice must be made between two or more goals, each of which has attractive and unattractive elements. For example, you may be offered a challenging job that appeals to you but that entails much traveling, which you consider a real drawback.

How many times have you been faced with two or more desirable choices and forced to choose one path? And how many times have you had to choose between unpleasant realities? Perhaps your major conflicts involve your choice of a lifestyle. For example, have you wrestled with the issue of being independent or blindly following the crowd? What about living a self-directed life or living by what others expect of you? Consider for a few minutes some of the major conflicts you have recently faced. How have these conflicts affected you? How do you typically deal with the stress you experience over value conflicts?

Change can be a key type of stress, especially life changes that involve read-justment in your living circumstances. Holmes and Rahe (1967) did a classic study on the relationship between stressful life events and physical illness. Their assumption is that changes in personal relationships, career changes, and financial changes are often stressful, even if these changes are positive. Disruptions in the routines of life can lead to stress. However, the demands for adjustment to these life changes are more important than the type of life changes alone.

Pressure, which involves expectations and demands for behaving in certain ways, is part of the "hurry sickness" of modern living. Also, we continually place internally created pressures on ourselves. Many people are extremely demanding of themselves, driving themselves and never quite feeling satisfied that they have done all they could or should have. Striving to live up to the expectations of others, coupled with self-imposed perfectionist demands, is a certain route to stress. If you find yourself in this situation, consider some of the faulty and unrealistic beliefs you hold. Are you overloading your circuits and heading for certain burnout? In what ways do you push yourself to perform, and for whom? How do you experience and deal with pressure in your daily life?

EFFECTS OF STRESS

Stress produces adverse physical effects. In our attempt to cope with everyday living, our bodies experience what is known as the "fight-or-flight" response. Our bodies go on constant alert status, ready for aggressive action to combat the many "enemies" we face. If we subject ourselves to too many stresses, the biochemical changes that occur during the fight-or-flight response may lead to chronic stress and anxiety. This causes bodily wear and tear, which can lead to a variety of what are known as psychosomatic or psychophysiological disorders. These are not a product of one's imagination. They are real bodily disorders manifested in disabling physical symptoms that are caused by emotional factors and the prolonged effects of stress. These symptoms range from minor discomfort to life-threatening conditions; most commonly they take the form of peptic ulcers, migraine and tension headaches, asthma and other respiratory disorders, high blood pressure, skin disorders, arthritis, digestive disorders, disturbed sleeping patterns, poor circulation, strokes, cancer, and heart disease. Explore how your physical symptoms may actually serve a purpose. Ask yourself how your life might be different if you were not ill.

Allan Abbott (a family-practice doctor) and Colony Abbott (a nurse) spent some time treating indigenous people in Peru. This experience stimulated their interest in the ways in which stress affects the body. The Abbotts became especially interested in coronary-prone behavior, which is so characteristic of the North American way of life. The leading causes of death in North America are cardiovascular diseases and cancer (diseases the Abbotts relate to stress), but these diseases rarely cause the death of Peruvian Indians, whose lives are relatively stress free.

In the Abbotts' view our bodies are paying a high price for the materialistic and stressful manner in which we live. Allan Abbott estimates that about 75% of the physical ailments he treats are psychologically and behaviorally related to stress. As an aside, he asserts that 90% of what he does as a physician that makes a significant difference is psychological in nature rather than medical. According to Abbott, belief in the doctor and in the process and procedures a doctor employs has a great deal to do with curing patients. Taking a blood test, having an X ray done, getting a shot, and simple conversation with the physician all appear to help patients improve. Indeed, faith healers work on this very principle, embracing the role of belief and its effect on the body.

The psychiatrist and founder of reality therapy, William Glasser (1998), maintains that a psychosomatic (or psychophysiological) illness is a creative process. In a chronic illness for which there is no known physical cause, our bodies are involved in a creative struggle to satisfy our needs. Because there is no specific medical treatment for these psychosomatic disorders, Glasser advises that the best course of action is to attempt to regain effective control over whatever is out of control in your life. Rather than accepting passive statements such as "I am depressed," Glasser helps clients realize their active role in *depressing*, *angering*, *headaching*, or *anxietying* themselves. He emphasizes that people choose these behaviors in an attempt to meet their needs and wants, and people have some control over what they continue to choose to do. Although it may be difficult to directly control your feelings and thoughts, Glasser maintains that you do have control over what you are *doing*. If you change what you are doing, you increase the chances that your feelings and thoughts will also change. For instance, if you are depressing over failing an exam, or even a course, it may be difficult to directly control your feelings. However, instead of not taking action and feeling miserable, you could work out an action plan (a schedule for studying) that will increase your chances of succeeding in the next exam or course. By actually engaging in new behavior, it is likely that you will eventually begin to think and feel differently about this situation.

In his book *Joy's Way*, Brugh Joy (1979) describes how a life-threatening illness was the catalyst for him to call an end to a prosperous and growing private practice as a physician and a position as a clinical professor of medicine. He dropped a role that had brought him a great deal of success and security but that had also sickened him in some key respects. After giving up traditional medicine, Joy traveled through Europe, Egypt, India, and Nepal for 9 months on his own pilgrimage toward spiritual reawakening, which led to his physical and psychological healing. Along with Bernie Siegel and other physicians, Joy believes we become sick because of the stresses associated with psychological and spiritual anomalies. From Joy's perspective, people generally become sick for one of two reasons: either because their life is too restricted for the person they potentially could become or because their life is too expansive and exceeds their potential.

In *Avalanche,* Joy (1990) elaborates further on the meaning of physical illness and death, describing some common occurrences. When the last child is leaving home, some mothers may develop a life-threatening illness, primarily (in Joy's view) because they have based their existence on their family and cannot view themselves as separate from this entity. Some men who face retirement, with the potential loss of power, may become ill. Joy, along with other physicians, has observed "a tendency for spouses to die within a two-year period following the death of a husband or wife. In such cases the surviving partner is unable to engage a sense of self that can sustain life without the other person" (p. 65). It is clear that an intimate connection exists between the body and the mind and that emotional restriction can lead to sickness.

In our counseling practice we see evidence of this connection between stress and psychosomatic ailments. We often work with people who deal with their emotions by denying or repressing them or finding some other indirect channel of expression. Consider Lou's situation. He is a young man who suffered from occasional asthmatic attacks. He discovered during the process of therapy that he became asthmatic whenever he was under emotional stress or was anxious. To his surprise, Lou found that he could control his symptoms when he began to express his feelings and talk about what was upsetting him. While continuing to receive medical supervision for his asthma, he improved his physical condition as he learned to more fully explore his emotional difficulties. As Lou let out his anger, fear, and pain, he was able to breathe freely again.

Other examples can be found that illustrate how our bodies pay the price for not coping with stress adequately. Consider Arista's account of how the stress of her perfectionist strivings resulted in severe headaches.

ARISTA'S STORY

I have often described myself as a perfectionist, yet this word implies that I am constantly striving for something I never reach. This is not accurate, as I almost always reach my goals. So I redefine myself as driven, ambitious, and focused. In today's world, these are assets associated with the highest powered executives in the United States.

As a graduate student in a counseling program, I have had my share of stress and pressure. Over the past three semesters, I noticed that my monthly headaches were increasing in frequency and duration. What was once a minor inconvenience if the weather was hot or the sun was in my eyes became a daily occurrence. At first I believed it was stress. But the headaches would wake me up from a deep sleep, my head pounding and hammering, and the hypochondriac in me sought medical attention, which was to no avail. There was no blood clot in my brain, nor did I suffer from any other terminal illness.

So I pushed on, each semester getting closer and closer to graduating with a degree that would bring me my dream of counseling and teaching. Being the empirical researcher that I am, I began systematically recording the time and date of each headache. When the last day of the semester arrived, I eagerly began my summer vacation. Weeks went by without so much as a twinge of pain in my head.

As the fall semester approaches, I am certain that my headaches will begin again. In anticipation, I have begun meditating and will try to learn to work with my pain, instead of against it, which often makes it worse. I hope to learn to play and relax with the same intensity that I bring to my work. Praising the side of me that works so hard by taking time for myself to meditate, watch soaps, shop, or lie in the sun, is a goal I have for myself. Life will inevitably feel out of control at times, and my body will cry out for a break when I push too hard.

Stories such as Arista's are not uncommon. Physical symptoms often decrease or disappear when we learn to identify and appropriately express our feelings or challenge unrealistic goals of perfectionism.

Some people seem especially resilient, coping with stress with little apparent disruption in their lives. Suzanne Ouellette (Kobasa, 1979a, 1979b, 1984) provides evidence that personality plays a significant role in helping people resist stress-related illnesses. Her studies addressed the question of who stays well and why. Ouellette identified a personality pattern she labeled "hardiness," which distinguishes people who succeed in coping with change without becoming ill. Hardiness is characterized by an appetite for challenge, a sense of commitment, and a strong sense of being in control of one's life. Individuals who possess a high level of hardiness tend to have a clearly defined sense of self and purpose. They perceive change as stimulating and as providing them with options for growth.

Not only do hardy personalities seem to be able to survive stress and life changes, but they actually appear to thrive under conditions of rapid and clustered changes. Based on her study of high-stress executives who remained healthy, Ouellette (Kobasa 1979b, 1984) identified these personality traits:

> **A liking for challenge.** Hardy executives tend to seek out and actively confront challenges. They thrive under conditions of challenge, difficulty, and adversity. Rather than viewing difficult situations as being catastrophic, they perceive them as an opportunity for growing and learning. For them, change is the norm of life. They view change as stimulating and as providing them with opportunities for growth. Instead of being riveted to the past, they welcome change and see it as a stimulus for creativity. Less hardy executives tend to view change as threatening.

> **A strong sense of commitment.** People who are committed have high self-esteem, a clearly defined sense of self, a zest for life, and a meaning for living. Stress-resistant executives display a clear sense of values, well-defined goals, and a commitment to putting forth the maximum effort to achieve

their goals. In contrast, less hardy executives lack direction and do not have a commitment to a value system.

> **An internal locus of control.** Individuals with an internal locus of control believe they can influence events and their reactions to events. Such individuals accept responsibility for their actions. They believe their successes and failures are determined by internal factors, such as their abilities and the actions they take. People with an external locus of control believe what happens to them is determined by factors external to themselves such as luck, fate, and chance. Hardy individuals tend to exhibit an internal locus of control, whereas less stress-resistant individuals feel powerless over events that happen to them.

Ouellette's work has been a catalyst for research on the way personality affects health and the ability to tolerate stress, and hardiness traits have shown up in many other studies. Her studies demonstrate that hardiness is a buffer against distress and illness in coping with the stresses associated with change (Ouellette, 1993).

Take Time to Reflect

1. What things do you most stress about?

_____

_____

2. What have you tried to do to manage these stressors?

_____

_____

3. What are some other steps you could take to more effectively manage your stress?

_____

_____

4. In this chapter we encourage you to assume personal responsibility for the way stress affects your body. For example, instead of saying "I have a headache," you

are asked to say "I am headaching." How might your life be different if you accepted responsibility for your bodily symptoms (such as stomachaches, headaches, and muscular tension)?

_____

_____

5. Having a "hardy personality" can help you stay healthy as you cope with change and stress. What personality characteristics do you have that either help or hinder you in dealing with stressful situations?

_____

_____

DESTRUCTIVE REACTIONS TO STRESS

Reactions to stress can be viewed on a continuum from being effective and adaptive, on one end, to being ineffective and maladaptive, on the other. If your reactions to stress are ineffective over a long period of time, physical and psychological harm is likely. Ineffective ways of dealing with stress include defensive behavior and abusing drugs or alcohol. Burnout is a common outcome of ineffectively coping with stress.

Defensive Behavior

If you experience stress associated with failure in school or work or in some aspect of your personal life, you may defend your self-concept by denying or distorting reality. Although defensive behavior does at times have adjustive value and can result in reducing the impact of stress, such behavior actually increases levels of stress in the long run. If you are more concerned with defending your bruised ego than with coping with reality, you are not taking the steps necessary to reduce the source of stress. In essence, you are denying that a problem situation exists or minimizing an unpleasant reality. One problem with relying too heavily on defensive behavior is that the more you use defense mechanisms the more you increase your anxiety. When this happens, your defenses become entrenched. This leads to a vicious cycle that is difficult to break and ultimately makes coping with stress most difficult. Take time to review the discussion on ego-defense mechanisms in Chapter 2 and reflect on the degree to which you use defense mechanisms to cope with the stresses in your life.

Drugs and Alcohol

Many people are conditioned to take an aspirin for a headache, to take a tranquilizer when they are anxious, to rely on stimulants to keep them up all night at the end of a term, and to use a variety of drugs to reduce other physical symptoms and emotional stresses. Some time back, I (Jerry) took a vigorous bike ride on rough mountain trails. I returned home with a headache, a condition that afflicts me only occasionally. Instead of recognizing that I had overexerted myself and needed to take a rest, my immediate reaction was to take aspirin and proceed with my usual work for the day. My body was sending me an important signal, which I was ready to ignore by numbing. Perhaps many of you can identify with this tendency to quickly eliminate symptoms rather than recognize them as a sign of the need to change certain behaviors. Americans rely heavily on drugs to alleviate symptoms of stress rather than looking at the lifestyle that produces this stress.

Most of us use drugs or alcohol in some form or another. We are especially vulnerable to relying on drugs when we feel out of control, for drugs offer the promise of helping us gain control. Consider some of the ways we attempt to control problems by relying on both legal and illegal drugs. If we are troubled with shyness, boredom, anxiety, depression, or stress, we may become chemically dependent to relieve these symptoms. A drawback to depending on these substances to gain control is that through them we numb ourselves physically and psychologically. Instead of paying attention to our bodily signals that all is not well, we deceive ourselves into believing we are something we are not.

When drugs or alcohol are used excessively to escape painful reality, the "solution" to a problem becomes another problem. As tolerance is built up for these substances, we tend to become increasingly dependent on them to anesthetize both physical and psychological pain, and addiction can result. Alcohol is perhaps the most widely used and abused drug of all. It is also the most dangerous and debilitating. This is true not only because of its effects on us physically and psychologically but also because it is legal, accessible, and socially acceptable.

Once the effects of the drugs or alcohol wear off, we are still confronted by the painful reality we sought to avoid. Although drugs and alcohol can distort reality, at the same time these substances prevent us from finding direct and effective means of coping with stress. The problem here is that stress is now controlling us instead of our controlling stress.

Binge drinking—drinking with the aim of getting drunk—is one form of abusing alcohol that is a major problem on college campuses. The Harvard School of Public Health found that binge drinking is increasing on college campuses, with 1 out of 4 students frequent binge drinkers today (Adler, 2000). It should be noted, however, that 1 out of 5 students are abstaining from using alcohol. In a 1999 study of 14,000 college students from 119 colleges across the country, 23% of the college students were so-called frequent binge drinkers, or those who drank excessively within a 2-week period of time (Adler, 2000). In this study a male binge drinker consumes five or more drinks in a short time. A female binge drinker imbibes four or more. A frequent binge drinker exhibits this behavior at least 3 times in a 2-week period. This kind of drinking behavior hurts both those who drink and others. Some of the problems students experience with frequent binge drinking include memory loss, damage to property, injury, drunken driving, failing to use protection when having sex, having unplanned sex, absenteeism from classes, and getting behind in schoolwork.

If your drinking is causing you problems, the first step toward changing this pattern is to recognize it and accept that you have a problem with alcohol. Ask yourself whether you use alcohol or any other legal or illegal substances to cope with stress. Perhaps the most difficult aspect of making this self-assessment is simply being honest with yourself. In the final analysis, people who use any drug must honestly consider what they are getting from it as well as the price they are paying for their decision. You must determine for yourself whether the toll on your physical and psychological well-being is too high.

Burnout as a Result of Continual Stress

Burnout is a state of physical, emotional, intellectual, and spiritual exhaustion characterized by feelings of helplessness and hopelessness. It is the result of repeated pressures, often associated with intense involvement with people over long periods of time. Striving for unrealistically high goals can lead to a chronic state of feeling frustrated and let down. People who are burned out have depleted themselves on all levels of human functioning. Although they have been willing to give of themselves to others, they have forgotten to take care of themselves and generally feel negative about themselves and others.

Burnout is a problem for workers and for students as well. Students say that burnout often catches them by surprise. Often students do not recognize the general hurry of their lifestyle, nor do they always notice the warning signs that they have pushed themselves to the breaking point. Many students devote the majority of their time to school and work while neglecting their friendships, not making quality time for their family, and not taking time for their own leisure pursuits. Semester after semester they crowd in too many credits, convincing themselves that they must push themselves to graduate so they can start making money. Sometimes they do not realize the price they are paying. Eventually they become apathetic, just waiting for the semester to end. They are physically and emotionally exhausted and often feel socially cut off.

What can you do if you feel a general sense of psychological and physical exhaustion? Once we recognize our state and seriously want to change it, the situation is not hopeless. Instead of working harder, we can "work smarter," which means changing the way we approach our jobs so we suffer less stress (see

Chapter 10). Setting realistic goals is another coping skill. We can also work at conquering feelings of helplessness, because such feelings lead to frustration and anger, which in turn result in our becoming exhausted and cynical. We can learn to relax, even if such breaks are short. Instead of taking personally all the problems we encounter, we can condition ourselves to assume a more objective perspective. Most important, we can learn that caring for ourselves is every bit as important as caring for others.

Although learning coping skills to deal with the effects of burnout is helpful, our energies are best directed toward preventing this condition. The real challenge is to learn ways to structure our lives so we can avoid burnout. Prevention is much easier than attempting to cure a condition of severe physical and psychological depletion. Prevention includes becoming sensitive to the first signs of burnout creeping up on us and finding ways to energize ourselves. Learning how to use leisure to nurture ourselves is important. Each of us will find a different path to staying alive personally, but we must slow down and monitor the way we are living to discover that path.

CONSTRUCTIVE RESPONSES TO STRESS

To cope with stress effectively you first need to face up to the causes of your problems, including your own part in creating them. Instead of adopting destructive reactions to stress, you can employ task-oriented constructive approaches aimed at realistically coping with stressful events. Let us emphasize that although there are many useful approaches to dealing with stress, most of these are not adequate measures and are not sufficient to bring about long-lasting change. Feuerstein and Bodian (1993) point out how essential it is that we understand the basic causes of stress reactions. Deeper levels of stress management must involve insights and self-discovery if we hope to manage stress in a profound, life-altering manner. If we do not address the emotional and mental origins of stress, then using coping techniques is like putting out a fire—only to come back and find it burning again. With this deeper understanding, it is possible for us to alter some of these basic causes and at the same time utilize a range of constructive coping strategies.

Weiten and Lloyd (2000) describe constructive coping as behavioral reactions to stress that tend to be relatively healthy or adaptive. Constructive coping strategies include these characteristics:

> Confronting a problem directly

> Staying in tune with reality

> Accurately and realistically appraising a stressful situation rather than distorting reality

> Learning to recognize and manage harmful emotional reactions to stress

Brisk walking for 20 to 30 minutes several times a week is an easy way to get regular exercise to help with stress management.

David Young-Wolff/PhotoEdit

> Consciously and rationally evaluating alternative courses of action
> Learning to exert behavioral self-control

In addition to these characteristics, three other strategies for constructively coping with stress are modifying your self-talk, learning to laugh and enjoy humor, and turning stress into strengths. Later in this chapter we discuss other healthy approaches to managing stress, but let's examine these three ideas in more detail now.

Changing Self-Defeating Thoughts and Messages

Your thoughts and what you tell yourself can contribute to your experience of stress. For example, these thoughts about using time often bring about stress: "When I take time for fun, I feel guilty." "I'm constantly feeling rushed, telling myself that I ought to be doing more and that I should be working faster." "If there were more hours in a day, I'd find more things to do in a day and feel even more stressed."

In Chapter 3 we discussed ways to challenge parental injunctions, cultural messages, and early decisions. Those same principles can be effectively applied to coping with the negative impact of stress. Most stress results from beliefs about the way life is or should be. For example, the pressures you experience to perform and to conform to external standards are greatly exacerbated by self-talk such as "I must do this job perfectly." You can use the cognitive techniques described in Chapter 3 to help you uproot faulty beliefs based on "shoulds," "oughts," and "musts." If you can change your self-defeating beliefs about living up to external expectations, you are in a position to behave in ways that produce less stress. Even if it is not always possible to change a difficult situation, you can modify your beliefs about the situation. Doing so can result in decreasing the stress you experience. By monitoring your self-talk, you can identify beliefs that create stress. From a personal perspective I (Jerry) know how difficult it is to change certain internalized messages.

I often listen to messages pertaining to doing more and making full use of my time. People who know me well see the following behavior patterns: being wedded to work, impatience, a loathing for waiting, doing several things at once, taking on more projects than there is time for, meeting self-imposed deadlines, and a desire to control the universe! Over the years I have realized that I cannot cram my life with activities all year, fragmenting myself with many stressful situations, and then expect a "day off" to rejuvenate my system. Even though I am a somewhat slow learner in this respect, a few years ago I recognized the need to find ways of reducing, if not eliminating, situations that cause stress and to deal differently with the stresses that are inevitable. It has been useful for me to identify my individual patterns, beliefs, and expectations that lead to stress. Furthermore, I am increasingly making conscious choices about my ways of behaving—recognizing that my choices can result in either stress or inner peace. I continue to learn that changing my thinking and behavior is an ongoing process of self-monitoring and making choices.

Acquiring a Sense of Humor

Workshops and conferences aimed at teaching people ways of having fun and learning to laugh are becoming popular. It is a sad commentary that we have to be taught how to laugh, but for many of us this no longer seems to come naturally. Too many of us take ourselves far too seriously and have a difficult time learning how to enjoy ourselves. If we are overly serious, there is very little room for expressing the child within us. Laughing at our own folly, our own inconsistencies, and at some of our pretentious ways can be highly therapeutic. Taking time for play can be the very medicine we need to combat the negative forces of stress. If we learn to "lighten up," the stresses that impinge upon us can seem far less pressing. Laughter is a healing force; humor can be a powerful antidote to physical illness and stress.

Humor not only acts as a buffer against stress but provides an outlet for frustration and anger. Studies exploring the physiological changes caused by laughter show that laughter can release endorphins, lower heart rate and blood pressure, stimulate respiratory activity and oxygen exchange, and enhance immune and endocrine functions (Vergeer, 1995). Vergeer states that humor can be considered a transformative agent of healing and an approach for putting stressful situations into a new perspective.

Tips for Managing Stress

Stress does not have to be a liability. You can transform stress into strength by taking steps to creatively cope with your stress. Although many strategies for stress reduction are based on simple commonsense principles, actually putting them into action involves self-discipline. As you examine these strategies, identify the ones you are interested in remembering and putting into daily practice.

> ❯ Find ways to simplify your life.
> ❯ Become more aware of the demands you place on yourself and on others.
> ❯ Make the time each day to do something that you enjoy.
> ❯ Practice consciously doing one thing at a time.
> ❯ When you feel stressed, pause to take a few deep breaths.
> ❯ Regularly practice one or more relaxation techniques.
> ❯ Strive to live in the present. If you become aware of regretting past actions or worrying about the future, tell yourself that this moment is what counts.
> ❯ Practice being kind to yourself and to others.
> ❯ Ask others to help you learn to deal effectively with stress.

To put these techniques into practice, write your favorite tips on a small card that you can look at throughout the day. Simply remembering to stop what you are doing at different times during the day to ask yourself what you are experiencing is a good beginning to significantly reduce your stress level. At these times you can identify your self-talk and experiment with giving yourself new and more constructive thoughts. Look for the humor in life and remember to smile and laugh more.

Even if it is not always possible to change a difficult situation, you can modify your beliefs about the situation.

A wide variety of stress reduction strategies can be helpful to you in managing the stress in your life. The following sections focus in more detail on a variety of stress buffers that are positive ways to deal with stress. These buffers include learning good time management, sound financial management practices, meditation, mindfulness, deep relaxation, yoga, and therapeutic massage. Take some time for quiet reflection and consider whether you might benefit from some of these practices.

TIME MANAGEMENT

You can learn to manage your time so you get what you want from your life. There is no one best way to budget your time; you have to find the system that works for you. Time management is not an end in itself. If your time management program begins to control you, it is time to reevaluate and reset your priorities. Although learning to manage time is essential, too many of us become overly fixated on clock time. In writing about relaxing with time, Mike George (1998) makes this thoughtful statement:

> INCREASINGLY, OUR LIVES ARE RULED BY THE CLOCK, but clock time is a human invention made to serve us. We must not allow the measurement of time to dominate our thinking, or we will sabotage ourselves in a self-fulfilling cycle of anxiety undermining success. (p. 120)

George admits that many aspects of our lives are necessarily clock-bound, but he suggests that we look for periods when we can pay more attention to the natural inclinations of our body clock rather than a mechanical clock. How many of us have a meal when we are hungry or go to bed when we are tired?

We all have the same amount of time: 24 hours a day, 168 hours a week, and 8,760 hours a year. How people use time varies greatly from individual to individual. Consider time as a valuable resource that enables you to do what you want in your life. The way you choose to use your time is a good indicator of what you value. If you are interested in making better use of your time, a good place to begin is by monitoring your time. Once you have identified how you spend your time, you will be able to make conscious choices of where you want to allocate your limited time.

Using your time wisely is related to living a balanced life and is thus a part of wellness. Ask yourself these questions:

❭ Am I making the time to eat properly, get adequate sleep, and maintain a regular exercise program?

❭ Do I know where I want to go in the next few months and years?

❭ Am I generally accomplishing what I have set out to do each day? Is it what I *wanted* to do?

> Do I take the time to balance fun with work? Do I tell myself I do not have time for fun?

> Am I feeling rushed?

> Do I make time for nurturing my significant relationships? If I tell myself that I do not have time for my friends, what is the message here?

> Is there time in my day for meeting my spiritual needs? Do I allow time for quiet reflection of my priorities in life?

> Do I generally like the way I am spending my time? What would I like to be doing more of? What would I like to reduce or cut out in my daily activities?

> How would I like to use time differently than I did last week?

Time management is a key strategy in managing stress. Indeed, much of the daily stress you experience is probably due to taking on too many projects at once, not using your time effectively, or procrastinating. Putting things off, especially if they need immediate attention, is a certain route to stress. Procrastination has some obvious short-term gains or so many would not be chronic procrastinators. But over the long term, procrastination typically leads to disappointment, feelings of failure, anxiety, and increased stress. Ask yourself if procrastination has sometimes gotten you into trouble. If it has, is there something you are willing to do to change this? If you want to change patterns of procrastination, here are a few suggestions to consider:

> Ask yourself if the tasks you are putting off are of value to you. If certain tasks are not meaningful to you, it may be best to drop them.

> Admit to yourself that you do have trouble completing certain tasks and decide what you are willing to do to make changes.

> Make a commitment to breaking a project down into smaller elements that you are willing to complete by a certain time.

> Let yourself visualize the completion of a project. How does it feel to tackle a task and finish it?

> Write down specific dates that you will begin and end a phase of your project. Make a contract with a friend to keep up to date with this schedule.

> If you do not follow through or feel discouraged, try to devote at least 10 or 15 minutes a day to some aspect of your project.

By following these suggestions, you can change your habits of procrastination. Even small changes may be important in taking a new direction.

If you are not in control of where your time is going, then time is in control of you. Once you have begun to conquer procrastination and other time-wasters, here are some suggestions for positive actions you can take to remain in charge of your time:

> Reflect on your long-range goals, prioritizing the steps you will take in reaching them. Establish clear and attainable goals. Set goals and reevaluate them periodically.

> Break down long-range goals into smaller goals. Develop a plan of action for reaching subgoals.

> Be realistic in deciding what you can accomplish in a given period of time. Think about Oprah Winfrey's saying: "You can do it all. You just can't do it all at once."

> Before accepting new projects, think about how realistic it is to fit one more thing into your schedule. Put yourself in the driver's seat and do not allow others to overload your circuits.

> Make use of a schedule book or a planner so that you can organize your time efficiently. Create a schedule that helps you get done what you want to accomplish. Make use of daily, weekly, monthly, and yearly planners. Make a daily "to do" list to keep yourself from becoming overwhelmed.

> Do not try to do everything yourself. Ask for help from others and learn to delegate.

> Be comfortable with what you accomplish. You cannot be productive every moment. Make time in your schedule for fun, exercise, meditation, socializing, and down time.

> If you do too many things at once, you increase your stress level. Concentrate on doing one thing at a time as well as you can.

> Schedule as much time for eating and sleeping as you require.

> Strive to live in the present moment and experience what is going on now as fully as possible. Avoid ruminating about what you could have done in the past or endlessly planning about the future. Living in the past or in the future makes it difficult to savor present experiences and tends to escalate stress.

As you are learning how to organize your time, you will surely meet with obstacles. You may underestimate how long a project will take, unexpected demands may chew up time you had blocked off for studying, or other external factors may throw off your plans. Be patient with yourself and tolerate some slip ups. Skills in time management take time to acquire. You may hear old voices in your head telling you that you never get done what is important to you. Learn to dispute those internal voices that stand between you and your goals.

MONEY MANAGEMENT

Financial pressures are consistently mentioned by students as a major stressor. Money, like time, is a limited resource that must be spent wisely, and many of the time management tips presented previously can be applied to money management as well. In learning to manage your time, the first step was to track where you spent your time. Likewise, the initial step in managing your financial resources is to discover where your money goes. To do this, monitor all of your expenses for at least one month. Carry a small note pad or an index card in your wallet and write down everything you spend each day. Then transfer these notes to your expense record at home at the end of the day. Fixed expenses, such as rent and tuition, can be recorded directly on your expense record. Keeping a complete expense record is an important step toward increasing your awareness of how you are spending money. Examine this month-long record and decide the degree to which you are satisfied with your spending habits. You are likely to be surprised at how much you spent in some categories.

The next step in managing your finances is to determine all the sources of income at your disposal. Your income may be greater in summer than during the school year, so it is a good idea to figure out your average monthly income. Once you establish how much you have in the pot, you have a better idea of what you can actually afford to take out of the pot.

The next step is to plan a budget. Evaluate whether the way you are spending your money fits your goals and values. A meaningful budget must be tailored to your means. Look at each category of expenses and ask yourself if the amount you are spending reflects your goals. One general guideline in budgeting is not to spend more money than you make. If you find that more money is going out than is coming in, you have three options: increase your income, decrease your spending, or both. If you need help developing your personal budget, courses and workshops in managing personal finances are available through the extended education programs at most colleges.

Credit card spending can also be a real source of stress. You may have the illusion that you are not spending money when you are using "plastic." But when your statement comes at the end of the month, you are likely to be jolted back to reality. Ideally, it is best to pay off your credit card debt at the end of each month. The rule of thumb for good money management is simple: if you don't have it, don't spend it! If you prepare a realistic budget and stick to it, you will decrease your level of stress a great deal. Effective money management can go a long way toward helping you reach your goals.

MEDITATION

Meditation is a process of directing our attention to a single, unchanging or repetitive stimulus. Meditation may include repetition of a word, sound, phrase, or prayer, but its main purpose is to eliminate mental distractions and relax the body. Fontana (1999) says: "Put simply, meditation is the experience of the limitless nature of the mind when it ceases to be dominated by its usual chatter"

(p. 16). Meditation sharpens our concentration and our thinking power and is aimed at personal transformation. In a little book on meditation, Sogyal Rinpoche (1994) writes:

> GENERALLY WE WASTE OUR LIVES, distracted from our true selves, in endless activity; meditation, on the other hand, is the way to bring us back to ourselves, where we can really experience and taste our full being, beyond all habitual patterns. Our lives are lived in intense and anxious struggle, in a swirl of speed and aggression, in competing, grasping, processing, and achieving, forever burdening ourselves with extraneous activities and preoccupations. Meditation is the exact opposite. (pp. 6–7)

Meditation is enjoying increased popularity among people of all ages. But it still has an aura of mysticism, and some people may shy away from it because it seems intricately bound up with elaborate Eastern rituals, strange language, strange clothing, and abstract philosophical and spiritual notions. It is useful to know what meditation is not, because there are many misconceptions surrounding meditative practices. In his book *Mindfulness in Plain English,* Gunaratana (1991, pp. 19–31) discusses and dissolves the following misconceptions about meditation:

〉 Meditation is just a relaxation technique.

〉 Meditation means going into a trance.

〉 Meditation is a mysterious practice that cannot be understood.

〉 The purpose of meditation is to become a psychic superbeing.

〉 Meditation is dangerous, and a prudent person should avoid it.

〉 Meditation is for holy people, but not for regular people.

〉 Meditation is running away from reality.

〉 Meditation is a great way to get high.

〉 Meditation is selfish.

〉 When you meditate, you sit around thinking lofty thoughts.

〉 A couple of weeks of meditation will solve all our problems.

During much of our waking time, we are thinking and engaging in some form of verbalization or inner dialogue. In fact, many of us find it difficult to quiet the internal chatter that typically goes on inside our heads. We are not used to attending to one thing at a time or to fully concentrating on a single action. Oftentimes we miss the present moment by thinking about what we did yesterday or what we will do tomorrow or next year. Meditation is a tool to increase awareness, become centered, and achieve an internal focus. In meditation our attention is focused, and we engage in a single behavior. Our attention is cleansed of preconceptions and distracting input so that we can perceive reality more freshly. Although we narrow our focus of attention when we meditate, the result is an enlarged sense of being.

One answer to our fragmented existence is to practice mindfulness, or "bringing the mind home" through meditation (Rinpoche, 1994). George (1998) uses the analogy of the mind being like a desktop—piled high with so much information that we are unable to function effectively. Our minds sometimes become cluttered with worries, regrets, negative self-images, memories, reactions, hopes, and fears, which leads to our true self getting buried deeper and deeper. Meditation is a way to sort out the confusion and to bring about tranquility, enabling us to focus on constructive thoughts and to discover positive images of ourselves. In George's words: "By relaxing our minds through meditation, we can clear our desks and experience a renewed sense of self. This will bring with it identity, clarity and freedom in a cascade of revolutionary thinking" (p. 125).

Meditation is effective in creating a deep state of relaxation in a fairly short time. The meditative state not only induces profound relaxation but also reduces physical and psychological fatigue. Its beneficial effects are numerous, and it has been shown to relieve anxiety and stress-related disease. People who consistently practice meditation show a substantial reduction in the frequency of stress-related symptoms. Some of the physical benefits that can result from the regular practice of meditation include relief from insomnia, lower blood pressure, improved posture, increased energy, and better management of pain (Fontana, 1999). There are also mental benefits of meditation, such as improved tranquility, patience, concentration, and memory and enhanced understanding and empathy for others. Notice how many of the benefits of meditation are strikingly similar to the benefits of regular exercise discussed in Chapter 4.

There are as many different ways to meditate as there are meditators. Some people allow an hour each morning for silence and internal centering. Others find that they can enter a meditative state while walking, jogging, bike riding, or doing T'ai Chi. You do not have to wear exotic garb and sit in a lotus position to meditate. Sitting quietly and letting your mind wander or looking within can be a simple form of meditation.

You may argue that you do not have time for morning meditation. However, if you do not carve out time for this centering activity, it is likely that you will be bounced around by events that happen to you throughout the day. To make meditation part of your daily pattern, discipline and consistent practice are required. Most writers on meditation recommend 20- to 30-minute sessions before breakfast and before dinner. Easwaran (1991) states that beginning meditators should meditate for half an hour each morning.

It is better to assume a sitting position for meditating rather than lying in bed, and meditating on an empty stomach is recommended for achieving deep meditative states. These exercises must be practiced for at least a month for meditation's more profound effects to be experienced. Several excellent guides to meditation include *Meditation* (Rinpoche, 1994), *Learn to Meditate* (Fontana, 1999), *Meditation* (Easwaran, 1991), and *Mindfulness in Plain English* (Gunaratana, 1991).

MINDFULNESS

Living by the values of accomplishing and producing, we sometimes forget the importance of experiencing the precious moment unfolding before us. By emphasizing *doing,* we forget the importance of *being.* The idea of mindfulness is that we experience each moment fully. Thich Nhat Hanh (1991) reminds us that we do a good job of *preparing* to live, but that "we have difficulty remembering that we are alive in the present moment, the only moment there is for us to be alive. Every breath we take, every step we make, can be filled with peace, joy, and serenity. We need only to be awake, alive in the present moment" (p. 5). Begin the practice of mindfulness by simply paying attention to your breathing. You can then extend this to other facets of your daily life, such as walking.

Mindfulness is like meditation in that the aim is to clear your mind and calm your body. Mindfulness helps us to slow down and experience what we are doing. It is a state of active attention that involves focusing on here-and-now awareness. Easwaran (1991) encourages us to slow down if we hope to acquire a mindful approach to living:

❭ If we are driven by a hectic and hurried pace, we become robotlike with little freedom and no choices.

❭ If we want freedom of action, good relations with others, health and vitality, a calm and clear mind, it is essential that we make strides in slowing down.

❭ As a way to develop mindfulness, it is crucial that we refrain from trying to perform several operations simultaneously.

❭ As we acquire the skills of mindfulness, our senses become keener, our thinking patterns become more lucid, and we increase our sensitivity to the needs of others.

Jon Kabat-Zinn (1990) describes some basic attitudes necessary to the practice of mindfulness:

❭ Do not judge. Become aware of automatic judging thoughts that pass through your mind.

❭ Be open to each moment, realizing that some things cannot be hurried.

❭ See everything as if you are looking at it for the first time.

❭ Learn to trust your intuitions.

❭ Rather than striving for results, focus on accepting things as they are.

❭ Develop an accepting attitude.

❭ Let go. Turn your mind off and simply let go of thoughts.

Mindfulness is not limited to periods of formal practice; rather, it is meant to become a way of life.

The ability to observe our physical, emotional, and mental activities with a degree of nonjudgmental detachment enables us to become increasingly aware of what we do and say. George (1998) reminds us that

> WE ALL HAVE A CHOICE. We can live life in the "fast lane," pushing ourselves hard from one experience to the next, until one day we can push ourselves no more; or we can turn off the superhighway to follow the quieter, slower roads that encourage our driving skills, rather than our driving speed. Ultimately, we may reach the same destination. However, the different routes by which we travel there will determine the state of our mind and body on arrival. (p. 11)

If you are living in the present moment, you are not ruminating about the past or worrying about the future. Living in the present allows you to gain full awareness of whatever actions you are engaged in and to be fully present when you are with another person.

DEEP RELAXATION

You don't have to settle for a range of psychophysiological problems such as indigestion, backaches, insomnia, and headaches as part of your life. If you can genuinely learn to relax and take care of yourself in positive and nurturing ways, you will enhance your life and the lives of the people close to you.

Take a few moments right now to become aware of your breathing. Breathing is our most natural instinct, but many of us have forgotten how to breathe. Relearning the correct way to breathe can have a significant impact on our well-being and can contribute to our ability to relax. If we are not able to breathe properly, we cannot fully relax our bodies and minds (George, 1998).

Now devote a few moments to reflecting on how you relax. Do you engage in certain forms of relaxation on a regular basis? What do you consider to be relaxing? Think about the quality of each of these forms of relaxation and how often you use it:

> Sitting in a quiet place for as few as 10 minutes a day and just letting your mind wander

> Listening to music and fully hearing and feeling it (without making it the background of another activity)

> Sleeping deeply and restfully

> Regulating your breathing

> Being involved in a hobby that gives you pleasure

> Engaging in sports that have the effect of calming you

> Asking for and receiving a massage
> Taking longer than usual in lovemaking
> Walking in the woods or on the beach
> Closing your eyes and listening to the sounds in nature
> Listening to the sounds of your breathing
> Practicing some form of meditation each day
> Relaxing in a hot tub
> Allowing yourself to have fun with friends
> Regularly practicing muscle-relaxation exercises
> Practicing some form of self-hypnosis to reduce stress and eliminate outside distractions

Williams and Knight (1994) describe a progressive muscular relaxation technique that they recommend be practiced for 10 to 20 minutes. This form of deep relaxation involves these steps:

> Get comfortable, be quiet, and close your eyes.
> Pay attention to your breathing. Breathe in slowly through your nose. Exhale slowly through your mouth.
> Clench and release your muscles. Tense and relax each part of your body two or more times. Clench while inhaling; release while exhaling.
> Tense and relax, proceeding through each muscle group.

Herbert Benson (1976, 1984), a Harvard cardiologist, described a simple meditative technique that has helped many people cope with stress. Benson's experiments revealed how it is possible to learn to control blood pressure, body temperature, respiration rate, heart rate, and oxygen consumption through the use of what he called the "relaxation response." Benson's work demonstrates that it is possible to make use of self-regulatory, noninvasive techniques in the prevention of stress-related illnesses. In his studies participants achieved a state of deep relaxation by repeating a mantra (a word used to focus attention, such as *om*). He described the following three factors as crucial to inducing this state:

> Find a quiet place with a minimum of external distractions. The quiet environment contributes to the effectiveness of the repeated word or phrase by making it easier to eliminate distracting thoughts.
> Find an object or mantra to focus your attention on and let thoughts simply pass by. What is important is to concentrate on one thing only and learn to eliminate internal mental distractions as well as external ones.
> Adopt a passive attitude, which includes letting go of thoughts and distractions and simply returning to the object you are dwelling on. A passive attitude implies a willingness to let go of evaluating yourself and to avoid the usual thinking and planning.

In writing about choosing a suitable relaxation technique, Feuerstein and Bodian (1993) make it clear that there is no perfect technique that will miraculously make stress disappear. All methods of deep relaxation require the individual to assume a great deal of responsibility. For most of us, it has taken years to build up tension patterns. It stands to reason that it will take effort and perseverance to overcome years of negative mental and physical conditioning. Feuerstein and Bodian provide this encouragement:

> IF YOU HAVE NEVER ENGAGED IN REGULAR PSYCHOPHYSICAL DISCIPLINE, you may be surprised at how long it can take you to develop the ability to relax deeply. In any case, don't lose heart. The importance of relaxation techniques in reducing stress and increasing immune system function has been well documented, so your patience will be well rewarded. (p. 117)

In the complex society most of us live in, you will inevitably encounter obstacles to fully relaxing. Even if you take a few moments in a busy schedule to unwind, your mind may be reeling with thoughts of past or future events. Another problem is simply finding a quiet and private place where you can relax and a time free from interruptions. Learn how to let go for even a few minutes so you can unwind while waiting in a line or riding on a bus. Deep relaxation is a powerful positive response to stress.

YOGA

Over the past three decades yoga has become quite popular throughout the Western world, and it appeals to a wide range of people, from children to the elderly, with all levels of abilities. This brief section on yoga consists of a summary of a few of the points Feuerstein and Bodian (1993) make about the practice of yoga in their book *Living Yoga: A Comprehensive Guide for Daily Life.*

Yoga is not simply a form of calisthenics, a system of meditation, or a religion. However, like meditation and mindfulness, yoga is a way of life. Yoga is about doing the best you can at that day or time, without comparing yourself to others. As a noncompetitive activity, yoga enables you to see the strengths you already have and to build on those strengths. Those who practice yoga have a personal goal. Some of the goals that motivate people to engage in yoga are to reduce stress, expand awareness, deepen spirituality, or provide greater flexibility. It is important to know your goals so you can choose a form of yoga that fits your needs.

In addition to managing stress, yoga provides numerous health benefits in both prevention and treatment of illnesses. For years Eastern health practitioners have known of the health value of practicing yoga, and now Western doctors are acknowledging the significant health benefits of yoga. Some of these benefits include lowering blood pressure and cholesterol levels and decreasing problems associated with chronic illnesses such as arthritis, rheumatism, back pain, digestive disorders, insomnia, diabetes, migraines and headaches, varicose veins, and obesity (Choudhury, 1978). Specific types of yoga can work on both internal and external organs as well as on the muscular and skeletal systems.

THERAPEUTIC MASSAGE

In many European countries, and in Eastern cultures as well, massage is a well-known way to enhance health. In fact, physicians often prescribe therapeutic massage and mineral baths to counter the negative effects of stress. Massage is a legitimate route to maintaining wellness and coping with stress, but use caution in selecting a reputable practitioner.

Earlier we talked of the need for touch to maintain the well-being of the body and mind, and we also mentioned how the body tells the truth. Massage is one way of meeting the need for touch; it is also a way to discover where and how you are holding onto the tension produced by stressful situations. Practitioners who have studied physical therapy and therapeutic massage say that the body is the place where changes need to be made if long-lasting psychological changes are to result.

Massage therapy has been popularized recently as a part of alternative medicine. The benefits of massage therapy include facilitating growth, reducing pain, increasing alertness, reducing depression, and enhancing immune function (Field, 1998). Therapeutic massage is an excellent way to develop awareness of the difference between tension and relaxation states and to learn how to release the muscular tightness that so often results when you encounter stress. It is also a good way to learn how to receive the caring touch of another.

Take Time to Reflect

1. Identify a few specific areas of your life that you find most stressful (for example, trying to balance school with work, attempting to do too much in too short a time, problems with relationships, critical self-talk).

   _____

   _____

What would help you to reduce your stress in these areas?

_____

_____

2. This self-inventory is designed to assist you in pinpointing some specific ways you might better manage stress. Check all of the statements that express a goal that has meaning for you or describes a form of behavior you would like to acquire.

_____ I avoid using drugs and alcohol as a way to cope with stressful situations.

_____ I am interested in paying attention to the subtle signs of burnout, so I can take action before advanced stages of burnout set in.

_____ Learning time management skills is a priority for me.

_____ I am willing to make a schedule as a way to better organize my time.

_____ My negative self-talk often results in stressing me out. I would like to identify those thoughts that get in my way and challenge my thinking.

_____ Meditation is a practice I would be willing to experiment with for at least a month as a way to center myself and better manage stress.

_____ Mindfulness requires experiencing each moment as fully as possible. I want to acquire the kind of attention that involves focusing on here-and-now awareness.

_____ Taking short relaxation breaks appeals to me, and I am willing to do what it takes to learn relaxation methods.

3. This time management inventory can help you recognize your own time traps. Decide whether each statement is more true or more false as it applies to you and place a T for true or an F for false in the space provided.

_____ I often find myself taking on tasks because I am the only one who can do them.

_____ I often feel overwhelmed because I try to do too much in too little time.

_____ No matter how much I do, I feel that I am always behind and never quite caught up.

_____ I frequently miss deadlines.

_____ I simply have too many irons in the fire.

_____ I am a chronic procrastinator.

_____ I tend to be a perfectionist, and this leaves me never feeling satisfied with what I accomplish.

_____ I am bothered by many unscheduled interruptions when doing important work.

_____ I am aware of hurrying much of the time and feeling hassled.

_____ I have a hard time getting to important tasks and sticking to them.

(continued)

4. What behaviors would you most like to improve with respect to managing your time?

_____

_____

_____

5. What beliefs or attitudes make it difficult for you to cope with stress? In other words, what do you sometimes tell yourself that increases your level of stress?

_____

_____

_____

6. What behaviors are you willing to work on to gain better control over the stressors in your life?

_____

_____

_____

Now that you have finished reading this chapter and completing this Take Time to Reflect, consider some of the ways you can manage the stresses you face. Reflect on the value you place on taking good care of yourself through practices such as meditation, relaxation exercise, paying attention to your spiritual life, participating in meaningful religious activities, maintaining good nutritional habits, getting adequate sleep and rest, and participating in a regular exercise program. Ask yourself whether your daily behavior provides evidence that you value your physical, psychological, social, and spiritual health. Once you have made this assessment, decide on a few areas you would like to improve. We strongly recommend that you record these goals in your journal. Then begin working on a plan to change one aspect at a time. Even small changes can lead to significant improvements for you and those close to you.

SUMMARY

One enemy of your overall well-being is excessive stress. You have learned that the way you process the stress of daily living has a lot to do with your mental attitude, yet stress affects you physically as well as psychologically. You cannot realistically expect to eliminate stress from your life, but you can modify your way of thinking and your behavior patterns to reduce stressful situations and manage stress more effectively.

Conquering stress requires a willingness to accept responsibility for what you are doing to your body. A central message is to listen to your body and respect what you hear. If you are feeling the effects of stress in your body, this is a signal to pay attention and change what you are thinking and doing. If you fail to heed the warning of your body, you may suffer a heart attack or some other form of illness. It is a shame that some people will not choose to slow down until they do become ill.

Remember that you are a whole being, which implies an integration of your physical, emotional, social, mental, and spiritual dimensions. If you neglect any one of these aspects of your self, you will feel the impact on the other dimensions of your being. Think again about how well you are taking care of yourself physically, emotionally, socially, and spiritually. Ask yourself the degree to which you know your priorities and are acting on them.

In this chapter we have described a number of strategies for effectively managing stress. There is no one right way to cope with stress, which means you are challenged to devise your own personal approach to handle the stresses of daily life. Although you may not be able to eliminate certain stressors in your life, there is a lot that you can do. By focusing on constructive reactions to stress and taking action, you gain personal power that enables you to manage stress instead of letting stress control you. You can apply the tools of time and financial management to attain your goals. You can identify and change your self-defeating thoughts that lead to stress. Acquiring a sense of humor will allow you to put many of your difficulties into perspective. Develop your own strategies and consistently work at applying them to a variety of situations in everyday living.

❭ Where Can I Go From Here?

1. How are you coping with stress? Keep an account in your journal for one week of the stressful situations you encounter. After each entry, note these items: To what degree was the situation stressful because of your thoughts, beliefs, and assumptions about the events? How were you affected? Do you see any ways of dealing with these stresses more effectively?

(continued)

> **Where Can I Go From Here?** *(continued)*

2. How are you using your time? Take an inventory of how you use your time. Be consistent in recording what you do. Keep a log of your activities for at least 1 week (2 weeks would be better) to see where your time is going. Carry a pocket notebook. Write down what you have done a couple of times each hour. After a week add up the hours you are spending on personal, social, job, and academic activities. Then ask yourself these questions:

   > Am I spending my time the way I want to?

   > Am I accomplishing what I have set out to do each day? Is it what I wanted to do?

   > Am I feeling rushed?

   > Am I spending too much time watching television?

   > Am I balancing activities that I need to do with ones that I enjoy?

   > How would I like to use time differently than I did last week?

   > How well am I currently managing time?

3. List three to five things you can do to feel better when you are experiencing stress (meditate, engage in deep breathing, exercise, talk to a friend, and so forth). Put this list where you can see it easily, and use it as a reminder that you have some ways to reduce stress.

4. Identify some environmental sources of stress or other stresses that are external to you. Finding a parking spot, navigating in rush hour traffic, and noise are all external factors that can put a strain on you. Once you have identified external stressors, write in your journal about how you might deal with them differently. What ways could a change in your thinking or adopting a new attitude change the impact of these external sources of stress?

5. How does stress affect your body? For at least 1 week (2 weeks would be better) record how daily stresses show up in bodily symptoms. Do you have headaches? Are you troubled with muscular aches? Do you have trouble sleeping? Does stress affect your appetite?

6. Consider the constructive ways to cope with stress presented in this chapter. Might some of these stress management strategies help you keep stress from getting the best of you? If you can select even two or three new stress management strategies and begin to practice them regularly (such as relaxation exercises, meditation, or humor), your ability to effectively curb the effects of stress are likely to be significantly improved. Write out a plan for practicing these techniques and make a commitment to a friend on what you are willing to do to better deal with your stress.

Resources for Future Study

Web Site Resources

STRESS AND YOU
http://www.chronicfatigue.org/History.html

This site is the realization of a long-held dream of Dr. Gerald E. Poesnecker. It is a part of the Chronic Fatigue Unmasked Web site and describes the biological effects of stress including the general adaptation syndrome, hypoadrenalism, and chronic fatigue. It discusses the signs of chronic fatigue and makes suggestions about getting help for it.

WESLEY SIME: STRESS MANAGEMENT AND PEAK PERFORMANCE
http://www.unl.edu/stress/

This site by professor and author Wesley E. Sime, Ph.D., MPH/Ph.D. offers great resources on the fundamentals of stress management and an educational online tutorial.

NATIONAL INSTITUTE ON ALCOHOL ABUSE AND ALCOHOLISM (NIAAA)
http://www.niaaa.nih.gov/

The NIAAA is a part of the National Institutes of Health and provides this site, which includes resources and references about alcohol abuse and alcoholism. Included are links to publications and databases such as the National Library of Medicine Databases and Electronic Sources, press releases, conferences, and research programs.

WEB OF ADDICTIONS
http://www.well.com/user/woa/

This site by Andrew L. Homer, Ph.D., and Dick Dillon is dedicated to providing accurate information about alcohol and other drug addictions, serving as a resource for teachers and students who "need factual information on abused drugs." It provides a collection of fact sheets arranged by drug, links to other resources, contact information for a variety of groups, meetings/conferences related to addictions, in-depth information on special topics, and places to get help with addictions.

STRESS AND WORKSTRESS DIRECTORY
http://web.inter.nl.net/hcc/P.Compernolle/strescat.htm

Theo Compernolle, M.D., Ph.D., offers extensive links to articles and other sites relating to stress in general and especially in the workplace.

APA HELPCENTER: PSYCHOLOGY AT WORK
http://helping.apa.org/work/index.html

The American Psychological Association provides this resource describing various aspects of work including the myths of stress, the different kinds of stress, and the "Road to Burnout."

THE ANXIETY-PANIC INTERNET RESOURCE: RELAXATION
http://www.algy.com/anxiety/relax.html

This is a great site that deals with anxiety, coping with panic, and stress. Many stress reduction techniques are given. They are currently working on publishing an "encyclopedia/compendium of anxiety and self-help information."

MIND TOOLS™
http://www.mindtools.com/index.html

Mind Tools is dedicated to "helping you to think your way to an excellent life." This site provides shareware and practical suggestions for problem solving, memory improvement, increasing creativity, mastering stress, time management, goal setting links to stress/time management book stores, and much more.

InfoTrac College Edition Resources

For additional readings, explore InfoTrac College Edition, our online library.

Go to **http://www.infotrac.college.com/wadsworth**

Hint: Enter the search terms:

stress management

time management

money management

meditation

mindfulness

yoga

burnout

psychosomatic illness

psychophysiological

Print Resources

Benson, H. (1984). *Beyond the relaxation response.* New York: Berkeley Books.

Easwaran, E. (1991). *Meditation.* Tomales, CA: Nilgiri Press.

Feuerstein, G., & Bodian, S. (Eds.). (1993). *Living yoga: A comprehensive guide for daily life.* New York: Jeremy P. Tarcher/Putnam Books.

Fontana, D. (1999). *Learn to meditate: A practical guide to self-discovery and fulfillment.* San Francisco: Chronicle Books.

George, M. (1988). *Learn to relax: A practical guide to easing tension and conquering stress.* San Francisco: Chronicle Books.

Gunaratana, J. (1991). *Mindfulness in plain English.* Boston: Wisdom Publications.

Hanh, T. N. (1997). *Peace is every step: The path of mindfulness in everyday life.* New York: Bantam Books.

Rice, P. L. (1999). *Stress and health* (3rd ed.). Pacific Grove, CA: Brooks/Cole.

Rinpoche, S. (1994). *Mediatation.* San Francisco: Harper.

If you want to live forever,
love someone—*Bernie Siegel*

Heidi Jo Corey

LOVE

6

> ## Where Am I Now?

Use this scale to respond to these statements:

  4 = This statement is true of me *most* of the time.
  3 = This statement is true of me *much* of the time.
  2 = This statement is true of me *some* of the time.
  1 = This statement is true of me *almost none* of the time.

_____ 1. My parents modeled healthy patterns of love.

_____ 2. I have a fear of losing others' love.

_____ 3. When I experience hurt or frustration in love, I find it more difficult to trust and love again.

_____ 4. I make myself known in significant ways to those I love.

_____ 5. I find it difficult to express loving feelings toward members of the same sex.

_____ 6. I am as afraid of being accepted by those I love as I am of being rejected.

_____ 7. I have to take some risks if I am to open myself to loving.

_____ 8. In my loving relationships there is complete trust and an absence of fear.

_____ 9. I accept those whom I love as they are, without expecting them to be different.

_____ 10. I need constant closeness and intimacy with those I love.

In this chapter we invite you to look carefully at your style of loving by examining your choices and decisions when giving and receiving love. People often say either that they have love in their lives or that they do not. We believe you have the capacity to become better at loving. Look at the situations you create for yourself and consider how conducive these are to sharing love. What are your attitudes toward love? How are love, intimacy, and sexuality interrelated? What is the difference between authentic and inauthentic love? Is love active or passive? Do we fall in and out of love? How much are we responsible for creating a climate in which we can love others and receive love from them? Do we have romantic and unrealistic ideals of what love should be? If so, how can we challenge them? In what ways does love change as we change? What are the myths surrounding love? Is it worth it to love?

Freud defined the healthy person as one who can work well and love well. Like work, love can make living worthwhile, even during bleak times. We can find meaning in actively caring for others and in helping them make their lives better. Our love for others or their love for us may enable us to continue living, even in conditions of extreme hardship. In the Nazi concentration camp where he was imprisoned, Frankl (1963) noted that some of those who kept alive the images of those they loved and retained some measure of hope survived the ordeal, whereas those who lost any memories of love perished. From his experiences Frankl concluded that "the salvation of man is through love and in love" (p. 59).

Love involves risk, especially the risk of loss or rejection. The act of reaching out to another person entails the possibility of that person's moving away, leaving you more painfully alone than you were before. Loving and living a full life may include pain, but the alternative is choosing not to live or to love fully. Love also involves commitment, which is the foundation of any genuinely loving relationship. Although commitment does not guarantee a successful relationship, it is perhaps one of the most important factors in nurturing and fostering a relationship. Another major characteristic of genuine love is separateness, so that the identity of those in the relationship is maintained and preserved. Love is also an exercise of free choice, for people who love each other are able to live without each other yet choose to live together. When we speak of love relations, we refer to the various kinds of love, such as love between parent and child, love between siblings, friendships, and romantic relationships. Admittedly, these various types of love have some very real differences, but all forms of genuine love embody these basic characteristics in one way or another.

One of the purposes of this chapter is to help you clarify your views and values pertaining to love. As you read, try to apply the discussion to your own experience of love, and consider the degree to which you are now able to appreciate and love yourself. We encourage you to review your own need for love as well as your fears of loving. If you do so, you are likely to recognize whether barriers within you are preventing you from fully experiencing love.

LOVE MAKES A DIFFERENCE

To fully develop as a person and enjoy a rich existence, we need to care about others and have them return this care to us. A loveless life is characterized by joyless isolation and alienation. Our need for love includes the need to know that our existence makes a difference in at least one other person's world. If we exclude ourselves from physical and emotional closeness with others, we pay the price in emotional and physical deprivation, which leads to isolation.

Love is eternal; the love that people have for each other does not end upon death. In *Tuesdays With Morrie*, Mitch Albom (1997) recounts a series of conversations with Morrie Schwartz, who talks about how our love for others keeps them alive in our memory. Before his death, Morrie Schwartz spoke about how "death ends a life, but not a relationship."

> AS LONG AS WE CAN LOVE EACH OTHER, and remember the feeling of love we had, we can die without ever really going away. All the love you created is still there. All the memories are still there. You live on—in the hearts of everyone you have touched and nurtured while you were here. (p. 174)

When Albom asked Morrie if he worried about being forgotten after he died, Morrie replied: "I don't think I will be. I've got so many people who have been involved with me in close, intimate ways. And love is how you stay alive, even after you are gone" (p. 133). Love can transcend death as others remember us and keep their love for us alive. Our influence in their lives may live on even after we die.

People express their need to love and to be loved in many ways, a few of which are revealed in these statements:

> I need to have someone in my life I can actively care for. I need to let that person know he [she] makes a difference in my life, and I need to know I make a difference in his [her] life.

> I want to feel loved and accepted for who I am now, not for what the other person thinks I should be to be worthy of acceptance.

> Although I enjoy my own company, I also have a need for people in my life. I want to reach out to certain people, and I hope they will want something from me.

> I am finding out that I need others and that I have more of a capacity to give something to others than I had thought.

> I am beginning to realize that I need to learn how to love myself more fully. Until now I have limited myself by discounting my worth. I want to learn how to appreciate myself and to accept myself in spite of my imperfections. Then maybe I will be able to really believe that others can love me.

> There are times when I want to share my joys, my dreams, my anxieties, and my uncertainties with another person, and at these times I want to feel heard and understood.

Active love is something we can choose to share with others.

Dale Durfee/Stone

Of course, we can harden ourselves so we do not experience a need for love. We can close ourselves off from needing anything from anybody; we can isolate ourselves by never reaching out to another; we can refuse to trust others and to make ourselves vulnerable; we can cling to an early decision that we are basically unlovable. In whatever way we deaden ourselves to our own need for love, we pay a price. The question you must ask yourself is whether the safety achieved is worth the price you have paid for it.

BARRIERS TO LOVING AND BEING LOVED

Myths and Misconceptions About Love

Our ability to love fully and to receive love from others may be inhibited by misconceptions we have about the nature of love. We may have unconsciously bought into some myths about love that prevent us from forming realistic views of the nature of love. Our culture, especially the media, influences the way we conceive of love. If we hope to challenge these myths, we must take a critical look at the messages we have received from society about the essence of love. In the following pages we present our views on some common beliefs that need to be challenged.

The Myth of Eternal Love Some people assume that if the romance in the relationship fades this is a sure sign that love never really existed. The notion that love will endure forever without any change is unrealistic. Although love can last over a period of time, love takes on different forms as the relationship matures. Love assumes many complexions and involves both joyful experiences and difficulties. The intensity and degree of your love change as you change. You may experience several stages of love with one person, deepening your love and finding new levels of richness. Conversely, you and your partner may grow in different directions or outgrow the love you once shared.

The Myth That Love Implies Constant Closeness Betina and Luis dated throughout junior high and high school, and they went to college together because they could not tolerate any separation. They are making no friends, either with the same or opposite sex, and they show extreme signs of jealousy when the other indicates even the slightest interest in wanting to be with others. Rather than creating a better balance of time with each other and time with others, the only alternative they see is to terminate their relationship. The mistaken assumption they are operating on is that if they loved each other they would be fused into one being.

Many of us can tolerate only so much closeness, and at times we are likely to need some distance from others. Gibran's (1923) words in *The Prophet* are still timely: "And stand together yet not too near together: For the pillars of the temple stand apart, and the oak tree and the cypress grow not in each other's shadow" (p. 17).

There are times when a separation from our loved one can be very healthy. At these times we can renew our need for the other person and also become centered again. If we fail to separate when we feel the need to do so, we will surely strain the relationship. As an example consider the case of Martin. He refused to spend a weekend without his wife and children, even though he said he wanted some time for himself. The myth of constant closeness and constant togetherness in love prevented Martin from taking private time. It might also have been that the myth covered up certain fears. What if he discovered that his wife and children could manage very well without him? What if he found that he could not stand his own company for a few days and that the reason for "togetherness" was to keep him from boring himself?

As a couple, we (Marianne and Jerry) sometimes travel separately. At times Marianne goes to Germany by herself for a visit. In the past, some of the townspeople have let her know that they thought our marriage must be in trouble if we were not always together. Once Marianne and her mother went on a cruise together for a week, and many people wondered why Marianne would go on a vacation without her husband. When Jerry travels alone, whether for personal or professional reasons, he rarely is asked why he is not with his wife. This notion that couples should be inseparable is certainly influenced by what society considers appropriate gender-role behavior. The truth is that we enjoy traveling together and also without each other.

The Myth That We Fall In and Out of Love A common notion is that people "fall" in love, that they passively wait for the right person to come along and sweep them off their feet. Part of this misconception is the belief that when love strikes it is so powerful that it renders people helpless and unable to control what they do. According to this view, love is something that happens to people. This belief keeps people from assuming personal responsibility for their behavior and decisions. In contrast, we view love as something people themselves create—people *make* love happen.

Buscaglia (1992) criticizes the phrase "to fall in love." He contends that it is more accurate to say that we grow in love, which implies choice and effort: "We really don't fall out of love any more than we fall into it. When love dies, one or both partners have neglected it, have failed to replenish and renew it. Like any other living, growing thing, love requires effort to keep it healthy" (p. 6). In *The Art of Loving,* Fromm (1956) also describes love as active: "In the most general way, the active character of love can be described by stating that love is primarily giving, not receiving" (p. 22). Although the notion of falling in love is popular, most serious writers on the subject deny that it can be the basis for a lasting and meaningful relationship.

People often say "I love you" and at the same time are hard pressed to describe the active way in which they show this love. Words can easily be overused and become hollow. The loved one may be more convinced by actions than by words. In our professional work with couples, we find that one person may rant and rave about his or her partner's shortcomings. We often ask, "If the situation is as bad as you describe, what keeps you together as a couple?" To this question people often reply that they love the other person. Yet they are slow in identifying ways that they show what their love actually means, and they go on to blame their partner for whatever is awry in their relationship.

Active love is something we can choose to share with others. Love is not lost by sharing but rather increased. This thought leads to the next myth.

The Myth of the Exclusiveness of Love Sometimes you may think of love as something you possess in a limited quantity and must conserve. You may believe you are capable of loving only one other person—that there is one right person for you. One of the signs of genuine love is that it is expansive rather than exclusive. By opening yourself to loving others, you also open yourself to loving one person more deeply.

It is our choice to make our love exclusive or special. For example, two persons may choose not to have sexual relationships with others because they realize that doing so might interfere with their capacity to freely open up and trust each other. Nevertheless, their sexual exclusivity does not have to mean that they cannot genuinely love others as well.

Jealousy is an emotion that often accompanies feelings of exclusiveness. For example, Drew may feel insecure if he discovers that his wife, Adriana, has friendships with other men. Even if Adriana and Drew have an agreement not to have sexual relationships with others, Drew might be threatened and angry over the fact that Adriana wants to maintain these friendships with other men. He may wrongly reason: "What is the matter with me that Adriana has to seek out these friends? Her interest in other men is a sign that something is wrong with me!" This kind of jealousy, based on ownership of the other, is really not flattering. In Drew's case, his jealousy is probably rooted in his feelings of inferiority and the threat posed to him because of the reality that Adriana wants to include others in her life.

It is equally wrong to equate an absence of jealousy with an absence of love. For example, Adriana might be upset if Drew did not display any jealousy toward her, insisting that this meant that he was indifferent to her or that he had come to take her for granted. The motivations for jealousy need to be understood.

The Myth That True Love Is Selfless Lily is a mother who has always given to her children. She never lets them know that she needs anything from them, yet she confides to her friends that she is very hurt that the children do not seem to appreciate her. She complains that if she did not initiate visits with them they would never see her. She would never say anything about her feelings to her children, nor would she ever tell them that she would like for them to contact her. If they really loved her, she thinks they would know what she needed without her having to ask for it.

People like Lily are "selfish givers"; that is, they have a high need to take care of others yet appear to have little tolerance for accepting what others want to give to them. Selfish givers create an inequality; the receivers tend to feel guilty because they do not have a chance to reciprocate. Although these receivers may feel guilty and angry, their feelings do not seem appropriate—how could they have angry feelings toward someone who does so much for them? At the same time, selfish givers may feel resentment toward those who are always taking from them, not recognizing how difficult they are making it to receive.

It is a myth that true love means giving selflessly. For one thing, love also means taking. If you cannot allow others to give to you and cannot take their expressions of love, you are likely to become drained or resentful. For another thing, in giving to others we do meet many of our own needs. There is not necessarily anything wrong in this, as long as we can admit it. For example, a mother who never says no to any demands made by her children may not be aware of the ways she has conditioned them to depend on her. They may be unaware that she has any needs of her own, for she hides them so well. In fact, she may set them up to take advantage of her out of her need to feel significant. In other words, her "giving" is actually an outgrowth of her need to feel like a good mother rather than an honest expression of love for her children. In *Care of the Soul* (1994) Thomas Moore addresses this notion of selflessness. One of his clients said, "I can't be selfish. My religious upbringing taught me never to be selfish" (p. 56). Moore observes that although she insisted on her selflessness she was quite preoccupied with herself. Selfless people often depend on others to maintain their feelings of selflessness.

Giving to others or the desire to express our love to others is not necessarily a problem. However, it is important that we recognize our own needs and consider the value of allowing others to take care of us and return the love we show them. One of us (Marianne) is finally learning the importance of letting others return favors.

MARIANNE'S STORY

*I*t has always been easy for me to show others kindness and take care of others, yet it has been a struggle for me to be on the receiving end. An old pattern of mine is to do everything by myself and not take the chance of imposing on others by asking for assistance. I have learned to ask others for help instead of insisting on doing everything by myself. More often than not, when I do ask for help, not only do others not feel any imposition but they express delight that I made the request and are pleased to reciprocate. I continue to learn that it takes a concerted effort to challenge ingrained beliefs about being a selfless giver. One way I am able to give to others is by letting others take care of me at times.

The Myth That Love and Anger Are Incompatible Many people are convinced that if they love someone they cannot get angry at them. When they do get angry, they tend to deny these feelings or express them in indirect ways. Unfortunately, denied or unexpressed anger can lead to the death of a relationship. Anger needs to be dealt with in a constructive way before it reaches explosive proportions.

Anger and love cannot be compartmentalized: If you deny your anger, you are negating your love. It is difficult to feel loving toward others if we harbor unexpressed grudges. These unresolved issues tend to poison the relationship and can actually prevent deeper intimacy. The harmful effects of unexpressed anger on relationships is explored in some detail by Harriet Goldhor Lerner in *The Dance of Anger* (1985) and *The Dance of Intimacy* (1989).

Self-Doubt and Lack of Self-Love

Despite our need for love, we often put barriers in the way of our attempts to give and receive love. One common obstacle consists of the messages we sometimes

Myrleen Ferguson/PhotoEdit

There is an uncon-
ditional quality about
love.

send to others concerning ourselves. If we enter relationships convinced that nobody could possibly love us, we will give this message to others in many subtle
ways. We create a self-fulfilling prophecy; we make the very thing we fear come
true by telling both ourselves and others that life can be no other way.

If you are convinced that you are unlovable, your conviction is probably related to decisions you made about yourself during your childhood or adolescent
years. At one time perhaps you decided that you would not be loved unless you
did certain expected things or lived up to another's design for your life. For example: "Unless I succeed, I won't be loved. To be loved, I must get good grades,
become successful, and make the most of my life." Such a decision can make it
difficult to convince yourself later in life that you can be loved even if you are
not successful.

Jay decided as a child that he would do whatever it took to meet the expectations of others and to gain their acceptance. He gives his all to please people and to get them to like him, yet he has few friends. Through his actions of desperately trying to win people over, he pushes them away even more. Although he thinks he is doing everything right, people are uncomfortable with the way he behaves around them. He is constantly depressed and complains about how hard life is for him. He seeks sympathy and receives rejection. He needs continual reassurance that he is capable, yet when he does get acceptance and reassurance, he negates it. He seems to work at convincing people that he is really unlovable, and eventually people who know him get frustrated and rebuff him. He may never realize that he has created the cycle of his own rejection. In some important ways he continues to live by the theme that no matter what he does or how hard he tries people will still not like him, much less love him.

Sometimes people have a difficult time believing they are lovable for who they are, and they may discount the love others give them. For example, think for a moment of how many times you have completed this sentence in any of the following ways: People love me only because I am . . .

> Pretty, bright, and witty.

> Good in sports.

> A good student.

> A fine provider.

> Attractive.

> Accomplished.

> Cooperative and considerate.

> A good father [mother].

> A good wife [husband].

If you have limited your ability to receive love from others by telling yourself (and by convincing others) that you are loved primarily for a single trait, it would be healthy to challenge this assumption. For example, if you say "You only love me because of my body," you might try to realize that your body is only one of your assets. You can learn to appreciate this asset without assuming that it is all there is to the person you are. If you have trouble seeing any desirable characteristics besides your physical attractiveness, you are likely to give others messages that your primary value is bound up in appearances. Ideally, you will come to accept that being a physically attractive person makes it easier for others to notice you and want to initiate contact with you. However, you do not need to limit yourself by depending exclusively on how you look; work at developing other traits. When you rely exclusively on any one trait as a source of gaining love from others (or from yourself), your ability to be loved is in a tenuous state.

Our Fear of Love

The Fear of Isolation Despite our need for love, we often fear loving and being loved. Our fear can lead us to seal off our need to experience love, and it can dull our capacity to care about others. In some families relatives have not spoken to one another for years. This act of shunning is generally deliberate and aimed at controlling and isolating those who do not live within the boundaries of acceptable norms. Those who are shunned often feel invisible. Within the Amish culture the practice of shunning is used to sanction members who violate certain norms and religious values. In its most severe form, shunning almost totally cuts off an individual from interaction within the community. Other members will not eat at the same table with those who are shunned, will not do business with them, and will not have anything to do with them socially (Good & Good, 1979). The fear of isolation as a result of being cut off emotionally is so overwhelming that many would not even think of going against their cultural norms. The need for love and acceptance may be far stronger than giving expression to your own individual desires. Have you ever faced an emotional cutoff? If so, what did you experience? Have you sometimes felt isolated because others that you cared about shunned you or treated you as though you were invisible?

The Fear of Being Discovered Some of us are afraid that if we get too close to others they will certainly discover who we really are. We may be anxious that the deepest core of our being is not attractive and that if people really knew us they would not want to have a relationship with us. Many people doubt the positive reactions they receive from others and have difficulty believing that others are really able to value them. Iyanla Vanzant (1998) realized that she wanted to be loved but was unwilling to risk being known:

> I ALSO ACKNOWLEDGED THAT I KEPT MOST PEOPLE I PROFESSED TO LOVE AT AN ARM'S DISTANCE, never allowing them to know too much or get too close, because I was afraid of being hurt. My mouth was saying I wanted to be loved, while my mind was thinking I was unworthy. I was sending out signals indicating that I wanted to be loved, but I would only let so much love in. My fear, which I am sure is the same fear for many of us, is that too much love would kill me. I would simply melt in its presence. (p. 227)

Reflect for a moment on how much love you are able to receive from others and answer this question: "How much love can I stand?" Do you have any fears that if people get to know you they will not like, appreciate, and love who you are?

The Uncertainty of Love Love does not come with guarantees. We cannot be sure that another person will always love us, and we do lose loved ones. As Hodge (1967) insists, we cannot eliminate the possibility that we will be hurt if we choose to love. Our loved ones may die or be injured or become painfully ill, or they may simply be mistrustful of our caring. "These are painful experiences, and we cannot avoid them if we choose to love. It is part of the human dilemma that love always includes the element of hurt" (p. 266).

Most of the common fears of risking in love are related to rejection, loss, the failure of love to be reciprocated, or uneasiness with intensity. Here are some of the ways these fears might be expressed:

> Since I once got badly hurt in a love relationship, I'm not willing to take the chance of trusting again.

> I fear allowing myself to love others because of the possibility that they will be seriously injured, contract a terrible illness, or die. I don't want to let them matter that much; that way, if I lose them, it won't hurt as much as if they really mattered.

> I'm afraid of loving others because they might want more from me than I'm willing to give, and I might feel suffocated.

> I'm afraid that I'm basically unlovable and that when you really get to know me you'll want little to do with me.

> If people tell me they care about me, I feel I've taken on a burden, and I'm afraid of letting them down.

> I've never really allowed myself to look at whether I'm lovable. My fear is that I will search deep within myself and find little for another to love.

Maribel has struggled in overcoming early childhood messages in her quest for loving and being loved. At her present age of 26 she is still learning to deal with the fear of love. Here she describes the experience of "wearing protective armor" around her heart.

MARIBEL'S STORY

*I*ntimacy and trust do not come easy for me. Physical contact and close intimate relationships were not present during my childhood. Yet there is nothing more incredible than sharing your life with someone you love and trust completely. Even after being together almost 4 years, my boyfriend Al and I are still often engaged in what I sometimes call an emotional tug-of-war. He gives a little, and I feel secure. I give a little and then feel like I'm the one giving it all. We are always struggling to find a balance.

I have become aware that I wear a protective armor around my heart. In my own personal therapy I have been exploring the ways in which this wall was helpful in my childhood but may keep people at a distance now. I put my boyfriend through a test every day. If he can take the time to look beneath the tough exterior, he passes the test, and the wall comes down. I sometimes wonder if the game will ever end.

I have come to realize the vicious cycle of ebb and flow in my relationship. At times things have gotten so difficult we've actually decided to end it. I sometimes use the analogy of a person on life support for our relationship. The loved ones hesitate on pulling the plug because the person could wake up any day. Sometimes hanging on is what you have to do, so you don't risk ending something that may come alive the very next day.

No matter what your own fears may be, you can learn, as Maribel has, to choose a different path and to open yourself to the potential for love that awaits you. Can you identify with Maribel's struggle in any way?

Take Time to Reflect

1. What did you learn about love in your family of origin?

_____

_____

2. How do you express your love to others?

_____

_____

3. How do you let another person know your own need to receive love, affection, and caring?

_____

_____

4. List some specific fears you have concerning loving others.

_____

_____

(continued)

5. What barriers within yourself prevent others from loving you or prevent you from fully receiving their love?

_____

_____

6. List some qualities you have that you deem lovable.

_____

_____

7. What are some specific ways in which you might become a more lovable person?

_____

_____

IS IT WORTH IT TO LOVE?

Often we hear people say, "Sure, I need to love and to be loved, but is it _really_ worth it?" Underlying this question is a series of other questions: "Can I survive without love?" "Is the risk of rejection and loss worth taking?" "Are the rewards of opening myself up as great as the risks?"

It would be comforting to have an absolute answer to these questions, but each of us must struggle to decide for ourselves whether it is worth it to love. Our first task is to decide whether we prefer isolation to intimacy. Of course, our choice is not between extreme isolation and constant intimacy; surely there are degrees of both. But we do need to decide whether to experiment with extending our narrow world to include significant others. We can increasingly open ourselves to others and discover for ourselves what that is like for us; alternatively, we can decide that people are basically unreliable and that it is better to be safe and go hungry emotionally.

Perhaps you feel unable to give love but would like to learn how to become more intimate. You might begin by acknowledging this reality to yourself, as well as to those in your life with whom you would like to become more intimate. In this way you can take a significant beginning step.

In answering the question of whether it is worth it to you to love, you can challenge some of your attitudes and beliefs concerning acceptance and rejection. We have encountered many people who believe it is not worth it to love because of the possibility of experiencing rejection. If you feel this way, you can decide whether to stop at this barrier. You can ask yourself: "What's so catastrophic about being rejected? Will I die if someone I love leaves me? Can I survive the emotional hurt that comes with disappointment in love?" Of course, being rejected is not a pleasant experience, yet we hope this possibility will not deter you from allowing yourself to love someone. If a love relationship ends for you, it would surely be worth it to honestly search for your part in contributing to this situation without being severely self-critical. Identify some ways in which you would like to change and learn from this experience. Elana had to learn to trust again after being deeply hurt in a relationship.

ELANA'S STORY

I had a mutual loving bond with Monte, yet most of my friends had a hard time understanding why I continued in this relationship. I guess I had an idealized picture of Monte and made excuses for his insensitive behavior. I became extremely dependent on Monte and preoccupied with trying to please him at all costs, even if it meant sacrificing my own happiness to keep peace with him. My friends let me know of their concern and tried to convince me that I deserved better treatment. My response was to cut myself off from my friends so I would not have to deal with their feedback. Eventually, Monte betrayed me, which led to a crisis. I ended my relationship with Monte, but I was quite fearful of loving again, and old wounds were reopened each time I met a new man. I approached new relationships with fear and distrust, which made it difficult to open myself to love again.

With concerted work on her part, Elana became aware of how clinging to her past hampered her ability to receive love and develop friendships. Elana's immediate impulses were to flee from getting close, yet she challenged her fears with the realization that the risk of rejection did not have to keep her helpless and guarded.

As adults we are no longer helpless; we can do something about rejection and hurt. We can choose to leave relationships that are not satisfying, we can learn to survive pain, and we can realize that being rejected does not mean we are fundamentally unlovable. Consider how the last line in Hodge's (1967) book, *Your Fear of Love,* may apply to you: "We can discover for ourselves that it is worth the risk to love, even though we tremble and even though we know we will sometimes experience the hurt we fear" (p. 270).

LEARNING TO LOVE AND APPRECIATE OURSELVES

In our counseling sessions clients are sometimes surprised when we ask them what they like and appreciate about themselves. They look uncomfortable and embarrassed, and it is obvious that they are not accustomed to speaking positively about themselves. An indirect way to get people to express some self-appreciation is to ask questions such as these: "If your best friends were here, how would they describe you?" "What characteristics would they ascribe to you?" "What reasons might they give for choosing you as a friend?" People appear to find it easier to talk about how they see themselves in positive ways when responding to these kinds of questions.

Some people are reluctant to speak of their self-love because they have been brought up to think of it as purely egocentric. But unless we learn how to love ourselves, we will encounter difficulties in loving others and in allowing them to express their love for us. We cannot very well give to others what we do not possess ourselves. If we cannot appreciate our own worth, how can we believe others when they say that they see value in us? When we are able to love ourselves, we open the door to loving others, even an enemy. Hanh (1997) speaks about self-love as a prerequisite for loving others: "If you are not yet able to love yourself, you will not be able to love your enemy. But when you are able to love yourself, you can love anyone" (p. 37).

Having love for ourselves does not mean having an exaggerated picture of our own importance or placing ourselves above others or at the center of the universe. Rather, it means having respect for ourselves even though we are imperfect. It entails caring about our lives and striving to become the people we are capable of becoming.

Many writers have stressed the necessity of self-love as a condition of love for others. In *The Art of Loving*, Fromm (1956) describes self-love as respect for our own integrity and uniqueness and maintains that it cannot be separated from love and understanding of others. We often ask clients who only give to others and who have a difficult time taking for themselves: "Do you deserve what you so freely give to others?" "If your own well runs dry, how will you be able to give to others?" We cannot give what we have not learned and experienced ourselves. Moore (1994) writes that those who try very hard to be loved do not succeed because they do not realize that they have to first love themselves as others before they can receive love from others.

As we grow to treat ourselves with increasing respect and regard, we increase our ability to fully accept the love others might want to give us; at the same time, we have the foundation for genuinely loving others. If we are unable to care for ourselves, we are unable to care for another person. Caring for ourselves and caring for others are mutually dependent.

INAUTHENTIC AND AUTHENTIC LOVE

"Love" That Stifles

Authentic love enhances us and those we love, but there is another kind of "love" that diminishes us and those to whom we attempt to give it. Some forms of pseudolove parade as real love but cripple us and those we say we love. Certain characteristics are typical of a type of love that stifles. This list is not definitive, but it may give you some ideas you can use in thinking about the quality of your love. A person whose love is inauthentic

> Needs to be in charge and make decisions for the other person.
> Has rigid and unrealistic expectations of how the other person must act to be worthy of love.
> Attaches strings to loving and loves conditionally.
> Puts little trust in the love relationship.
> Perceives personal change as a threat to the continuation of the relationship.
> Is possessive.
> Depends on the other person to fill a void in life.
> Lacks commitment.
> Is unwilling to share important thoughts and feelings about the relationship.
> Resorts to manipulation to get the other person to respond in a predetermined manner.

Most of us can find some of these manifestations of inauthentic love in our relationships, yet this does not mean that our love is necessarily fraudulent. For instance, at times you may be reluctant to let another person know about your private life, you may have excessive expectations of another person, or you may attempt to impose your own agenda. It is essential to be honest with yourself and to recognize when you are not expressing genuine love, then you can choose to change these patterns.

Some Meanings of Authentic Love

So far we have discussed mostly what we think love is not. Now we would like to share some of the positive meanings love has for us.

Love means that I *know* the person I love. I am aware of the many facets of the other person—not just the beautiful side but also the limitations, inconsistencies, and flaws. I have an awareness of the other's feelings and thoughts, and I experience something of the core of that person. I can penetrate social masks and roles and see the other person on a deeper level.

Love means that I *care* about the welfare of the person I love. To the extent that it is genuine, my caring is not a smothering of the person or a possessive clinging. On the contrary, my caring liberates both of us. If I care about you, I am concerned about your growth, and I hope you will become all that you can become. Consequently, I do not put up roadblocks to what you do that enhances you as a person, even though it may result in my discomfort at times.

Love means having *respect* for the *dignity* of the person I love. If I love you, I can see you as a separate person, with your own values and thoughts and feelings, and I do not insist that you surrender your identity and conform to an image of what I expect you to be for me. I can allow and encourage you to stand alone and to be who you are, and I avoid treating you as an object or using you primarily to gratify my own needs.

Love means having a *responsibility* toward the person I love. If I love you, I am responsive to most of your major needs as a person. This responsibility does not entail my doing for you what you are capable of doing for yourself; nor does it mean that I run your life for you. It does mean acknowledging that what I am and what I do affects you; I am directly involved in your happiness and your misery. A lover does have the capacity to hurt or neglect the loved one, and in this sense I see that love entails acceptance of some responsibility for the impact my way of being has on you.

Love means *growth* for both me and the person I love. If I love you, I am growing as a result of my love. You are a stimulant for me to become more fully what I might become, and my loving enhances your being as well. We each grow as a result of caring and being cared for; we each share in an enriching experience that does not detract from our being. Buscaglia (1992) puts this idea well when he writes: "We must not only respect the need for our lover's growth, we must encourage it, even at the risk of losing them. It seems ironic, but it is true, that only in continuing to grow separately is there any hope of individuals growing together" (p. 22).

Love means making a *commitment* to the person I love. This commitment does not entail surrendering our total selves to each other; nor does it imply that the relationship is necessarily permanent. It does entail a willingness to stay with each other in times of pain, uncertainty, struggle, and despair, as well as in times of calm and enjoyment. In his book, *Passionate Marriage*, Schnarch (1997) writes: "Loving is not for the weak, nor for those who have to be carefully kept, nor for the faint of heart. That's why there's so little of it in the world. Love requires being steadfast through many difficulties" (p. 404).

Love means that I am *vulnerable*. If I open myself up to you in trust, I may experience hurt, rejection, and loss. Love involves allowing you to matter to me in

Jim Whitmer/Stock, Boston

Love means making a commitment.

spite of my fear of losing you. Because you are not perfect, you have the capacity to hurt me. There are no guarantees in love, and there is no security that your love will endure. Loving involves sharing with and experiencing with the person I love. My love for you implies that I want to spend time with you and share meaningful aspects of your life with you. It also implies that I have a desire to share significant aspects of myself with you.

Love means *trusting the person you love.* If I love you, I trust that you will accept my caring and my love and that you will not deliberately hurt me. I trust that you will find me lovable and that you will not abandon me; I trust the reciprocal nature of our love. If we trust each other, we are willing to be open to each other and can shed masks and pretenses and reveal our true selves.

Love means *trusting yourself.* In relationships a great deal is made of trusting the person you love, yet the ability to trust yourself is equally important. Indeed, if your trust in yourself wavers, you may not be able to believe or trust in the love another wants to share with you: "The biggest trust issue in marriage isn't about trusting your partner. It's about whether or not you can really trust yourself" (Schnarch, 1997, p. 404). We need to trust ourselves to be able to soothe ourselves. "It's not safe to love your partner more than you can self-soothe, especially if you always need him or her to 'be there for you.' Your partner won't be there to hold your hand and comfort you through his or her death. You'll go through that alone" (p. 404).

Love allows for accepting *imperfection*. In a love relationship there are times of boredom, times when I may feel like giving up, times of strain, and times I feel stuck. Authentic love does not provide perpetual happiness. I can stay during rough times, however, because I can remember what we had together in the past and can envision what we will have together in our future if we care enough to face our problems and work them through.

Love is *freeing*. Love is freely given. At the same time, my love for you is not contingent on whether you fulfill my expectations of you. Authentic love does not mean "I'll love you when you become perfect or when you become what I expect you to become." Authentic love is not given with strings attached. There is an unconditional quality about love.

Love is *expansive*. If I love you, I encourage you to reach out and develop other relationships. Although our love for each other and our commitment to each other might preclude certain actions on our parts, we are not totally and exclusively wedded to each other. Only a pseudo-love cements one person to another in such a way that he or she is not given room to grow.

Love means having a *want* for the person I love without having a need for that person to be complete. If I am nothing without you, then I am not really free to love you. If I love you and you leave, I will experience a loss and be sad and lonely, but I will still be able to survive. If I am overly dependent on you for my meaning and my survival, I am not free to challenge our relationship; nor am I free to challenge and confront you. Because of my fear of losing you, I will settle for less than I want, and this settling will surely lead to feelings of resentment.

Love means *identifying* with the person I love. If I love you, I can empathize with you and see the world through your eyes. I can identify with you because I am able to see myself in you and you in me. This closeness does not imply a continual "togetherness," for distance and separation are sometimes essential in a loving relationship. Distance can intensify a loving bond, and it can help us rediscover ourselves, so that we are able to meet each other in a new way. "Mature love is union under the condition of preserving one's integrity, one's individuality. In love this paradox occurs that two beings become one and yet remain two" (Fromm, 1956, pp. 20–21).

Love involves *self-acceptance*. I can only love you if I genuinely love, value, appreciate, accept, and respect myself. If I am empty, all I can give you is my emptiness. If I feel that I am complete and worthwhile in myself, I am able to give to you out of my fullness. One of the best ways for me to give you love is by fully enjoying myself with you.

Love involves *seeing the potential* within the person I love. If I love you, I am able to see you as the person you can become, while still accepting who you are now. Goethe's observation is relevant here: "By taking people as they are, we make them worse, but by treating them as if they already were what they ought to be, we help make them better."

Love means *letting go* of the illusion of total control of ourselves, others, and our environment. The more I strive for complete control, the more out of control I am. Loving implies a surrender of control and being open to life's events. It implies the capacity to be surprised. Bringing surprise to love, says Buscaglia (1992), is a way to keep a relationship alive: "Love withers with predictability; its very essence is surprise and amazement. To make love a prisoner of the mundane is to take away its passion and lose it forever" (p. 19).

We conclude this discussion of the meanings that authentic love has for us by sharing the prayer of Saint Francis of Assisi, which to us embodies the essence of authentic love. Some authors have cited this prayer as illustrative of a heart that is filled with unconditional love (Maier, 1991). In his book, *Meditation*, Eknath Easwaran (1991) recommends memorizing the prayer of Saint Francis of Assisi and using this as a basis for daily meditation. He believes the words of this prayer have an almost universal appeal. Regardless of one's possible religious affiliation or spiritual beliefs, there is an in-depth message in this prayer. For Easwaran the word "Lord" is not something outside of us or separate from us. Instead, it is within the core of our being.

> LORD, MAKE ME AN INSTRUMENT OF THY PEACE.
> Where there is hatred, let me sow love;
> Where there is injury, pardon;
> Where there is doubt, faith;
> Where there is despair, hope;
> Where there is darkness, light;
> Where there is sadness, joy;
> O divine Master, grant that I may not
>   so much seek
> To be consoled as to console;
> To be understood as to understand;
> To be loved, as to love;
> For it is in giving that we receive;
> It is in pardoning that we are pardoned;
> It is in dying to self that we are born
>   to eternal life.
> (as cited in Easwaran, 1991, pp. 29–30)

This prayer is a source of meditation and personal reflection, but it can also be useful as a basis for journal writing.

Take Time to Reflect

1. Examine your thoughts about opening yourself to loving another person, and complete these sentences:

   It is worth it to love, because _____

   _____

It is not worth it to love because _____

_____

2. Review the list of meanings love has for us, and then list some of the meanings love has for you.

_____

_____

_____

_____

3. Think of someone you love. What specifically do you love about that person? Then list some ways or times when you withhold love from that person.

_____

_____

_____

4. What are some concrete steps you can take to allow others to love you more fully?

_____

_____

_____

5. What are some steps you can take to demonstrate your love for others?

_____

_____

_____

6. Reflect on the prayer of Saint Francis of Assisi, looking for aspects in this prayer that capture the essence of what it means to actively love others. What personal meaning does this prayer have for you?

_____

_____

SUMMARY

We have a need to love and to be loved, but most of us encounter barriers to meeting these needs. Our doubt that we are worthy of being loved can be a major roadblock to loving others and receiving their love. Although many of us have been brought up believing that self-love is egotistical, in reality we are not able to love others unless we love and appreciate ourselves. How can we give to others something we do not possess ourselves? Our fear of love is another major impediment to loving. Many people would like guarantees that their love for special people will last as long as they live, but the stark reality is that there are no guarantees. It helps to realize that loving and trembling go together and to accept that we must learn to love despite our fears.

Myths and misconceptions about love make it difficult to be open to giving and receiving love. A few of these are the myth of eternal love, the myth that love implies constant closeness, the myth of the exclusiveness of love, the myth that true love is selfless, and the myth of falling in love. Although genuine love results in the growth of both persons, some "love" is stifling. Not all that poses as real love is authentic, and one of the major challenges is to decide for ourselves the meanings of authentic love. By recognizing our attitudes about loving, we can increase our ability to choose the ways in which we behave in our love relationships.

❭ Where Can I Go From Here?

1. Think about some early decisions you made regarding your own ability to love or to be loved. Have you ever had any of these thoughts?

❭ I'm not lovable unless I meet others' expectations.

❭ I won't love another because of my fears of rejection.

❭ I'm not worthy of being loved.

(continued)

> **Where Can I Go From Here?** *(continued)*

Write down some of the messages you have received and perhaps accepted uncritically. What message have you received from your family of origin? How has your ability to feel loved or to give love been restricted by these messages and decisions?

2. For a period of at least a week, pay close attention to the messages conveyed by the media concerning love. What picture of love do you get from television? What do popular songs portray about love? Make a list of some common myths or misconceptions regarding love that you see promoted by the media.

3. Do you agree with the proposition that you cannot fully love others unless you first love yourself? How does this apply to you? In your journal write some notes to yourself concerning situations in which you do not appreciate yourself. Also record the times and events when you do value and respect yourself.

4. How important is love in your life right now? Do you feel that you love others in the ways you would like to? Do you feel that you are loved by others in the ways you want to be?

5. Are you an active or a passive lover? Write down the ways in which you demonstrate your caring for those you love and then ask them to read your list and discuss with you how they see your style of loving.

Resources for Future Study

Web Site Resource

LOVE PAGE
http://www.tc.umn.edu/nlhome/g296/parkx032/LVindex.html

The Love Page was created by James Park, an existential philosopher and advocate of freedom and authenticity in relationships. This site offers many articles that challenge more traditional notions of romantic love and includes a 60-page preview of his book *New Ways of Loving*. There are also bibliographies on a wide variety of topics dealing with love and relationships.

 InfoTrac College Edition Resources

For additional readings, explore InfoTrac College Edition, our online library.

Go to **http://www.infotrac.college.com/wadsworth**

Hint: Enter the search terms:

> love
> self acceptance
> humanitarian love
> self-love
> brotherly love
> jealousy

Print Resources

Albom, M. (1997). *Tuesdays with Morrie.* New York: Doubleday.

Buscaglia, L. (1972). *Love.* Thorofare, NJ: Charles B. Slack.

Buscaglia, L. (1992). *Born for love: Reflections on loving.* New York: Fawcett Columbine.

Easwaran, E. (1991). *Meditation.* Tomales, CA: Nilgiri Press.

Fromm, E. (1956). *The art of loving.* New York: Harper & Row (Colophon). (Paperback edition published 1974)

Hanh, T. N. (1997). *Teachings on love.* Berkeley, CA: Parallax Press.

Jampolsky, G. G. (1981). *Love is letting go of fear.* New York: Bantam Books.

Moore, T. (1994). *Care of the soul: A guide for cultivating depth and sacredness in everyday life.* New York: Harper Perennial.

Schnarch, D. (1997). *Passionate marriage.* New York: Henry Holt & Co.

Vanzant, I. (1998). *One day my soul just opened up.* New York: Fireside Book (Simon and Schuster).

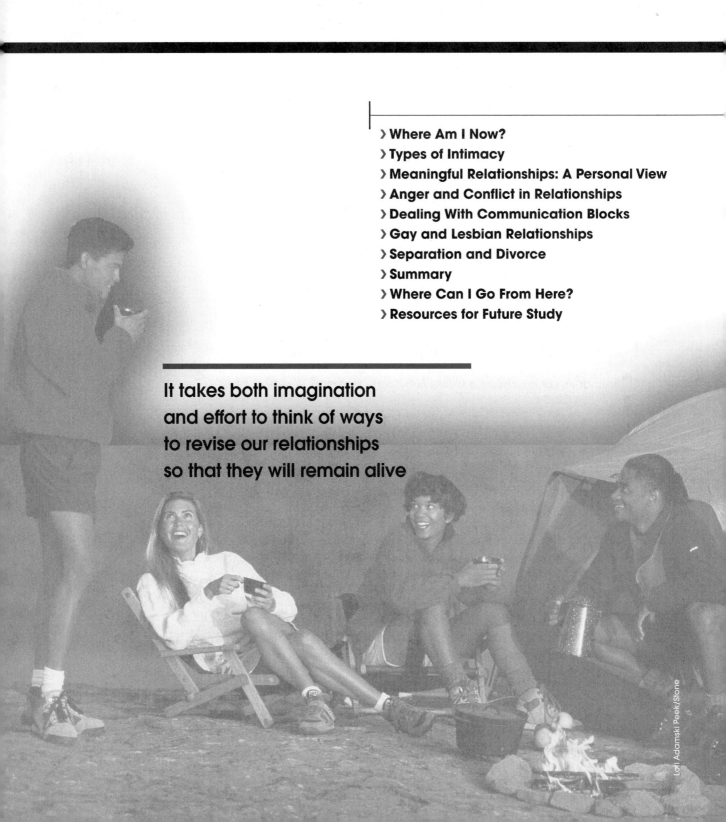

It takes both imagination
and effort to think of ways
to revise our relationships
so that they will remain alive

Lori Adamski Peek/Stone

RELATIONSHIPS

Use this scale to respond to these statements:

   4 = This statement is true of me *most* of the time.
   3 = This statement is true of me *much* of the time.
   2 = This statement is true of me *some* of the time.
   1 = This statement is true of me *almost none* of the time.

_____ 1. I consider the absence of conflict and crisis to be a sign of a good relationship.

_____ 2. It is difficult for me to have many close relationships at one time.

_____ 3. If I am involved in a satisfactory relationship, I won't feel attracted to others besides my partner.

_____ 4. I believe the mark of a successful relationship is that I enjoy being both with and without the other person.

_____ 5. I would like to find intimacy with one other person.

_____ 6. At times, wanting too much from another person causes me difficulties in the relationship.

_____ 7. I feel confident in what I have to offer in a relationship.

_____ 8. I am comfortable with the amount of energy I spend in my relationships.

_____ 9. I feel satisfied with my connection with others.

_____ 10. I can be emotionally intimate with another person without being physically intimate with that person.

Relationships play a significant role in our lives. In this chapter we deal with friendships, marital relationships, intimacy between people who are not married, dating relationships, relationships between parents and children, same-gender relationships as well as opposite-gender relationships, and other meaningful personal relationships.

Whether you choose to marry or not, whether your primary relationship is with someone of the same or the opposite gender, you will face many of the same relationship challenges. What is true for marriage is largely true for these other intimate relationships as well. The signs of growth and meaningfulness are much the same, and so are the problems. You can use the ideas in this chapter as a basis for thinking about the role relationships play in your life. In this chapter we hope to encourage you to reflect on what you want from your relationships, and we will assist you in examining the quality of these relationships.

TYPES OF INTIMACY

The challenge of forming intimate relationships is the major task of early adulthood (Erikson, 1963). Being able to share significant aspects of yourself with others, understanding the barriers to intimacy, and learning ways of enhancing intimacy can help you better understand the many different types of relationships in your life. The ideas in this chapter are useful tools in rethinking what kind of relationships you want, as well as in clarifying some new choices you may want to make. Take a fresh look at your relationships, including both their frustrations and their delights, and decide whether you might want to initiate some changes. Consider the case of Donald, who told us about how little closeness he had experienced with his father.

DONALD'S STORY

*M*y father seems uncaring, aloof, and preoccupied with his own concerns. I deeply wish to be physically and emotionally closer to my father, but I have no idea of how to bring this about. I decided to talk to my father and tell him how I feel and what I want. My father appeared to listen, and his eyes moistened, but then without saying much he quickly left the room. I am pretty hurt and disappointed that my father wasn't more responsive when I talked to him. I just don't know what else I can do.

Donald was missing the subtle yet significant signs that his father had been touched and was not as uncaring as he had imagined. That his father listened to him, that he responded with even a few clumsy words, that he touched Donald on the shoulder, and that he became emotional were all manifestations that Donald's overtures had been received. Donald needs to understand that his father is probably very uncomfortable talking about his feelings. His father may well be every bit as afraid of his son's rejection as Donald is of his father's rebuffs. Donald will need to show patience and continue "hanging in there" with his father if he is really interested in changing the way they relate to each other.

The experience Donald had with his father could have occurred in any intimate relationship. We can experience feelings of awkwardness, unexpressed desires, and fears of rejection with our friends, lovers, spouses, parents, or children. A key point is that we have the power to bring about change if we ourselves change and do not insist that the other person make quick and total changes. It is up to us to teach others specific ways of becoming more personal. It does little good to invest our energy in lamenting all the ways in which the other person is not fulfilling our expectations, nor is it helpful to focus on remaking others. Time and again in this chapter we will encourage you to focus on your own wants, to look at what you are doing, and to make some decisions about how you can assume increased control of your relationships. When you take a passive stance and simply hope the other person will change in the ways that you would like, you are giving away your own power.

The intimacy we share with another person can be emotional, intellectual, physical, spiritual, or any combination of these. It can be exclusive or nonexclusive, long-term or brief. For example, many of the participants in the personal-growth groups we conduct develop genuine closeness with one another, even though they may not keep in touch after the termination of the group. This closeness does not come about magically or automatically. They earn it by daring to be different in how they relate. Instead of keeping their thoughts, feelings, and reactions to themselves, they let others know them in ways that they typically do not allow outside of the group setting. The cohesion comes about when people discover that they have very similar feelings and when they are willing to share their pain, anger, frustration—and their joys. Many people are reluctant to open themselves up emotionally in such short-term situations because they want to avoid the sadness of parting. Bonds of intimacy and friendship can be formed in a short period, however, and subsequent distance in space and time need not diminish the quality of the friendships we form. We caution that developing intimacy with people in the group should not be the final goal. What is important is that the members translate this learning to their outside lives.

When we avoid intimacy, we only rob ourselves. We may pass up the chance to really get to know neighbors and new acquaintances because we fear that either we or our new friends will move and that the friendship will come to an end. Similarly, we may not want to open ourselves to intimacy with sick or dying persons because we fear the pain of losing them. Although such fears may be natural ones, too often we allow them to cheat us of the uniquely rich experience of being truly close to another person. We can enhance our lives greatly by daring to care about others and fully savoring the time we can share with them now.

The idea that we most want to stress is that you can choose the kinds of relationships you want to experience. Often, we fail to make our own choices and instead fall into a certain type of relationship because we think "this is the way it is supposed to be." For example, some people marry who in reality might prefer to remain single—this is particularly true for women who feel the pressure to have a family because it is "natural" for them to do so. Sometimes people choose a heterosexual relationship because they think that it is what is expected of them, but they would really prefer a same-gender relationship. This chapter challenges you to look at your choices regarding the types of intimacy that have meaning for you.

As you read the remainder of this chapter, spend some time thinking about the quality of all the various kinds of intimacy you are experiencing in your life. Are you involved in the kinds of relationships that you want? How can you enhance your relationships? What are you willing to do to improve them? What is your view of a growing relationship? The Take Time to Reflect exercises presented here you with an opportunity to address these questions and clarify what you are looking for in your relationships.

Take Time to Reflect

1. What do you look for in a person you would like to form an intimate relationship with? For each item, put a 1 in the space if the quality is very important to you, a 2 if it is somewhat important, and a 3 if it is not very important.

_____ intelligence
_____ character (a strong sense of values)
_____ physical appearance and attractiveness
_____ money and possessions
_____ charm
_____ prestige and status
_____ a strong sense of identity
_____ expressiveness and a tendency to be outgoing
_____ a sense of humor
_____ caring and sensitivity
_____ power
_____ independence
_____ a quiet person
_____ someone who will make decisions for me
_____ someone I can lean on
_____ someone who will lean on me
_____ someone I can't live without
_____ someone who works hard and is disciplined
_____ someone who likes to play and have fun

_____ someone who has values similar to mine
_____ someone I'd like to grow old with

Now list the three qualities that you value most in a person when you are considering an intimate relationship.

_____

_____

_____

2. What would a person discover in an intimate relationship with you? List the qualities you see yourself as having.

_____

_____

_____

3. Identify the kinds of intimate relationships you have chosen so far in your life. What have you learned from them? If you are not now involved in an intimate relationship, what stops you?

_____

_____

_____

4. What are the challenges and difficulties you face in being in a significant relationship? What do you get from being involved in a significant relationship?

_____

_____

_____

MEANINGFUL RELATIONSHIPS: A PERSONAL VIEW

In this section we share some of our ideas about the characteristics of a meaningful relationship. Although these guidelines pertain to couples, they are also relevant to other personal relationships. Take, for example, the guideline "The persons involved are willing to work at keeping their relationship alive." Parents and children often take each other for granted, rarely spending time talking about how they are getting along. Either parent or child may expect the other to assume the major responsibility for their relationship. The same principle applies to friends or to partners in a primary relationship. As you look over our list, adapt it to your own relationships, keeping in mind your particular cultural values. Your cultural background plays an influential role in your relationships, and you may need to adapt our ideas to better fit your core values. As you review our list, ask yourself what qualities you think are most important in your relationships.

We see relationships as most meaningful when they are dynamic and evolving rather than fixed or final. Thus, any relationship may have periods of joy and excitement followed by times of struggle, pain, and distance. As long as the individuals in a relationship are growing and changing, their relationship is bound to change as well. The following qualities of a relationship seem most important to us.

❯ *Each person in the relationship has a separate identity.* Kahlil Gibran (1923) expresses this thought well: "But let there be spaces in your togetherness, and let the winds of the heavens dance between you" (p. 16). Making long-term relationships work is difficult because it is necessary to create and maintain a balance between separateness and togetherness (Lerner, 1985). If there is not enough togetherness in a relationship, people typically feel isolated and do not share feelings and experiences. If there is not enough separateness, they give up a sense of their own identity and control, devoting much effort to becoming what the other person expects.

❯ *Although each person desires the other, each can survive without the other.* This characteristic is an extension of the prior one, and it implies that people are in a relationship by choice. They are not so tightly bound together that if they are separated one or the other becomes lost and empty. Thus, if a young man says "I simply can't live without my girlfriend," he is indeed in trouble. His dependency should not be interpreted as love but as seeking for an object to make him feel complete.

❯ *Each is able to talk openly with the other about matters of significance to the relationship.* Both people can openly express grievances and let each other know the changes they desire. They ask for what they want rather than expecting the other to intuitively know what they want and give it to them. For example, assume that you are not satisfied with how you and your mother spend time to-

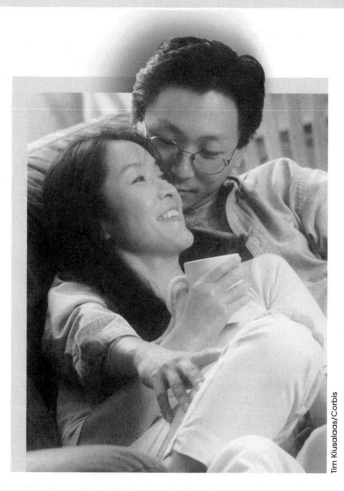

In a meaningful relationship, the persons involved are willing to work at keeping their relationship alive.

Tim Kiusalaas/Corbis

gether. You can take the first step by letting her know, in a nonjudgmental way, that you would like to talk more personally. Rather than telling her how she is, you can focus more on telling her how you are in your relationship with her.

❯ *Each person assumes responsibility for his or her own level of happiness and refrains from blaming the other if he or she is unhappy.* Of course, in a close relationship or friendship the unhappiness of the other person is bound to affect you, but you should not expect another person to make you happy, fulfilled, or excited. Although the way others feel will influence your life, they do not create or cause your feelings. Ultimately, you are responsible for defining your goals and your life, and you can take actions to change what you are doing if you are unhappy with a situation.

❯ *Both people are willing to work at keeping their relationship alive.* If we hope to keep a relationship vital, we must reevaluate and revise our way of being with each other from time to time. Consider how this guideline fits for your friendships. If you take a good friend for granted and show little interest in doing what is necessary to maintain your friendship, that person may soon grow disenchanted and wonder what kind of friend you are. Buscaglia (1992) puts this notion as follows: "If we want love in our relationships, then we are directly responsible for creating and maintaining it" (p. 190).

❭ *They are able to have fun and to play together; they enjoy doing things with each other.* It is easy to become so serious that we forget to take time to enjoy those we love. One way of changing drab relationships is to become aware of the infrequency of playful moments and then determine what things are getting in the way of enjoying life. Again, think of this guideline as it applies to your close friends.

❭ *Each person is growing, changing, and opening up to new experiences.* When you rely on others for your personal fulfillment and confirmation as a person, you are in trouble. The best way to build solid relationships with others is to work on developing your own personality.

❭ *If the relationship contains a sexual component, each person makes some attempt to keep the romance alive.* Although sexual partners may not always experience the intensity and novelty of the early period of their relationship, they can devise ways of creating a climate of romance and closeness. They may go to places they have not been before or otherwise vary their routine in some ways. They recognize when life is getting dull and look for ways to eliminate its boring aspects. In their lovemaking they are sensitive to each other's needs and desires; at the same time, they are able to ask each other for what they want and need.

❭ *The two people are equal in the relationship.* People who feel that they are typically the "givers" and that their partners are usually unavailable when they need them might question the balance in their relationships. In some relationships one person may feel compelled to assume a superior position relative to the other—for example, to be very willing to listen and give advice yet unwilling to go to the other person and show any vulnerability or need. Both parties need to be willing to look at aspects of inequality and demonstrate a willingness to negotiate changes.

❭ *Each person actively demonstrates concern for the other.* In a vital relationship the participants do more than just talk about how much they value each other. Their actions show their care and concern more eloquently than any words. Each person has a desire to give to the other. They have an interest in each other's welfare and a desire to see that the other person is fulfilled.

❭ *Each person finds meaning and sources of nourishment outside the relationship.* Sometimes people become very possessive in their friendships. A sign of a healthy relationship is that each avoids assuming an attitude of ownership toward the other. Although they may experience jealousy at times, they do not demand that the other person deaden his or her feelings for others. Their lives did not begin when they met each other, nor would their lives end if they should part.

❯ *Each person is moving in a direction in life that is personally meaningful.* They are both excited about the quality of their lives and their projects. Applied to couples, this guideline implies that both individuals feel that their needs are being met within the relationship, but they also feel a sense of engagement in their work, play, and relationships with other friends and family members.

❯ *If they are in a committed relationship, they maintain this relationship by choice, not simply for the sake of any children involved, out of duty, or because of convenience.* They choose to keep their ties with each other even if things get rough or if they sometimes experience emptiness in the relationship. Because they share common purposes and values, they are willing to look at what is lacking in their relationship and to work on changing undesirable situations.

❯ *They are able to cope with anger in their relationship.* Couples often seek relationship counseling with the expectation that they will learn to stop fighting and that conflict will end. This is not a realistic goal. More important than the absence of fighting is learning how to fight cleanly and constructively, which entails an ongoing process of expressing anger and frustrations.

❯ *Each person recognizes the need for solitude and is willing to create the time in which to be alone. Each allows the other a sense of privacy.* Because they recognize each other's individual integrity, they avoid prying into every thought or manipulating the other to disclose what he or she wants to keep private. Sometimes parents are guilty of not respecting the privacy of their children. A father may be hurt if his daughter does not want to talk with him at any time that he feels like talking. He needs to realize that she is a separate person with her own needs and that she may be needing time alone when he wants to talk.

❯ *They do not expect the other to do for them what they are capable of doing for themselves.* They do not expect the other person to make them feel alive, take away their boredom, assume their risks, or make them feel valued and important. Each is working toward creating his or her own autonomous identity. Consequently, neither person depends on the other for confirmation of his or her personal worth; nor does one walk in the shadow of the other.

❯ *They encourage each other to become all that they are capable of becoming.* Unfortunately, people often have an investment in keeping those with whom they are intimately involved from changing. Their expectations and needs may lead them to resist changes in their partner and thus make it difficult for their partner to grow. If they recognize their fears, however, they can challenge their need to block their partner's progress.

❯ *Each has a commitment to the other.* Commitment is a vital part of an intimate relationship. It means that the people involved have an investment in their future together and that they are willing to stay with each other in times of crisis and conflict. Although many people express an aversion to any long-term commitment in a relationship, how deeply will they allow themselves to be loved if they believe the relationship can be dissolved on a whim when things look bleak? Perhaps, for some people, a fear of intimacy gets in the way of developing a sense of commitment. Loving and being loved is both exciting and frightening, and we may have to struggle with the issue of how much anxiety we want to tolerate. Commitment to another person involves risks and carries a price, but it is an essential part of an intimate relationship.

Creating and maintaining friendships, especially intimate relationships, is a primary interest among many college students. There is no single or easy prescription for success; developing meaningful relationships entails the willingness to struggle. You may have encountered difficulties keeping your relationships alive. Many students say that they do not have enough time to maintain their friendships and other relationships. If this fits for you, realize that your relationships and friendships are likely to dissolve if you neglect them. Time must be devoted to nourishing and revitalizing your relationships if you expect them to last.

You can make choices that will increase your chances of developing lasting friendships:

> Be accepting of differences between your friends and yourself.

> Learn to become aware of conflicts and deal with them constructively.

> Be willing to let the other person know how you are affected in the relationship.

> Stay in the relationship even though you may experience a fear of rejection.

> Check out your assumptions with others instead of deciding for them what they are thinking and feeling.

> Be willing to make yourself vulnerable and to take risks.

> Avoid the temptation to live up to others' expectations instead of being true to yourself.

John Gottman, cofounder and codirector of the Seattle Marital and Family Institute, has conducted extensive research to determine what factors are associated with successful marital relationships. In their book, *The Seven Principles for Making Marriage Work*, Gottman and Nan Silver (1999) describe some key characteristics of a successful relationship.

> *Intimate familiarity:* Couples know each other's goals, concerns, and hopes.

> *Fondness and admiration:* When couples no longer feel honor and respect for one another, it is extremely difficult to revitalize the relationship.

> *Connectedness:* When individuals honor each other, they are generally able to appreciate each other's perspective.

> *Shared sense of power:* When couples disagree, they look for common ground rather than insisting their way has to be supreme.

> *Shared goals:* Partners incorporate each other's goals into their concept of what their intimate relationship is about.

> *Open communication:* Each person in the relationship can talk fully and honestly about his or her convictions and core beliefs.

Developing meaningful intimate relationships requires time, work, and the willingness to ride out hard times. Further, to be a good friend to another, you must first be a good friend to yourself, which implies knowing yourself and caring about yourself. In this Take Time to Reflect, we ask you to focus on some of the ways you see yourself as an alive and growing person, which is the foundation for building meaningful relationships.

Take Time to Reflect

1. What are some ways in which you see yourself as evolving in your relationships?

_____

_____

_____

2. Are you resisting growth and change by sticking with some old and comfortable patterns, even if they don't work? What are they?

_____

_____

_____

3. How is the person with whom you are most intimate changing or resisting change?

_____

_____

_____

(continued)

4. If you are involved in a couple relationship, in what ways do you think you and your partner are growing closer? In what ways are you going in different directions?

_____

_____

_____

5. Are you satisfied with the relationship you have just described? If not, what would you most like to change? How might you go about it?

_____

_____

_____

6. To what extent do you have an identity apart from the relationship? How much do you need (and depend on) the other person? Imagine that he or she is no longer in your life, and write down how your life might be different.

_____

_____

_____

A suggestion: If you are involved in a relationship, have the other person respond to the questions on a separate sheet of paper. Then compare your answers and discuss areas of agreement and disagreement.

ANGER AND CONFLICT IN RELATIONSHIPS

"We have never had a fight!" say some people proudly of their long-term relationships. Perhaps this is true, but the reasons couples do not fight can be complex. Buscaglia (1992) claims that many people try to disguise anger, sublimate it, suppress it, or project it where it does not belong. He adds that expressing anger often takes care of the situation, whereas repressed anger festers until it explodes. Iyanla Vanzant (1998) identifies anger as one of the most powerful emotions we can experience. She views passion as the driving force for life and also as the impetus for anger. Take a moment to think about how you view anger. How did you see anger expressed when you were a child? How do you deal with anger today? Are you able to express your anger? Do you deny your anger?

Expressing anger or dealing with a conflict situation may be difficult for you because of what you have learned and the messages you have heard about anger, conflict, and confrontation. Some of you have been told outright not to be angry. You may have observed harmful and destructive anger and made an early decision never to express these emotions (see the discussion of injunctions and early decisions in Chapter 3). You may have had mostly negative and frightening outcomes in situations involving conflict. If so, it may be necessary for you to challenge some of the messages you received from your family of origin about feeling and expressing anger.

> How was anger expressed in your home?

> Who got angry and what typically occurred?

> Did dealing with conflict and anger bring people closer together or move them farther apart?

> Is what you learned as a child about expressing anger and dealing with conflict helping or hindering you at this time in your life?

It is generally helpful to express persistent annoyances rather than pretend they do not exist. Ideally, sources of anger are best recognized and expressed in a direct and honest way. To be able to express your anger, however, there must be safety in the relationship that will enable you to share and deal with your feelings. If you cannot trust how your reactions will be received, chances are that you will not be willing to open yourself to the other person. To us, a sign of a healthy relationship is that people are able to express feelings and thoughts that may be difficult for the other to hear, yet the message is delivered in such a way that it does not assassinate the other person's character.

Clearly, recognizing and expressing anger can be valuable in relationships, but anger can also be destructive or dangerous at times. On a daily basis we see evidence that misdirected anger is harmful and destructive. Expressing anger in relationships is not always appropriate, is not always safe, nor does it always bring about closeness.

For many people the expression of anger becomes a reflex behavior that is easily escalated. It happens without thinking, and it takes much effort to change this pattern. Some of you may have learned that anger leads to withdrawal of a person's love. One of our colleagues talks about the violence of silence, which is a form of destructive anger. Dealing with anger by growing silent generally does not help the situation; rather, both parties tend to pay a price for withholding their feelings. Sweeping conflict under the rug may appear to work in the short term, but over time it typically exacerbates the situation.

Some people may be incapable of handling even the slightest confrontation, and no matter how sensitively you deliver your message, the outcome could be detrimental. If you find yourself in an abusive relationship where the outcome of anger is most often destructive, you will need to exercise great caution in how you confront that person. In such situations it may never be safe for you to express your feelings. If you recognize that anger is a problem in your relationship, we hope you will be willing to seek professional help. Many college counseling centers offer anger management workshops to assist individuals and couples in this area.

Ask yourself if you or your partner may have a problem dealing with anger and conflict. Recognizing these signs that indicate trouble may be the first step in bringing about change. Do you recognize yourself or your partner in any of these statements?

> What you say and what you feel are not congruent. For instance, you tell the other person that you are fine, yet you are feeling angry.

> You overreact to what is said to you, and your responses are extreme to anything that is difficult to hear.

> You typically walk away from conflict situations, or you avoid conflict at all costs.

> You respond without thinking and often have regrets later about what you said.

> You often have physical symptoms such as headaches and stomachaches.

> You know you hurt the other person, yet you are unwilling to acknowledge this to that person.

> You rarely resolve a conflict, assuming that time alone will take care of the situation.

> You focus on what the other person does wrong and rarely on what you could be doing differently.

> During every altercation, you bring up a litany of old grievances.

> You hold grudges and are unwilling to forgive.

It is difficult to change that which you are not aware of. But with awareness you can catch yourself in reflex behavior and begin to modify what you say and do. If some of these strategies are no longer working for you, try implementing these guidelines.

> *Recognize that conflict can be a healthy sign of individual differences.* Both individuals in a relationship can be strong. When this leads to differences of opinion, it is not necessarily true that one is right and the other is wrong. Two people can be right, and they can agree that they see an issue differently.

❯ *See confrontation as a caring act, not an attack on the other person.* Confront a person if you care and if you are interested in bettering your relationship. Rather than being delivered as an attack, confrontation can be an invitation to examine some aspect of a relationship. Even though the tendency is to get defensive and attempt to fault the other person, strive to really listen and understand the point of view of the other person.

❯ *If you do confront a person, know why.* Are you doing so out of concern? Are you expecting change in the way you deal with each other? Is your motivation to get even? Do you hope to enhance your relationship?

❯ *In confronting another, be careful not to issue dogmatic statements of who and what the other person is.* Instead of telling others how they are, say how they affect you. It is so easy for us to judge others and focus on all that they are doing wrong. It is more difficult to focus on ourselves and how we might change our response in difficult situations.

❯ *Resist the temptation to plan your next argument as another is speaking to you.* Learning to manage conflict situations is not about one person winning and another person losing. Successfully working through conflicts allows all the parties involved to be winners.

❯ *Deliver your message in a way that you would want to listen to if you were on the receiving end.* Would you want to stay and listen? Would you be inclined to talk more? Would you want to run away?

❯ *Accept responsibility for your own feelings.* Be aware of wanting to blame others for whatever you feel. At times it is easy to lash out at someone close to you simply because he or she is convenient. Be willing to examine the source of your feelings. Even though others may contribute to some of your feelings in a situation, this is very different from making others responsible for how you feel or how you relate to a situation.

❯ *Tell others how you are struggling with them.* Too often we leave out all the information that leads to a particular reaction. Instead, we give only the bottom line. We say, "You are insensitive and uncaring." Let others know all that you have been thinking and feeling as it pertains to them. It is not helpful to withhold your thoughts and feelings and then suddenly hit them with rejecting and judgmental comments.

❯ *Don't walk away from conflict.* Walking away from conflict does not solve the problem. However, when emotions are very highly charged and you are unable to resolve a conflict, it may be best to agree to resume discussing this issue at a later time. But do not pretend that the situation is resolved. Make a commitment to continue talking about the differences that may be separating you at a later time when both of you are able to listen to each other.

❯ *Recognize the importance of forgiving others who have hurt you.* If you desire intimacy with an individual, nursing grudges and pain will get in the way of closeness. Letting go of old grievances and forgiving others is essential in maintaining intimacy. Forgiveness does not imply that you have forgotten what was done to you. However, you no longer harbor feelings of resentment, nor do you seek to get even.

❯ *Recognize that it is essential to forgive yourself.* Sometimes others are willing to forgive us for causing them hurt, yet we may refuse to forgive ourselves for our wrongs. Morrie Schwartz (1996) offers this sage advice: "Learn to forgive yourself and to forgive others. Ask for forgiveness from others. Forgiveness can soften the heart, drain the bitterness, and dissolve your guilt" (p. 55). It is not just other people that we need to forgive—we need to forgive ourselves. As Gerald Jampolsky (1999) states, "I believe with all my heart that peace will come to the world when each of us takes the responsibility of forgiving everyone, including ourselves, completely" (p. 123).

In her commentary on forgiveness, Vanzant (1998) speaks of forgiveness as a release and a letting go. She writes: "Most people believe that when you forgive someone, you are doing something for them. The truth is, when you forgive, you are doing it for yourself. As it relates to forgiveness you must give up what you do not want in order to make room for what you do want (p. 168). Jampolsky (1999) believes forgiving others is the first step to forgiving ourselves. For Jampolsky, the purpose of forgiveness is to release us from the past. Forgiveness can free us from the grievances we hold toward others. He writes: "We can look upon forgiveness as a journey across an imaginary bridge from a world where we are always recycling our anger to a place of peace" (p. 18). He adds that through forgiveness we can let go of fear and anger. The process of forgiving heals the wounds associated with past grievances.

In *The Art of Dying,* Weenolsen (1996) lists a number of reasons it makes sense to forgive. Here are a few of those reasons:

❯ An unforgiven injury is a ballast that holds you down from a destined flight. When you let go, you will soar.

❯ People forgive at the end of life because it is their last chance to do so.

❯ Forgiveness can lead to a resurrection of love.

❯ Forgiveness is somewhat like "spiritual surgery" on the soul. It cuts away the rotten parts so that there is room for healthy growth.

Without doubt, one of the major stumbling blocks people involved in close relationships must face is learning how to deal with anger in realistic and appropriate ways. If we avoid putting one another down and avoid being emotionally or physically abusive, anger does not have to rupture the relationship. Once conflict is recognized and dealt with appropriately, forgiveness is possible, and we can let go of lingering resentments. This opens communication pathways that can deepen the relationship. In the next section, we examine some other communication blocks.

Take Time to Reflect

1. How did your family of origin deal with conflict? What did this teach you?

_____

_____

2. How do you deal with anger directed toward you?

_____

_____

3. How do you express your own anger in your current relationships?

_____

_____

4. What changes would you like to make, if any, in the manner in which you deal with conflicts in your relationships?

_____

_____

5. What importance do you place on forgiveness as a way to enhance significant relationships?

_____

_____

6. To what degree are you able to forgive yourself for any of your past regrets? How does this influence your ability to establish meaningful connections with others?

_____

_____

DEALING WITH COMMUNICATION BLOCKS

A number of barriers to effective communication can inhibit developing and maintaining intimate relationships. Here are some common communication barriers:

> Failing to really listen to another person

> Selective listening—that is, hearing only what you want to hear

> Being overly concerned with getting your point across without considering the other's views

> Silently rehearsing what you will say next as you are "listening"

> Becoming defensive, with self-protection your primary concern

> Attempting to change others rather than first attempting to understand them

> Telling others how they are rather than telling them how they affect you

> Reacting to people on the basis of stereotypes

> Being blinded by prejudice

> Bringing old patterns into the present and not allowing the other person to change

> Overreacting to a person

> Failing to state what your needs are and expecting others to know intuitively

> Making assumptions about another person without checking them out

> Using sarcasm and hostility instead of being direct

> Speaking in vague terms such as "You manipulate me!"

These barriers make it very difficult to have authentic encounters in which both people are open with themselves and each other, expressing what they think and feel and making genuine contact. Barriers between people who are attempting to communicate typically leave the participants feeling distant from each other.

In *That's Not What I Meant*, Deborah Tannen (1987) focuses on how conversational styles can make or break a relationship. She maintains that male–female communication can be considered cross-cultural. The language we use as we are growing up is influenced by our gender, ethnicity, class and cultural background, and location. Boys and girls grow up in different worlds, even if they are part of the same family. Furthermore, they carry many of the patterns they established in childhood into their transactions as adults. For Tannen, these cultural differences include different expectations about the role of communication in relationships, and the subtle gender differences in communication style can lead to overwhelming misunderstandings and disappointments. Although conversational style differences do not explain all the conflicts in relationships between women and men, many problems result because partners are expressing their thoughts and feelings in different ways (Tannen, 1991). If we can sort out these

Barriers make it very difficult to have authentic encounters in which both people are open with themselves and each other.

Scott Roper/Corbis

differences based on conversational style, Tannen believes we will be better able to confront real conflicts and find a form of communication that will enable us to negotiate these differences.

Rogers (1961) has written extensively on ways to improve personal relationships. For him, the main block to effective communication is our tendency to evaluate and judge the statements of others. He believes that what gets in the way of understanding another is the tendency to approve or disapprove, the unwillingness to put ourselves in the other's frame of reference, and the fear of being changed ourselves if we really listen to and understand a person with a viewpoint different from our own. Rogers suggests that the next time you get into an argument with your partner, your friend, or a small group of friends, stop the discussion for a moment and institute this rule: "Each person can speak up for himself only after he has restated the ideas and feelings of the previous speaker accurately, and to that speaker's satisfaction" (p. 332).

Carrying out this experiment requires that you strive to genuinely understand another person and achieve his or her perspective. Although this may sound simple, it can be extremely difficult to put into practice. It involves challenging yourself to go beyond what you find convenient to hear, examining your assumptions and prejudices, not attributing to statements meanings that were not intended, and not coming to quick conclusions based on superficial listening. If you are successful in challenging yourself in these ways, you can enter the subjective world of the significant person in your life; that is, you can acquire empathy, which is the necessary foundation for all intimate relationships. Rogers (1980) contends that the sensitive companionship offered by an empathic person is healing and that such a deep understanding is a precious gift to another.

Stereotypes as Barriers to Interpersonal Communication

A stereotype is a judgmental generalization applied to an individual without regard to his or her own uniqueness. Here are a few examples of stereotypes: "Men are unemotional and uncaring." "Lesbians hate men." "Asians are talented in mathematics." "Italians are emotional." "Women are passive." Stereotypes are very common in our society, partly because they make complex problems seem simple. But putting people in boxes is hardly treating them as individuals, and most of us would resist being categorized this way.

Stereotypes create boundaries that prevent us from seeing our interconnectedness as members of the human family. This social isolation limits our capacity to experience the richness that can be part of diverse human relationships. Unless challenged, our stereotypes can keep us separate and prevent us from getting to know people who could enhance our lives.

Prevailing assumptions are generally held onto tenaciously. People have a tendency to see evidence that supports their assumptions more clearly than evidence that challenges those assumptions. They are likely to call someone an "exception" rather than change a stereotype. For example, if you believe all men are "macho," you are likely to look for and find macho men. However, if you take on the challenge of disproving this generalization, you will likely find the opposite to be true also. In our professional work, we often challenge people who make unfounded assumptions or generalizations to look for evidence to disprove their hypotheses—or to prove the other side they tend not to consider.

Ask yourself how stereotypes get in your way of understanding people on an individual basis. Consider stereotypes you may hold and reflect on ways that they serve as barriers to getting to know another person:

❯ How are you affected by having certain characteristics assigned to you based on your gender, sexual orientation, ethnicity, culture, religion, age, or ability?

❯ How does the act of placing a label on you or on others affect your relationships?

Once you become aware of some stereotypes you may have bought into, explore where you acquired those beliefs. If you are interested in identifying and challenging any stereotypes you hold, the place to begin is to recognize specific instances when the way you think or behave is influenced by stereotyping. One thing you can do is to begin to look for evidence that will disconfirm the expectations you have about a particular group of people. Did you get messages from your parents? From people in your community? From your friends? From your teachers? Although you may have acquired stereotypes on a less than conscious level, once you become aware of their existence you are in a position to question their validity.

Effective Personal Communication

Your culture influences both the content and the process of your communication. Some cultures prize direct communication; other cultures see this behavior as rude and insensitive. In certain cultures direct eye contact is as insulting as the avoidance of eye contact is in other cultures. Harmony within the family is a cardinal value in certain cultures, and it may be inappropriate for adult children to confront their parents. As you read the following discussion, recognize that variations do exist among cultures. Our discussion has a Euro-American slant, which makes it essential that you adapt the principles we present to your own cultural framework. Examine the ways your communication style has been influenced by your culture, and decide if you want to modify certain patterns that you have learned. For example, your culture might have taught you to control your feelings. You might decide to become more emotionally expressive if you discover that this pattern is restricting you.

From our perspective, when two people are communicating meaningfully, they are involved in many of the following processes:

> They are facing each other and making eye contact, and one is listening while the other speaks.

> They do not rehearse their response while the other is speaking. The listener is able to summarize accurately what the speaker has said. ("So you're hurt when I don't call to tell you that I'll be late.")

> The language is specific and concrete. (A vague statement is "I feel manipulated." A concrete statement is "I don't like it when you bring me flowers and then expect me to do something for you that I already told you I didn't want to do.")

> The speaker makes personal statements instead of bombarding the other with impersonal questions. (A questioning statement is "Where were you last night, and why did you come home so late?" A personal statement is "I was worried and scared because I didn't know where you were last night.")

> The listener takes a moment before responding to reflect on what was said and on how he or she is affected. There is a sincere effort to walk in the shoes of the other person. ("It must have been very hard for you when you didn't know where I was last night and thought I might have been in an accident.")

❯ Although each has reactions to what the other is saying, there is an absence of critical judgment. (A critical judgment is "You never think about anybody but yourself, and you're totally irresponsible." A more appropriate reaction would be "I appreciate it when you think to call me, knowing that I may be worried.")

❯ Each of the parties can be honest and direct without insensitively damaging the other's dignity. Each makes "I" statements, rather than second-guessing and speaking for the other. ("Sometimes I worry that you don't care about me, and I want to check that out with you, rather than assuming that it's true.")

❯ There is respect for each other's differences and an avoidance of pressuring each other to accept a point of view. ("I look at this matter very differently than you do, but I understand that you have your own opinion.")

❯ There is congruence (or matching) between the verbal and nonverbal messages. (If she is expressing anger, she is not smiling.)

❯ Each person is open about how he or she is affected by the other. (An ineffective response is "You have no right to criticize me." An effective response is "I'm very disappointed that you don't like the work I've done.")

❯ Neither person is being mysterious, expecting the other to decode his or her messages.

These processes are essential for fostering any meaningful relationship. You might try observing yourself while you are communicating and take note of the degree to which you practice these principles. Decide if the quality of your relationships is satisfying to you. If you determine that you want to improve certain relationships, it will be helpful to begin by working on one of these skills at a time.

Communicating With Your Parents

Many of the people we counsel cling to an expectation of having perfect parents. They do not give their parents much room to be imperfect. Time and again they blame their parents for having done or having failed to do something. In the group they express this blame in a symbolic way, such as in role-playing exercises. But before they got involved in a group, they might have been engaging in blaming behavior for years.

If you desire intimacy with your parents, it is a good idea to put aside your need to remake them and to accept any small changes that they may make. Furthermore, rather than expecting your parents to make the first move, it would be more realistic to take the first step by initiating the changes in yourself that you are hoping they will make. For example, if you hope for more physical signs of affection between you and your parents, you might initiate touching. If you want more time with your mother and are angry that she does not ask for this time, ask yourself what is stopping you from taking this time with her. Persistence in asking for what you want sometimes does pay off. Too many people withdraw quickly when their expectations of others are not fully and immediately met.

Our experience with personal-growth groups has taught us how central our relationship with our parents is and how it affects all of our other interpersonal relationships. We learn from our parents how to deal with the rest of the world. We are often unaware of the impact our parents had, and continue to have, on us. Our groups are made up of people of various ages, sociocultural backgrounds, life experiences, and vocations; yet many of the members have ongoing struggles with their parents. It is not uncommon to have a 60-year-old man and a 20-year-old woman both expressing their frustration over not being accepted and affirmed by their parents. They are both intent on obtaining parental approval that they are convinced they need.

It is important to recognize the present effect that your parents are having on you and to decide the degree to which you like this effect. On one hand, you may have problems letting them be other than they were when you were a child. Although they may continue to treat you as a child, it could be that you behave around them as you did as a child and provoke this response. On the other hand, parents at times are reluctant to give up old parental roles; this does not mean that you cannot be different with them. You might become angry at your parents for the very things you are not willing to do, such as initiating closer contact or making time for the relationship. If you really want to be able to talk with your parents more intimately, you can take the first step. You can apply the principles of effective communication to enrich the time you spend with your parents.

GAY AND LESBIAN RELATIONSHIPS

Same-gender primary relationships are preferred by many people, but gay and lesbian relationships are not accepted as normal in our society. Our intention in including a discussion of gay and lesbian relationships is to dispel the myth that these relationships are basically different from heterosexual relationships. Common factors underlie all forms of intimate relationships; the guidelines for meaningful relationships presented earlier can be applied to friendships, parent–child relationships, and relationships between couples who are married or unmarried, gay or straight.

This section is not designed to be a comprehensive discussion of such a complex issue; rather, it is aimed at dispelling some of the myths and challenging some of the prejudices that lead to homophobia. You may be struggling over making a decision to declare your gay inclinations to others (or to acknowledge and accept them in yourself). You may be affected by the prejudices of others, and you may be trying to clarify your values and decide how you want to behave. We hope that this discussion will assist you in thinking about your views, assumptions, values, and possible prejudices.

Bruce Ayres/Stone

Same-gender sexual orientation can be regarded as another style of expressing sexuality.

Psychological Views of Homosexuality

How sexual orientation is established is still not understood. Some experts argue that sexual orientation is at least partly a function of genetic or physiological factors, and others contend that homosexuality is entirely a learned behavior. Some maintain that both an internal predisposition and an environmental dimension come together to shape one's sexual orientation. And there are those who assert that sexual identity is strictly a matter of personal choice. Many gay men, lesbians, and bisexuals report that they did not actively choose their sexual orientation anymore than they did their sex. Where they see choice entering the picture is in deciding how they will act on their inclinations. Some will see that they have a choice of keeping their sexual orientation a secret or "coming out" and claiming their affectional preference.

The American Psychiatric Association in 1973 and the American Psychological Association in 1975 stopped labeling homosexuality a form of mental illness, ending a long and bitter dispute. Along with these changes came the challenge to mental health professions to modify their thinking and practice to reflect a view of homosexuality as normal and healthy. Same-gender sexual orientation can be regarded as another style of expressing sexuality. And, as with any form of sexual expression, this style can be healthy or unhealthy, depending on the person and the social and psychological dynamics.

In our field of counseling we are surprised at the number of heterosexual counselors who see their proper role as actively trying to convert gay couples or gay individuals to a heterosexual preference, even if these clients do not have a problem with their sexual orientation. Mary Sykes Wylie (2000) writes that the current position of many evangelicals is that homosexuals cannot help being what they are and that their desire for same-gender partners is an "orientation," not a "choice." However, they believe *acting* on that unchosen orientation is both a choice and a sin. Wylie reports that "reparation therapy" is the goal of some Christian counselors who have the goal of loving gay people right out of their lifestyle and back into the straight Christian community.

Many gay people are not interested in changing their sexual orientation but seek counseling for many of the same reasons as do nongay people. In our consulting with counselors, we make our views quite clear. We see the counselor's job as helping clients clarify their own values and decide for themselves the course of action to take. We strongly oppose the notion that it is the role of counselors to impose their values on their clients, to tell others how to live, or to make their decisions for them. We believe it is unethical for counselors who are opposed to homosexuality on moral grounds to work with gay clients if they are unable to retain the objectivity necessary to effectively help them. The ethical course would be to acknowledge their bias and provide referrals to other professionals who are in a position to work with these clients objectively. It is not the counselor's job to persuade these individuals to change.

Prejudice and Discrimination Against Lesbians and Gay Men

In the past many people felt ashamed and abnormal because they had homosexual feelings. Heterosexuals frequently categorized them as deviants and as sick or immoral. For these and other reasons many gay and lesbian individuals were forced to conceal their preferences, perhaps even to themselves. Today, the gay liberation movement is actively challenging the stigma attached to sexual orientation, and those with same-gender partners are increasingly asserting their rights to live as they choose, without discrimination. However, just as gay men, lesbians, and bisexuals had won some rights and were more willing to disclose their sexual orientation, the AIDS crisis arose, once again creating animosity, fear, and antipathy toward the gay population. Much of the public continues to cling to stereotypes, prejudices, and misconceptions regarding behavior between same-gender couples.

In writing about being a gay adolescent male, Pollack (1998) maintains that the tough problems they face are caused not by homosexuality but rather by society's misunderstanding of homosexuality. According to Pollack, the stereotypes and stigma that burden gay people are very much like those faced by other minorities. Like any minority group, lesbians, gay men, and bisexual individuals are subjected to discrimination, which manifests itself when gay people seek employment or a place of residence. For instance, the Department of Defense does not allow openly homosexual individuals in the military. The "Don't ask, don't tell" policy still does not allow military personnel to be open about their sexual orientation. A special issue that lesbians, gay men, and bisexuals often bring to counseling is the struggle of concealing their identity versus "coming out." Dealing with other family members is of special importance to gay couples. They may want to be honest with their parents, yet they may fear hurting their parents or receiving negative reactions from them.

Ann and Berit, friends of ours from Norway, wrote this personal account of the development of their relationship.

ANN AND BERIT'S STORY

We met when we were in our early 20s while attending a teacher education program in Norway. Over the years we became close friends and spent more and more time together. Even though neither of us ever married, both of us had various relationships with men, which for the most part, were not very satisfying. As our friendship deepened, our interest in male companionship diminished and, when it was there, it seemed to be more in response to a societal "should" than an inner need.

Our families and friends often expressed concern and disapproval about the closeness of our relationship, which didn't appear "natural" or "normal" to them and which, they thought, might interfere with our "settling down with a good man" and starting a family. So we tried to keep our feelings for each other a secret for fear of rejection.

At one point, our relationship became a sexual one, a fact that brought out many of our self-doubts and vulnerabilities and the concern that, should we become separated, being sexually involved would make the parting even more difficult. Even though the sexual aspect didn't last long because of our concerns and doubts, our relationship continued. But the burden of pretending to be other than we were became increasingly heavy for us. We felt insincere and dishonest both toward each other and toward our families and friends, and we found the need to invent pat answers when others asked us why we were still single. We both felt that, if we had been honest, we would have said instead, "I'm not interested at all in a traditional marriage. I have a significant other, and I wish I didn't have to hide this very important part of my life."

Ann and Berit's situation was complicated by the fact that Ann lived in a small rural community near her extended family, which made it almost impossible to maintain a sense of privacy. Although Berit did not live near her family, she too felt she could not openly acknowledge her relationship with Ann for fear of being rejected by family, friends, and coworkers. In her early 30s Berit developed a range of anxiety symptoms over driving, being in a store, or even just going out of the house.

BERIT'S STORY

*B*ecause of my anxiety attacks, I went into therapy, and soon afterward my symptoms decreased greatly. I never felt a need to explore my preference for women, but I did spend a good deal of time on the conflict between my need to do what I thought was right for me and my need to give in to external pressure to be "normal."

At the age of 40, we made the decision that we could no longer live with the duplicity and that something had to be done. Either we would go separate ways, or we would share a life and acknowledge our situation openly. We decided to do the latter. After years of struggling, we were finally able to face ourselves, each other, and then the other significant people in our lives. Much to our surprise, when we did disclose the truth about our relationship, most of our relatives and friends were supportive and understanding, and some even told us that they knew of our "special" relationship. We felt a great burden had been lifted from us and began to experience a new sense of peace and happiness.

Just last year we got married. Ann's mother's first reaction to this was somewhat negative, probably because of her concern over what the neighbors and other relatives would think. However, when Ann's mother experienced nothing but positive reactions from her friends and family, her attitude changed and she accepted our marriage. My parents acted as if the marriage never took place. No remarks were ever made about the event, but they continued to treat both of us with respect, friendliness, and hospitality.

We got married first and foremost to protect each other financially. Although neither of us thought marriage would make any difference in our relationship, we now see that the marriage itself has been an important aspect in our lives. It has made us feel more confident being the "number one" in each other's lives. It also makes a difference as to how others view us as a couple. We are both happy to live in Norway, a country that allows people of the same sex to marry.

Ann and Berit's case illustrates the struggle that many couples go through as they make the choice of how they will live. Many of the issues that concern Ann and Berit are the same interpersonal conflicts that any couple will eventually face and need to resolve. However, they must also deal with the pressure of being part of a segment of society that many consider unacceptable. Thus, being involved in a gay or lesbian relationship is not simply a matter of sexual preference; it involves a whole spectrum of interpersonal and practical issues. All the concerns about friendships, heterosexual relationships, and traditional marriage that we explore in this chapter apply to gay and lesbian relationships as well. Indeed, barriers to effective communication are found in every kind of intimate relationship. The challenge is to find ways of removing the blocks that obstruct communication and intimacy.

In categorizing relationships as heterosexual or homosexual, we sometimes forget that sex is not the only aspect of a relationship. Whatever choice we make, we need to examine whether it is the best choice for us and whether it is compatible with our own values. Some people choose or reject specific gender roles because of others' expectations, and in the same fashion people may reject being gay merely because others condemn it or adopt it merely because they are unquestioningly following a liberation movement. What we think is important is that you define yourself, that you assume responsibility and accept the consequences for your own choices, and that you live out your choices with peace and inner integrity.

Take Time to Reflect

1. What are your reactions to people who have a same-gender sexual orientation?

_____

_____

_____

2. What are your views concerning the gay liberation movement? Do you believe the rights of gay men and lesbians have been denied? Should people who openly admit they are gay have rights equal to those of heterosexuals?

_____

_____

_____

3. Do you think anyone should be denied a specific job because of his or her sexual orientation alone?

_____

_____

_____

SEPARATION AND DIVORCE

The principles we discuss here can be applied to separations between people who are friends, to unmarried people involved in an intimate relationship, or to married couples who are contemplating a divorce. The fear of being alone forever often keeps people from dissolving a relationship, even when they agree that there is little left in that relationship. People may say something like this: "I know what I have, and at least I have somebody. So maybe it's better to have that than nothing at all." Because of their fears, many people remain stuck in stagnant relationships.

Freeing Ourselves From Deadening Ways of Being Together

An alternative to separating or stagnating is to remain in the relationship but challenge both yourself and your partner to create a different way of relating to each other. Often people are not very creative when it comes to finding new ways of living with each other, and they tend to fall into the same ruts day after day, year after year.

At its best, marriage is a relationship that generates change through dialogue. Instead of being threatened by change, we can welcome it as necessary for keeping the relationship alive. In this way an impasse can become a turning point that enables two people to create a new way of life together. If both partners care enough about their investment in each other, and if they are committed to doing the work necessary to change old patterns and establish more productive ones, a crisis can actually save their relationship. People often terminate their relationships without really giving themselves or others a chance to face a particular crisis and work it through. For example, a man begins to see how deadening his marriage is for him and to realize how he has contributed to his own unhappiness in it. As a result of changes in his perceptions and attitudes, he decides that he no longer wants to live with a woman in this deadening fashion. However, rather than deciding to simply end the marriage, he might allow his partner to really see and experience him as the different person he is becoming. Moreover, he might encourage her to change as well instead of giving up on her too quickly. His progress toward becoming a more integrated person might well inspire her to work actively toward her own internal changes. This kind of work on the part of both people takes understanding and patience, but they may find that they can meet each other as new and changing persons and form a very different kind of relationship.

Sometimes, of course, ending a relationship is the wisest course. Ending a relationship can be an act of courage that makes a new beginning possible. Our concern is that too many people may not be committed enough to each other to stay together in times of crisis and struggle. As a result, they may separate at the very time when they could be making a new start together.

When to Separate or Terminate a Significant Relationship

How do two people know when a separation is the best solution? No categorical answer can be given to this question. However, before two people decide to terminate their relationship, they might consider these questions:

❭ *Has each of you sought personal therapy or counseling?* Perhaps self-exploration would lead to changes that would allow you and your partner to renew or strengthen your relationship.

❭ *Have you considered seeking relationship counseling?* If you do get involved in relationship counseling of any type, it is important that both of you do so willingly. If one of you is merely going along to placate the other, little therapeutic work can be done.

❭ *Are you both really interested in maintaining your relationship?* Perhaps one or both of you are no longer interested in keeping the old relationship, but you both at least want time together. We routinely ask both partners in a significant relationship who are experiencing difficulties to decide whether they even want to preserve their relationship. Some of the responses people give include: "I don't really know. I've lost hope for any real change, and at this point I find it difficult to care whether we stay together or not." "I'm sure that I don't want to live with this person anymore; I just don't care enough to work on improving things between us. I'm here so that we can separate cleanly and finish the business between us." "Even though we're going through some turmoil right now, I would very much like to care enough to make things better. Frankly, I'm not too hopeful, but I'm willing to give it a try." Whatever your response, it is imperative that each of you knows how the other feels about the possibility of renewing the relationship.

❭ *Have you each taken the time to be alone, to get in focus, and to decide what kind of life you want for yourself and with others?* Few couples in troubled relationships arrange for time alone with each other. It is almost as if couples fear discovering that they really have little to say to each other. This discovery in itself might be very useful, for at least you might be able to do something about the situation if you confronted it; but many couples seem to arrange their lives in such a way that they block any possibilities for intimacy. They eat dinner together with the television set blasting, or they spend all their time together taking care of their children, or they simply refuse to make time to be together.

❭ *If you are married, what do you each expect from the divorce?* Frequently, problems in a marriage are reflections of internal conflicts within the individuals in that marriage. In general, unless there are some changes within the individuals, the problems they experienced may not end with the divorce. In fact, many who do divorce with the expectation of finding increased joy and freedom discover instead that they are still miserable, lonely, depressed, and anxious. Lacking insight into themselves, they may soon find a new partner very much like the one they divorced and repeat the same dynamics. Thus, a woman who finally decides to leave a man she thinks of as weak and passive may find a similar man to live with again, unless she comes to understand why she needs or wants to align herself with this type of person. Or a man who contends that he has "put up with" his wife for more than 20 years may find a similar person unless he understands what motivated him to stay with his first wife for so long. It is essential, therefore, that you come to know as clearly as possible why you are divorcing and that you look at the changes you may need to make in yourself as well as in your circumstances.

Sometimes one or both members of a couple identify strong reasons for separating but say that, for one reason or another, they are not free to do so. This kind of reasoning is always worth examining; an attitude of "I couldn't possibly leave" will not help either partner make a free and sound choice. Here are some of the reasons people give for refusing to call an end to their relationship:

❯ "I have an investment of 15 years with this person, and to end our relationship now would mean that these 15 years have been wasted." A person who feels this way might ask: "If I really don't see much potential for change, and if my partner has consistently and over a long period of time rebuffed any moves that might lead to improving our relationship, should I stay another 15 years and have 30 years to regret?"

❯ "I can't leave because of the kids, but I do plan to leave as soon as they get into high school." This kind of thinking often burdens children with unnecessary guilt. In a sense, it makes them responsible for the unhappiness of their parents. Why place the burden on the children if you stay in a place where you say you do not want to be? And will you find another reason to cement yourself to your partner once your children grow up?

"Since the children need both a mother and a father, I cannot consider breaking up our marriage." True, children do need both a father and a mother, but it is worth asking whether they will get much of value from either parent if they see them despising each other. How useful is the model that parents present when they stay together and the children see how little joy they experience? Might they not get more from two parents separately? Parents can set a better and more honest example if they openly admitted that they no longer choose to remain together.

❯ One man in a gay relationship may say, "I'm afraid to break off the relationship because I might be even more lonely than I am now." Certainly, loneliness is a real possibility. There are no guarantees that a new relationship will be established after one relationship is terminated. He might be reluctant to leave the relationship because his parents warned him of the problems he was getting into when he decided on an arrangement of living together. However, he might be more lonely living with someone he does not like, much less love, than he would be if he were living alone. Living alone might bring far more serenity and inner strength than remaining in a relationship that is no longer right for him. If he refuses to get out of a relationship because of what his parents might say about his original choice, he is almost certain to experience more alienation than he already does.

❭ "One thing that holds me back from separating is that I might discover that I left too soon and that I didn't give us a fair chance." To avoid this regret, partners should explore all the possibilities for creating a new relationship before making the decision to dissolve their relationship. There does come a point, however, at which a person must finally take a stand and decide. Once the decision to separate is made, it is fruitless to brood continually over whether he or she did the right thing.

At times, people find themselves in relationships that are emotionally or physically abusive, yet they are hesitant to leave these relationships. Abusive relationships have been getting a great deal of media attention, and people who have left abusive relationships often report that they did not recognize the full extent to which the relationship was toxic. Although they may have had opportunities to terminate the relationship, they rationalized that their situation was not really so bad. They often excuse the partner's behavior and find fault with themselves for bringing about the abuse. The individual doing the abuse might well demonstrate regret for hurting the partner and give promises to reform. However, soon afterward the same cycle repeats itself, and one person in the relationship feels trapped. Many times people stay in a relationship that is less than desirable because they do not know where else to go, nor do they know who can help them. Here are some signs that could indicate an abusive relationship:

❭ Verbal put downs
❭ Withholding love and affection
❭ Striking, hitting, pushing, shoving
❭ Using physical or psychological threats
❭ Making promises, yet never keeping them
❭ Unpredictable behavior
❭ Extreme jealousy and possessiveness
❭ Chronic hostility and sarcasm

Not all abusive relationships involve physical violence. Subtle emotional abuse over a period of time can also erode a relationship. Remaining in such a relationship generally makes it difficult for an individual to want to reach out and form new friendships. He or she often becomes numb and is cautious about trusting again for some time.

People sometimes remain in unhealthy relationships in the hopes that their situation will improve. Perhaps one of the partners believes he or she can change the other person. Frequently, this attempt ends in frustration. If you think you are involved in an abusive relationship, you need not remain a victim. Recognize what you are not getting with your partner, and do not discount reality.

We limit our options unnecessarily whenever we tell ourselves that we *cannot possibly* take a certain course of action. Before deciding to terminate a relationship, ask whether you have really given the other person (and yourself) a chance to establish something new. By the same token, if you decide that you want to end the relationship but cannot, it is worth asking whether you are not simply evading the responsibility for creating your own happiness. Neither keeping a relationship alive and growing nor ending one that is no longer right for you is easy, and it is tempting to find ways to put the responsibility for your decisions on your children, your mate, or circumstances. You take a real step toward genuine freedom when you fully accept that the choice is yours to make.

Coping With Ending a Long-Term Relationship

When a long-term relationship comes to an end, a mixture of feelings, ranging from a sense of loss and regret to relief, may be present. Betty, an unmarried college student in her mid-20s, is going through some typical reactions to the breakup of a 3-year relationship with her boyfriend Isaac.

BETTY'S STORY

*A*t first I felt abandoned and was afraid of never finding a suitable replacement. I kept wondering who was at fault. I switched back and forth between blaming myself and blaming Isaac. I was depressed, and I wasn't eating or sleeping well. Then I began to withdraw from other relationships too. I felt worthless and inadequate. Because my relationship with Isaac didn't work out, it proves that I'm a failure and unlovable and that I won't be able to establish and keep any other relationships. It is a sure sign that I'll never get along with any man. Isaac found me undesirable, and I don't think I can stand the pain of this rejection.

Internal dialogue such as this kept Betty miserable and kept her from taking any action that could change her situation. It was not the breakup itself that was causing Betty's reactions; rather, her beliefs about and her interpretations of the breakup were giving her trouble.

There are no easy ways to ending a long-standing relationship. After a breakup or loss of a friend or significant other, you will have feelings of pain, anger, and grief. However, if you find yourself in such a situation, we hope you will realize that there are some attitudes you can assume and some behaviors you can choose that are likely to help you work through your feelings associated with the breakup. Here are some suggestions for dealing effectively with the termination of a meaningful relationship:

> *Allow yourself to grieve.* Although grieving can be both overwhelming and painful, the alternative of cutting off your feelings will keep you stuck and make it difficult to move on.

> *Give yourself time.* As the saying goes, "Time heals all wounds." However long or short it takes, it is important to permit yourself to grieve based

on your own time clock and not because others feel you should be over it by now.

> *Express your anger.* Sometimes breakups leave us feeling angry and bitter. Remember that anger is a normal reaction, yet if unexpressed or overindulged in, it can poison you.

> *Depersonalize your partner's actions.* Often, when one person ends a relationship, the other is left feeling rejected and as if they were a failure for not making the relationship work. A person's decision to end a relationship may be more a reflection of them than it is of you.

> *Take responsibility for your own part in the relationship.* It may be easier to find fault in the other person, but exploring your own behaviors can be helpful in your healing process. The point is not to find blame but to gain insight into how you relate to people in both negative and positive ways.

> *Find a support network.* Whether you are shy or social, having people there to support you can provide you with some level of stability in a time of loss and change. Seek counseling or professional help if you feel that you cannot cope with the loss on your own. Most universities offer free student counseling.

> *Keep busy.* Setting aside time to grieve is important, yet obsessing over your situation does not change it. Pushing yourself to engage in some form of activity can help you stay connected to the aspects of your life that continue outside the relationship.

> *Write in your journal.* Writing can help you release emotions even if you are not able to talk to others about how you are feeling. Later, it can be useful to reread what you wrote and see how you may have grown since then.

> *Make amends.* Making amends and forgiving both yourself and your partner can free you from carrying the pain and anger into future relationships.

> *Get closure.* Coming to some type of closure is essential to moving forward. To one person it may mean forgiveness and for another it may include some type of a ritual or final letter.

> *Love and learn.* At some point you will find that it can be freeing to reflect on what you have learned from the experience. Even the most abusive or unhealthy relationship can teach us something about ourselves and the types of relationships we want to have.

Take Time to Reflect Complete the following sentences by writing down the first responses that come to mind. Suggestion: Ask your partner or a close friend to do the exercise on a separate sheet of paper; then compare and discuss your responses.

1. To me, intimacy means _____

_____

2. The most important thing in making an intimate relationship successful is

_____

_____

3. The thing I most fear about an intimate relationship is _____

_____

4. When an intimate relationship becomes stale, I usually _____

_____

5. One of the reasons I need another person is _____

_____

6. One conflict that I have concerning intimate relationships is _____

_____

7. In an intimate relationship, it is unrealistic to expect that _____

_____

8. To me, commitment means _____

_____

9. I have encouraged my partner to grow by _____

_____

10. My partner has encouraged me to grow by _____

_____

SUMMARY

In this chapter we have encouraged you to think about what characterizes a growing, meaningful relationship and to ask yourself these questions: "Do I have what I want in my various relationships?" "Do I desire more (or less) intimacy?" "What changes would I most like to make in my intimate relationships?" "In each of my relationships, can both the other person and I maintain our separate identities and at the same time develop a strong bond that enhances us as individuals?"

The themes explored in this chapter can be applied to all intimate relationships, regardless of one's sexual orientation. Although same-gender relationships are not well accepted in our society, it is important to realize that all couples share some common challenges. Rather than judging lesbians and gay men because of their sexual orientation, focus on understanding concerns and struggles that we all share.

A major barrier to developing and maintaining relationships is our tendency to evaluate and judge others. By attempting to change others we typically increase their defensiveness. A key characteristic of a meaningful relationship is the ability of the people involved to listen and to respond to each other. They are able to communicate effectively, and they are committed to staying in the relationship even when communication appears to have broken down. It is important to pay attention to both cultural and gender differences that make up our conversational style. Many misunderstandings are due to the different ways women and men express their thoughts and feelings.

Maintaining a relationship entails dedication and hard work. Although there are many sources of conflict in intimate relationships, a major problem is a sense of predictability that comes with knowing another person well. It takes both imagination and effort to think of ways to revise our relationships so that they remain alive. At times people decide that a relationship is "dead," and they give serious consideration to separating. Although this may be a solution for some situations, a relationship that has lost life can also be reinvented. Again, commitment is essential, because time will be required to resolve certain issues that are divisive and that cause conflict.

The ideal picture we have drawn of a growing relationship is not a dogmatic or necessarily complete one; nor will your relationships, however good they are, always approximate it. Our hope is that these reflections will stimulate your own independent thinking. You can begin by honestly assessing the present state of your intimate relationships and recognizing how they really are (as opposed to how you wish they were). Then you can consider the choices that can lead to positive change in those areas over which you are dissatisfied.

Throughout this chapter we have emphasized that we must actively work to recognize problems in ourselves and in our relationships if we are to make intimacy as rewarding as it can be. You can choose the quality of the relationships you want in your life.

❯ Where Can I Go From Here?

Some of these activities can be done on your own; others are designed for two persons in an intimate relationship to do together. Select the ones that have the most meaning for you, and consider sharing the results with the other members of your class.

1. In your journal write down some reflections on your parents' relationship. Consider these questions:
   ❯ Would you like the same kind of relationship your parents have had?

❯ Where Can I Go From Here? *(continued)*

> ❯ What are some of the things you like best about their relationship?
> ❯ What are some features of their relationship that you would not want in your own relationships?
> ❯ How have your own views, attitudes, and practices regarding intimacy been affected by your parents' relationship?

2. How much self-disclosure, honesty, and openness do you want in your intimate relationships? Reflect in your journal on how much you would share your feelings concerning each of the following with your partner. Then discuss how you would like your partner to respond to this same question.

> ❯ Your need for support from your partner
> ❯ Your angry feelings
> ❯ Your dreams
> ❯ Your friendships with other persons
> ❯ Your ideas on religion and your philosophy of life
> ❯ The times when you feel inadequate as a person
> ❯ The times when you feel extremely close and loving toward your partner
> ❯ The times in your relationship when you feel boredom, staleness, hostility, or detachment

Now think about how open you want your partner to be with you. If your partner were doing this exercise, what answers do you wish he or she would give for each of the items?

3. Over a period of about a week, do some writing about the evolution of your relationship and ask your partner to do the same. Consider why you were initially attracted to each other, and how you have changed since first meeting. Do you like these changes? What would you most like to change about your life together? List the best things about your relationship and some problem areas you need to explore. If you could do it over again, would you select the same person? What's the future of your life together? After you have each written about these and any other questions that are significant for you, read each other's work and discuss where you want to go from here. This activity can stimulate you to talk more openly with each other and can also give each of you the chance to see how the other perceives the quality of your relationship.

4. As you look at various television shows, keep a record of the messages you get regarding marriage, family life, and intimacy. What are some common stereotypes? What sex roles are portrayed? What myths do you think are being presented? Keep a record for a couple of weeks or so, and write down some of the attitudes you have incorporated from television and other media about marriage, family life, and intimacy. Do you want to rethink any of them?

Resources for Future Study

Web Site Resources

RELATIONSHIPS: THE COUNSELING CENTER, UNIVERSITY AT BUFFALO
http://ub-counseling.buffalo.edu/Relationships/

The counseling center at the University at Buffalo offers information on topics such as starting and ending relationships, communication, rape and surviving, and about men and women and lesbian, gay, bisexual, and transgendered people.

WHOLEFAMILY
http://www.wholefamily.com/

This site offers extensive information and resources on family life including the Marriage Center, the Parent Center, the Teen Center, the WholeFamily Room (where the family meets to get each other's points of view), the Senior Center, weekly dilemmas, publications, and articles on mothering.

DIVORCE CENTRAL
http://www.divorcecentral.com/

Divorce central provides information and advice on legal, emotional, and financial issues for individuals who are considering or going through a divorce. You can use all of their services and can become a member of their online community for free. Links to other divorce-related sites are also available here.

PARTNERS TASK FORCE FOR GAY AND LESBIAN COUPLES
http://www.buddybuddy.com/toc-cont.html

Partners Task Force for Gay and Lesbian Couples is a national resource for same-sex couples, supporting the diverse community of committed gay and lesbian partners through a variety of media. This frequently updated Web site contains more than 200 essays, surveys, legal articles, and resources on legal marriage, ceremonies, domestic partner benefits, relationship tips, parenting, and immigration.

 **InfoTrac College Edition Resources**

For additional readings, explore InfoTrac College Edition, our online library.

Go to **http://www.infotrac.college.com/wadsworth**

Hint: Enter the search terms:

   intimate relationships
   interpersonal relationships

intimacy

anger

anger management

conflict resolution

interpersonal communication

forgiveness

gay relationship

lesbian relationship

homosexuality

heterosexuality

divorce

Print Resources

Dworkin, S. H., & Gutierrez, F. J. (Eds.) (1992). *Counseling gay men and lesbians: Journey to the end of the rainbow.* Alexandria, VA: American Counseling Association.

Hendrick, S. (1995). *Close relationships: What couple therapists can learn.* Pacific Grove, CA: Brooks/Cole.

Jampolsky, G. G. (1999). *Forgiveness: The greatest healer of all.* Hillsboro, OR: Beyond Words.

Lerner, H. G. (1985). *The dance of anger: A woman's guide to changing the patterns of intimate relationships.* New York: Harper & Row (Perennial).

Lerner, H. G. (1989). *The dance of intimacy: A woman's guide to courageous acts of change in key relationships.* New York: Harper & Row (Perennial).

Napier, A. Y. (1990). *The fragile bond: In search of equal, intimate and enduring marriage.* New York: Harper & Row (Perennial).

Schwartz, M. (1996). *Morrie: In his own words.* New York: Dell (Delta Book).

Vanzant, I. (1998). *One day my soul just opened up.* New York: Simon & Schuster (Fireside).

Webb, D. (1996). *Divorce and separation recovery.* Portsmouth, NH: Randall.

Webb, D. (2000). *50 ways to love your leaver: Getting on with your life after the breakup.* Atascadero, CA: Impact.

When gender transcendence occurs, people can be just people—*Basow*

Bob Daemmrich/The Image Works

BECOMING THE WOMAN
OR MAN YOU WANT TO BE

> **Where Am I Now?**

Use this scale to respond to these statements:

4 = This statement is true of me *most* of the time.

3 = This statement is true of me *much* of the time.

2 = This statement is true of me *some* of the time.

1 = This statement is true of me *almost none* of the time.

_____ 1. It is important to me to be perceived as feminine (masculine).

_____ 2. I have a clear sense of what it means to be a man (woman).

_____ 3. It is relatively easy for me to be both logical and emotional, tough and tender, objective and subjective.

_____ 4. I have trouble accepting both women who show masculine qualities and men who show feminine qualities.

_____ 5. It is difficult for me to accept in myself traits that are often associated with the other sex.

_____ 6. I welcome the change toward more flexibility in gender roles.

_____ 7. I think I am becoming the kind of woman (man) I want to become, regardless of anyone else's ideas about what is expected of my sex.

_____ 8. I am glad that I am the gender that I am.

_____ 9. I feel discriminated against because of my gender.

_____ 10. My parents provided good models of what it means to be a woman and a man.

All of us are the product of our cultural conditioning to some extent. Behavior depends not on gender but on prior experience, learned attitudes, cultural expectations, sanctions, opportunities for practice, and situational demands. We learn behavior that is appropriate for our gender by interacting in society. Socialization is a process of learning those behaviors (norms and roles) that are expected of people in a particular society. Learning about gender differences does not cease with childhood; rather, it is a lifelong process.

In this chapter we invite you to examine the experiences that have directly and indirectly influenced your gender-role identity. This is a good time to ask questions such as "What did I learn about gender roles from my parents?" "From my culture?" "What attitudes prevailed in my home about gender roles, and how does this influence the woman or man I am today?" With increased awareness, you will be able to assess both the positive and negative effects your gender-role socialization is having on all aspects of your life. Then you can decide what changes, if any, you want to make. We encourage you to think critically about gender-role stereotypes and to form your own standards of the woman or man you could be and want to be. This assessment requires patience and an appreciation of the difficulties involved in overcoming ingrained attitudes. The real challenge is to translate the new attitudes that you may acquire into your actual behavior.

As you read this chapter, reflect on the models that have influenced your views of what it means to be a woman or a man and on the choices that are available to you. Societal norms provide one set of standards, but you can decide for yourself what kind of person you want to be based on what you truly value.

MALE ROLES

Increasingly, men are unwilling to be cast in the rigid male roles that were a basic part of their socialization. Rather, they are giving expression to both masculine and feminine dimensions of their personalities. However, far too many men in our society still live a restricted and deadening life, accepting the cultural myths about what it means to be "manly." These men are so involved in the many roles they play that they no longer know what they are like inside. They have put all their energy into maintaining an acceptable male image.

The pressures on men to behave in ways that conflict with traditional masculine models have never been greater. According to Ronald Levant (1996), men now face pressures to make commitments in relationships, to share housework, to view sexuality in the context of loving relationships, and to curb aggression. These pressures "have shaken traditional masculinity ideology to such an extent there is now a masculinity crisis in which many feel bewildered and confused, and pride associated with being a man is lower than at any time in the recent past" (p. 259). Traditional male roles certainly pose problems for men who dare to venture from what is considered to be "masculine" in our society.

Gender-role socialization begins early in life. Men's problems have their origin in what they learned as boys. In his discussion of society's messages to boys, Terrance Real (1998) states that boys learn early on that they should have fewer emotional needs than girls. While girls are encouraged to fully develop connection and relationship, boys are discouraged from developing their relational, emotional selves. Boys are encouraged to develop their assertive selves, while girls are discouraged from developing assertive action.

As toddlers, boys are pressured to leave their close relationship with their mothers so they can begin to become independent and self-reliant little men. William Pollack (1998) suggests that the sadness and disconnection men often experience stems from the loss of this relationship. Pollack describes boys in his clinical practice who appear adequate on the surface but who are suffering silently inside. They experience confusion, a sense of isolation, loneliness, despair, detachment from themselves, and alienation from parents, siblings, and peers. Real (1998) asserts that boys and men need social connection to the same degree as girls and women. Boys and men will not heal from their wounds of disconnection until they learn to place themselves inside relationships rather than above them:

> UNTIL A MAN HAS HALTED THE ACTING OUT OF HIS DISTRESS, dealt with his relationship to himself, and brought his mature self to acknowledge and deal with early wounds that remain very much alive within him, he will be inescapably impaired in his capacity to sustain a fully satisfying relationship. (p. 290)

During adolescence, boys are often subjected to shaming, and these messages are powerfully reinforced by "locker-room" experiences wherein boys are teased or isolated when expressing vulnerable feelings. Pollack (1998) asserts that because boys feel ashamed of their vulnerability they often mask their emotions and ultimately their true selves. Because society's prevailing myths about boys do not allow for emotions such as feeling alone, helpless, and fearful, boys frequently feel that they do not measure up. Eventually, their sensitivity is submerged until they lose touch with themselves and become "tough" in the way society expects them to be. The result of this socialization process is a gender straightjacket.

Pollack (1998) asserts that boys should be encouraged to show *all* of their emotions. In short, boys need to hear the message that all of their feelings are normal and "masculine."

> THEY NEED TO BE TAUGHT CONNECTION rather than disconnection. They need to be treated with the same kind of caring and affection we hope they'll be able to express when they become men in the next century. They need to be convinced, above all, that both their strengths and their vulnerabilities are good, that all sides of them will be celebrated, that we'll love them through and through for being the boys they really are. (p. 398)

In our work with men we find that many of them show a variety of the characteristics we will describe as part of the traditional male role. We see signs that many men are struggling to live up to culturally defined standards for male behavior. In the safe environment that group therapy can provide, we also see a strong desire in these men to modify some of the ways in which they feel they must live. For instance, they are willing to let other group members know that they do not always feel strong and that they are scared at times. As trust builds within the therapeutic group, these men become increasingly willing to share their deep personal pain and longings, and they struggle to accept this dimension of themselves. As these men become more honest with women, they typically discover that women are more able to accept, respect, and love them. The very traits that men fear to reveal to women are the characteristics that draw others closer to them. This often results in removing some of the barriers that prevent intimacy between the sexes.

Many men and women live a restricted life because they have accepted certain cultural judgments about what it means to be male or female. Unfortunately, too many people are caught in rigid roles and expect sanctions when they deviate from those roles. People often become so involved in their roles that they become alienated from themselves. They no longer know what they are like inside because they put so much energy into maintaining an acceptable image. This was certainly the case for Abraham, who learned traditional male attitudes and behaviors from his father.

ABRAHAM'S STORY

*M*y father was hard-working, distant with us children, stoic, and prized himself for being a self-reliant individual. I learned from my father what a man is supposed to be and what behaviors are acceptable, and these attitudes were reinforced in school and by society. For a long time I did not even realize I was being restricted psychologically by these expectations, but then I faced a crisis in midlife. My father had a heart attack, and I was shocked to realize the toll that living by traditional roles had taken on him.

I began to look at the impact my definition of maleness was having on all aspects of my life, and I decided to make some changes. I realized that I had never questioned my attitudes about gender-role behavior and that I was behaving unconsciously and automatically rather than by choice. I wanted to become more expressive, but I had to struggle against years of conditioning that restricted the range of my emotional responses. I did increase my level of consciousness intellectually through reading and personal counseling, but I seem to be having trouble catching up emotionally and behaviorally. It is more difficult than I thought it would be to turn these insights into new behaviors.

Both Abraham and his father suffer from "gender-role strain" (Pleck, 1995). Societal norms for gender ideals are often contradictory, inconsistent, and unattainable. When men are unable to live up to these unrealistic societal expectations, they are subject to many psychological problems. Men who experience gender-role conflict and stress are more likely to be depressed, anxious, express hostility in interpersonal behaviors, have poor self-esteem, harbor anger, misuse substances, and engage in high-risk behavior (Mahalik, 1999a).

The next section considers some of the aspects of the traditional masculine ideology by examining stereotypes of males and by identifying messages that men are given about appropriate role behavior.

Stereotypical View of Males

In general, the stereotypical male is cool, detached, objective, rational, worldly, competitive, and strong. A man who attempts to fit the stereotype will suppress most of his feelings, for he sees the subjective world of feelings as being essentially feminine. A number of writers have identified the characteristics of a man living by the stereotype and the feelings he may attempt to suppress or deny: Basow (1992), Goldberg (1983, 1987), Harris (1995), Jourard (1971), Keen (1991), Kimmel (1996), Lerner (1985, 1989), Lott (1994), Mahalik (1999a, 1999b), Mornell (1979), Pleck (1995), Pollack (1998), Rabinowitz and Cochran (1994), Real (1998), Rosen (1999), Weiten and Lloyd (2000), and Witkin (1994). Keep in mind that the following discussion is about the *stereotypical* view of males, and certainly many men do not fit this narrow characterization. It would be a mistake to conclude that this picture is an accurate portrayal of the way most men are. However, men in our society tend to hear messages that dictate ways they should think, feel, and act. The limited view of the traditional male role that many men have accepted, to a greater or lesser degree, is characterized by these traits.

> *Emotional unavailability.* A man tends to show his affection by being a "good provider." Frequently, he is not emotionally available to his female partner. Because of this, she may complain that she feels shut out by him. He also has a difficult time dealing with her feelings. If she cries, he becomes uncomfortable and quickly wants to "fix her" so she will stop crying.

> *Independence.* A man is socialized with the message that he should not look for help from anyone other than himself and to do things alone (Harris, 1995). Rather than admitting that he needs anything from anyone, he may lead a life of exaggerated independence. He feels that he should be able to do by himself whatever needs to be done, and he finds it hard to reach out to others by asking for emotional support or nurturing.

> *Power and aggressiveness.* A man hears the message that he must be powerful physically, sexually, intellectually, and financially. He is told that he must take risks, be adventurous, and resort to violence if necessary. He feels that he must

be continually active, aggressive, assertive, and striving. He views the opposites of these traits as signs of weakness, and he fears being seen as soft.

❯ *Denial of fears.* A man hears the message that it is important to appear brave even in situations where he is frightened. He will not recognize his fears, much less express them. He has the distorted notion that to be afraid means that he lacks courage, so he hides his fears from himself and from others. He lacks the courage to risk being seen as frightened. He fears being ashamed or humiliated in front of other men or being dominated by stronger men (Kimmel, 1996).

❯ *Protection of his inner self.* With other men he keeps himself hidden because they are competitors and in this sense potential enemies. He does not disclose himself to women because he is afraid they will think him unmanly if they see his inner core. A woman may complain that a man hides his feelings from her, yet it is probably more accurate to say that he is hiding his feelings from himself. A man's tendency to protect his inner self begins when he is a boy and learns to hide his inner core with an image of toughness, stoicism, and strength (Pollack, 1998).

❯ *Invulnerability.* He cannot make himself vulnerable, as is evidenced by his general unwillingness to disclose much of his inner experience. He will not let himself feel and express sadness, nor will he cry. He interprets any expression of emotional vulnerability as a sign of weakness. To protect himself, he becomes emotionally insulated and puts on a mask of toughness, competence, and decisiveness.

❯ *Lack of bodily self-awareness.* Common physical stress signals that men identify include headaches, nausea, heartburn, muscle aches, backaches, and high blood pressure. However, a man often ignores these stress symptoms, deny their potential consequences, and avoid addressing their causes. He doesn't recognize bodily cues that may signal danger. For example, it is well known that heart disease and cardiovascular disease death rates are significantly higher in men than women. According to Real (1998), men die early because they do not take care of themselves. They are slow to recognize when they are sick, take longer to get help, and even after getting treatment tend not to cooperate with it as well as women do. Too often a man will drive himself unmercifully and view his body as some kind of machine that will not break down or wear out. He may not pay attention to his exhaustion until he collapses from it.

❯ *Remoteness with other men.* Although he may have plenty of acquaintances, he does not confide in many male friends. Men have difficulty creating and sustaining same-gender friendships or communicating their emotional problems or vulnerability (Rosen, 1999). It is not uncommon for men to state that they do not have a single male friend with whom they can be intimate. He can talk to other men about things but finds it hard to be personal. When men talk to each other, it is often about planning what they are going to do.

❯ *Driven to succeed.* A man is told that it is important to win and be competitive to get recognition, respect, and status. He has been socialized to believe success at work is the measure of his value as a man. He feels he is expected to succeed and produce, to be "the best," and to get ahead and stay ahead. He measures his worth by the money he makes or by his job title. Real (1998) contends men measure themselves with unrealistically narrow and perfectionistic standards of masculinity that leave them feeling that they never sufficiently measure up. One of the heaviest burdens a man carries is his need to continually prove his masculinity to himself and to others. This drive to prove himself is a mask for deeper feelings of low self-esteem and insecurity (Rosen, 1999).

❯ *Denial of "feminine" qualities.* Men are frequently shut off from their emotional selves. From infancy through adulthood men are socialized to give short shrift to their emotions (Rabinowitz & Cochran, 1994). A man hears the message that he should always be in full control of his emotions. He cannot be a man and at the same time possess (or reveal) traits usually attributed to women. Therefore, he is highly controlled, cool, detached, and shuts out much of what he could experience, which results in an impoverished emotional life. He finds it difficult to express warmth and tenderness or to publicly display tenderness or compassion.

❯ *Avoidance of physical contact.* A man has a difficult time touching freely or expressing affection and caring for other men. He thinks he should touch a woman only if it will lead to sex, and he fears touching other men because he does not want to be perceived as effeminate.

❯ *Rigid perceptions.* A man tends to view gender roles as rigid categories. Women should be weak, emotional, passive, and submissive; men are expected to be tough, logical, active, and aggressive. He does not act in any way that might be perceived as feminine. He does not give himself much latitude to deviate from a narrow band of expression.

❯ *Devotion to work.* A man is socialized with the message that work is the most important part of his identity. He puts much of his energy into external signs of success through his achievements at work. Thus, little is left over for his wife and children, or even for leisure pursuits. A man's obsession with defining himself mainly through work provides an acceptable outlet for pent-up energy. The result of getting lost in his work is forgetting to make contact with his inner spiritual self and intimate contact with others (Rabinowitz & Cochran, 1994).

❯ *Loss of the male spirit and experience of depression.* Because he is cut off from his inner self, he has lost a way to make intuitive sense of the world. Relying on society's definitions and rules about masculinity rather than his own leaves him feeling empty, and he experiences guilt, shame, anxiety, and depression (Keen, 1991). The secret legacy of male depression is a silent epidemic in men, a condition they hide from their family, friends, and themselves to avoid the stigma of "unmanliness" (Real, 1998). Recovery from depression entails the willingness of a man to face his pain and learn to cherish and take care of himself. Not until a man captures his own spirit will he be able to value and care for others.

Men often hide their feelings of vulnerability and are ever watchful of others' reactions, looking for indications that they might be exposed to ridicule. Hiding their true nature is characteristic of many men, regardless of their racial, ethnic, and cultural background, but the dilemma of masculine identity is especially challenging for African American men who must reclaim the manhood stolen from them by slavery and oppression (Rosen, 1999). Literary images of freed Black slaves at the turn of the century address the familiar idea of the self-made man who would reclaim his manhood (Kimmel, 1996).

Audrey Chapman (1993), a therapist with a good deal of experience working with African American men, sees their desire to connect with someone after years of frustration at not "getting it right." These men are skilled at hiding their feelings, and they see crying as the ultimate affront to manhood. Underneath their surface bravado is likely to be a scared and lonely person. Chapman emphasizes how important it is to learn to listen and be patient when these men do express what they are feeling or thinking: "If I could stress only one issue with black women, it would be the necessity of understanding and accepting the fragility of our men's psyche. They desire and need bonding as much as we do, but they need a road map to get where they long to be" (p. 225).

The Price Men Pay for Remaining in Traditional Roles

What price must a man pay for denying aspects of himself and living up to an image that is not true of himself? First, he loses a sense of himself because of his concern with being the way he thinks he *should* be as a male. Many men find it difficult to love and be loved. As we have seen, they hide their loneliness, anxiety, and hunger for affection, making it difficult for anyone to love them as they really are. Part of the price these guarded males pay for remaining hidden is that they must always be alert for fear that someone might discover their inner feelings and what lies beneath the image.

Second, adhering to a rigid model of what it means to be a man keeps men looking for the perfect job, house, and partner to make them happy (Rabinowitz & Cochran, 1994). In this process men avoid knowing themselves and appreciating the richness of life. According to Weiten and Lloyd (2000), the principal costs to men of remaining tied to traditional gender roles are excessive pressure to succeed, an inability to express emotions, and sexual difficulties. Christopher Kilmartin (1994) addresses the costs of the masculine ideology:

> THE TRADITIONAL MAN can never get enough, and thus he can never really enjoy what he has. . . . Such a lifestyle often results in stress-related physical and psychological symptoms. . . . The damage that male gender roles do to the quality of connectedness to other people and to feelings about the self can hardly be overestimated. Many men feel alienated from their partners, children, and other men, and these feelings are often mutual. (p. 13)

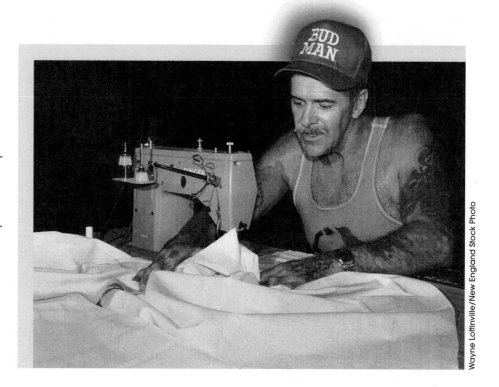

Some men are willing to break out of the rigid patterns of masculine behavior.

Wayne Lottinville/New England Stock Photo

If you are a man, ask yourself to what degree you are tied into your socialization regarding expected male patterns. What costs do you experience in striving to live up to what is expected of you as a man? Now might be a good time to reevaluate the costs associated with your gender-role identity and to consider in what ways, if any, you may want to alter your picture of what it means to be a man.

Challenging Traditional Male Roles

Are the traditional notions of what a man is supposed to be really changing in our society? Recent trends support the idea of an evolution of male consciousness, but change is a slow process. Some men are recognizing how lethal some of the messages they received are—not only for themselves but also for their relationships—and many others are challenging their childhood conditioning and are struggling to overcome stereotypes and to redefine what it takes to be a man. In our personal-growth groups we continue to encounter men who are willing to break out of the rigid patterns of masculine behavior they had adopted to conform to society's view. Leroy is one of those men.

LEROY'S STORY

*T*o me, life was a constant struggle, and I could never let down. I was a driving and driven man, and my single goal in life was to prove myself and become a financial and business success. Life was a series of performances that involved me pleasing others and then waiting for the applause to come. But the applause was never enough, and I felt empty when the applause would die down. So I continued to push myself to give more performances, and I worked 70 to 90 hours a week. I was on my way to becoming the president of a corporation, and I was thinking that I had it made. When I got my W-2 form, I became aware that I had made more money than was in my plan for success, yet I had had a miserable year.

Then one day I became ill, landed in the hospital, and almost died. I began to look at my life and slow down, and I realized there is a world out there that does not solely involve my work. I decided that I wanted to experience life, to smell more flowers, and to not kill myself with a program I had never consciously chosen for myself. I decided to work no more than 50 hours a week. With that extra time, I decided to smell life—there are a lot of roses in life, and the scent is enticing and exciting to me. I'll thrive on it as long as I can breathe.

At age 54 Leroy showed the courage to reverse some of the self-destructive patterns that were killing him. He began deciding for himself what kind of man he wanted to be rather than living by an image of the man others thought he should be.

Like Leroy, many men are showing a clear interest in men's consciousness-raising workshops. There is a great increase in the number of conferences, workshops, retreats, and gatherings for men. Some key books have provided impetus for the men's movement. One is the poet Robert Bly's best-selling book, *Iron John* (1990). According to Bly, men suffer from "father hunger," which results in unhappiness, emotional immaturity, and a search for substitute father figures. Bly writes and talks about the ways that having an absent, abusive, or alcoholic father results in the wounding of the sons. Bly says that many mothers look to their sons to meet their own emotional needs, which are often denied to them by their husbands, and that boys feel ashamed when they are not able to psychologically fill their mothers' longing.

Some men expect the women in their lives to heal their boyhood wounds caused by their fathers, but the wounded must be the ones who do the healing. One of the bases of men's gatherings is to share common struggles, reveal their stories, and find healing in the men's collective. Sam Keen (1991) focuses on men who lacked adequate male models who demonstrated healthy male behavior and talks about the importance of men writing their autobiographies in ways that can help them become aware of their family scripts and move away from the myths that formed their socialization. The fact that men from all walks of life are becoming interested in talking about their socialization from boyhood to manhood indicates that many men are rebelling against the steep price they have paid for subscribing to traditional role behavior.

Traditional gender roles are not completely unhealthy for everyone, but we want to promote the notion of individual choice in determining what aspects of these roles you may want to retain and what aspects you may choose to modify. To make this choice, you must first be aware of how you have been influenced by gender-role socialization.

Traditional males should not be told that they *must* change if they hope to be healthy and happy; indeed, many aspects of traditional roles may be very satisfying. However, many men are reinventing themselves without discarding many of the traits traditionally attributed to them. Look at the potential costs associated with your gender-role identity, and decide if you like being the way you are. The Take Time to Reflect exercises may help you discover some areas in your life that are ripe for change.

Take Time to Reflect

1. The following characteristics have been identified as gender stereotypes, some associated with women and others with men. Describe the degree to which you see each trait as a part of yourself. If you do not have this trait, explain why you would or would not like to incorporate this trait into your personality.

Emotional unavailability _____

_____

Independence _____

_____

Dependence _____

_____

Aggressiveness _____

_____

Denial of fears _____

_____

Emotional expressiveness _____

_____

Passive and submissive

_____

(continued)

Lack of bodily awareness _____

_____

Drive to succeed _____

_____

Avoidance of physical contact _____

_____

Rigid perceptions _____

_____

Devotion to work _____

_____

2. What are your thoughts about the price you pay for accepting traditional roles?

_____

_____

3. What are some specific qualities associated with each gender that you would most like in yourself?

_____

_____

FEMALE ROLES

Women today are questioning many of the attitudes they have incorporated and are resisting the pressures to conform to traditional gender-role behaviors. Gender roles are in a state of transition and will likely remain that way for some time to come (Weiten & Lloyd, 2000). Women are pursuing careers that in earlier times were closed to them. They are demanding equal pay for equal work. Many women are making the choice to postpone marriage and child-rearing until they have established themselves in careers, and some are deciding not to have children. Choosing a single life is now an acceptable option. Women are increasingly assuming positions of leadership in government and business. Women are refusing to stay in stifling or abusive relationships, and in dual-career marriages responsibilities previously allocated to one gender or the other are now often shared.

Despite these changes, women have not achieved equality with men in this society. For example, women's role in family life still places a great share of the responsibility on her. Women tend to be blamed for the breakdown of family solidarity, for abandoning their children, and for destroying their family by their selfishness in considering their own needs first. Even when both the woman and man work full time outside of the home, the majority of household labor still falls on the woman. Other family members still tend to believe that when they do participate in house work they are helping the woman with a responsibility that should primarily be hers (McGoldrick, 1999). Women's lives have always required great improvisation, but never more than today.

Like men, women in our society have suffered from gender stereotypes. Gender roles and stereotypes lead to a variety of negative outcomes with respect to self-concept, psychological well-being, and physical health (Basow, 1992). People tend to adapt their behavior to fit gender-role expectations, and women have been encouraged to lower their aspirations for achievement in the competitive world. Many women are concerned that they will be perceived as unfeminine if they strive for success with too much zeal. Women pay a price for living by narrowly defined rules of what women should be. Typically, women who achieve career success continue to carry the major responsibilities of parent and spouse, and an increasing number of women are expected to become caretakers of their own and their spouse's aging parents as well (Weiten & Lloyd, 2000).

Traditional Roles for Women

Traditional gender stereotypes categorize women as passive, dependent, and unaccomplished. But women are increasingly beginning to risk operating outside these narrow limits. As you examine these stereotypic characteristics of the traditional portrait of femininity, think about your own assumptions about appropriate gender roles.

> *Women are warm, expressive, and nurturing.* In their relationships with other women and with men, women are expected to be kind, thoughtful, and caring. Women are so attuned to giving that they often do not allow themselves to receive nurturance. Until recently, women's development was defined by the men in their lives. Their role was defined by their position in another's life, such as mother, daughter, sister, or grandmother. Rarely has there been acceptance of the notion of a woman having a right to a life for herself (McGoldrick, 1999).

> *Women are not aggressive or independent.* If women act in an assertive manner, they may be viewed as being hard and aggressive. If women display independence, men may accuse them of trying to "prove themselves" by taking on

masculine roles. Those women who are independent often struggle within themselves over being too powerful or not needing others.

❯ *Women are emotional and intuitive.* Women who defy their socialization may have trouble getting their emotional needs recognized. But women can be emotional and rational at the same time. Having an intuitive nature does not rule out being able to think and reason logically.

❯ *Women are passive and submissive.* A home orientation, being prone to tears and excitability in minor crises, indecisiveness, religiosity, and tactfulness are expected of the female role. If women deviate from these behavior patterns, they run the risk of being "unfeminine."

❯ *Women are more interested in relationships than in professional accomplishments.* Rather than competing or striving to get ahead, women are expected to maintain relationships. Many women are concerned about the quality of their relationships, but at the same time they are also interested in accomplishing goals they set for themselves.

Some of the problems associated with the traditional female role include diminished aspiration, juggling multiple roles, problems stemming from unequal sharing of role responsibilities, ambivalence about sexuality, and facing sexism and discrimination in the world of work (Weiten & Lloyd, 2000). Just as subscribing to traditional male roles stifles creativity in men, unthinkingly accepting traditional roles can result in greatly restricting the range of women. Women can be both dependent and independent, give to others and be open to receiving, think and feel, and be tender and firm. Women who are rejecting traditional roles are embracing this complex range of characteristics.

If you are a woman, ask yourself to what degree you are tied to your socialization regarding expected female patterns. Now might be a good time to reevaluate the costs associated with your gender-role identity and to consider whether you want to alter your picture of what it means to be a woman.

If you are a man, reflect on how you have been affected by female roles and ways you may want to change in relation to women. Consider the flexibility you might gain if women had a wider range of traits and behaviors available to them.

Challenging Traditional Female Roles

Basow (1992) cites considerable research evidence supporting the existence of gender stereotypes, but there are signs that women are increasingly recognizing the price they have been paying for staying within the limited boundaries set for them by their culture. We are realizing that gender stereotypes influence societal practices, discrimination, individual beliefs, and sexual behavior itself. Basow emphasizes that gender stereotypes are powerful forces of social control but that women can choose either to be socially acceptable and conform or to rebel and deal with the consequences of being socially unacceptable. Sensitizing ourselves

Challenging traditional
female roles.

Ranald Mackechnie/Stone

to the process of gender-role development can help us make choices about modifying the results of our socialization. Women are beginning to take actions that grow out of their awareness.

The changing structure of gender relations has altered what women expect of men and the role men play in women's lives. According to Kathleen Gerson (1987), the so-called traditional family has given way to a variety of family and household forms, and it becomes difficult to argue that the traditional division of labor between the sexes is natural, inevitable, or morally superior. There is no single standard of family life. Among the new options are equity in parenting and freedom from family commitments. Gerson writes that the larger social changes are promising women new sources of power but also bringing about new insecurities. In *Composing a Life,* Mary Catherine Bateson (1990) claims that the guidelines for composing a life are no longer clear for either sex. Especially for women, previous generations can no longer be used as a model. For women, some of the basic concepts used to design a life—work, home, love, commitment—have different meanings today. Becoming a fulfilled women entails challenging both societal and internal barriers. Lin's story reveals a woman who fought traditional socialization.

I grew up in a family where my parents' gender roles were at times reversed, and at other times mixed and ambiguous, but never traditional. This affected me in several ways. I developed into a girl whose behavior and dress was nontraditional. I experienced conflict within myself relating to the nontraditional roles my parents played. There was anger at times at both my mother and my father for not being like "other" parents.

I wasn't raised as a little boy or as a little girl. This was not deliberate or conscious, it was just how two adults whose own roles were mixed would raise children. I ended up being a tom boy—wearing a baseball cap and pants under my dresses. I climbed trees and played for hours in my self-made mud pools. Fortunately, I was never criticized or discouraged. It seemed that the way I was acting out my gender role was not an issue for my parents. I don't ever remember being told to "act like a young lady" or "girls shouldn't do that," although one time my mother reprimanded me for taking such wide strides when I walk. I remember it being a bit of a shock to me because I had never noticed my stride before. To this day, I'm conscious at times of my stride.

It wasn't until around the age of 12 that I began to feel the discomfort of not behaving like all the other girls. The discomfort was internal. I don't remember it ever being noticed or brought up by other kids. I felt different because the other girls seemed different. I just didn't ever feel "girly."

I didn't experience any external pressures until I had my first boyfriend. These pressures were limited to my sister's macho boyfriend who would state that I "was the one who wore the pants" and I was "the boss." These comments would feed into my own insecurities and conflicts about not being the type of girl I was "supposed" to be—and about having a boyfriend who was not being the type of man he was "supposed" to be. I often feel too strong, and my boyfriends seem too weak. I'm embarrassed sometimes because I "control" the relationship. And I'm embarrassed because the woman is not supposed to be in control. I don't choose this position; it just happens naturally, or so it seems.

I feel this internal conflict in my workplace also. I feel like I'm supposed to be wearing skirts, dresses, and heels. But I don't wear these things, and at times I feel like I'm somehow less of a woman. I sometimes feel bad that I'm not as chatty as most of the women I work with. I've heard that people think I'm arrogant—and I assume it's because I don't stop and talk to everyone who walks across my path. I think that a good percentage of men would not like me because I'm not feminine enough. I'm too strong and too opinionated. I'm not passive. And I doubt that I'd ever be described as a "sweet girl/woman."

I have bouts of hating that I am all these things. Society seems to be whispering that I am a bitch if I am not sweet and selfless. My bouts of disliking that I am who I am are closely matched by my strength, which says: Who cares! I am who I am. I'm proud that I am strong and able and smart and opinionated. As I surround myself with more and more women who are like me, I am calmed. I'm proud of these women and continually try to remind myself that I should be proud of myself too.

Women and Work Choices

The number and proportion of women employed in the workplace is increasing, and more women are now looking to an occupation outside the home as a major source of their identity (Lock, 2000a). By 2020, women are expected to make up half of the United States labor force (Judy & D'Amico, 1997). Many women work not only out of choice but also out of necessity. Some feel the pressure of taking care of the home and holding down an outside job to help support the family. In writing about women and work, McGoldrick (1999) makes it clear that there are many social pressures against women feeling good about working outside of the home. She notes that it is not merely the number of activities that is burdensome to a woman's well-being. Instead, it is her inability to choose her roles in meeting the demands she faces. McGoldrick adds that paid work actually improves the health of women. Women who work outside the home tend to show fewer symptoms of psychological and physical distress.

Single parents often face tremendous pressures in providing for their families and have no other viable option other than working. Consider the case of Deborah, who after her divorce said, "I know I can survive, but it's scary for me to face the world alone. Before, my job was an additional source of income and something I did strictly out of choice. Now a job is my livelihood and the means to support my children."

Although women are found working in virtually all areas of the economy, their numbers are still small in jobs traditionally performed by men. And although some progress has been made with respect to gender equity in the world of work, many challenges must still be met before women achieve equality with men in the workforce. In *Backlash*, Susan Faludi (1991) points out that about a third of the new jobs for women were at or below the poverty level—jobs that men turned down. In addition, the average woman earns considerably less than the average man in the same occupational category, receives fewer benefits, and works under poorer conditions.

According to Carney and Wells (1999), surveys indicate that social change is accelerating as different options are becoming available to women who want to combine a career with marriage and a family. The challenge for these women is learning how to balance the difficult demands of a two-career family. Changes in women's choices do influence the attitudes of both women and men with respect to work, marriage, and children. Increasing numbers of women are postponing marriage and having children so they can pursue an education and a career. It appears that homemakers and workers of both genders are returning to school or to work after their 20s to launch new careers. Women are assuming greater influence in corporate settings.

Other women are making the choice to find their fulfillment primarily through the roles of wife, mother, and homemaker. These women are not assuming these roles because they feel that they must or because they feel that they cannot enter the world of work; they want to devote most of their time to their family. These women often struggle with feeling that they should want a career outside the home, because they have heard so much about finding satisfaction in that way. But they do not feel incomplete without an outside career, and they need to learn how to feel comfortable with their choice.

One woman we know, Valerie, talks about the importance of accepting her choice, despite reactions from others that she should not settle for being "merely" a mother. Valerie and her husband, Phil, had agreed that after they had children both would continue working.

VALERIE'S STORY

*W*hen our first child was born, I continued to work as planned. What I had not foreseen was the amount of energy and time it took to care for our son, Dustin. Most important, I hadn't realized how emotionally attached I would become to him. My work schedule was extremely demanding, and I was only able to see Dustin awake for one hour a day. Phil was being Mr. Mom in the evening until I returned home, which eventually strained our marriage. I felt torn. When I was working, I felt I should be at home. I began to feel jealous of the babysitter, who had more time with Dustin than I did.

When our second son, Vernon, was born, I quit my job. Because we primarily depended on Phil's income, we thought it best that I stay home with our children. Some of my friends are pursuing a career while they take care of a family. For me, it was too difficult to manage both to my satisfaction. It means a lot to me to be involved in my sons' activities and have an influence on their lives. I have been active as a volunteer in their school, which I find very rewarding. Some of my friends cannot understand why I stay home, but I know I'm in the place where I need to be—for them and for me.

I do intend to return to my career once Vernon and Dustin begin high school, and at times I miss the stimulation my job provided. But overall I have no regrets about our decision.

Women in Dual-Career Families

One of the realities of our time is that more married women now have full-time jobs outside the home. Although a career meets the needs of many women who want something more than taking care of their families, it dramatically increases their responsibilities. Unless their husbands are willing to share in the day-to-day tasks of maintaining a home and rearing children, these women often experience fragmentation. Some women burden themselves with the expectation that they should perform perfectly as workers, mothers, and wives. Women who feel the pressures of doing too much need to reevaluate their priorities and decide how they want to live. Eventually, many women realize that they simply cannot continue to balance career and home responsibilities, and they finally exclaim that enough is enough! For women who are trying to do it all, Betty Friedan's advice is worth considering: Yes, women can have it all, but just not all at once.

Women in dual career families face high self-expectations.

Raoul Minsart/Corbis

Maureen, a physician, is another woman facing the challenge of a dual career. She holds a teaching position at a hospital. In addition to practicing medicine, she must teach interns, keep current in her field, and publish.

MAUREEN'S STORY

I enjoy pretty much everything I'm doing, but I do feel a lot of pressure in doing all that needs to be done. Much of the pressure I feel is over my conviction that I have to be an outstanding practitioner, teacher, and researcher and must also be fully available as a mother and a wife. There is also pressure from my husband, Daniel, to assume the bulk of the responsibility for taking care of our son and for maintaining the household. With some difficulty Daniel could arrange his schedule to take an increased share of the responsibility, but he expects me to consider his professional career above my own. I need to leave my job early each day to pick up our son from the day-care center. I fight traffic and get myself worked up as I try to get to the center before it closes. I put myself under a great deal of stress holding up all my roles. I feel the toll balancing family and work responsibilities is taking on my physical and emotional well-being.

Some women experience a lack of support and an actual resistance from the men in their lives when they do step outside traditional roles and exercise their options. Although Maureen did not get much resistance from her husband about maintaining her career, she received very little active support to make balancing her double life possible. The power resided with her husband, and she was expected to make decisions that would not inconvenience him greatly. Basow (1992) notes that men typically have been the dominant sex, with most of the power, and it is difficult for them to share this power with women. Those husbands who see themselves as liberated are put to the test when they are expected to assume increased responsibilities at home. They may say that they want their wives to "emerge and become fulfilled persons" but also send messages such as: "Don't go too far! If you want, have a life outside of the home, but don't give up any of what you are doing at home." A woman who has to fight her husband's resistance may have an even more difficult fight with herself. Both husband and wife may need to reevaluate how realistic it is to expect that she can have a career and also assume the primary responsibility for the children, along with doing all the tasks to keep a home going. Both parties need to redefine and renegotiate what each is willing to do and what each considers essential. Ideally, women and men should be free to choose which, if either, spouse stays at home. But we have yet to reach this ideal state.

Dual-career couples are often challenged to renegotiate the rules that governed the early phase of their relationship. Such is the case with Deloras and Carlos. Deloras, a reentry college student who also works, reports that she generally likes most aspects of her life, yet her relationship with her husband is strained because of the direction in which she is moving.

DELORAS'S STORY

*W*here I struggle is with my husband, who would prefer a traditional stay-at-home wife and mother. Now that I am older, I want to discover who I am. What is sad and painful for me is that Carlos doesn't seem to appreciate the woman I am becoming. He prefers the old "doer" that I was. But I won't go back to the compliant person I was, and I will not sacrifice my true feelings and thoughts to please others.

I appreciate the importance of negotiation and listening to my husband. I still love and care for him, but I am grieving because I don't have the relationship I long for. I desire a good and honest relationship where both of us are willing to be challenged and are open to change. I will be disappointed if we never get to that place.

In both of the cases just described, the husbands are resisting the growth of their wives. They do not see their wives as equal partners.

In dual-career families, both partners must be willing to renegotiate their relationship. Belinda and Burt have tried to establish a more equal partnership. Belinda is a professional woman with a husband and three young children. Her husband, Burt, shows a great deal of interest in Belinda's personal and professional advancement. She often tells her colleagues at work how much support she gets from him. When Bert was offered a higher paying job that entailed a move to another state, he declined the offer after a full discussion with his wife and children. They decided that the move would be too disruptive for all concerned. During the times when Belinda is experiencing the most pressure at work, Bert is especially sensitive and takes on more responsibility for household chores and for taking care of their children. This is an example of a dual-career couple who have created a more equitable division of responsibilities.

Just as a woman can question the traditional female stereotype, she can also question the myth that a successful and independent woman doesn't need anyone and can make it entirely on her own. This trap is very much like the trap that many males fall into and may even represent an assimilation of traditional male values. Ideally, a woman will learn that she can achieve independence, exhibit strength, and succeed while at times being dependent and in need of nurturing. Real strength allows either a woman or a man to be needy and to ask for help without feeling personally inadequate.

Relationships are often challenged as one person in the relationship moves beyond restrictive role conformity. Guiza is one of the many women struggling to break out of rigid traditional roles and move toward greater choice and self-expression. She describes the nature of her struggle.

GUIZA'S STORY

*I*n high school I was an exceptional student and had aspirations to go to college, but I was discouraged by my family. Instead, they encouraged me to marry the "nice guy" I had been dating through high school, letting me know that I would risk losing David if I went off to college. My parents told me that David could provide a good future for me and that it was not necessary for me to pursue college or a career. Without much questioning of what I was told, I got married and had two children. Others thought I had a good life, that I was well provided for and that my husband David and I were getting along well. For me, I remember first feeling restless and dissatisfied with my life when my children went to school. David was advancing in his career and was getting most of his satisfaction from his work. Around him, I felt rather dull and had a vague feeling that something was missing from my life. I had never forgotten my aspiration to attend college, and I eventually enrolled. Although David was not supportive initially, he later encouraged me to complete my education. But he made it perfectly clear that he expected me not to neglect my primary responsibilities to the family.

(continued)

As I was pursuing my college education, I often had to make difficult choices among multiple and sometimes conflicting roles. Sometimes I felt guilty about how much I enjoyed being away from my family. For the first time in my life I was being known as Guiza and not as someone's daughter or wife. Although at times David felt threatened by my increasing independence from him, he did like and respect the person I was becoming.

Guiza's situation illustrates that women can successfully shed traditional roles they have followed for many years and define new roles for themselves. Some of the themes that she and many women like her struggle with are dependence versus independence, fear of success, looking outside of yourself for support and direction, expecting to be taken care of, and questioning the expectations of others.

Take Time to Reflect

1. Examine your stance on topics pertaining to roles of women. In the blank, write "A" if you agree and "D" if you disagree with the statement.

_____ Women's socialization discourages achievement in a competitive world.

_____ Like men, women pay a price for living by narrowly defined rules of what women should be.

_____ Many women are labeled unfeminine if they strive for success, especially by men.

_____ Women traditionally are encouraged to be passive and dependent.

_____ Women are naturally more nurturing than men.

_____ Women tend to respond emotionally to a situation, and because of that are often times considered to be irrational.

_____ Women are still subject to discrimination in our society.

_____ Women have more opportunity today to attain equality with men in the workplace.

_____ Most women tend to feel more fulfilled if they work in and out of the home.

_____ Many women today reject rigid gender roles.

2. What challenges must women face in dual-career families? What are the challenges men face in dual-career families?

_____

_____

3. What challenges do marriages face in dual-career families?

_____

_____

4. What are your thoughts about the price women must pay for accepting traditional roles?

_____

_____

5. What specific qualities do you most respect in women?

_____

_____

ALTERNATIVES TO RIGID GENDER-ROLE EXPECTATIONS

The prevalence of certain male and female stereotypes in our culture does not mean that all men and women live within these narrow confines. Tavris (1992) rejects the idea that men and women have a set of fixed personality characteristics (masculine or feminine traits) that define them. It is freeing to recognize that the qualities and behaviors expected of women and men may vary, depending on situations. Tavris suggests that the challenge is for women and men to work together in rethinking how they want to be so that they will be able to have the kind of relationships they want.

We can actively define our own standards of what we want to be like as women or as men. We do not have to blindly accept roles and expectations that have been imposed on us or remain victims of our early conditioning—or of our own self-socialization. It is possible for us to begin achieving autonomy in our gender identity by looking at how we have formed our ideals and standards and who our models have been; then we can decide whether these are the standards we want to use in defining our gender-role identity now.

We are in a transitional period in which men and women are redefining themselves and ridding themselves of old stereotypes; yet too often we needlessly fight with each other when we could be helping each other be patient as we learn new patterns of thought and behavior. Women and men need to remain open to each other and be willing to change their attitudes if they are interested in releasing themselves from stereotyped and rigid roles. As women and men alike pay closer attention to deeply ingrained attitudes, they may find that they have not caught up emotionally with their intellectual level of awareness. Although we might well be "liberated" intellectually and know what we want, many of us have difficulty feeling OK about what we want. The challenge is getting the two together.

Monica McGoldrick (1999) maintains that traditional gender roles will not change until we have worked out a new structure in relationships that is not based on the patriarchal family hierarchy. She hopes that "both men and women will be able to develop their potential without regard for the constraints of gender stereotyping that have been so constricting of human experience until now" (p. 122).

Androgyny as an Alternative

One alternative to rigid gender stereotypes is the concept of androgyny, the coexistence of male and female personality traits and characteristics in the same person. Androgyny refers to the flexible integration of strong "masculine" and "feminine" traits in unique ways: Androgynous people are able to recognize and express both "feminine" and "masculine" dimensions. To understand androgyny, it is essential to remember that both biological characteristics and learned behavior play a part in how gender roles are actualized. We all secrete both male and female hormones, and we all have both feminine and masculine psychological characteristics, which Carl Jung labeled the *animus* and the *anima.* Taken together, the animus and the anima reflect Jung's conception of humans as androgynous (see Harris, 1996, for a more complete discussion of Jung's theory of personality).

Because women share some of the psychological characteristics of men (through their animus) and men possess some feminine aspects (through their anima), both can better understand the other. Jung was very insistent that women and men must express both dimensions of their personality. Failure to do so means that part of our nature is denied, which results in one-sided development. Becoming fully human requires that we accept the full range of our personality characteristics.

Androgynous individuals are able to adjust their behavior to what the situation requires in integrated and flexible ways. They are not bound by rigid, stereotyped behavior. Androgynous people have a wider range of capacities and can give expression to a richer range of behaviors than those who are entrapped by gender-typed expectations. Thus, they may perceive themselves as being both understanding, affectionate, and considerate and self-reliant, independent, and firm. The same person has the capacity to be an empathic listener to a friend with a problem, a forceful leader when a project needs to be moved into action, and an assertive supervisor. This fluid ability to access many qualities has been shown to correlate with good psychological health and appears to be good for both women and men (Real, 1998).

Masculinity and femininity continue to be regarded as distinctive and separate ways of behaving, yet such a dualistic view of human personality is not supported by evidence. Julia (2000) points out that the concept of gender is rooted in the premise that the sexes are diametrically defined as "female" and male." Gender-role socialization reinforces distinct and often unequal sets of behaviors for each gender. But there are wide individual differences within genders as well as across genders. In reality we are multidimensional beings, and polarities of behavioral traits are rare. People do have both feminine and masculine aspects within them. To become fully human, we need to realize the rich and complex dimensions of our being.

Gender-Role Transcendence

To transcend gender-roles we must move beyond them to reach a new synthesis. According to Basow (1992), androgyny may be one step on the path to transcending gender roles, but it is not the only nor necessarily the best way for personal change to occur. Basow suggests that we need to define healthy human functioning independently of gender-related characteristics. In this view the world is not divided into polarities of masculinity and femininity; rather, people have a range of potentials that can be adapted to various situations. As Basow puts it: "When gender transcendence occurs, people can be just people—individuals in their own right, accepted and evaluated on their own terms" (p. 327). When individuals go beyond the restrictions imposed by gender roles and stereotypes, they experience a sense of uniqueness because each person has different capabilities and interests. The transcendence model separates personality traits from biological sex. Those who advocate gender-role transcendence claim that this practice will enable individuals to free themselves from linking specific behavior patterns with a gender. If there were less emphasis on gender as a means of categorizing traits, they argue that individuals would be freer to develop their own unique potentials (Weiten & Lloyd, 2000).

Take Time to Reflect

1. The following statements may help you assess how you see yourself in relation to gender roles. Place a "T" before each statement that generally applies to you and an "F" before each one that generally does not apply to you. Be sure to respond as you are now rather than as you would like to be.

———— Under pressure I tend to withdraw rather than express myself.

———— I'm more an active person than a passive person.

———— I'm more cooperative than I am competitive.

———— I have clear gender expectations.

———— Under pressure I tend to be competitive.

———— I see myself as possessing both masculine and feminine characteristics.

———— I'm adventurous in most situations.

———— I feel OK about expressing difficult feelings.

(continued)

_____ I'm very success-oriented.
_____ I fear making mistakes.

Now look over your responses. Which characteristics, if any, would you like to change in yourself?

_____

_____

2. What are your reactions to the changes in women's views of their gender role? What impact do you think the feminist movement has had on women? On men?

_____

_____

3. Would you like to possess more of the qualities you associate with the other sex? If so, what are they? Are there any ways in which you feel limited or restricted by rigid gender-role definitions and expectations?

_____

_____

SUMMARY

The gender-role standard of our culture has encouraged a static notion of clear roles into which all biological males and females must fit. Masculinity has become associated with power, authority, and mastery; femininity has become associated with passivity and subordination. These concepts of masculinity and femininity are historically and socially conditioned. They are not part of a woman's or a man's basic nature.

Many men have become prisoners of a stereotypical role that they feel they must live by. Writers who address the problems of traditional male roles have focused on characteristics such as independence, aggressiveness, worldliness, directness, objectivity, activity, logic, denial of fears, self-protection, lack of emotional expressiveness, lack of bodily awareness, denial of "feminine" qualities, rigidity, obsession with work, and fear of intimacy. Fortunately, an increasing number of men are challenging the restrictions of these traditional roles. Books on men's issues have recently appeared that describe the challenges men face in breaking out of rigid roles and defining themselves in new ways.

Women, too, have been restricted by their cultural conditioning and by accepting gender-role stereotypes that keep them in an inferior position. Adjectives often associated with women include gentle, tactful, neat, sensitive, talkative, emotional, unassertive, indirect, and caring. Too often women have defined their own preferences as being the same as those of their partners, and they have had to gain their identity by protecting, helping, nurturing, and comforting. Despite the staying power of these traditional female role expectations, more and more women are rejecting the limited vision of what a woman is "expected" to be. Like men, they are gaining increased intellectual awareness of alternative roles, yet they often struggle emotionally to feel and act in ways that differ from their upbringing. The challenge for both sexes is to keep pace on an emotional level with what they know intellectually about living more freely.

We described androgyny as one path toward uprooting gender-role stereotypes. However, it is not the only way, or even the best way, to bring about this change. Ideally, you will be able to transcend rigid categories of "femininity" and "masculinity" and achieve a personal synthesis whereby you can behave responsively as a function of the situation. The real challenge is for you to choose the kind of woman or man you want to be rather than to passively accept a cultural stereotype or blindly identify with some form of rebellion. When you examine the basis of your gender-role identity and your concept of what constitutes a woman or a man, you can decide for yourself what kind of person you want to be instead of conforming to the expectations of others.

In this chapter we have encouraged you to think about your attitudes and values concerning gender roles and to take a close look at how you developed them. Even though cultural pressures are strong toward adopting given roles as a woman or a man, you are not hopelessly cemented into a rigid way of being. You can challenge role expectations that restrict you and determine whether the costs of having adopted certain roles are worth the potential gains.

❯ Where Can I Go From Here?

1. Write down the characteristics you associate with being a woman (or feminine) and being a man (or masculine). Then think about how you acquired these views and to what degree you are satisfied with them.

2. Men and women are challenging traditional roles. Based on your own observations, to what extent do you find this to be true? Do your friends typically accept traditional roles, or do they tend to challenge society's expectations?

3. Interview some people from a cultural group different from your own. Describe some of the common gender stereotypes mentioned in this chapter and determine if such stereotypes are true of the other cultural group.

(continued)

> ## Where Can I Go From Here? *(continued)*

4. Make a list of gender-role stereotypes that apply to men and a list of those that apply to women. Then select people of various ages and ask them to say how much they agree or disagree with each of these stereotypes. If several people bring their results to class, you might have the basis of an interesting panel discussion.

5. For a week or two, pay close attention to the messages you see on television, both in programs and in commercials, regarding gender roles and expectations of women and men. Record your impressions in your journal.

Resources for Future Study

Web Site Resources

SPSMM (Society for the Psychological Study of Men and Masculinity)
http://web.indstate.edu:80/spsmm/

A division of the American Psychological Association, SPSMM promotes the "critical study of how gender shapes and constricts men's lives" and is "committed to the enhancement of men's capacity to experience their full human potential." This site presents contemporary psychological approaches to masculinity and includes extensive links to other related Web resources.

Gender and Race in Media
http://www.uiowa.edu/~comnstud/resources/GenderMedia/index.html

The University of Iowa's Communication Studies program presents a number of articles and links about the ways in which gender and racial differences are expressed in various media. Articles include topics such as advertising, African American, Asian American, assorted gender and media links, cyberspace, feminist media, indexes and directories, Latin American, lesbian/bisexual/gay, Native American and other indigenous peoples, print media, television and film, other media, and mixed media.

The Wellesley Centers for Women
http://www.wellesley.edu/WCW/

The Wellesley Centers for Women works with the Center for Research on Women and the Stone Center for Developmental Services and Studies by "facilitating the development of new research, increasing efficiency, and expanding the Centers' outreach." It shares with them "a joint mission to educate, inform and expand the ways we think about women in the world." Resources for research and purchasing publications are offered.

WOMEN'S STUDIES DATABASE
http://www.inform.umd.edu/EdRes/Topic/WomensStudies/

The Women's Studies Database by the University of Maryland is a resource with links to many different areas of interest such as conferences, computing, employment, government and history, film reviews, program support, publications, and other Web sites.

FEMINIST MAJORITY FOUNDATION ONLINE
http://www.feminist.org/

This site offers many links to a variety of feminist issues including news and events, the National Center for Women and Policing, global feminism, and a feminist online store.

InfoTrac College Edition Resources

For additional readings, explore InfoTrac College Edition, our online library.

Go to **http://www.infotrac.college.com/wadsworth**

Hint: Enter the search terms:

gender-role socialization
gender stereotypes
gender-role identity
traditional male role
traditional female role
dual career family
androgyny
gender-role transcendence

Print Resources

Carter, B., & McGoldrick, M. (Eds.). (1999). *The expanded family life cycle: Individual, family, and social perspectives* (3rd ed.). Boston: Allyn & Bacon.

Julia, M. (2000). *Constructing gender: Multicultural perspectives in working women.* Pacific Grove, CA: Brooks/Cole.

Pollack, W. (1998). *Real boys.* New York: Henry Holt & Co.

Real, T. (1998). *I don't want to talk about it: Overcoming the secret legacy of male depression.* New York: Simon & Schuster (Fireside).

Tavris, C. (1992). *The mismeasure of women.* New York: Simon & Schuster (Touchstone).

It is no easier to achieve sexual autonomy than it is to achieve autonomy in other areas of your life

C. Moore/Corbis

SEXUALITY

Use this scale to respond to these statements:

4 = This statement is true of me *most* of the time.
3 = This statement is true of me *much* of the time.
2 = This statement is true of me *some* of the time.
1 = This statement is true of me *almost none* of the time.

_____ 1. The quality of a sexual relationship usually depends on the general quality of the relationship.

_____ 2. I find it easy to talk openly and honestly about sexuality with at least one other person.

_____ 3. For me, sex without love is unsatisfying.

_____ 4. I experience guilt or shame over sexuality.

_____ 5. I have found that gender-role definitions and stereotypes get in the way of mutually satisfying sexual relations.

_____ 6. Sensual experiences do not necessarily have to be sexual.

_____ 7. Performance standards and expectations get in the way of my enjoying sensual and sexual experiences.

_____ 8. I have struggled to find my own values pertaining to sexual behavior.

_____ 9. I acquired healthy attitudes about sexuality from my parents.

_____ 10. I worry a lot about HIV/AIDS and other sexually transmitted diseases.

People of all ages may experience difficulty talking openly about sexual matters. This lack of communication contributes to the perpetuation of myths and misinformation about sexuality despite the fact that the media are giving increased attention to all aspects of sexual behavior, literally bombarding us with new information and trends. Almost nothing is unmentionable in the popular media. Yet this increased knowledge regarding sexuality does not appear to have resulted in encouraging all people to talk more freely about their own sexual concerns, nor has it always reduced their anxiety about sexuality. For many people sex remains a delicate topic, and they find it difficult to communicate their sexual wants, especially to a person close to them. Discussing sexual matters in a classroom setting requires sensitivity and respect for the boundaries of students. Although many students want to find out how others think about sexual issues, some have reservations about sharing what are deeply personal matters.

One of our goals for this chapter is to help you learn how to recognize and appropriately express your sexual concerns. Too many people suffer from needless guilt, shame, worries, and inhibition merely because they keep their concerns about sexuality secret, largely out of embarrassment. Moreover, keeping your concerns to yourself can hinder your efforts to determine your own values regarding sex. The reality of the HIV/AIDS crisis challenges sexually active individuals to rethink their priorities and their sexual behavior. Thus, we address information necessary to prevent HIV infection, and we look at some misconceptions surrounding HIV and AIDS. In this chapter we ask you to examine your values and attitudes toward sexuality and to determine what choices you want to make in this area of your life.

MISCONCEPTIONS ABOUT SEXUALITY

We consider the following statements to be misconceptions about sex. As you read over this list, ask yourself what your attitudes are and where you developed these beliefs. Are they working for you? Could any of these statements apply to you? How might some of these statements affect your ability to make free choices concerning sexuality?

> If I allow myself to become sexual, I will get into trouble.

> Women are not as sexually desirable when they initiate sex.

> Men need to prove themselves through sexual conquests.

> As I get older, I am bound to lose interest in sex.

> If my partner really loved me, I would not have to tell him or her what I liked or wanted. My partner should know what I need intuitively without my asking.

> I cannot hope to overcome any negative conditioning I received about sex as I was growing up.

> Acting without any guilt or restrictions is what is meant by being sexually free.

> Being sexually attracted to a person other than my partner implies that I don't really find my partner sexually exciting.

> Being attracted to someone of the same gender is abnormal.

> The more physically attractive a person is, the more sexually exciting he or she is.

> With the passage of time, any sexual relationship is bound to become less exciting.

DEVELOPING YOUR OWN SEXUAL VALUES

The possibility of contracting a sexually transmitted disease or the risk of an unwanted pregnancy have long been considered as individuals make decisions regarding their own sexuality. Increasingly, people have openly questioned society's sexual standards and practices, and the AIDS epidemic has challenged our sexual attitudes and behaviors. Individuals can and should decide what sexual practices are acceptable for them, and this decision making is enhanced when sexual issues are talked about freely without guilt or shame.

It is also important that your sexual behavior be consistent with your value system. Take a few minutes to reflect on your attitudes about sexual behavior and consider these questions in exploring the pros and cons of being sexually active:

> How do I feel about my decision?

> Does my choice to be sexually active interfere with my religious beliefs or cultural values?

> Do I feel pressured into having sex?

> What are my reasons for choosing to have sex at this time?

> Am I willing to talk openly with my partner about sex prior to initiating a sexual relationship?

> Am I prepared for the emotional complications of a sexual relationship?

> If birth control is an issue, have I considered my options and chosen a safe and effective method?

> Have my partner and I discussed our sexual histories?

> Am I prepared to discuss and effectively use protection against sexually transmitted diseases?

Celibacy as an Option

If you decide that abstaining from sexual intercourse until marriage is congruent with your value system, you need not apologize for your choice. A recent news special reported that between 50% and 75% of adolescents engage in sexual intercourse before they graduate from high school, but there is also a growing group of young people committed to sexual abstinence until marriage. Purity seminars providing support for the choice of celibacy are part of this outreach program. Choosing celibacy or abstinence is a viable option. Some choose it out of moral or cultural convictions, others out of various fears about sex. Fear is not necessarily a bad reason. For example, the fear of driving under the influence of drugs and alcohol makes good sense. So does the fear of an unwanted pregnancy. Whatever your reasons for choosing to abstain from sex, you should know that you are not alone.

If you are choosing celibacy, answering these questions will help you understand the values that support your decision. "What meaning do I attach to celibacy?" "Is my choice to be celibate based on a full acceptance of my body?" "Do I believe I am a sexually desirable person?" "Do I fear that being celibate stands in the way of the level of intimacy I desire?"

Even in marriage or other committed relationships, celibacy is sometimes necessary due to illness or other physical conditions. It is important to cultivate emotional intimacy without physical intimacy.

Formulating Your Sexual Ethics

Designing a personal and meaningful set of sexual ethics is not an easy task. It can be accomplished only through a process of honest questioning. Examine the role of your family of origin and your culture as the background of your sexual ethics. Are the values you received from your family and your culture congruent with your views of yourself in other areas of your life? Which of them are important in enabling you to live responsibly and with enjoyment? Which should you reject or modify?

Achieving freedom does not require shedding all of your past beliefs or values. Whether you keep or reject them in whole or in part, you can refuse to allow others to make decisions for you. It can be tempting to allow others (whether past authorities or present acquaintances) to tell us what is right and wrong, but it is well to remember that sometimes we learn our ethics through our mistakes. If you fail to create your own values and choose for yourself, you surrender your autonomy.

Developing your own values means assuming responsibility for yourself, which includes taking into consideration how others may be affected by your choices while allowing them to take responsibility for themselves. For instance, some people struggle with wanting to act out sexually with many partners, even though this behavior goes against their personal value system. Their struggle is between giving behavioral expression to their sexual desires and feeling guilty because they are not living by their values. In an adult relationship, the parties involved are capable of taking personal responsibility for their own actions. For example, in the case of premarital or extramarital sex, each person must weigh these questions: "Do I really want to pursue a sexual relationship with this person at this time?" "Is the price worth it?" "What are my commitments?" "Who else is involved, and who could be hurt?" "Might this be a positive or a negative experience?" "How does my decision fit in with my values generally?"

It is no easier to achieve sexual autonomy than it is to achieve autonomy in other areas of your life. While challenging your values, you need to take a careful look at how you could easily engage in self-deception by adjusting your behavior to whatever you might desire at the moment. Pay attention to how you feel about yourself in regard to your past sexual experience. Perhaps, in doing so, you can use your level of self-respect as one important guide to your future behavior. You might ask: "Do I feel enhanced or diminished by my past experience?"

Sex can be a positive or a negative force, depending on how it is used. At its best, our sexuality provides a deep source of enjoyment, brings pleasure, enhances overall well-being, and demonstrates love, caring, and affection. At its worst, sex can be used to hurt others. Sex is abused when it is manipulative, used as a punishing force, used to get favors, is the tool of aggression and control, is aimed at dominating another, or when it evokes guilt. In the next section, we consider some of the ways sex is frequently abused and used as a ploy to assume power and control over others.

Take Time to Reflect

1. What influences have shaped your attitudes and values concerning sexuality? In the following list, indicate the importance of each factor by placing a 1 in the blank if it was *very important*, a 2 if it was *somewhat important*, and a 3 if it was *unimportant*. For each item you mark with a 1 or a 2, briefly indicate the nature of that influence.

_____ parents _____

_____ church _____

_____ friends _____

_____ siblings _____

_____ movies _____

_____ school _____

_____ books _____

(continued)

_____ television _____

_____ spouse _____

_____ grandparents _____

_____ your own experiences _____

_____ other influential factors _____

_____

2. Try making a list of specific values that guide you in dealing with sexual issues. As a beginning, respond to the following questions:

   a. How do you feel about sex with multiple partners versus monogamous sex?

   _____

   _____

   b. What is your view of sex outside of marriage or a committed relationship?

   _____

   _____

   c. How would it affect you if you separated love from sex?

   _____

   _____

LEARNING TO TALK OPENLY ABOUT SEXUAL ISSUES

As in other areas of your life, you may saddle yourself with beliefs about sex that you have not given much thought to. Open discussions with those you are intimate with, as well as an honest exchange of views in your class, can do a lot to help you challenge the unexamined attitudes you have about this significant area of your life.

Although you might expect that people today would be able to discuss openly and frankly the concerns they have about sex, this is not the case. Students will discuss attitudes about sexual behavior in a general way, but they show considerable resistance to speaking of their own sexual concerns, fears, and conflicts. It is of value to simply provide a climate in which people can feel free to examine their personal concerns. In the groups that we lead, we have found it useful to give women and men an opportunity to discuss sexual issues in separate groups and then come together to share the concerns they have discovered. Typically, both men and women appreciate the chance to explore their sexual fears, expectations, and wishes, as well as their concerns about the normality of their bodies and feelings. When the male and female groups come together, the participants usually find much common ground, and the experience of making this discovery can be very therapeutic. For instance, men may fear becoming impotent, not performing up to some expected standard, of being inadequate lovers, or not being "man enough." When the men and women meet as one group, the men may be surprised to discover that women worry about having to achieve orgasm (or several of them) every time they have sex and that they, too, have fears about their sexual desirability. When people talk about these concerns in a direct way, they often experience a sense of relief through hearing about the feelings of others.

In the past there was clearly a taboo against openly discussing sexual topics. Today, bookstores are flooded with paperbacks devoted to enhancing sexuality. Although people may have a greater awareness of sexuality, it is clear that many of them have not been able to translate their knowledge into a more satisfying sex life. In fact, an increased awareness of what is normal for women and men may have compounded their problems. Couples are often very uncomfortable communicating their sexual likes and dislikes, their personal fears, and the shame and guilt they sometimes have about sex. Many still operate on the old myth that if their mate really loves them he or she should know intuitively what gives them pleasure. To ask for what you want sexually is often seen as diminishing the value of what is received.

Nevertheless, the outlook in this area is not totally negative. Whereas in the past a couple might have kept their sexual problems locked behind their bedroom door, the trend now is toward acknowledging these problems and seeking help. Typical concerns openly aired by both men and women in discussion groups we have participated in include those on this list:

> I often wonder what excites my partner and what she [he] would like, yet I seldom ask. Am I responsible if my partner is dissatisfied? I suppose it is important for me to learn how to initiate by asking and also how to tell the other person what I enjoy.

> I am concerned about sexually transmitted diseases.

> Sex can be fun, I suppose, but it is really difficult for me to be playful and spontaneous.

> ❯ I would really like to know how other women feel after a sexual experience.

> ❯ As a man, I frequently worry about performance standards, and that gets in the way of my making love freely and spontaneously.

> ❯ There are times when I think I am running into a sexual relationship because I feel lonely.

> ❯ There are times when I really do not want intercourse but would still like to be held and touched and caressed. I wish my partner could understand this about me and not take it as a personal rejection.

These are common concerns about sexuality. Knowing that many others have these concerns, we hope you will feel less alone with some of your anxieties about sex. Look over the list again and identify the statements that seem to fit for you. Ask yourself if you are ready to reexamine your beliefs about some of these issues.

SEX AND GUILT

Guilt Over Sexual Feelings

As in the case of shame over our bodies, we need to become aware of our guilt and reexamine it to determine whether we are needlessly burdening ourselves. Not all guilt is unhealthy and irrational, of course, but there is a real value in learning to challenge guilt feelings and to rid ourselves of those that are unrealistic.

Many people express very real fears as they begin to recognize and accept their sexuality. It is important to learn that we can accept the full range of our sexual feelings yet decide for ourselves what we will do about them. For instance, we remember a man who said that he felt satisfied with his marriage and found his wife exciting but was troubled because he found other women appealing and sometimes desired them. Even though he had made a decision not to have extramarital affairs, he still experienced a high level of anxiety over having sexual feelings toward other women. At some level he believed he might be more likely to act on his feelings if he fully accepted that he had them. It was important for him to learn to discriminate between having sexual feelings and deciding to take certain actions and that he learn to trust his own decisions.

In making responsible, inner-directed choices about whether to act on your sexual feelings, consider these questions:

> ❯ Will my actions hurt another person or myself?

> ❯ Will my actions limit another person's freedom?

> ❯ Will my actions exploit another's rights?

> ❯ Are my actions consistent with my commitments?

Each of us must decide on our own moral guidelines, but it is unrealistic to expect that we can or should control our feelings in the same way we control our actions. By controlling our actions, we define who we are; by denying or banishing our feelings, we only become alienated from ourselves.

Guilt Over Sexual Experiences

Although some people are convinced that in these sexually liberated times college students do not suffer guilt feelings over their sexual behaviors, our observations show us that this is not the case. College students, whether single or married, young or middle-aged, report a variety of experiences over which they feel guilty. Guilt may be related to masturbation, extramarital (or "extrapartner") affairs, same-sex behavior, sexual practices that are sometimes considered deviant, or sexual promiscuity.

Our early sexual learning is a crucial factor in later sexual adjustment because current guilt feelings often stem from both unconscious and conscious decisions made in response to verbal and nonverbal messages about sexuality. Children are often not given the proper words for their body parts and for erotic activities. If parents restrict their vocabulary by referring to the genitals as simply organs of excretion, children tend to assume that sexual pleasure is "dirty" or unnatural. An acquaintance once was shocked and upset when she heard one of our daughters use the word *penis*. When we asked her how she referred to genitals with her children, she replied, "Of course, I call it a weenie!" Such distortions or omissions of information can create an underlying negative attitude through which later information tends to be filtered.

Peers often fill the void left by parents. However, reliance on the same-sex peer group usually results in learning inaccurate sexual information, which can later lead to fears and guilt over sexual feelings and activities. Most sex information from the peer group is imparted during the early teen years, and we carry into adulthood many distorted notions about sex.

Movies, television, magazines, and newspapers provide information that is often a source of negative learning about sexuality. Material dealing with rape, violent sex, and venereal disease is blatantly presented to children. This slanted information often produces unrealistic and unbalanced attitudes about sexuality and ultimately fosters fears and guilt that can have a powerful impact on the ability to enjoy sex as an adult.

We acquire a sense of guilt over sexual feelings and experiences as a result of a wide diversity of sources of information and misinformation. Not all guilt is neurotic, nor should it necessarily be eliminated. When we violate our value system, guilt is a consequence. This guilt can serve a useful purpose, motivating us to change the behavior that is not congruent with our ethical standards. In freeing ourselves of unearned guilt, the first step is to become aware of early verbal and nonverbal messages about sexuality and gender-role behavior. Once we become aware of these messages, we can explore them to determine in what ways we might want to modify them.

Take Time to Reflect

1. Complete the following statements pertaining to sexuality:

   a. I first learned about sex through ————————————————

   ————————————————————————————————

   b. My earliest memory about sex is ——————————————

   ————————————————————————————————

   c. The way this memory affects me now is ————————————

   ————————————————————————————————

   d. One verbal sexual message I received from my parents was ————

   ————————————————————————————————

   e. One nonverbal sexual message I received from my parents was ————

   ————————————————————————————————

   f. An expectation I have about sex is ——————————————

   ————————————————————————————————

   g. When the topic of sexuality comes up I usually ————————

   ————————————————————————————————

   h. While I was growing up, a sexual taboo I internalized was ————

   ————————————————————————————————

2. Are there any steps you would like to take toward learning to accept your body and your sexuality more than you do now? If so, what are they?

   ————————————————————————————————

   ————————————————————————————————

3. Do you experience guilt over sexual feelings? If so, what specific feelings lead to guilt?

_____

_____

4. How openly are you able to discuss sexuality in a personal way? Would you like to be more open in discussing your sexuality or sexual issues? If so, what is preventing this openness?

_____

_____

5. How have your cultural, spiritual, and religious background and values affected your view of sex?

_____

_____

LEARNING TO ENJOY SENSUALITY AND SEXUALITY

Sensual experiences involve all of our senses and can be enjoyed separately from sexual experiences. People often confuse sensuality with sexuality, especially by concluding that sensuality necessarily leads to sexual experiences. Although sexuality involves sensual experiences, sensuality often does not lead to sexual activity.

Performance standards and expectations often get in the way of sensual and sexual pleasure, particularly for men. Some men think they must be supermen, particularly in the area of sexual attractiveness and performance. They measure themselves by unrealistic standards and may greatly fear losing their sexual power. In spite of the appearance of a drug such as Viagra, men continue to be concerned about their ability to sexually respond. Instead of enjoying sexual and sensual experiences, many men become oriented toward orgasm. For some men, the fact that they or their partner experiences an orgasm signifies that they have performed adequately. They may expect their partner always to have an orgasm during intercourse, primarily out of their need to prove their sexual adequacy. For example, Roland stated in his human sexuality class that he would not continue to

Intimacy can be conceived of as a close emotional relationship characterized by a deep level of caring for another person and is a basic component of all loving relationships.

W. Hill, Jr./The Image Works

date a woman who did not have an orgasm with him. Several of the other male students were in full agreement with Roland's attitude. With this type of orientation toward sex, it is not surprising that these men harbor intense fears of impotence.

Listening to Our Bodies

Recent media attention devoted to impotence, also referred to as *erectile dysfunction,* includes former Senator Robert Dole talking openly about erectile dysfunction and dispelling some of the myths surrounding it. Television commercials promoting Viagra have also changed the way many men think about their ability to be sexually responsive.

Sexual dysfunction can occur for any one of a number of reasons, including, in some cases, physical ones, and impotence can be a side effect of certain prescription drugs. But in the majority of cases impotence is due to psychological factors such as feelings of guilt, prolonged depression, hostility or resentment, anxiety about personal adequacy, or a generally low level of self-esteem. Most men for whom impotence becomes a problem might be well advised to ask themselves "What is my body telling me?"

When we are unable to be sexually responsive, our bodies are often sending us an important message about our emotional health. Although impotence is one of the most anxiety-provoking situations men can experience, it paradoxically creates and promotes the potential for making significant changes, for it can lead to cracking their armor. Goldberg (1987) contends that impotence is a lifesaving and life-giving response. If the context is properly understood, and if the man's fragile masculine self-image is able to tolerate the anxiety over not performing adequately, he has the opportunity to become aware of his flawed emotional interaction. His impotence can thus be the only authentic response he has left to measure the defects in the interchange. Although he is telling himself that he should be close, his body is telling the real truth, for it knows that he does not want to be close. Impotence is a pathway to a man's deeper feelings because it represents a central threat to his ego, makes him vulnerable, and motivates him to seek help. If men are able to pay attention to their body signals, they can see that the penis serves as a monitoring device in the relationship. Goldberg likens impotence to a psychological heart attack, which can either result in psychological death or be a catalyst for the man to restructure his patterns of living.

Some women have difficulty responding sexually, especially experiencing orgasm. Stress is a major factor that can easily interfere with being in a frame of mind that will allow a woman's body to respond. Although her partner may climax and feel some degree of satisfaction, she might be left frustrated. This is particularly true if the couple engages in sex late at night when they are both tired or if they have been under considerable stress. If her body is not responding, it could well be a sign that stress and fatigue are making it difficult for her to relax and give in to a full psychological and physical release. Rather than interpreting her lack of responsiveness as a sign of sexual inadequacy, she would be wise to pay attention to what her body is expressing. Her body is probably saying, "I'm too tired to enjoy this."

Asking for What We Want

Paying attention to the messages of our body is only a first step. We still need to learn how to express to our partner specifically what we like and do not like sexually. Women and men both tend to keep their sexual preferences and dislikes to themselves instead of sharing them with their partner. They have accepted the misconception that their partner should know intuitively what they like, and they resist telling their partner what feels good to them out of fear that their lovemaking will become mechanical or that their partner will only be trying to please them.

Often a woman will complain that she does not derive as much enjoyment from sex as she might because the man is too concerned with his own pleasure or is orgasm-oriented. Many men see touching, holding, and caressing only as necessary duties they must perform to obtain "the real thing." A woman may find that her partner rolls over in bed as soon as he is satisfied, even if she is left frustrated. Although she may require touching and considerable foreplay and afterplay, he may not recognize her needs. Therefore, it may be helpful for her to express to him what it feels like to be left unsatisfied, but in a way that does not feel to him like an attack. It needs to be mentioned that in some cultures there is an injunction against women asking for what they want in a sexual relationship. Thus, it is essential to consider the cultural context here.

It is not uncommon for a woman to ask a question such as "Does touching always have to lead to sex?" She is probably implying that there is a significant dimension missing for her in lovemaking—namely, the sensual aspect. The case of Tiffani and Ron illustrates this common conflict in lovemaking.

TIFFANI'S STORY

*A*nytime I want to be affectionate with Ron, he wants to have sexual intercourse. I really resent Ron's inability to respond to my need for affection without making a sexual demand. When I sense that Ron wants to be sexual with me, I start a fight to create distance. In turn, he feels rejected, humiliated, and angry. I want to feel close to Ron both physically and emotionally, but his all-or-nothing response makes me afraid to be affectionate with him.

It is important to learn how to negotiate for what you want in sex. Being sensual is an important part of a sexual experience. Sensuality pertains to fully experiencing all of our senses, not just sensations in our genitals. Many parts of the body are sensual and can contribute to our enjoyment of sex. Although there is great enjoyment in the orgasmic experience, many people are missing out on other sources of enjoyment by not giving pleasure to themselves and their partners with other stimulation. A range of sexual behavior is open to couples if they make their expectations clear and if they talk about sexuality as part of their relationship.

SEX AND INTIMACY

Intimacy can be conceived of as a close emotional relationship characterized by a deep level of caring for another person and is a basic component of all loving relationships. Although intimacy is part of all loving relationships, it is a mistake to assume that sexuality is part of all loving and intimate relationships. In Chapter 7 we explored many forms of intimate relationships that do not involve sex. Here we address the links between sex and intimacy.

Increasing our sexual awareness can include becoming more sensitive to the ways in which we sometimes engage in sex as a means to some end. For instance, sexual activity can be used as a way to actually prevent the development of intimacy. It can also be a way to avoid experiencing our aloneness, our isolation, and our feelings of distance from others. Sex can be an escape into activity, a way of avoiding inner emptiness. When used in any of these ways, sex takes on a driving or compulsive quality that detracts from its spontaneity and leaves us unfulfilled. Used as a way of filling inner emptiness, sex becomes a mechanical act, divorced from any passion, feeling, or caring. Then it only deepens our feelings of isolation and detachment.

In our professional work with clients and college students we have observed a trend away from casual sexual encounters without any emotional attachment. Those who have left sexually exclusive relationships may look forward to sex with a variety of partners for a time, and some may be drawn to "sport sex" as they experience their newfound "freedom." Many report, however, that they eventually tire of such relationships and find themselves searching for intimacy as a vital part of their sexual involvements. Of course, the impact of AIDS on sexual behavior probably accounts for some of the caution in getting involved with multiple partners. The fear of becoming infected certainly makes casual sex much less attractive than it might otherwise be. As one student put it, "When you are sexually intimate with someone, it could be a life-or-death matter. You are really trusting them with your life." In our discussions with college students, we are finding that they are seeking to be loved by a special person, and they want to trust giving their love in return.

Take a moment to reflect on what sex means to you and how sex can be used to either enhance or diminish you and your partner as persons. Is sex a form of stress release? Does it make you feel secure? Loved? Accepted? Nurtured? Is it fun? Does it signify commitment? Is it abusive? Pleasurable? Is it shameful or positive? Ask yourself: "Are my intimate relationships based on a need to conquer or exert power over someone else? Or are they based on a genuine desire to become intimate, to share, to experience joy and pleasure, to both give and receive?" Asking yourself what you want in your relationships and what uses sex serves for you may also help you avoid the overemphasis on technique and performance that frequently detracts from sexual experiences. Although technique and knowledge are important, they are not ends in themselves, and overemphasizing them can cause us to become oblivious to the persons we have sex with. An abundance of anxiety over performance and technique can only impede sexual enjoyment and rob us of the experience of genuine intimacy and caring. It may be helpful for you to examine where your views about sex come from and the meaning you attach to sexuality. Knowing where you stand can make it easier to make choices about what you do and do not want sexually.

Take Time to Reflect

1. Complete the following sentences:

   a. To me, being sensual means _____

   _____

   b. To me, being sexual means _____

   _____

   c. Sex without intimacy is _____

   _____

   d. Sex can be an empty experience when _____

   _____

   e. Sex can be most fulfilling when _____

   _____

2. Look over the following list, quickly checking the words that you associate with sex:

_____ fun	_____ dirty	_____ routine
_____ ecstasy	_____ shameful	_____ closeness
_____ procreation	_____ joy	_____ release
_____ beautiful	_____ pressure	_____ sinful
_____ duty	_____ performance	_____ guilty
_____ trust	_____ experimentation	_____ vulnerability

   Now look over the words you have checked and see whether there are any significant patterns in your responses. What can you say by way of summary about your attitudes toward sex?

   _____

   _____

AIDS: A CONTEMPORARY CRISIS

If you have not already done so, you will inevitably come in contact with people who have tested positive for HIV, people who have AIDS, people who have had sexual contact with someone who has tested HIV-positive, and people who are close to individuals with HIV or AIDS.*

AIDS already affects a wide population and will continue to be a major health problem. You simply cannot afford to be unaware of the personal and societal implications of this epidemic. Unless you are educated about the problem, you are likely to engage in risky behaviors or live needlessly in fear. Accurate information is vital if you are to deal with the personal and societal implications of the AIDS epidemic.

You need to be able to differentiate between fact and fiction about the virus and about this disease. Because this is a relatively new disease, we continue to discover new information. Thus, the material we provide here is continually being updated and expanded. You can contact the Centers for Disease Control and Prevention (CDC) National AIDS Hotline (1-800-342-AIDS) for free written material, for updated information, and for answers to your questions.

Ignorance and fear of AIDS is fueled by conflicting reports and misinformation about the ways in which the disease is spread. But there is no reason to remain ignorant today because the basic information you need about this disease is available from the CDC and through AIDS workshops or by contacting your local public health department or one of the many HIV clinics that are being started all over the country.

As well as finding out about HIV and AIDS, we urge you to explore your own sexual practices, drug behaviors, and your attitudes, values, and fears pertaining to HIV/AIDS. Better understanding on all fronts will better equip you to make informed, wise choices.

Basic Facts About AIDS

What Is AIDS? Acquired immunodeficiency syndrome (AIDS) is the last stage of a disease caused by the human immunodeficiency virus (HIV), which attacks and weakens the body's natural immune system. Without a working immune system, the body gets infections and cancers that it would normally be able to fight off. By the time an individual develops AIDS, the virus has damaged the body's defenses (immune system). HIV was first isolated by French and American scientists in late 1983 and early 1984. People who have AIDS are vulnerable

---

*We want to acknowledge the helpful suggestions of Jerome Wright and Michael Moulton in providing an updated perspective on the AIDS issue.

to serious illnesses that would not be a threat to anyone whose immune system was functioning normally. These illnesses are referred to as "opportunistic" infections or diseases. AIDS weakens the body's immune system against invasive agents so that other diseases can prey on the body. The course of HIV infection is unpredictable. Some individuals progress to full-blown AIDS and die within several months. Others have no symptoms as long as 10 years or more after being infected with HIV (Edlin, Golanty, & Brown, 2000).

What Do We Know About HIV/AIDS? At this time, much is known about how HIV is transmitted and how it can be avoided. What is not known is how to destroy the virus. Although there is not yet a vaccine, treatment is improving with early detection and intervention. The vast majority of people with HIV infection will eventually develop AIDS. However, with early treatment, the HIV infection can generally be retarded and the onset of AIDS can be delayed. HIV-positive individuals can live relatively symptom free lives for many years, and new medications are now available to treat the opportunistic infections that often kill people with AIDS. Without treatment, half of HIV-infected people will develop an AIDS-related illness within 10 years (CDC, 1994c). Once the HIV virus infects a person's body, the immune system attempts to fight the virus, but it is unable to destroy it. Because of the way the HIV virus attacks the immune system, it becomes less effective in fighting off other infections that the body is exposed to or is carrying. Gradually, the immune system becomes weaker and weaker. Many people who were infected with HIV in the early 1980s have yet to be diagnosed with AIDS. There is still a great deal we do not know about the virus and whether everyone infected will eventually develop AIDS. But most people who become infected become ill to some degree within 5 to 15 years after infection. Recent research from the Centers for Disease Control and Prevention has determined that many factors play a role in the progression of HIV infection to other illness (including AIDS). Health behaviors known to be cofactors for facilitating the progression of HIV include these:

> Restricted breathing patterns

> Low levels of fluid or water intake

> Poor appetite or inadequate nutrition

> Inadequate or disrupted sleep

> Excessive use of alcohol and other drugs

> Lack of physical exercise

> High levels of stress

By changing their behavior to reduce the number of cofactors, people with HIV can slow and possibly stop the progression of their infection.

How Is HIV Transmitted? HIV can be transmitted by unprotected sexual intercourse (vaginal or anal) with a person infected with the virus or by sharing needles with an infected person during intravenous drug use. Babies born to HIV-infected women may become infected before or during birth or through breast-feeding after birth. Although some cases have developed through blood transfusions, this risk has been practically eliminated since 1985 when careful and widespread screening and testing of the blood supply for evidence of HIV became standard practice (CDC, 1994c). "High concentration" agents of transmission of HIV include blood, semen, vaginal secretions, and breast milk. The virus can be spread by women or men through heterosexual or homosexual contact. It may also be possible to become infected with HIV through oral intercourse because the act often involves semen and vaginal secretions that may contain HIV. The virus can enter the body through the vagina, penis, rectum, or mouth or through breaks in the skin. The risk of infection with the virus is increased by having multiple sexual partners and by sharing needles among those using drugs. People are most able to infect someone in the first few months of being infected themselves. This is a major problem because individuals may test HIV-negative during this time. It is possible for people carrying the virus to infect others even if they do not know they are infected. They may feel fine and be without symptoms of the illness yet still be HIV-positive and be able to transmit HIV infection.

The virus has been found in "low concentration" in a number of body fluids and secretions, such as saliva, urine, and tears. However, you do not "catch" AIDS in the same way you catch a cold or the flu. It cannot be passed through a glass or eating utensils. The AIDS virus is not transmitted through everyday contact with people around you in the workplace, at school, or at social functions. You cannot get AIDS by being near someone who carries the virus. The virus is hard to get and easily avoided. It is a misconception that it is spread through casual contact or from a mosquito bite, a casual kiss, swimming pools, eating food prepared by someone who is HIV infected, or a toilet seat. HIV infection is best prevented by abstinence, fidelity between noninfected partners, avoiding sharing needles, and by consistently using latex condoms.

Who Gets AIDS? Some people who are infected with HIV have not developed AIDS. Most of the AIDS public health effort has been focused on persons with high-risk behavior such as bisexual and gay men, intravenous drug users, and blood transfusion recipients. Some people have been lulled into feeling safe because they believe they are not associated with a high-risk group. But this epidemic is shifting and is spreading to women, youth, and minorities. Indeed, most cases of HIV infection worldwide are due to unprotected heterosexual intercourse. Here are the statistics provided by the World Health Organization:

> 80% transmitted through heterosexual intercourse

> 10% transmitted through homosexual intercourse

> 5% to 10% transmitted through injection drug use

> 3% transmitted through breast-feeding and blood transfusions

AIDS has been called an "equal opportunity disease" because it is found among people of all ages, genders, races, and sexual orientations. Unlike people, AIDS does not discriminate. It is behavior that puts people at risk—not the group to which they belong. The largest growth in HIV infection is occurring among women. In 1999 there were 39 million HIV infections worldwide. There are 16,000 new HIV infections each day. This is more than 3 million infections per year, which means there are about 5 infections per minute.

What Symptoms Are Associated With HIV Infection? HIV may live in the human body for years before symptoms appear. These people are asymptomatic.

Although many individuals infected with the virus have no symptoms, some people develop severe and prolonged fatigue, night sweats, fever, loss of appetite and weight, diarrhea, and enlarged lymph glands in the neck. Anyone having one or more of these symptoms for more than 2 weeks should see a health care provider. Of course, other diseases besides HIV can cause similar symptoms.

What Kind of Test Is There for HIV Infection? An HIV antibody test looks for antibodies, not the virus. People can test negative but be positive during a 6-month window period. This is why it is important to get a second test about 6 months after a person thinks he or she might have been exposed to the virus. Many people who test positive either remain symptom free or develop less serious illnesses. Two separate tests for HIV (called ELISA and Western blot), when used together, are accurate more than 99% of the time (CDC, 1994b, 1994c). The ELISA test can be performed relatively quickly and easily. If the results are positive, the test is repeated to check it. Edlin, Golanty, and Brown (2000) report that the most accurate test for HIV infection is the Western blot, which provides an indirect measure of HIV infection. It does not measure whether a person has AIDS or will get AIDS, and the test cannot tell whether the individual will eventually develop signs of illness related to the viral infection or, if so, how serious the illness might be. Testing is completely anonymous and confidential, but you should inquire if the test site provides these safeguards. It is generally free if you go to the health department in your county.

Early intervention is the key. One of the problems with AIDS antibody tests is that false-positive results can create unnecessary anxiety. Any positive HIV test result should be rechecked (Edlin, Golanty, & Brown, 2000). A positive result does not mean that you have AIDS. It means that you have been infected with the HIV virus, that your body has developed a reaction to it, and that you can transmit it to others. If you suspect that you have been exposed to the virus, it is crucial that you get tested as soon as possible because there are clear benefits to early medical attention for HIV infection. If you are infected with HIV, the virus slowly weakens your ability to fight illness, but early medical care and medicines can help your body resist the virus. Medicines do this by slowing the growth of HIV and delaying or preventing certain life-threatening conditions (CDC, 1994c).

What Are Common Reactions to Testing HIV-Positive? Upon learning that they are HIV-positive, it is not uncommon for people to experience a gamut of emotional reactions from shock, to anger, to fear and anxiety, to grieving for the loss of sexual freedom, to alarm over the uncertain future. Some feel that they have been given a death sentence. They will need to find a support system to help them cope with the troubled times that lie ahead.

HIV-positive individuals can live long and relatively symptom-free lives. Many new medications are now available to treat the opportunistic infections that often killed people with AIDS in years gone by. Today much more is known about the disease than was the case when AIDS was first discovered, and research toward a cure is continuing.

Why Is a Stigma Attached to AIDS? Both those who have AIDS and those who discover that they have the HIV virus within them struggle with the stigma attached to this disease. People who are HIV-positive live with the anxiety of wondering whether they will come down with this incurable disease. Most of them also struggle with the stigma attached to AIDS. They live in fear not only of developing a life-threatening disease but also of being discovered and thus being rejected by society in general and by significant persons in their lives. Of course, those who develop AIDS must also deal with this stigma.

Many of the social fears felt by people with HIV or AIDS are realistic. Some family members actually disown the person with AIDS out of fear. This type of treatment naturally inspires anger, depression, and feelings of hopelessness in the person who has been rejected. He or she may express this anger by asking, over and over: "What did I do to deserve this? Why me?" This anger is sometimes directed at God for letting this happen, and then the person may feel guilty for having reacted this way. Anger is also directed toward others, especially those who are likely to have transmitted the virus.

How Is HIV/AIDS Treated? At this point, those who carry the virus are likely to have it for the rest of their lives. No drugs currently available will completely destroy HIV, but new drugs and vaccines are being tested. Although optimism for treating HIV infections has increased, a cure for AIDS is still a remote hope (Edlin, Golanty, & Brown, 2000). Although not a cure, antiviral agents including azidothymidine (AZT), dideoxyinosine, and others appear to retard the progress of the disease in some patients. Several experimental drugs have also shown efficacy in delaying the onset of AIDS. According to Edlin, Golanty, and Brown (2000), the majority of HIV-infected patients require powerful drugs to keep HIV in check and prevent progression to AIDS. They list three classes of drugs that block HIV multiplication in infected individuals: reverse transcriptase inhibitors (AZT and 3TC), nonnucleoside reverse transcriptase inhibitors (Nevirapine, Delavirdine, and Loviride), and newly developed protease inhibitors (Saquinavir, Rotonavir, and Indinavir). These and other drugs must be taken daily to prevent HIV from infecting additional cells. Although no treatment has yet been successful in restoring the immune system, doctors have been able to treat the various acute illnesses affecting those with AIDS.

How Can the Spread of HIV Be Prevented? Pollack (1998) reports that AIDS is now the second leading cause of death in the United States among people ages 25 to 44. He adds that 1 in 5 of all reported AIDS cases are diagnosed in the 20- to 29-year age group. Most people who are diagnosed with AIDS in their 20s were probably teenagers when they first became infected. What this means is that an increasing number of teenagers are being infected with HIV each year and that by the time they reach their 20s many of them may develop the symptoms of AIDS. Because the impact of AIDS has been devastating, Pollack urges parents and schools to teach children and adolescents about sex and sexuality, including the reality of AIDS and ways to prevent this disease. Because this reality unravels and even ends human life, Pollack feels it is absolutely critical that young people receive objective information and are exposed to an honest discussion that may enable them to make better choices regarding their sexual behavior.

Designing prevention programs that really work is a real challenge. Conflicting reports and evidence about AIDS and misinformation about the ways in which the disease is spread can block programs aimed at prevention. But the HIV/AIDS crisis shows no signs of decreasing, and education to stop the spread of the disease is the key to prevention. Individuals can do a lot to avoid contracting the disease. These specific steps aimed at prevention have been taken from a number of sources:

❯ All sexually active individuals need to know the basic facts about this disease and how to avoid the risk of infection.

❯ Engaging in sex with multiple partners is high-risk behavior. The more partners you have, the more you increase your risk. Restricting intercourse to only one uninfected partner is low-risk or no-risk behavior.

❯ Having sex with persons with AIDS, with those at risk for AIDS, or with those who have tested positive on the HIV antibody test is high-risk behavior.

❯ Effective and consistent use of latex condoms and spermicidal barriers will reduce the possibility of transmitting the virus, but they are not 100% effective in preventing HIV or other sexually transmitted diseases (STDs). It is essential that latex condoms be used correctly from start to finish with each act of intercourse. When condoms are used reliably, not only do they prevent pregnancy up to 98% of the time, but they provide a high degree of protection against a variety of sexually transmitted diseases, including HIV infection. For more detailed information about condoms, see the CDC (1999a) publication *Condoms and Their Use in Preventing HIV Infection and Other STDs.*

❯ Making responsible choices is of the utmost importance in avoiding sexually transmitted diseases, including HIV infection. Sexual abstinence is certainly a safe course to follow. If you choose to practice abstinence as a way to prevent infection, this strategy will be effective only if you always abstain.

❯ If you intend to have unprotected sexual intercourse, you are engaging in unsafe behavior and subjecting yourself to the risks of infection. Any form of unprotected sex is risky, including oral sex. Rather than thinking in terms of "safe sex," it is helpful to consider practices that are "unsafe," "relatively safe," and "safer." In *What You Can Do to Avoid AIDS* (1992), Earvin "Magic" Johnson emphasizes that "the most responsible thing you can do is to act as though you yourself and anybody you want to have sex with could have HIV and to practice safer sex every time" (p. 67).

❯ It is wise to talk with your partner about his or her past and present sexual practices, STD history, and sex history. It is important to negotiate safer sex with your partner.

❯ Safer sex behavior includes choosing not to be sexually active; restricting sex to one mutually faithful, uninfected partner; and not injecting drugs. Safer sex practices are especially critical if you sense that your partner may not be totally honest about his or her past or present sexual practices.

❯ If you use intravenous drugs, do not share needles.

❯ Avoid using drugs and alcohol, which cloud your judgment. Many college students attend parties in which there is a great deal of peer pressure to "drink and have fun." Intoxication lessens inhibitions, which often leads to unprotected sex. It takes a good bit of courage to take a stand and not engage in irresponsible use of drugs and alcohol, especially when many of your friends may be drinking excessively. Furthermore, if you are drunk and have unprotected sex, the chances are increased that you will be infected if your partner is carrying the virus because your immune system is lowered.

❯ People who carry the HIV virus often are not sick and may be unaware that they are infected. You can be HIV-positive and still look fine and feel well. If you have engaged in a high-risk behavior, get an HIV test to determine your health status.

Educate Yourself

Simply having information will not prevent you from getting AIDS (or from contracting other STDs), but it will help you make sound behavioral choices. In the early days of the AIDS epidemic, the emphasis was on providing information and education. But information is changing rapidly today, and it is difficult for some people who are at risk to trust what they hear from the medical profession. Some individuals do not believe the information they are given and become defensive. Others may remain in a state of denial because they do not want to change their sexual behavior. Education is only one step in the change process; information alone is not sufficient to create the environment for individuals to change. Behavior change is tough, especially when dealing with very personal behaviors such as sexuality. Assess your own knowledge about HIV/AIDS and determine whether you are practicing safer sex. What can you do to protect yourself and your sexual partners from contact with this virus?

More information about AIDS and HIV-related illnesses can be obtained from your doctor, your state or local health department, your local chapter of the American Red Cross, and the Public Health Service's toll-free HIV and AIDS hotline (1-800-342-AIDS). This national hotline is for anyone with questions about HIV and AIDS, and it functions 24 hours a day in every state. These information specialists are well trained, respect privacy, and can provide information and referrals to appropriate sources. The National AIDS Clearinghouse (1-800-458-5231) also provides information on HIV/AIDS. Updated pamphlets (some of which are listed at the end of this chapter) can also be requested by contacting either of these hotlines. Additional sources of information on HIV/AIDS and other STDs include these agencies:

> HIV/AIDS Treatment Information Service, 1-800-HIV-0440
> National Gay and Lesbian Task Force AIDS Information Line, 1-800-221-7044
> AIDS National Interfaith Network, 202-546-0807
> Public Health Service AIDS Hotline, 1-800-342-AIDS
> National Institute on Drug Abuse Hotline, 1-800-662-HELP
> National Sexually Transmitted Diseases Hotline, 1-800-227-8922
> Centers for Disease Control and Prevention, 404-639-3534
> American Red Cross, 1-800-375-2040
> World Health Organization, 202-861-4354

Magic Johnson (1992) sums up the message we have attempted to convey in this section on HIV and AIDS. His message deserves reflection.

> TAKE RESPONSIBILITY. It's your life. Remember: The safest sex is no sex, but if you choose to have sex, have safer sex each and every time. HIV happened to me, so I know it could happen to you. I want you to stay safe. Your life is worth it. (p. 156)

OTHER SEXUALLY TRANSMITTED DISEASES

It is a reality that unprotected sexual practices frequently result in contracting some form of sexually transmitted disease. Some of the more common STDs include pubic lice, herpes, genital warts, chlamydial infection, gonorrhea, and syphilis. Some STDs can be transmitted without direct genital-to-genital contact. Effective and consistent protection is necessary to protect yourself and your partner. All STDs are treatable, yet all are not curable. If you or someone you know discovers symptoms associated with STDs, seek medical treatment as soon as possible. If STDs go untreated, they can cause sterility, organ damage, and life-threatening complications.

The safest way to prevent the transmission of STDs is abstinence and other activities that do not include the exchange of body fluids. One alternative to abstinence is to consider long-term monogamy, where both partners have been tested for STDs. As a way to reduce the risk, it is a good practice to avoid using drugs and alcohol, which can interfere with your judgment and may cause you to make unsafe choices about sex. Another approach to reducing the risk is to use preventive measures (such as condoms) consistently and effectively. The

National Sexually Transmitted Diseases Hotline (1-800-227-8922) can provide you with additional information on STDs.

What it boils down to is this: If you choose to be sexually active, in addition to getting information and educating yourself about a safer sex plan, it is essential that you develop the skills to negotiate your safer sex plan with your partner. Magic Johnson (1992) has some outstanding advice for those who are considering becoming sexually active. He suggests asking yourself these questions:

> Am I prepared to practice safer sex each time I have sex?
> Am I prepared to consistently and effectively use contraception each time I have heterosexual sex?
> Am I prepared to deal with the consequences if I or my partner becomes infected with HIV or another STD or becomes pregnant?
> Am I prepared to say "no" when I think it is not right for me?

If you cannot answer "yes" to each of these questions, you are ill prepared to take on the responsibilities that are basic to this level of intimacy.

Young adults often feel that they are immune to any harm, and thus they tend to disregard good advice. Others may remain in a state of denial because they do not want to change their sexual lifestyle. In his keynote address at the Evolution of Psychotherapy conference, Elliot Aronson (2000) spoke about the value of self-persuasion as opposed to direct persuasion by others as a way to reduce risky sexual behavior in young adults. Only a small percentage of young people who are sexually active use condoms with regularity, and fear-arousing campaigns are not effective in changing these patterns of sexual behavior. Aronson encourages young adults to persuade themselves to change dysfunctional attitudes and behavior, and his work in schools teaching self-persuasion has had results far superior to traditional external approaches. If people learn to challenge their own beliefs and make new decisions based on internal motivation, they have gained personal power over their lives. By persuading yourself to act in accordance with what you know, you can lessen your chances of contracting a sexually transmitted disease.

Take Time to Reflect

1. What are your attitudes, values, and fears pertaining to HIV/AIDS and other STDs?

_____

_____

2. What steps are you willing to take to avoid contracting HIV and other STDs?

_____

_____

3. Have you known anyone who is HIV-positive or who has AIDS? How did you react when you first heard this news? Has your relationship with this person changed because of this?

_____

_____

4. What kind of education about HIV/AIDS have you been exposed to? What kind of education do you think is most needed?

_____

_____

5. Simply having information will not prevent you from contracting HIV or other STDs. What other factors, besides education, will help you make sound behavioral choices?

_____

_____

SEXUAL ABUSE AND HARASSMENT

In this section we discuss three topics that involve some form of abuse of sexuality: incest, rape, and sexual harassment. In each of these cases, power is misused or a trusting relationship is betrayed for the purpose of gaining control over the individual. Individuals are robbed of choice—except for the choice of how to react to being violated. Incest, date and acquaintance rape, and sexual harassment all entail abusive power, control, destructiveness, and violence. As such, these practices are never justifiable. In all of these forms of sexual abuse, a common denominator is the reluctance of victims to disclose that they have been wronged. In fact, many victims suffer from undue guilt and believe they were responsible for what occurred. This guilt is exacerbated by segments of society that contribute to the "blaming the victim" syndrome. The victims should not be given further insult by being blamed for cooperating or contributing to the violence that was forced upon them. Survivors of sexual abuse often carry psychological scars from these experiences that stifle their ability to accept and express the full range of their sexuality, as well as many other aspects of their lives.

Incest: A Betrayal of Trust

In our therapeutic groups we continue to meet women who suffer tremendous guilt related to early incestuous experiences. To a lesser extent, we come across men who have been subjected to incest or some form of molestation. Today this subject is being given much-deserved attention by both helping professionals and the general public, and it appears that incest is far more widespread than ever before thought. Incest occurs on all social, economic, educational, and professional levels, and at least 1 out of 10 children is molested by a trusted family member (Forward & Buck, 1988). This number of victims is conservative because many incidents are never reported, and many women do not remember their incestuous experiences until something triggers a certain memory in their adult years (Maltz & Holman, 1987). Incest is a betrayal of trust and a misuse of power and control. It can never be rationalized away. The responsibility of the perpetrator can never be diminished.

In our personal-growth groups for relatively well-functioning people, we find a startling number of women who report incidents of incest and sexual experimentation with fathers, uncles, stepfathers, grandfathers, and brothers. Incest involves any form of inappropriate sexual behavior that is brought about by coercion or deception. Vanderbilt (1992) defines incest as "any sexual abuse of a child by a relative or other person in a position of trust and authority over the child. It is the violation of the child where he or she lives—literally and metaphorically" (p. 51). Vanderbilt indicates that incest is a felony offense in all 50 states, although its definition varies from state to state, as does the punishment. Although females are more often incest victims, males also suffer the effects of incestual experiences.

In our therapy groups many women bring up the matter of incest because they feel burdened with guilt, rage, hurt, and confusion over having been taken advantage of sexually and emotionally. Some feel both confused and guilty. They feel like they are victims, but they also see themselves as conspirators. They may believe they were to blame—a belief that is often reinforced by others. They may have liked the affection and love they received even though they were probably repulsed by the sexual component. Because children realize that adults have power over them, they tend to be compliant, even in situations that seem strange. Typically, these experiences happen in childhood or early adolescence; the women remember feeling helpless at the time, not knowing how to stop the man, and also being afraid to tell anyone. Some of the reasons children give for not telling others about the abuse include not knowing that it was wrong, feeling ashamed, being frightened of the consequences of telling, fearing that others might not believe that such abuse occurred, and hoping to protect other siblings from incest. However, once they bring out these past experiences, intense, pent-up emotions surface, including hatred and rage for having been treated in such a way and feelings of having been raped and used.

In *Betrayal of Innocence,* Forward and Buck (1988) describe recurring themes that emerge from the incest experiences of almost every victim. From the victim's perspective, these themes include a desire to be loved by the perpetrator; a tendency to put up little resistance; an atmosphere of secrecy surrounding the incest; feelings of repulsion, fear, and guilt; the experience of pain and confusion; fears of being punished or removed from the home; and feelings of tremendous isolation and of having no one to turn to in a time of need. Most often the victim feels responsible for what occurred.

Children who have been sexually abused by someone in their family feel betrayed and typically develop a mistrust of others who are in a position to take advantage of them. Oftentimes the sexual abuse is only one facet of a dysfunctional family. There may also be physical abuse, neglect, alcoholism, and other problems. These children are often unaware of how psychologically abusive their family atmosphere really is for all members of the family.

The effects of these early childhood experiences can carry over into adulthood, for both women and men. Men often have many of the same patterns that are carried over because of the trauma of sexual abuse. For now we address the impact of childhood sexual abuse on the woman. The woman's ability to form sexually satisfying relationships may be impaired by events she has kept inside for many years. She may resent all men, associating them with the father or other man who initially took advantage of her. If she could not trust her own father, then what man can she trust? She may have a hard time trusting men who express affection for her, thinking that they, too, will take advantage of her. She may keep control of relationships by not letting herself be open or sexually playful and free with men. She may rarely or never allow herself to fully give in to sexual pleasure during intercourse. Her fear is that if she gives up her control, she will be hurt again. Her guilt over sexual feelings and her negative conditioning prevent her from being open to enjoying a satisfying sexual relationship. She may blame all men for her feelings of guilt and her betrayal and victimization. She may develop severe problems with establishing and maintaining intimate relationships, not only with her partner but also with her own children. In adulthood she may marry a man who will later victimize their own children, which perpetuates the pattern of her experiences in growing up. In this way the dynamics from childhood are repeated in adulthood.

Veronika Tracy (1993) conducted a research study to determine the impact of childhood sexual abuse on women's sexuality. Her study compared a group of women who were sexually abused with a group of women who had not experienced sexual abuse. She found that the women with a reported history of sexual abuse in childhood tended to have lower self-esteem, a greater number of sexual problems, less sexual satisfaction with a partner, less interest in engaging in sex, a higher propensity for sexual fantasies that involved force, and more guilt feelings about their sexual fantasies. Many of the women who were sexually abused reported that they were not able to achieve orgasm with a partner, but only by themselves. Her research revealed that women who were sexual abuse survivors often blocked out their negative experiences, only to remember the sexual abuse as they became sexually active. Paradoxically, as the women began to feel safer with a partner, their sexual activity often triggered memories of the abuse, which tended to interfere with their ability to maintain satisfying intimate relationships.

In our work with people in groups, we have found that it is therapeutic for most women and men who have a history of sexual abuse to share the burden associated with their abuse that they have been carrying alone for so many years. In a climate of support, trust, care, and respect, these individuals can begin a healing process that will eventually enable them to shed needless guilt. Before this healing can occur, they generally need to fully express bottled-up feelings, usually of anger and hatred. A major part of their therapy consists of accepting the reality that they were indeed victims and learning to direct their anger outward, rather than blaming themselves. We stress that it is important for this catharsis to occur in the group in symbolic ways. With the assistance of their therapist, they may be able to confront the perpetrator and those who did not protect them. Sometimes the perpetrator in question will no longer be alive, or the individual may decide that he or she does not want to confront the aggressor.

As we mentioned, it is not uncommon for people to assume the guilt and responsibility for these inappropriate sexual activities. Even though they may have been only 7 years old, they firmly believe they should have prevented the abuse from happening. They fail to realize that the adults in their lives were violating them and did not provide the safe environment in which they could have developed and matured as sexual beings. A very moving account that describes a long period of incest between a lonely and disturbed man and his daughter is the subject of *If I Should Die Before I Wake* by Michelle Morris (1984). This book depicts the terror experienced by the victim and shows the psychological scars she carried beyond childhood.

The process of recovery from the psychological wounds of incest varies from individual to individual, depending on a number of complex factors. Many incest victims cut off their feelings as a survival tactic. Part of the recovery process involves regaining the ability to feel, getting in touch with buried memories, and speaking truths. They will likely have to deal with these questions: "What is wrong with me?" "Why did this happen in my life?" "Why didn't I stop it?" "What will my future be like?" Victims may vacillate between denying the incestuous experiences and accepting what occurred. As they work through their memories surrounding the events, they eventually accept the fact that they were involved in incest. They typically feel sadness, grief, and then rage. It is hoped that eventually they are able to shift the responsibility to the perpetrator and to release themselves from this responsibility and guilt.

According to Forward and Buck (1988), one of the greatest gifts that therapy can bestow is a full and realistic reversal of blame and responsibility from the victim to the victimizers. In her therapeutic practice with victims of incest, Susan Forward attempts to achieve three major goals:

> Assist the client in externalizing the guilt, rage, shame, hurt, fear, and confusion that are stored up within her.

> Help the survivor place the responsibility for the events primarily with the aggressor and secondarily with the silent partner.

> Help the client realize that although incest has damaged her dignity and self-esteem she does not have to remain psychologically victimized for the rest of her life.

Through role playing, release of feelings, and sharing her conflicts with others in the group, the survivor often finds that she is not alone in her plight, and she begins to put these experiences into a new perspective. Although she will never forget these experiences, she can begin the process of letting go of feelings of self-blame and eventually arrive at a place where she is not controlled by these past experiences. In doing so, she is also freeing herself of the control that these sexual experiences (and the feelings associated with them) have had over her ability to form an intimate relationship with her partner.

We have worked with some adult men who were incest victims during childhood and adolescence. Regardless of gender or cultural background, the dynamics of incest are similar, and thus the therapeutic work is much the same for both women and men. If you have been sexually abused in any way, we encourage you to seek counseling. It is not uncommon for people to block out experiences such as sexual abuse, only to have memories and feelings surface in a course that deals with the subject. Counseling can provide you with an opportunity to deal with unresolved feelings and problems that may linger because of earlier experiences. Support groups for incest survivors also can be most beneficial. These self-help resources may also be useful for victims of child sexual abuse (Vanderbilt, 1992):

> Self-Help Clearinghouse, St. Clare's-Riverside Medical Center, Denville, NJ 07834 (201-625-9565) publishes *The Self-Help Directory,* a guide to mutual-aid self-help groups and how to form them.

> Incest Survivors Anonymous, P.O. Box 5613, Long Beach, CA 90805-0613 (213-428-5599) assists in forming 12-step groups.

> SARA (Sexual Assault Recovery Anonymous) Society, P.O. Box 16, Surrey, British Columbia V3T 4W4 Canada (604-584-2626) provides self-help information for adults and teens who were sexually abused as children.

The National Council on Child Abuse and Family Violence, 1155 Connecticut Avenue NW, Suite 400, Washington, DC 20036 (202-429-6695) may also be helpful.

In addition to counseling or support groups, many fine books deal with sexual abuse, which can be of value. If you are interested in doing further reading on the psychological aspects of incest, including its causes, effects, and treatment approaches, a number of recommended readings are listed at the end of this chapter.

Date and Acquaintance Rape

In our contacts with college students it has become clear to us that date rape is prevalent on the campus. Acquaintance rape takes place when a woman is forced to have unwanted sex with someone she knows. This might involve friends, coworkers, neighbors, or relatives. Date rape occurs in those situations where a woman is forced to have unwanted intercourse with a person in the context of dating. Rape is an act of aggressive sexuality. Contrary to popular belief, about 80% of rapes are committed by acquaintances (Weiten & Lloyd, 2000).

Earlier in this chapter we identified some misconceptions about sexuality. One of these misconceptions is that men are by nature sexually aggressive. Thus, men may feel that they are expected to be this way. As a consequence, they may misinterpret a woman's "no" as a "maybe" or a sign of initial resistance that can be broken down. Dating partners may not say what they really mean, or they may not mean what they say. This phenomenon is reinforced by the linkage of sex with domination and submission. In our society masculinity is equated with power, dominance, and sexual aggressiveness, and femininity is associated with pleasing men, sexual passivity, and lack of assertiveness (Basow, 1992).

Weiten and Lloyd (2000) offer a number of suggestions to people in dating relationships as a way of reducing date rape:

❯ Recognize that date rape is an act of sexual aggression.

❯ Familiarize yourself with the characteristics of men who are likely to engage in date rape, and avoid dating such men.

❯ Beware of using excessive alcohol or drugs, which can lower your resistance and distort your judgment.

❯ Exercise control over your environment—agree to go only to public places until you know someone well.

❯ Clarify your values and attitudes about sex *before* you are in a situation where you have to make a decision about sexual behavior.

❯ Communicate your feelings, thoughts, and expectations about sex in a clear and open manner.

❯ Listen carefully to each other and respect each other's values, decisions, and boundaries.

❯ Be prepared to act aggressively if assertive refusals do not stop unwanted sexual advances.

Both date rape and acquaintance rape can be considered as a betrayal of trust. Much like in incest, when a woman is forced to have sex against her will, her dignity as a person is violated. Not believing that she is in danger, she may make herself vulnerable to a man, and then experience hurt. She might have explicit trust in a man she knows, only to discover that he is intent on getting what he wants, regardless of the cost to her. The emotional scars that are a part of date rape are similar to the wounds inflicted by incest. As is the case with incest victims, women who are raped by people they know often take responsibility and blame themselves for what occurred, and they are often embarrassed about or afraid of reporting the incident.

Currently, many college campuses offer education directed at the prevention of date rape. The focus of this education is on the importance of being consistent and clear about what you want or do not want with your dating partner, as well as providing information about factors contributing to date rape. Rape prevention programs are increasing, and these programs are designed for women, men, and both women and men. Programs for women are designed for women to increase their awareness of high-risk situations and behaviors and to teach them how to protect themselves. Those targeted for men emphasize responsibility and respect for women. It is the man's responsibility to avoid forcing a woman to have sex with him, and he must learn that her "no" really does mean "no." It is clear that campus preventive programs need to be designed for both women and men. Both women and men can benefit from discussion groups or workshops on rape prevention. In such programs the focus is generally on topics such as interpersonal communication and predicting potential problem areas.

Sexual Harassment

Sexual harassment is repeated and unwanted sexually oriented behavior in the form of comments, gestures, or physical contacts. This phenomenon is of concern on the college campus, in the workplace, and in the military. Women experience sexual harassment more frequently than do men. Sexual harassment is abuse of the power differential between two people. Those who have more power tend to engage in sexual harassment more frequently than those with less power (Basow, 1992). You may have witnessed, or been the victim of, some of these forms of sexual harassment:

> Comments about one's body or clothes
> Physical or verbal conduct of a sexual nature
> Jokes about sex or gender-specific traits
> Repeated and unwanted staring, comments, or propositions of a sexual nature
> Demeaning references to one's gender
> Unwanted touching or attention of a sexual nature
> Conversations tinted with sexually suggestive innuendoes or double meanings
> Questions about one's sexual behavior

Men sometimes make the assumption that women like sexual attention, when in fact they resent being related to in strictly sexual terms. Sexual harassment diminishes choice, and surely it is not flattering. Harassment reduces people to objects to be demeaned. The person doing the harassing may not see this behavior as being problematic and may even joke about it. Yet it is never a laughing matter. Those on the receiving end of harassment often report feeling responsible. However, as in the case of incest and date rape, the victim should never be blamed.

PhotoDisc

Because sexual harassment is never appropriate, you have every right to break the pattern.

As is true in cases of incest and date or acquaintance rape, many incidences of sexual harassment go unreported because the individuals involved fear the consequences, such as getting fired, being denied a promotion, risking a low grade in a course, or encountering barriers to pursuing their careers. Fear of reprisals is a foremost barrier to reporting.

If you are on the receiving end of unwanted behavior, you are not powerless. Because sexual harassment is never appropriate, you have every right to break the pattern. Make it clear to the person doing the harassing that his or her behavior is unacceptable to you and that you want it stopped. If this does not work, or if you feel it would be too much of a risk to confront this individual, you can talk to someone else. If the offensive behavior does not stop, keep a detailed record of what is taking place. This will be useful in showing a pattern of unwanted behavior when you issue a complaint.

Most work settings and colleges have policies and procedures for dealing with sexual harassment complaints. You do not have to deal with this matter alone if your rights are violated. Realize that the college community does not take abusing power lightly and that procedures are designed to correct abuses. When you report a problematic situation, know that your college most likely has staff members who will assist you in bringing resolution to this situation. As is true for preserving the secret of incest, it will not help if you keep the harassment a secret. By telling someone else, you are breaking the pattern of silence that burdens sexual harassment victims.

Take Time to Reflect

1. Recent legislation requires that information identifying registered (convicted) sex offenders be made available to the public. What is your reaction to this ruling? How do you think you would react if you knew one of your neighbors had been convicted of molesting children?

_____

_____

2. Of the suggestions discussed in this chapter for reducing date or acquaintance rape, which strategies make the most sense to you? Are you using any of these strategies currently?

_____

_____

3. Sexual harassment is common on both college campuses and in the workplace. What specific behaviors that you would deem sexual harassment have you witnessed or experienced yourself?

_____

_____

SUMMARY

Sexuality is part of our personhood and should not be thought of as an activity divorced from our feelings, values, and relationships. Although childhood and adolescent experiences do have an impact on shaping our present attitudes toward sex and our sexual behavior, we are in a position to modify our attitudes and behavior if we are not satisfied with ourselves as sexual beings.

One significant step toward evaluating your sexual attitudes is to become aware of the myths and misconceptions you may harbor. Review where and how you acquired your views about sexuality. Have the sources of your sexual knowledge and values been healthy models? Have you questioned how your attitudes affect the way you feel about yourself sexually? Is your sexuality an expression of yourself as a complete person? The place that sex occupies in your life and the attitudes you have toward it are very much a matter of free choice. It is no easier to achieve sexual autonomy than it is to achieve autonomy in other areas of your life.

Another step toward developing your own sexual views is to learn to be open in talking about sexual concerns, including your fears and desires, with at least one other person you trust. Guilt feelings may be based on irrational premises, and you may be burdening yourself needlessly by feeling guilty about normal feelings and behavior. You may feel very alone when it comes to your sexual feelings, fantasies, fears, and actions. By sharing some of these concerns with others, you are likely to find out that you are not the only one with such concerns.

If we are successful in dealing with barriers that prevent us from acknowledging, experiencing, and expressing our sexuality, we increase our chances of learning how to enjoy both sensuality and sexuality. Sensuality can be a significant path toward creating satisfying sexual relationships, and we can learn to become sensual beings even if we decide not to have sexual relationships with others. Sensuality implies a full awareness of and a sensitivity to the pleasures of sight, sound, smell, taste, and touch. We can enjoy sensuality without being sexual, and it is a mistake to conclude that sensuality necessarily leads to sexual behavior. Nevertheless, sensuality is very important in enhancing sexual relationships. Intimacy, or the emotional sharing with a person we care for, is another ingredient of joyful sex. As a habitual style, sex without intimacy tends to lead to a basic sense of frustration, emptiness, and emotional deadness.

The AIDS crisis has had a significant impact on sexual behavior. Although ignorance and fear of AIDS are rampant, education can be the key to dispelling them. There are many misconceptions pertaining to who gets AIDS, how it is transmitted, and the stigma attached to it. Along with a better understanding of this disease and of other STDs, education can put you in a good position to make informed choices in expressing your sexuality.

Incest, date or acquaintance rape, and sexual harassment are all forms of sexual abuse that have the capacity to render the victims powerless and helpless. They are all embedded in gender and power dynamics. Incest and date rape are examples of betrayals of trust, sexual aggression, and violence. Those involved do not have much choice in a situation that is foisted upon them. The consequences are potentially dire both physically and psychologically, for the victims often have difficulty forming trusting relationships and enjoying sexuality.

The themes explored in the chapters on love and relationships are really impossible to separate from the themes of this chapter. Think about love, sex, and relationships as an integrated dimension of a rich and full life.

❯ Where Can I Go From Here?

1. Write down some of your major questions or concerns regarding sexuality. Consider discussing these issues with a friend, your partner (if you are involved in an intimate relationship), or your class group.

2. In your journal trace the evolution of your sexual history. What were some important experiences for you, and what did you learn from these experiences?

3. What sexual modeling did you see in your parents? What attitudes and values about sex did they convey to you, both implicitly and explicitly? What would you most want to communicate to your children about sex?

4. List as many common slang words as you are able to think of pertaining to (a) the male genitals, (b) the female genitals, and (c) sexual intercourse. Review this list and ask yourself what sexual attitudes seem to be expressed. What do you think this list implies about your culture's attitude toward sexuality? Reflect for a moment on the particular slang words regarding sex that are used in your culture. What attitudes about sex are conveyed by these words?

5. Go to a community family-planning agency or the campus health center. Pick up pamphlets on HIV, AIDS, STDs, and safer sex practices. Recruit a health educator as a guest speaker for some group you belong to or for your class.

6. Incest is a universal taboo. Explore some of the reasons for this taboo. You might investigate cross-cultural attitudes pertaining to incest. Do you view sexual experimentation between siblings during childhood as incest? Discuss.

7. The media are giving increasing attention to the topics of incest and sexual abuse of children. What do you think this current interest in these subjects implies?

Resources for Future Study

Web Site Resources

SEXUAL HEALTH NETWORK
http://www.sexualhealth.com/

This site is "dedicated to providing easy access to sexuality information, education, counseling, therapy, medical attention, and other sexuality resources," especially for people with disabilities, illness, or other health-related problems.

SEX EDUCATION RESOURCES ON THE WORLD-WIDE-WEB: RECOMMENDED SITES
http://www.jagunet.com/~dgotlib/meanstreets.htm

This site contains some excellent online resources about sexuality.

SIECUS (SEXUALITY INFORMATION AND EDUCATION COUNCIL OF THE UNITED STATES)
http://www.siecus.org/

This organization is devoted to providing information on a range of topics pertaining to sexuality.

QUEER RESOURCES DIRECTORY (QRD)
http://www.qrd.org/QRD/

The QRD is about issues relating to sexual minorities: "groups which have traditionally been labeled as 'queer' and systematically discriminated against." This site is "an electronic library with news clippings, political contact information, newsletters, essays, images, hyperlinks, and every other kind of information resource of interest to the gay, lesbian, and bisexual community."

HIV/AIDS AEGIS
http://www.aegis.com/

This is the largest and one of the most important Internet resources dealing with HIV and AIDS. This site provides an extensive collection of related links, documents, and news articles.

SEXUAL ASSAULT INFORMATION PAGE
http://www.cs.utk.edu/~bartley/saInfoPage.html

This excellent site provides a wide variety of links and information "concerning acquaintance rape, child sexual abuse/assault, incest, rape, ritual abuse, sexual assault, and sexual harassment."

 **InfoTrac College Edition Resources**

For additional readings, explore InfoTrac College Edition, our online library.

Go to **http://www.infotrac.college.com/wadsworth**

Hint: Enter the search terms:

> sexuality
> sensuality
> celibacy
> acquired immunodeficiency syndrome
> human immunodeficiency virus
> sexually transmitted disease

safe sex

sexual harassment

incest

date rape

Print Resources

Bass, E., & Davis, L. (1994). *The courage to heal: A guide for women survivors of child sexual abuse* (3rd ed.). New York: Harper Perennial.

Black, C. (1987). *It will never happen to me.* New York: Ballantine.

Centers for Disease Control and Prevention. (1994). *Voluntary HIV counseling and testing: Facts, issues, and answers.* Rockville, MD: Author.

Centers for Disease Control and Prevention. (1999). *Condoms and their use in preventing HIV infection and other STDs.* Rockville, MD: Author.

Centers for Disease Control and Prevention. (1999). *HIV and its transmission.* Rockville, MD: Author.

Crooks, R., & Baur, K. (1996). *Our sexuality* (6th ed.). Pacific Grove, CA: Brooks/Cole.

Finklehorn, D. (1984). *Child sexual abuse: New theory and research.* New York: Free Press.

Forward, S., & Buck, C. S. (1988). *Betrayal of innocence: Incest and its devastation.* New York: Penguin.

Johnson, E. M. (1992). *What you can do to avoid AIDS.* New York: Times Books.

Jones, L. (1996). *HIV/AIDS: What to do about it.* Pacific Grove, CA: Brooks/Cole.

King, B. M. (1999). *Human sexuality today* (3rd ed.). Upper Saddle River, NJ: Prentice-Hall.

Maltz, W. (1991). *The sexual healing journey: A guide for women and men survivors of sexual abuse.* New York: HarperCollins.

Meiselman, K. C. (1990). *Resolving the trauma of incest: Reintegration therapy with survivors.* San Francisco: Jossey-Bass.

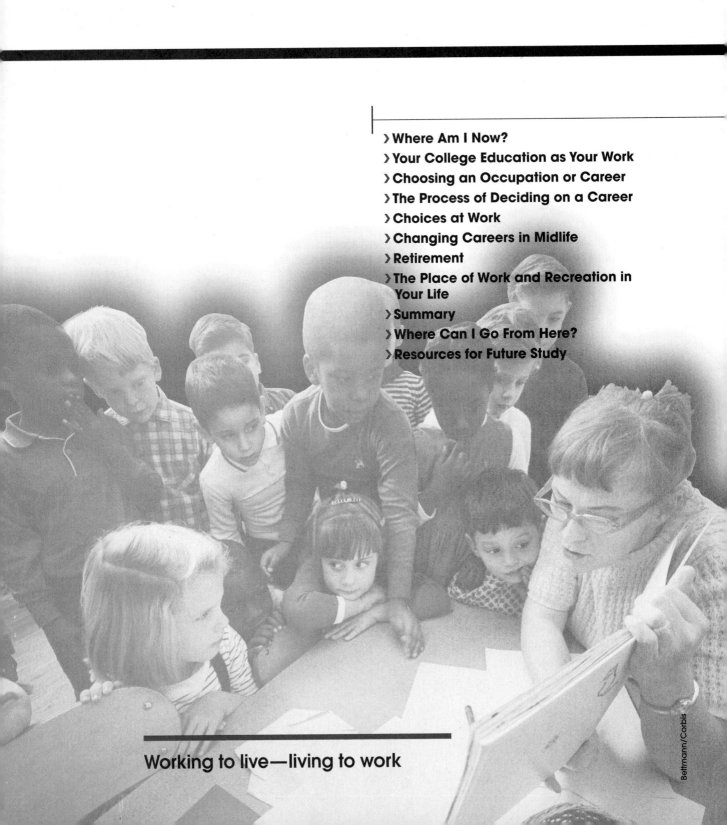

Working to live—living to work

Bethmann/Corbis

10

WORK AND RECREATION

> **Where Am I Now?**

Use this scale to respond to these statements:

4 = This statement is true of me *most* of the time.
3 = This statement is true of me *much* of the time.
2 = This statement is true of me *some* of the time.
1 = This statement is true of me *almost none* of the time.

_____ 1. I am in college because it is necessary for the career I want.

_____ 2. My primary reasons for being in college are to grow as a person and to fulfill my potential.

_____ 3. I am in college to give me time to decide what to do with my life.

_____ 4. I would not work if I did not need the money.

_____ 5. Work is a very important means of expressing myself.

_____ 6. I expect to change jobs several times during my life.

_____ 7. A secure job is more important to me than an exciting one.

_____ 8. If I am unhappy in my job, it is probably my fault, not the job's.

_____ 9. I expect my work to fulfill many of my needs and to be an important source of meaning in my life.

_____ 10. I have a good balance between my work and my recreation.

Deriving satisfaction from work and recreation are of paramount importance. As you will see, work has an impact in many areas of our lives; and the balance we find between work and recreation can contribute to our personal vitality or be a stressful experience that ultimately results in burnout. Recreation is derived from "re-create," which is defined as to restore, to refresh, to put new life into, and to create anew. Recreation involves leisure time and what we do away from work.

Work is a good deal more than an activity that takes up a certain number of hours each week. If you feel good about your work, the quality of your life will improve. If you hate your job and dread the hours you spend at it, your relationships and your feelings about yourself are bound to be affected. It is important to reflect on the attitudes we have toward work and recreation and to be aware of the impact of these attitudes on our lives. It is certainly worth the effort to think about ways to improve the quality of the many hours you devote to work and to recreation in your daily life.

If you are a reentry student, you may already have a career. You may be working at a job, carrying out responsibilities in the home, and also being either a part-time or a full-time college student. Your college work may be preparing you for a career change or a job promotion. If you have not yet begun a career, you can use this chapter to examine your expectations about work. Make an assessment of your personal interests, needs, values, and abilities, and begin the process of matching these personal characteristics with occupational information and trends in the world of work. In *Taking Charge of Your Career Direction*, Robert Lock (2000c) acknowledges that choosing an occupation is not easy. Externally, the working world is constantly changing; internally, your expectations, needs, motivations, values, and interests may change. Deciding on a career involves integrating the realities of these two worlds. Lock emphasizes the importance of *actively choosing* a career.

> YOU MUST ACCEPT THE RESPONSIBILITY of choosing an occupation for yourself and then be willing to live with the consequences of that decision. These words are easily said but difficult to practice. There will be times when you want to escape the responsibility that freedom of choice brings, but no good counselor, parent, friend, or test interpreter will allow you to abdicate that responsibility. (p. 6)

One way to assume an active role in deciding on a career is to talk to other people about their job satisfaction. However, it is essential that you explore your thoughts about a career. One of the major factors that might prevent you from becoming active in planning for a career is the temptation to put off doing what needs to be done to choose your work. Rather than actively choosing a career, some people allow themselves to merely "fall into" a job.

Career development researchers have found that most people go through a series of stages when choosing an occupation or, more typically, several occupations to pursue. As with life-span stages, different factors emerge or become influential at different times throughout this process. Therefore, it could well be a mistake to think about selecting *one* occupation that will last a lifetime. It may be more fruitful to choose a general type of work or a broad field of endeavor that appeals to you. You can consider your present job or field of study as a means of gaining experience and opening doors to new possibilities, and you can focus on what you want to learn from this experience. It can be liberating to realize that your decisions about work can be part of a developmental process and that your jobs can change as you change or can lead to related occupations within your chosen field.

The fast pace of social and technological change in today's world is forcing people to adapt to a changing world of work. The average American entering the workforce today will change careers, not just jobs, three times (Bolles, 1999; Naisbitt & Aburdene, 1991). This means that people entering the workforce need to have more than specific knowledge and skills; they need to be able to adapt to change. One career may pave the way to another.

Before continuing with this chapter, let's clarify the terms "career," "occupation," "job," and "work." A *career* can be thought of as your life's work. A career spans a period of time and may involve one or several occupations; it is the sequence of a person's work experience over time. An *occupation* is your vocation, profession, business, or trade, and you may change your occupation several times during your lifetime. A *job* is your position of employment within an occupation. Over a period of time you may have several jobs within the same occupation. A job is what you do to earn money to survive and to do the things you would like to do. *Work* is a broad concept that refers to something you do because you want to, and we hope, because you enjoy it. Ideally, your job and your work involve similar activities. Work is fulfilling when you feel you are being compensated adequately and when you like what you are doing.

YOUR COLLEGE EDUCATION AS YOUR WORK

You may already have made several vocational decisions and held a number of different jobs, you may be changing careers, or you may be in the process of exploring career options and preparing yourself for a career. If you are in the midst of considering what occupations might best suit you, it would be helpful to review the meaning that going to college has for you now. There is certainly some relationship between how you approach your college experience and how you will someday approach your career.

School may be your primary line of work for the present, but for those of you who are engaged in a career and have families, school is not likely to be your main source of work. Regardless of your commitments outside of college, it is a good idea to reflect on why you are in college. Ask yourself these questions:

"Why am I in college?" "Is it my choice or someone else's choice for me?" "Do I enjoy most of my time as a student?" "Is my work as a student satisfying and meaningful?" "Would I rather be somewhere else or doing something other than being a student? If so, why am I staying in college?"

The reasons for attending college are many and varied, but studies suggest that student motivations can be summarized under the following three categories (Herr & Cramer, 1988):

> *Self-fulfillers.* If you are in this category, your primary concern is searching for a personal identity and using your college experience as a means of self-fulfillment. You expect school to provide a supportive environment for self-expansion through academic pursuits.

> *Careerists.* If you are in this category, you are attending college mainly for vocational reasons. School is a means to an end rather than an end in itself. Although you may have other motivations, they are secondary to your major goal of adequately preparing yourself for a selected occupation.

> *Avoiders.* The decision to go to college is sometimes more an avoidance maneuver than a conscious striving for a career goal or for self-development. You may be in college largely as a result of pressure from parents or peers. You also may not be quite certain what you want to do with your life and may hope that you can clarify your thoughts. Some attend college as a delaying tactic. Others are interested primarily in the social life.

Herr and Cramer maintain that many students in each of these categories can benefit from career counseling. Self-fulfillers may eventually realize that even though personal growth is a laudable goal they will have to work. Careerists may discover that their original career choice is inappropriate and that they need to search out alternatives. Avoiders eventually realize that they cannot endlessly put off their career choice. Whatever your motivation for going to college, career-development assistance can provide you with the tools you need to make good career decisions.

Brandi's story illustrates how motivations for going to college can change. Brandi, now age 21, initially enrolled in college on a scholarship to participate in the gymnastics team. Brandi made choices to broaden her life beyond gymnastics, as you can see from her account.

BRANDI'S STORY

I had been a gymnast since I was 4 years old, and I didn't know any kind of life without it. My body was consistently failing me though, and going to practice every day was becoming harder and harder. It was frustrating not to be able to do what I was once capable of, and I found I was becoming very unhappy as a gymnast. I had been a gymnast all my life, and I wanted the chance to be a normal student for a while.

Knowing that I was not going to be able to continue as a gymnast much longer, I decided it was important to end my gymnastics career while I still liked my sport. My coach expected a lot from me, and I expected a lot from myself. However, I felt as though I was not going to be able to reach these expectations. I was also tired of waking up and wondering how much I was going to be hurting physically every day. There were many pressures on me, such as struggles to be thin, get good grades, and practice at a level that was equivalent to what my coach wanted.

Gymnastics took an enormous amount of time and energy. I found myself wanting to put my time and energy into my college education as I began to set new goals for myself. It was the first time in my life that I really wanted to accomplish something that did not involve gymnastics. My choice to leave the team was very difficult and scary. I was so used to gymnastics being such a large part of my life and such a large part of who I was. I am very happy with the choice I made, and even though I miss gymnastics at times, I now have my education and other things in my life to accomplish and look forward to.

In Chapter 1 we asked you to review your experiences as a learner and your learning style. You were encouraged to take steps to become an active and involved student. This would be a good time to review the goals you set and determine how well you are progressing toward them. If you established a contract to take increased responsibility for your own learning and to get personally involved in this book and the course, reevaluate how you are doing. This is an ideal time to set new goals, to modify your original goals, or to try new behavior in reaching your goals.

If you like the meaning your college experience has for you as well as your part in creating this meaning, you are likely to assume responsibility for making your job satisfying. If you typically do more than is required as a student, you are likely to be willing to go beyond doing what is expected of you in your job. If you are the kind of student who fears making mistakes and will not risk saying what you think in class, you may carry this behavior into a job. You may be afraid of jeopardizing your grades by being assertive, and someday you may very well be unassertive in the work world out of fear of losing your job or not advancing. If you have taken on too many courses and other projects, planned poorly, procrastinated, and fallen behind, you may feel utter frustration and exhaustion by semester's end. Might you not display this same behavior in your work?

Make an honest inventory of your role as a student. If you are not satisfied with yourself as a student, the situation is far from being hopeless. If you decide that your present major is not what really interests you, you are no more wedded to your course of study than you are to one particular job in the future. Determine for yourself why you are in college and what you are getting from and giving to this project.

The fast pace of social and technological change in today's world is forcing people to adapt to a changing world of work.

Roger Tully/Stone

CHOOSING AN OCCUPATION OR CAREER

What do you expect from work? What factors do you stress in selecting a career or an occupation? In working with college students, we find that many of you have not thought seriously about why you are choosing a given vocation. For some, parental pressure or encouragement is the major reason for being in college. Others have idealized views of what it would be like to be a lawyer, an engineer, or a doctor. Many college students have not looked at what they value the most and whether these values can be attained in their chosen vocation. John Holland's (1997) theory of career decision making is based on the assumption that career choices are an expression of personality. Holland believes the choice of an occupation should reflect the person's motivation, knowledge, personality, and ability. Occupations represent a way of life. Dave's personal story illustrates this search for a satisfying career. Dave chose college without knowing what he wanted. Eventually he found a direction by pursuing what interested him.

DAVE'S STORY

I went to college right out of high school even though I wasn't sure that college was for me. I went because I thought I needed a college degree to get a good job and to succeed.

My first year was a bit rough because of the new surroundings. In my classes I felt like a number, and it didn't seem to matter if I attended classes or not. College provided a wide range of freedom. I was the one who was responsible to show up for class. It was hard for me to handle this freedom. I found it easier to go off with my friends. Needless to say, my grades took a nose dive. I was placed on academic probation. As a result, I decided to go to a community college. But my pattern of not taking school seriously remained the same.

Although I wanted to eventually finish college, I knew that university life was not right for me at this time. I decided to move out of my parents' home and worked full time. Although I was working, I managed to take a few night classes at a community college. I knew that if I left college completely it would be harder to ever return.

Eventually I accepted a job with a promotional marketing firm. I was given more responsible assignments, and I really enjoyed what I was doing. I asked myself: "How could I apply what I enjoyed doing and make it a career?" This question led me to doing research on the sports entertainment field to discover a career path.

My research convinced me of the importance of returning to college full time. Now I was focused and determined to receive my degree and to pursue a career in the sports entertainment industry. Knowing what I wanted as a career made selecting a major relatively easy. I majored in business with a marketing emphasis and did extremely well. My journey took me from academic disqualification to graduating with honors.

After graduation I accepted a job from the same marketing firm where I had worked earlier, only this time it was a higher level job that included travel. After many interviews I accepted a job with a professional baseball team. After working there for more than 2 years, I was offered a job with a national sport's team in the sales and marketing department, where I am currently employed. I sell advertising, sponsorships, and various ticket packages. My work involves implementing much of what I learned in my major. This position is ideal because it allows me to do what I enjoy and use what I learned in college.

Following my interests has led to an exciting career. I look forward to getting up and going to work, which is both fun and challenging. I am able to combine my sports hobbies with my profession. This work is personally rewarding, and I feel energized and motivated on the job. My work doesn't seem like "work." To me, this is one of the keys to a meaningful life.

The Disadvantages of Choosing an Occupation Too Soon

So much emphasis is placed on what you will do "for a living" that you may feel compelled to choose an occupation or a career before you are really ready to do so. In our society we are pressured from an early age to grow up, and we are encouraged to identify with some occupation. Children are often asked: "What are you going to be when you grow up?" Embedded in this question is the implication that we are not grown up until we have decided to be something. By late adolescence or young adulthood, the pressure is on to make decisions and commitments. Young adults are expected to make choices that will affect the rest of their lives, even though they may not feel ready to make these commitments. Our society expects young people to identify their values, choose a vocation and a lifestyle, and then settle down (Carney & Wells, 1999). The implication is that once young people make the "right decision" they should be set for life. Yet deciding on a career is not that simple.

One of the disadvantages of focusing on a particular occupation too soon is that students' interest patterns are often not sufficiently reliable or stable in high school or sometimes even in the college years to predict job success and satisfaction. Furthermore, the typical student does not have enough self-knowledge or knowledge of educational offerings and vocational opportunities to make realistic decisions. The pressure to make premature vocational decisions often results in choosing an occupation in which one does not have the interests and abilities required for success. At the other extreme are those who engage in delay, defensive avoidance, and procrastination. An individual on this end of the scale drifts endlessly and aimlessly, and life may be pretty well over when he or she asks, "Where am I going?" It is clear that either extreme is problematic. We need to be cautious in resisting pressures from the outside to decide too quickly on a life's vocation, yet we also need to be alert to the tendencies within ourselves to expect that what we want will come to us easily. You may remember from Chapter 2 that Erikson calls for a psychological moratorium during adolescence to enable young people to get some distance from the pressure of choosing a career too soon. A moratorium can reduce the pressure of having to make key life choices without sufficient data. As young people gain experience, they are likely to develop a new perspective about what they want from a career and from life.

Factors in Vocational Decision Making

Factors that have been shown to be important in the occupational decision-making process include motivation and achievement; attitudes about occupations; abilities; interests; values; self-concept; temperament and personality styles; socioeconomic level; parental influence; ethnic identity; gender; and physical, mental, emotional, and social handicaps. In choosing your vocation (or in evaluating the choices you have made previously), consider which factors really mean the most to you. Let's take a closer look at how some of these factors may influence your vocational choice, keeping in mind that vocational choice is a process, not an event.

Motivation and Achievement Setting goals is at the core of the process of deciding on a vocation. If you have goals but do not have the energy and persistence to pursue them, your goals will not be met. Your need to achieve along with your achievements to date are related to your motivation to translate goals into action plans. In thinking about your career choices, identify those areas where your drive is the greatest. Also, reflect on specific achievements. What have you accomplished that you feel particularly proud of? What are you doing now that moves you in the direction of achieving what is important to you? What are some of the things you dream about doing in the future? Did you ever have a dream of what you wanted to be when you grew up? What happened to that dream? Were others encouraging or discouraging of this dream? Thinking about your goals, needs, motivations, and achievements is a good way to get a clearer focus on your career direction.

Attitudes About Occupations We develop our attitudes toward the status of occupations by learning from the people in our environment. Typical first graders are not aware of the differential status of occupations, yet in a few years these children begin to rank occupations in a manner similar to that of adults. As students advance to higher grades, they reject more and more occupations as unacceptable. Unfortunately, they rule out some of the very jobs from which they may have to choose if they are to find employment as adults. It is difficult for people to feel positive about themselves if they have to accept an occupation they perceive as low in status. At this point ask yourself: "What did I learn about work from my parents? What did I learn about work from my culture?"

Abilities Ability or aptitude has received a great deal of attention in the career decision-making process, and it is probably used more often than any other factor to evaluate potential for success. Ability refers to your competence in an activity; aptitude is your ability to learn. Both general and specific abilities should be considered in making career choices, but scholastic aptitude or IQ—a general ability typically considered to consist of both verbal and numerical aptitudes—is particularly significant because it largely determines who will be able to obtain the level of education required for entrance into higher status occupations. You can measure and compare your abilities with the skills required for various professions and academic areas of interest to you. Ask yourself: "How did I determine what abilities I have? What influence did my family of origin have on my perception of my abilities? How did others, such as teachers and friends, influence my perception?"

Interests Your interests reflect your experiences or ideas pertaining to work-related activities that you like or dislike. Interest measurement has become increasingly popular and is used extensively in career planning. Vocational planning should give primary consideration to interests. First, determine your areas of vocational interest. Next, identify occupations in your interest areas. Then, determine which occupations correspond to your abilities.

Occupational interest surveys can be used to compare your interests with those of others who have found job satisfaction in a given area (Carney & Wells, 1999). Researchers have shown that a significant relationship exists between interests and abilities. Abilities and interests are two integral components of career decision making, and understanding how these factors are related is essential (Randahl, 1991). But remember that interest alone does not necessarily mean that you have the ability to succeed in a particular occupation.

Several interest inventories are available to help you assess your vocational interests. If you were going to select just one instrument, we recommend Holland's Self-Directed Search (SDS) Interest Inventory, which is probably the most widely used interest inventory. Other interest and personality inventories you may want to consider taking are the Vocational Preference Inventory, the Strong Interest Inventory, the Kuder Occupational Interest Inventory, and the Myers-Briggs Type Indicator. This last instrument assesses types of human personality. For further information about such inventories, contact the counseling center at your college.

Values   Your values indicate what is important to you and what you want from life. It is important to assess, identify, and clarify your values so you will be able to choose a career that enables you to achieve what you value. An inventory of your values can help you discern patterns in your life and see how your values have emerged, taken shape, and changed over time.

Your work values pertain to what you hope to accomplish through your role in an occupation. Work values are an important aspect of your total value system, and knowing those things that bring meaning to your life is crucial if you hope to find a career that has personal value for you. A few examples of work values include helping others, influencing people, finding meaning, prestige, status, competition, friendships, creativity, stability, recognition, adventure, physical challenge, change and variety, opportunity for travel, moral fulfillment, and independence. Because specific work values are often related to particular occupations, they can be the basis of a good match between you and a position.

Self-Concept   People with a poor self-concept are not likely to envision themselves in a meaningful or important job. They are likely to keep their aspirations low, and thus their achievements will probably be low. They may select and remain in a job they do not enjoy or derive satisfaction from because they are convinced this is all they are worthy of. Choosing a vocation can be thought of as a public declaration of the kind of person we see ourselves as being.

Personality Types and Choosing a Career

People who exhibit certain values and particular personality traits are a good match with certain career areas. John Holland (1997) has identified six worker personality types, and his topology is widely used as the basis for books on career development, vocational tests used in career counseling centers, and self-help approaches for making career decisions.* Because his work has been so influential in vocational theory, it is worth going into some detail about it here. As you read the descriptions of Holland's six personality types, take the time to think about the patterns that fit you best.

---

*Holland's (1997) six personality types are realistic, investigative, artistic, social, enterprising, and conventional. Our discussion of these six types is based on Holland's work as refined by Jim Morrow (retired professor of counseling, Western Carolina University, North Carolina). For more information about Holland's personality types and implications for selecting a career, we highly recommend John Holland's (1994) *Self-Directed Search (Form R)*. For further information contact: Psychological Assessment Resources, Inc., P.O. Box 998, Odessa, FL 33556 or telephone (1-800-331-TEST).

As you read about these six personality types, remember that most people do not fall neatly into one category but have characteristics from several types. When you come across a phrase that describes you, put a check mark in the space provided. Then look again at the six personality types and select the three types (in rank order) that best describe the way you see yourself. As you become more aware of the type of person you are, you can apply these insights in your own career decision-making process.

Realistic Types

_____ are attracted to outdoor, mechanical, and physical activities, hobbies, and occupations

_____ like to work with things, objects, and animals rather than with ideas, data, and people

_____ tend to have mechanical and athletic abilities

_____ like to construct, shape, and restructure and repair things around them

_____ like to use equipment and machinery and to see tangible results

_____ are persistent and industrious builders but seldom creative and original, preferring familiar methods and established patterns

_____ tend to think in terms of absolutes, dislike ambiguity, and prefer not to deal with abstract, theoretical, and philosophical issues

_____ are materialistic, traditional, and conservative

_____ do not have strong interpersonal and verbal skills and are often uncomfortable in situations in which attention is centered on them

_____ tend to find it difficult to express their feelings and may be regarded as shy

Investigative Types

_____ are naturally curious and inquisitive

_____ need to understand, explain, and predict what goes on around them

_____ are scholarly and scientific and tend to be pessimistic and critical about nonscientific, simplistic, or supernatural explanations

_____ tend to become engrossed in whatever they are doing and may appear to be oblivious to everything else

_____ are independent and like to work alone

_____ prefer neither to supervise others nor to be supervised

_____ are theoretical and analytic in outlook and find abstract and ambiguous problems and situations challenging

_____ are original and creative and often find it difficult to accept traditional attitudes and values

_____ avoid highly structured situations with externally imposed rules but are themselves internally well-disciplined, precise, and systematic

_____ have confidence in their intellectual abilities but often feel inadequate in social situations

_____ tend to lack leadership and persuasive skills

_____ tend to be reserved and formal in interpersonal relationships

_____ are not typically expressive emotionally and may not be considered friendly

Artistic Types

_____ are creative, expressive, original, intuitive, and individualistic

_____ like to be different and strive to stand out from the crowd

_____ like to express their personalities by creating new and different things with words, music, materials, and physical expression like acting and dancing

_____ want attention and praise but are sensitive to criticism

_____ tend to be uninhibited and nonconforming in dress, speech, and action

_____ prefer to work without supervision

_____ are impulsive in outlook

_____ place great value on beauty and esthetic qualities

_____ tend to be emotional and complicated

_____ prefer abstract tasks and unstructured situations

_____ find it difficult to function well in highly ordered and systematic situations

_____ seek acceptance and approval from others but often find close interpersonal relationships so stressful that they avoid them

_____ compensate for their resulting feelings of estrangement or alienation by relating to others primarily indirectly through art

_____ tend to be introspective

Social Types

_____ are friendly, enthusiastic, outgoing, and cooperative

_____ enjoy the company of other people

_____ are understanding and insightful about others' feelings and problems

_____ like helping and facilitating roles like teacher, mediator, adviser, or counselor

_____ express themselves well and are persuasive in interpersonal relationships

_____ like attention and enjoy being at or near the center of the group

_____ are idealistic, sensitive, and conscientious about life and in dealings with others

_____ like to deal with philosophical issues such as the nature and purpose of life, religion, and morality

_____ dislike working with machines or data and at highly organized, routine, and repetitive tasks

_____ get along well with others and find it natural to express their emotions

_____ are tactful in relating to others and are considered to be kind, supportive, and caring

Enterprising Types

_____ are outgoing, self-confident, persuasive, and optimistic

_____ like to organize, direct, manage, and control the activities of groups toward personal or organizational goals

_____ are ambitious and like to be in charge

_____ place a high value on status, power, money, and material possessions

_____ like to feel in control and responsible for making things happen

_____ are energetic and enthusiastic in initiating and supervising activities

_____ like to influence others

_____ are adventurous, impulsive, assertive, and verbally persuasive

_____ enjoy social gatherings and like to associate with well-known and influential people

_____ like to travel and explore and often have exciting and expensive hobbies

_____ see themselves as popular

_____ tend to dislike activities requiring scientific abilities and systematic and theoretical thinking

_____ avoid activities that require attention to detail and a set routine

Conventional Types

_____ are well-organized, persistent, and practical

_____ enjoy clerical and computational activities that follow set procedures

_____ are dependable, efficient, and conscientious

_____ enjoy the security of belonging to groups and organizations and make good team members

_____ are status-conscious but usually do not aspire to high positions of leadership

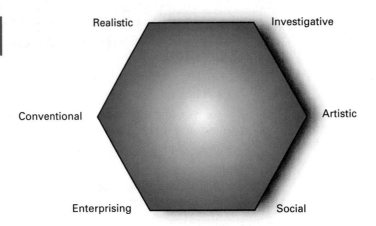

Figure 10.1
Holland's Hexagon

_____ are most comfortable when they know what is expected of them

_____ tend to be conservative and traditional

_____ usually conform to expected standards and follow the lead of those in positions of authority, with whom they identify

_____ like to work indoors in pleasant surroundings and place value on material comforts and possessions

_____ are self-controlled and low-key in expressing their feelings

_____ avoid intense personal relationships in favor of more casual ones

_____ are most comfortable among people they know well

_____ like for things to go as planned and prefer not to change routines

Relationships Among the Personality Types As you were reading the descriptions of the six personality types, you probably noticed that each type shares some characteristics with some other types and also is quite different from some of the others. To help you compare and contrast the six types, Holland's "hexagon" illustrates the order of the relationships among the types.

Each type shares some characteristics with those types adjacent to it on the hexagon. Each type has only a little in common with those types two positions removed from it, and it is quite unlike the type opposite it on the hexagon. For example, the investigative type shares some characteristics with the realistic and artistic types, has little in common with the conventional and social types, and is quite different from the enterprising type. If you read the descriptions of the six types once more with the hexagon in mind, the relationships among the types will become clearer.

People who feel that they resemble two or three types that are not adjacent on the hexagon may find it difficult to reconcile the conflicting elements in those type descriptions. It is important to remember that the descriptions provided are for "pure" types and that very few people resemble a single type to the exclusion of all others. This is why we ask you to select the three types that you think best describe you.

Once you have compared your personal traits with the characteristics of each of the six types, it is possible to find a general area of work that most matches your personal qualities, interests, and values. This topic is addressed in the next section. The Take Time to Reflect exercise will assist you in assessing your personality type. It is important to have someone you know assess you as well as doing so yourself.

Take Time to Reflect

This exercise will help you become familiar with Holland's personality types.

1. Read the descriptions and other information furnished about Holland's six personality types at least two or three times.

2. Which of the six personality types best describes you? No one type will be completely "right" for you, but one of them will probably sound more like you than the others. Consider the overall descriptions of the types; do not concentrate on just one or two characteristics of a type. As soon as you are satisfied that one type describes you better than the others, write that type down on the space for number 1 at the end of this exercise.

3. Which of the six types next best describes you? Write that type down in the space for number 2. Write down the type that next best describes you in the space for number 3.

4. Next, give the descriptions of the six types to someone who knows you very well. Ask them to read the descriptions carefully and order them in terms of their resemblance to you, just as you have done. Do not show or tell them how you rated yourself.

5. After the other person finishes rating you, compare your own rating with theirs. If there is not close agreement among the three types on both lists, ask the other person to give examples of your behaviors that prompted his or her ratings. The other person may not have rated you very accurately, or your behavior may not portray you to others as you see yourself. The purpose of this exercise is to familiarize you with Holland's personality types. It may have a "bonus" effect of better familiarizing you with yourself.

Your rating of yourself:

1. _____

2. _____

3. _____

Rating by someone who knows you well:

1. _____

2. _____

3. _____

Brooks/Cole

The process of selecting a career is more than a simple matter of matching information about the world of work with your personality type.

THE PROCESS OF DECIDING ON A CAREER

Holland (1997) originally developed his system as a way of helping people make occupational choices. After you have identified the three personality types that most closely describe you, this information can be used in your career decision-making process.

It is more likely that you will be successful in your career if your own personality types match those of people who have already proven themselves in the career that you hope to pursue. Holland has developed elaborate materials that can help you assess your personality type and compare it with the dominant types in various occupations. Here is a list of possible occupations associated with each personality type.

Realistic Type: carpenter, electronics engineer, emergency medical technology, mechanical engineering, industrial design, sculpture, law enforcement, photography, wildlife conservation management, orthodontics assistant, culinary arts, locomotive engineer, camera repair, cement masonry, jewelry repair, diesel mechanics, optician, floral design, marine surveying, automotive technology.

Investigative Type: economics, marketing, linguistics, biology, dentistry, food technology, optometry, medicine, physician's assistant, pollution control and technology, surveying, quality control management, meteorology, public health administration, highway engineering, veterinary medicine, biochemistry, cardiology, chemistry.

Artistic Type: acting/theater, creative writing, dance, journalism, commercial art, music, technical writing, fashion illustration, art education, graphic arts and design, cosmetology, fashion design, audiovisual technology, furniture design, interior decorating and design, photography, architecture, landscape architecture, stage design.

Social Type: education, motion pictures/cinema, probation and parole, recreation education/leadership, social work, hospital administration, rehabilitation counseling, nursing, psychology, school administration, labor relations, religious education, television production, library assistant, air traffic control, real estate, physical therapy, home economics, beautician, dental assistant.

Enterprising Type: accounting, travel agency management, park administration, dietetics, laboratory science, banking and finance, industrial engineering, international engineering, fire science management, records management, fashion merchandising, business administration, travel administration, marketing, law, international relations, marketing, outdoor recreation.

Conventional Type: computer and data processing, office machine technology, bookkeeping, building inspection, computer operator, court reporter, library assistant, medical records technology, personnel clerk, secretarial science, quality control technology, orthodontics assistant, electrical technology, medical secretary.

This process of selecting a career is more than a simple matter of matching information about the world of work with your personality type. You will find it useful to go through some of these steps several times. For example, gathering and assessing information is a continual process rather than a step to be completed.

> **Begin by focusing on yourself.** Continue to identify your interests, abilities, values, beliefs, wants, and preferences. Keep these questions in mind: "Who am I?" "How do I want to live?" "Where do I want to live?" "What kind of work environment do I want?" "What do I want to do for a living?" This self-assessment includes taking into consideration your personality style. Ask yourself: "Do I function well in a system that is structured or unstructured?" "How much and what type of supervision do I need?" "Do I prefer to work alone or with others?"

> **Generate alternative solutions.** This stage is closely related to the next two. Rather than first narrowing your options, consider a number of alternatives or different potential occupations that you are drawn to. In this step it is wise to consider your work values and interests, especially as they apply to Holland's six personality types.

❯ **Gather and assess information about the alternatives generated.** In the process of expanding your list of career possibilities, recognize that you will likely devote a great deal of time to your occupation. Be willing to research the occupations that attract you. Doing so will increase the chances of you being able to live the way you want. Ask yourself, "Where do I best fit?" "Will the occupation I am considering be psychologically and financially satisfying to me?" "Do I have the resources to meet the challenges and responsibilities of the occupation?" "What are the typical characteristics of people who enter into this occupation?" Find an occupation that matches your interests, values, and talents, and read about the educational requirements of the occupation. Talk to as many people as you can who are involved in the occupations you are considering. Ask them how their occupation may be changing in the years to come. Examine the social, political, economic, and geographic environment as a basis for assessing factors that influence your career choice.

❯ **Weigh and prioritize your alternatives.** After you arrive at a list of alternatives, spend adequate time prioritizing them. Consider the practical aspects of your decisions. Integrate occupational information and the wishes and views of others with your knowledge of yourself.

❯ **Make the decision and formulate a plan.** It is best to think of a series of many decisions at various turning points. In formulating a plan, read about the preparation required for your chosen alternative. Ask, "How can I best get to where I want to go?"

❯ **Carry out the decision.** After deciding, take practical steps to make your vision become a reality. Realize that committing yourself to implementing your decision does not mean that you will have no fears. The important thing is not to allow these fears to keep you frozen. You will never know if you are ready to meet a challenge unless you put your plan into action. This action plan includes knowing how to market your skills to employers. You need to learn how to identify employment sources, prepare resumes, and meet the challenges of job interviews.

❯ **Get feedback.** After taking practical steps to carry out your decision, you will need to determine whether your choices are viable for you. Both the world of work and you will change over time, and what may look appealing to you now may not seem appropriate at some future time. Remember that career development is an ongoing process, and it will be important to commit yourself to repeating at least part of the process as your needs change or as occupational opportunities open up or decline.

For a more detailed discussion of the steps we have outlined above, see *Taking Charge of Your Career Direction* (Lock, 2000c). Lock emphasizes these key components of the career-planning process: being aware and committed, studying the environment, studying yourself, generating occupational alternatives, gathering information about occupational prospects, making decisions, implementing a plan of action, and obtaining feedback or reevaluating this career decision-making process.

Take Time to Reflect   This survey is aimed at getting you to reflect on your basic attitudes, values, abilities, and interests in regard to occupational choice.

1. Rate each item, using the following code: 1 = this is a *most important* consideration; 2 = this is *important* to me, but not a top priority; 3 = this is *slightly important*; 4 = this is of *little* or *no importance* to me.

_____ financial rewards

_____ security

_____ challenge

_____ prestige and status

_____ the opportunity to express my creativity

_____ autonomy—freedom to direct my project

_____ opportunity for advancement

_____ variety within the job

_____ recognition

_____ friendship and relations with coworkers

_____ serving people

_____ a source of meaning

_____ the chance to continue learning

_____ structure and routine

Once you have finished the assessment, review the list and write down the three most important values you associate with selecting a career or occupation.

_____

_____

2. In what area(s) do you see your strongest abilities?

_____

_____

3. What are a few of your major interests?

_____

_____

(continued)

4. Which one value of yours do you see as having some bearing on your choice of a vocation?

_____

_____

5. At this point, what work do you see as most suitable to your interests, abilities, and values?

_____

_____

CHOICES AT WORK

Just as choosing a career is a process, so is creating meaning in our work. If we grow stale in our jobs or do not find avenues of self-expression through the work we do, we eventually lose our vitality. In this section we look at ways to find meaning in work and at approaches to keeping our options open.

The Dynamics of Discontent in Work

If you are dissatisfied with your job, one recourse is to look for a new one. Change alone, however, might not produce different results. In general it is a mistake to assume that change necessarily cures dissatisfactions, and this very much applies to changing jobs. To know whether a new job would be helpful, you need to understand as clearly as you can why your present job is not satisfactory to you. Consider some of the external factors that can devitalize you in your job and the very real pressures your job often creates. It is also critical to deal with those factors within yourself that lead to discontent at work. The emphasis of our discussion will be on what you can do to change some of these factors in the job and in yourself.

You may like your work and derive satisfaction from it yet at the same time feel drained because of irritations produced by factors that are not intrinsic to the work itself. Such factors may include low morale or actual conflict and disharmony among fellow workers, authoritarian supervisors who make it difficult for you to feel any sense of freedom on the job, or organizational blocks to your creativity. Countless pressures and demands can sap your energy and lead you to feel dissatisfied with your job. These include having to meet deadlines and quotas, having to compete with others instead of simply doing your best, facing the threat of losing your job, feeling stuck in a job that offers little opportunity for growth or that you deem dehumanizing, dealing with difficult customers or clients, or having to work long hours or perform exhausting or tedious work. A stress that is particularly insidious—because it can compound all the other dissatisfactions you might feel—is the threat of cutbacks or layoffs, an anxiety that becomes more acute when you think of your commitments and responsibilities. In addition to the strains you may experience on the job, you may also have the daily stress of commuting to and from work. You may be tense before you even get to work, and the trip home may only increase the level of tension or anxiety you bring home with you. One real problem for many is that relationships with others are negatively affected by this kind of pressure. If your work is draining and deenergizing, you may have little to give your children, spouse, and friends, and you may not be receptive to their efforts to give to you. You may not be able to avoid working in a less than desirable job, but you cannot afford to ignore the effects this may have on your overall life. If you are in an unsatisfying and draining work situation, look for other ways of nourishing yourself.

All these factors can contribute to a general discontent that robs your work of whatever positive benefits it might otherwise have. In the face of such discontent, you might just plod along, hating your job and spoiling much of the rest of your life as well. The alternative is to look at the specific things that contribute to your unhappiness or tension and to ask yourself what you can do about them. You can also ask what you can do about your own attitudes toward those pressures and sources of tension.

Self-Esteem and Work

With downsizing and layoffs, people sometimes find themselves out of work due to circumstances beyond their control. Unemployment is a reality that can erode self-esteem. Maria's story illustrates how self-esteem and identity are often anchored to your ability to engage in meaningful work, and how losing your job can be devastating.

MARIA'S STORY

*T*wo years ago I had an accident at work that forever changed who I was and required that I modify my future goals and plans. After hurting my back, I was told that I was no longer able to continue in the job that I had been engaged in for 16 years. I didn't want to believe this, and for a time I was in denial. When this harsh reality eventually hit me, I became depressed.

I didn't know who I was anymore. Working had been my life. It was my identity. I felt lost and very empty inside, and my self-esteem plummeted. I found myself making

(continued)

very little money, and at my age this was a failure. Being on worker's compensation, I was required to get training in a different line of work. Changing careers at this point in my life was a most difficult task. I was both angry and scared.

As the emptiness inside me deepened, I realized the hardest part for me was that I had little control over what I was going through. I had to rely on the decisions of my doctors and the insurance company. I felt as though I had lost all control over my life. To make matters even worse, I had to live at home with my parents. This felt like another loss of identity, because I ceased to be the head of my own household. Instead, I was the child of my parents again. I was no longer in charge of my own life.

Coping with these circumstances was difficult, yet not impossible. The first thing I did was pray that God would help me through this crisis, making me stronger and restoring my self-esteem. I also relied on my friends, who gave me support and encouragement. Most important, I tried to keep on talking to myself daily. I told myself that I was a good person, no matter what the circumstances. It took hard work, help from others, and positive thinking to keep my self-esteem afloat.

Maria's story demonstrates how losing a job had a negative impact on her life. But she learned a crucial lesson. Maria learned to separate her worth as a person from her job performance. She realized that she was a good person even though her options had been limited by losing her job.

Creating Meaning in Work

Work can be a major part of your quest for meaning, but it can also be a source of meaninglessness. Work can be an expression of yourself; it can be "love made visible" (Gibran, 1923, p. 27). It can be a way for you to be productive and to find enjoyment in daily life. Through your work you may be making a significant difference in the quality of your life or the lives of others, and this may give you real satisfaction. But work can also be devoid of any self-expressive value. It can be merely a means to survival and a drain on your energy. Instead of giving life meaning, it can actually be a destructive force that contributes to burnout and even an early death. Ask yourself: "Is my work life-giving?" "Does it bring meaning to my life? If not, what can I do about it?" "Is my most meaningful activity—my true work—something I do away from the job?"

If you find your work meaningless, what can you do about it? If your job drains you physically and emotionally instead of energizing you, what can you do about it? What are your options if you feel stuck in a dead-end job? Are there some ways that you can constructively deal with the sources of dissatisfaction within your job? When might it be time for you to change jobs as a way of finding meaning?

One way to examine the issue of meaninglessness and dissatisfaction in work is to look at how you really spend your time. It would be useful to keep a running account for a week to a month of what you do and how you relate to

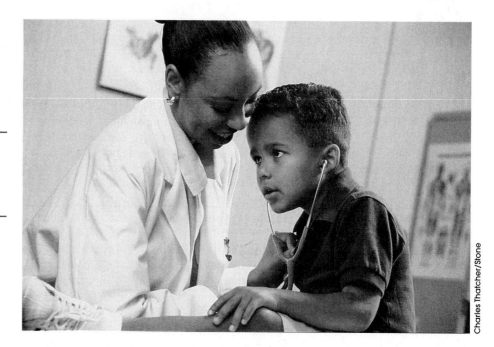

Through your work you may be making a significant difference in the quality of your life or the lives of others.

each of your activities. Which of them are draining you, and which are energizing you? Although you may not be able to change everything about your job that you do not like, you might be surprised by the significant changes you can make to increase your satisfaction. Some people adopt a passive stance in which they complain about the way things are and dwell on those aspects that they cannot change. Instead, a more constructive approach is to focus on those factors within your job that you *can* change. Even in cases where it is impractical to change jobs, you can still change your attitude and how you respond to a less than ideal situation.

Perhaps you can redefine the hopes you have for the job. Of course, you may also be able to think of the satisfactions you would most like to aim for in a job and then consider whether another job more clearly meets your needs and what steps you must take to obtain it. You might be able to find ways of advancing within your present job, making new contacts, or acquiring the skills that eventually will enable you to move on.

Although making changes in your present job might increase your satisfaction in the short term, the time may come when these resources no longer work and you find yourself stuck in a dead-end job that leads toward frustration. Changing jobs as a way to create meaning is possible, but you have to be prepared to pay the price. Changing jobs might increase your satisfaction with work, but changing jobs after a period of years can entail even more risk and uncertainty than making your first job selection.

You may be enthusiastic about some type of work for years and yet eventually become dissatisfied because of the changes that occur within you. With these changes comes the possibility that a once-fulfilling job will become monotonous and draining. If you outgrow your job, you can learn new skills and in other ways increase your options. Because your own attitudes are crucial, when a feeling of dissatisfaction sets in, it is wise to spend time rethinking what you want from a job and how you can most productively use your talents. Look carefully at how much the initiative rests with you—your expectations, your attitudes, and your sense of purpose and perspective.

CHANGING CAREERS IN MIDLIFE

Being aware of options can be an important asset at midlife. Most of the people we know have changed their jobs several times; you might think about whether this pattern fits any people you know. And whether or not you have reached middle age, ask yourself about your own beliefs and attitudes toward changing careers. Although making large changes in our lives is rarely easy, it can be a good deal harder if our own attitudes and fears are left unquestioned and unexamined.

A common example of midlife change is the woman who decides to return to college or the job market after her children reach high school age. Many community colleges and state universities are enrolling women who realize that they would like to develop new facets of themselves. This phenomenon is not unique to women. Many middle-age men are reentry students pursuing an advanced degree or a new degree. Some men quit a job they have had for years, even if they are successful, because they want new challenges. Men often define themselves by the work they do, and work thus becomes a major source of the purpose in their lives. If they feel successful in their work, they may feel successful as persons. If they become stagnant in work, they may feel that they are ineffectual in other areas. People sometimes decide on a career change even as they approach late adulthood.

Thomas Bonacum was drafted into the army at age 21 and became a drill instructor. After leaving the army, Tom completed his degree in engineering, which led to a job as an industrial engineer. A few years later he was laid off and then joined the police department. During the time he was a police officer, he returned to college to get another degree in criminal justice. He became a police sergeant and eventually taught criminal justice for 4 years in the police academy during his 22 years in police work.

After the death of his wife of 35 years, "Father Tom" made a significant change of careers. With the support and encouragement of his four grown children, he entered the seminary in his late 50s and was ordained as a Catholic priest at age 60.

Even after Father Tom retired, at the age of 77, he still kept active in the church and conducted services on weekends as long as his health allowed him to do so. He died at the age of 81.

Father Tom is an example of a person who was able to translate a dream into reality. When he graduated from high school, he tried to become a priest but discovered that he was not ready for some of the people in church, and they were not ready for him. He exemplifies a man who was willing to make career changes throughout his life and who dared to pursue what might have seemed like an impossible career choice. Many of us would not even conceive of such a drastic career change, yet Father Tom not only entertained this vision but also realized his dream.

For many it may be extremely risky and seemingly unrealistic to give up their job, even if they hate it, because it provides them with a measure of financial security. This is especially true during economically difficult times. The costs involved in achieving optimal job satisfaction may be too high. People might choose to stay with a less-than-desirable career yet at the same time discover other avenues for satisfaction. People who feel stuck in their jobs would do well to ask themselves these questions: "Does my personal dissatisfaction outweigh the financial rewards?" "Is the price of my mental anguish, which may have resulted in physical symptoms, worth the price of keeping this job?"

RETIREMENT

Many people look forward to retirement as a time for them to take up new projects. Others fear this prospect and wonder how they will spend their time if they are not working. The real challenge of this period, especially for those who retire early, is to find a way to remain active in a meaningful way. Some people consciously choose early retirement because they have found more significant and valuable pursuits. For other people, however, retirement does not turn out as expected, and it can be traumatic. Can people who have relied largely on their job for meaning or structure in their lives deal with having much time and little to do? How can people retain their sense of purpose and value apart from their occupation?

Options at Retirement It is a mistake to think of retired people as sitting around doing nothing. Many retired individuals keep themselves actively involved in community affairs, volunteer work, pursuit of new careers, engaging in recreation more fully and with more enjoyment, and having a fuller life than when they were employed full time. At the age of 76 Angela finally retired. Soon after her retirement, she became deeply involved in managing a retirement community. Doing this as a volunteer did not lessen the meaning of this kind of work for Angela.

For people who were in positions of power, the adjustment to retirement is sometimes difficult. They need to come to terms with the reality that once they retire they may no longer have the respect and admiration that they received in their professional roles. If most of the meaning of their lives was derived from their work position, they may be at a loss when they are without the work that filled so many of their needs. It is important to prepare for retirement and to find other sources of meaning so that you remain engaged with life.

Adjustments at Retirement Some individuals are at a loss when they retire, and they really did not want to quit working as soon as they did. Ray, a 73-year-old retired person, worked for 32 years as a salesman for a large dairy company. Here is Ray's description of his experience with work and retirement.

RAY'S STORY

I loved my work. My job was my life. I looked forward to going to work, I liked helping people, and I thrived on the challenges of my career. I worked for 50 hours a week, and at age 57 I stopped very abruptly. While I had made some plans for my financial retirement, I was not prepared for the emotional toll that not working would take on me. My work was my identity, and it helped me to feel worthwhile. For at least 2 years, I did not know what to do with myself. I sat around and began feeling depressed. It took me some time to adjust to this new phase in my life, but eventually I began to feel that I mattered. With the help of some friends I began to take on small jobs outside the home. I managed rentals, did repair work, and did some volunteer work at my church. Simply getting out of the house every day gave me another opportunity to contribute, which changed my attitude.

Today, at 73, I can honestly say that I like my life. Leisure is something I value now, rather than fearing it, which was the case in my younger years. There are plenty of work projects to keep me busy. There are always things to fix, work to be done in my shop, and plenty of chores. I don't seem to run out of things to do. Fortunately, I love fishing and golfing. Each year I go on several fishing trips, and my wife and I do a lot of traveling. By being active in the church, I've learned the value of fellowship and sharing with friends. I've found that I don't have to work 50 hours a week to be a productive human being. Just because I'm retired doesn't mean that I want to sit in a rocking chair most of the day. While I retired from my career, I have not retired from life.

Although many people take early retirement in their 50s, retirement generally comes later in life than was the case a couple of decades ago. Most people who are over 65 will continue to find some form of work, even if they decide to retire from a full-time job. They may work part time, serve as community volunteers, become consultants, or become self-employed. People in their 60s and 70s may seek work not only because they want to feel a sense of purpose but because they want to support themselves for greatly elongated later lives (Sheehy, 1995).

Retirement can usher in new opportunities to redesign your life and tap unused potentials, or it can be a coasting period where people simply mark time until their end. A couple who did not deal well with retirement are Leona and Marvin. Both had very active careers and retired relatively early. They began to spend most of their time with each other. After about 2 years they grew to dislike each other's company. They both began to have physical symptoms and became overly preoccupied with their health. Leona chronically complained that Marvin did not talk to her, to which he usually retorted, "I have nothing to say, and you should leave me alone." They were referred by their physician for marital counseling. One of the outcomes of this counseling was that they both secured part-time work. They found that by spending time apart they had a greater interest in talking to each other about their experiences at work. They also began to increase their social activities and started to develop some friendships, both separately and together. Marvin and Leona recognized that they had retired too early from life as well as from work.

Just because people no longer work at a job does not mean that they have to cease being active. Many options are open to retired people who would like to stay active in meaningful ways. This is the time for them to get involved with the projects they have so often put on the back burner due to their busy schedules. A high school teacher who retired at 55 is now making wooden toys for underprivileged children with a group of men. This offers both companionship and doing something productive for those in need. It is essential for retirees to keep themselves vital as physical, psychological, and social beings. Here are some other ways retired people can stay active:

> Go back to school to take classes simply for interest or to prepare themselves for a new career.
> Become an integral part of community activities.
> Share their expertise, experiences, and wisdom with others.
> Become more interested in and care for their grandchildren.
> Take trips to places that they have wanted to see.
> Visit relatives and friends.
> Take time for more physical activity.
> Cultivate hobbies that they have neglected.
> Join a senior citizens' center.

This list is not exhaustive. What can you add to it?

Retirees do have choices and can create meaning in their lives. They may discover that retirement is not an end but rather a new beginning. One 93-year-old woman, who had lived alone since her husband died until a year ago when she found it necessary to have a live-in caretaker assist her and do routine chores in the house, has a routine that involves talking with friends, watching her favorite shows on television, and doing crossword puzzles. When her grandchildren ask her if she is lonely, she quickly responds by letting them know that she enjoys her solitude and that her days are full. She likes not having to answer to anyone but herself, and she looks forward to each day. She does not brood over the past, nor does she wish that things had been different. Instead, she accepts both her accomplishments and her mistakes, and she still finds life meaningful.

THE PLACE OF WORK AND RECREATION IN YOUR LIFE

One way to look at the place that work and recreation occupy in your life is to consider how you divide up your time. In an average day, most people spend about 8 hours sleeping, another 8 hours working, and the other 8 hours in routines such as eating, traveling to work, and leisure. If your work is something that you enjoy, then at least half of your waking existence is spent in meaningful activities. Yet if you dread getting up and hate going to work, those 8 hours can easily have a negative impact on the other 8 hours you are awake.

Work and the Meaning of Your Life

If you expect your work to be a primary source of meaning but feel that your life is not as rich with meaning as you would like, you may be saying, "If only I had a job that I liked, then I'd be fulfilled." This type of thinking can lead you to believe that somehow the secret of finding purpose in your life depends on something outside yourself.

If you decide that you must remain in a job that allows little scope for personal effort and satisfaction, you may need to accept the fact that you will not find much meaning in the hours you spend on the job. It is important, then, to be aware of the effects that your time spent on the job have on the rest of your life and to minimize them. More positively, it is crucial to find something outside your job that fulfills your need for recognition, significance, productivity, and excitement. By doing so, you may develop a sense of your true work as something different from what you are paid to do.

Your job may provide you with the means for the productive activities you engage in away from the job, whether they take the form of hobbies, creative pursuits, volunteer work, or spending time with friends and family. One high school teacher we know finds himself discouraged over how little his students are interested in learning. Rather than expecting to get all his rewards from teaching, he finds meaning in making things and remodeling his house. He loves to travel, work on antiques, and read. Although he enjoys aspects of his teaching profession, he finds many of his rewards outside the classroom. If this person did not find his own rewards—many of them beyond his job—he would soon feel trapped in an unfulfilling job. The point is to turn things around so that you are the master rather than the victim of your job. Too many people are so negatively affected by their job that their frustration and sense of emptiness spoil their eat-

Peter Winter/Corbis

Work alone does not generally result in fulfillment.

ing, leisure time, family life, sex life, and relationships with friends. For some, job dissatisfaction can be so great that it results in physical or psychological illness.

If you can regain control of your own attitudes toward your job and find dignity and pride elsewhere in your life, you may be able to lessen these negative effects. Seeking counseling is one means to achieve greater control of your life. It can be an excellent way for you to deal with the frustrating and negative effects that work has on you and those around you. Counseling often helps people recognize the stagnant roles they are caught up in both at work and in their personal relationships—and then assists them in creating more satisfying ways of being.

Recreation and the Meaning of Your Life

Work alone does not generally result in fulfillment. Even rewarding work takes energy, and most people need some break from it. Recreation involves creating ourselves anew and is a vital path to vitality. Leisure is "free time," the time that we control and can use for ourselves. Whereas work requires a certain degree of perseverance and drive, recreation requires the ability to let go, to be spontaneous, and to avoid getting caught in the trap of being obsessed with what we "should" be doing. Recreation implies flowing with the river rather than pushing against it and making something happen. Compulsiveness dampens the enjoyment of leisure time, and planned spontaneity is almost a contradiction in terms.

The balance between work and recreation depends on the needs of the individual. Some people schedule recreational activities in such a manner that they actually miss the point of recreation. They "work hard at having a good time." Others become quickly bored when they are not doing something. For Bob and Jill, leisure is more of a burden than a joy. He is a laborer, she is a hairstylist, and both of them work hard all week. They say they like a weekend trip to the river, but their "vacation" includes driving in a car with two whiny children who constantly ask when they will get there. After coping with traffic, they often feel more stressed once they return home from the river. They need to assess whether their leisure is providing them with what they want.

As a couple, we attribute different meanings to our leisure time. I (Jerry) tend to plan most of the things in my life, including my leisure time. I often combine work and leisure. Until recently, I seemed to require less leisure than some people, because most of my satisfactions in life came from my work. Many of my "hobbies" are still work-related, and although my scope tends to be somewhat narrow, this has been largely by choice. I am aware that I have had trouble with unstructured time. I am quite certain that leisure has represented a personal threat; as if any time unaccounted for is not being put to the best and most productive use. However, I am learning how to appreciate the reality that time is not simply to be used in doing, producing, accomplishing, and moving mountains. Although it is a lesson that I am learning relatively late in life, I am increasingly relishing times of being and experiencing, as well as time spent on accomplishing tasks. Experiencing sunsets, watching the beauty in nature, and being open to what moments can teach me are ways of using time that I am coming to cherish. Although work is still a very important part of my life, I am realizing that this is only a part of my life, not the totality of it. In essence, I am learning the importance of making time for leisure pursuits, which are essential for revitalization.

Marianne, in contrast, wants and needs unstructured and spontaneous time for unwinding. I (Marianne) am uncomfortable when schedules are imposed on me. I do not particularly like to make detailed life plans, for this gets in the way of my relaxing. Although I plan for trips and times of recreation, I do not like to have everything I am going to do on the trip planned in advance. I like the element of surprise. It feels good to flow with moments and let things happen rather than working hard at making things happen. Also, I do not particularly like to combine work and leisure. For me, work involves considerable responsi-

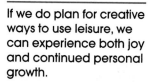

If we do plan for creative ways to use leisure, we can experience both joy and continued personal growth.

Gerald Corey

bility, and it is hard for me to enjoy leisure if it is tainted with the demands of work, or if I know that I will soon have to function in a professional role.

The objectives of planning for a career and planning for creative use of leisure time are basically the same: to help us develop feelings of self-esteem, reach our potential, and improve the quality of our lives. If we do not learn how to pursue interests apart from work, we may well face a crisis when we retire. In fact, many people die soon after their retirement (Joy, 1990; Siegel, 1988, 1989). If we do plan for creative ways to use leisure, we can experience both joy and continued personal growth.

A Couple Who Are Able to Balance Work and Recreation

Judy and Frank have found a good balance between work and recreation. Although they both enjoy their work, they have also arranged their lives to make time for leisure.

Judy and Frank were married when she was 16 and he was 20. They now have two grown sons and a couple of grandchildren. At 59 Frank works for an electrical company as a lineman, a job he has held for close to 35 years. Judy, who is now 55, delivers meals to schools.

Judy went to work when her two sons were in elementary school. Although she felt no financial pressure to do so, she took the job because she liked the extras their family could afford with her salary. She was interested in doing something away from home. Judy continues her work primarily because she likes the contact with both her coworkers and the children and adolescents whom she meets daily. However, she would like more time to enjoy her grandchildren and would like a longer weekend.

Frank is satisfied with his work, and he looks forward to going to the job. Considering that he stopped his education at high school, he feels he has a good job that both pays well and offers many fringe benefits. Although he is a bright person, he expresses no ambition to increase his formal education. A few of the things Frank likes about his work are the companionship with his coworkers, the physical aspects of his job, the security it affords, and the routine. As a mechanically inclined person, he is both curious about and challenged by how things work, what makes them malfunction, and how to repair them.

Judy and Frank have separate interests and hobbies, yet they also spend time together. Both of them are hardworking, and they have achieved success financially and personally. They feel pleased about their success and can see the fruits of their labor. They spend most of their weekends at their mountain cabin, which both of them helped build. He fishes, hikes, rides his motorcycle, cuts wood, fixes the house, and visits with friends. She is talented in arts and crafts, repairing the cars, house painting, and preparing delicious meals. Together they enjoy their grandchildren, their friends, and themselves.

Judy and Frank enjoy their work life and their leisure life, both as individuals and as a couple. A challenge that many of us will face is finding ways of using our leisure as well as they do. In a high-technology age, the question of how we can creatively use our increased leisure time must be addressed. Just as our work can have either a positive or a negative influence on our life, so, too, can leisure. These Take Time to Reflect exercises will help you consolidate your thoughts on how work and leisure are integrated in your life.

Take Time to Reflect

1. List a few of the most important benefits that you get (or expect to get) from work or college.

   _____

   _____

2. To what extent do you allow for leisure time? What was modeled by way of leisure time and recreation in your family of origin?

   _____

   _____

3. Are there any ways that you would like to spend your leisure time differently?

_____

_____

4. What nonwork activities have made you feel creative, happy, or energetic?

_____

_____

5. Could you obtain a job that would incorporate some of the activities you have just listed? Or does your job already account for them?

_____

_____

6. What do you think would happen to you if you could not work? Write what first comes to mind.

_____

_____

SUMMARY

Some people are motivated to go to college because it offers opportunities for personal development and the pursuit of knowledge. Others are in college primarily to attain their career objectives, and some go because they are avoiding making other choices in their lives. Clarifying your own reasons for being in college can be useful in the process of long-range career planning.

Choosing a career is best thought of as a process, not a one-time event. The term *career decision* is misleading, because it implies that we make one choice that we stay with permanently. Most of us will probably have several occupations over our lifetimes, which is a good argument for a general education. If we prepare too narrowly for a specialization, that job may become obsolete, as will our training. In selecting a career or an occupation, it is important to first assess our attitudes, abilities, interests, and values. The next step is to explore a wide range of occupational options to see what jobs would best fit our personality. Becoming familiar with Holland's six personality types is an excellent way to consider the match between your personality style and the work alternatives you are considering. Choosing an occupation too soon can be risky, because our interests change as we move into adulthood. Passively falling into a job rather than carefully considering where we might best find meaning and satisfaction can lead to dissatisfaction and frustration.

Because we devote about half of our waking hours to our work, it behooves us to actively choose a form of work that can express who we are as a person. Much of the other half of our waking time can be used for leisure. With the trend toward increased leisure time, cultivating interests apart from work becomes a real challenge. Just as our work can profoundly affect all aspects of our lives, so, too, can leisure have a positive or negative influence on our existence. Our leisure time can be a source of boredom that drains us, or it can be a source of replenishment that energizes us and enriches our lives.

Although work is seen as an important source of meaning in our lives, it is not the job itself that provides this meaning. The satisfaction we derive depends to a great extent on the way we relate to our job, the manner in which we do it, and the meaning that we attribute to it. Perhaps the most important idea in this chapter is that we must look to ourselves if we are dissatisfied with our work. We can increase our power to change unfavorable circumstances by recognizing that we are mainly responsible for making our lives and our work meaningful.

❯ Where Can I Go From Here?

1. Interview a person you know who dislikes his or her career or occupation. Here are some questions you might ask to get started:

   ❯ If you don't find your job satisfying, why do you stay in it?

   ❯ Do you feel that you have much of a choice about whether you'll stay with the job or take a new one?

   ❯ What aspects of your job bother you the most?

   ❯ How does your attitude toward your job affect the other areas of your life?

> ## Where Can I Go From Here? *(continued)*

2. Interview a person you know who feels fulfilled and excited by his or her work. Begin with these questions:

   ❯ What does your work do for you? What meaning does your work have for the other aspects of your life?

   ❯ What are the main satisfactions for you in your work?

   ❯ How do you think you would be affected if you could no longer pursue your career?

3. Interview your parents and determine what meaning their work has for them. How satisfied are they with the work aspects of their lives? How much choice do they feel they have in selecting their work? In what ways do they think the other aspects of their lives are affected by their attitudes toward work? After you have talked with them, determine how your attitudes and beliefs about work have been influenced by your parents. Are you pursuing a career that your parents can understand and respect? Is their reaction to your career choice important to you? Are your attitudes and values concerning work like or unlike those of your parents?

4. If your college has a vocational counseling program available to you, consider talking with a counselor about your plans. You might want to explore taking vocational interest and aptitude tests. If you are deciding on a career, consider discussing how realistic your vocational plans are. For example:

   ❯ What are your interests?

   ❯ Do your interests match the careers you are thinking about pursuing?

   ❯ Do you have the knowledge you need to make a career choice?

   ❯ Do you have the aptitude and skills for the careers you have in mind?

   ❯ What are the future possibilities in the careers you are considering?

5. If you are leaning toward a particular occupation or career, seek out a person who is actively engaged in that type of work and arrange for a time to talk with him or her. You might even see if job shadowing is a possibility. Ask questions concerning the chances of gaining employment, the experience necessary, the satisfactions and drawbacks of the position, and so on. In this way, you can make the process of deciding on a type of work more realistic and perhaps avoid disappointment if your expectations do not match reality.

6. Most career guidance centers in colleges and universities now offer one or more computer-based programs to help students decide on a career. One popular program is known as the System of Interactive Guidance and Information, more commonly referred to as SIGI. This program assesses and categorizes your work values in these 10 areas: income, prestige, independence, helping others, security, variety, leadership, leisure, working in one's field of interest, and early entry. Taking the SIGI will aid you

(continued)

❭ **Where Can I Go From Here?** *(continued)*

in identifying specific occupations you might want to explore. SIGI Plus is an updated version of the original SIGI.

Schedule an appointment in the career counseling center at your college to participate in a computer-based occupational guidance program. In addition to SIGI, other programs are the Career Information System (CIS), the Guidance Information System (GIS), Choices, and Discover. Each of these programs develops lists of occupations to explore. Other instruments assess values. One is the Allport, Vernon, and Lindzey Study of Values. Another is Super's Work Values Inventory. Consider taking the Myers-Briggs Type Indicator, which is an inventory that indicates your temperament style. You can take the Keirsey Temperament Sorter online (www.Keirsey.com). Meet with a career counselor to discuss these value assessment instruments.

7. The abbreviated description of Holland's six personality types and the exercise in this chapter should not be thought of as a complete and accurate way to assess your personality. If you are interested in a more complete self-assessment method that also describes the relationship between your type and possible occupations or fields of study, we strongly recommend that you take Form R of the *Self-Directed Search* (Holland, 1994). The *Self-Directed Search* (SDS) consists of a test as well as these booklets designed to accompany this test: (1) You and Your Career, (2) The Occupations Finder, (3) The Educational Opportunities Finder, (4) The Leisure Activities Finder, and (5) Assessment Booklet: A Guide to Educational and Career Planning. All of these resources are available from Psychological Assessment Resources, P.O. Box 998, Odessa, FL 33556 or by telephone (1-800-331-8378). In addition to the SDS, other inventories that are useful in constructing a list of occupational alternatives from which to choose a career include the *Career Decision-Making System* (CDM) and the *Career Occupational Preference System* (COPS).

8. Here are some steps you can take when exploring the choice of a major and a career. Place a check before each item you are willing to seriously consider. I am willing to:

_____ talk to an adviser about my intended major

_____ interview at least one instructor regarding selecting a major

_____ interview at least one person I know in a career that I am interested in

_____ make a trip to the career development center and just look around

_____ inquire about taking a series of interest and work values tests in the career development center

_____ take the SIGI or some similar computer-based instrument

_____ take an interest inventory

_____ talk to my parents about the meaning work has for them

_____ write in my journal about my values as they pertain to work

_____ browse through books that deal with careers

_____ read a book on careers

❯ Where Can I Go From Here? *(continued)*

9. Apply the seven steps of the career-planning process to your own career planning. Set realistic goals to do one or more of the following or some other appropriate activity:

> ❯ Choose a major that most fully taps my interests and abilities.
> ❯ Take time to investigate a career by gathering further information.
> ❯ Develop contacts with people who can help me meet my goals.
> ❯ Take steps that will enable me to increase my exposure to a field of interest.

In your journal, write down at least a tentative plan for action. Begin by identifying some of the key factors associated with selecting a career. Write down the steps you are willing to take at this time. (Your plan will be most useful if you identify specific steps you are willing to take. Include seeking the help of others somewhere in your plan.)

Resources for Future Study

Web Site Resources

THE OCCUPATIONAL OUTLOOK HANDBOOK
http://stats.bls.gov/ocohome.htm

The *Occupational Outlook Handbook* is a "nationally recognized source of career information, designed to provide valuable assistance to individuals making decisions about their future work lives" and it "describes what workers do on the job, working conditions, the training and education needed, earnings, and expected job prospects in a wide range of occupations." Users can download pages on the careers of their choice.

THE CATAPULT ON JOB WEB
http://www.jobweb.org/catapult/catapult.htm

The National Association of Colleges and Employers has created a comprehensive set of resources for job seekers and job offerings. The site includes searching employment listings, resources for career practitioners, career library resources, and professional development resources.

U.S. DEPARTMENT OF LABOR
http://www.dol.gov/

This online site serves as a way to explore topics such as wages, worker productivity, unsafe working conditions, and the legal rights of workers, including protection from sexual harassment.

APA HELPCENTER: PSYCHOLOGY AT WORK
http://helping.apa.org/work/index.html

The American Psychological Association publishes this resource describing various aspects of work including doing more with less, downsizing survivors, working moms, and a focus on stress.

CAREERS.WSJ.COM
http://careers.wsj.com/

This site contains daily updates of employment issues and more than 1,000 job-seeking articles.

ELDERHOSTEL
http://www/elderhostel.org

This site provides "adventures in lifelong learning" for adults ages 55 and older. It is a not-for-profit organization with a catalog of high-quality, affordable, educational programs lasting 1 to 4 weeks year round and throughout the world.

InfoTrac College Edition Resources

For additional readings, explore InfoTrac College Edition, our online library.

Go to **http://www.infotrac.college.com/wadsworth**

Hint: Enter the search terms:

career development
career decision making
career decision
occupational interest
occupational ability
personality type
leisure time

Print Resources

Bolles, R. N. (1999). *What color is your parachute? A practical manual for job hunters and career changers.* Berkeley, CA: Ten Speed Press.

Carney, C. G., & Wells, C. F. (1999). *Working well, living well: Discover the career within you* (5th ed.). Pacific Grove, CA: Brooks/Cole.

Holland, J. L. (1997). *Making vocational choices: A theory of vocational personalities and work environments* (3rd ed.). Odessa, FL: Psychological Assessment Resources, Inc.

Lock, R. D. (2000). *Job search: Career planning guide, Book 2* (4th ed.). Pacific Grove, CA: Brooks/Cole.

Lock, R. D. (2000). *Taking charge of your career direction: Career planning guide, Book 1* (4th ed.). Pacific Grove, CA: Brooks/Cole.

Sharf, R. S. (1993). *Occupational information overview.* Pacific Grove, CA: Brooks/Cole.

Terkel, S. (1975). *Working.* New York: Avon.

U.S. Department of Labor. (1998). *Occupational outlook handbook, 1998–1999.* Washington, DC: U.S. Government Printing Office.

In solitude we make the time to be with ourselves, to discover who we are, and to renew ourselves

Dale Durfee/Stone

11

LONELINESS AND SOLITUDE

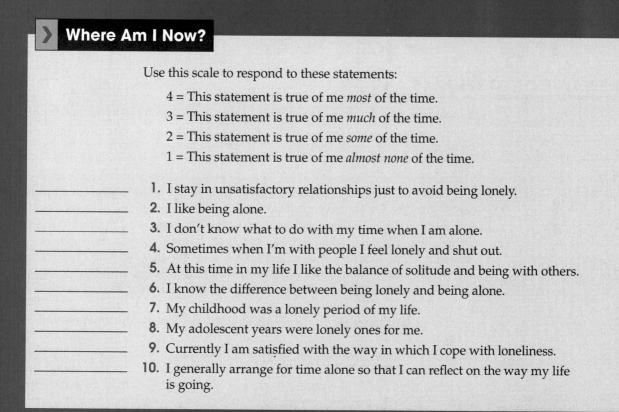

Use this scale to respond to these statements:

4 = This statement is true of me *most* of the time.

3 = This statement is true of me *much* of the time.

2 = This statement is true of me *some* of the time.

1 = This statement is true of me *almost none* of the time.

_____ 1. I stay in unsatisfactory relationships just to avoid being lonely.

_____ 2. I like being alone.

_____ 3. I don't know what to do with my time when I am alone.

_____ 4. Sometimes when I'm with people I feel lonely and shut out.

_____ 5. At this time in my life I like the balance of solitude and being with others.

_____ 6. I know the difference between being lonely and being alone.

_____ 7. My childhood was a lonely period of my life.

_____ 8. My adolescent years were lonely ones for me.

_____ 9. Currently I am satisfied with the way in which I cope with loneliness.

_____ 10. I generally arrange for time alone so that I can reflect on the way my life is going.

Being with others and being with ourselves are best understood as two sides of the same coin. If we do not like our own company, why should others want to be with us? If we are not able to enjoy time alone, it will be difficult to truly enjoy time with others. If we have a good relationship with ourselves and enjoy our solitude, we have a far greater chance of creating solid, give-and-take relationships with others. Although the presence of others can surely enhance our lives, no one else can completely become us or share our unique world of feelings, thoughts, hopes, and memories. In some respects we are alone, even though we may have meaningful connections with others.

We invite you to think of being alone as a natural and potentially valuable part of human experience. It is important to distinguish between being alone and being lonely. Casey and Vanceburg (1985) write about being alone, but not lonely, as we search for understanding, serenity, and certainly about the path of life we are traveling. All of us are ultimately alone in the world. Appreciating our aloneness can enrich our experience of life.

THE VALUE OF LONELINESS AND SOLITUDE

Loneliness and solitude are different experiences, and each has its own potential value. Loneliness generally results from certain events in life—the death of someone we love, the decision of another person to leave us for someone else, a move to a new city, a long stay in a hospital, or making a key decision in life. Loneliness can occur when we feel set apart in some way from everyone around us. We also experience loneliness when our network of social relationships is lacking or when there are strains on these relationships. Sometimes feelings of loneliness are simply an indication of the extent to which we have failed to listen to ourselves and to our own feelings. However it occurs, loneliness is generally something that happens to us rather than something we choose to experience, but we can choose the attitude we take toward it. If we allow ourselves to experience our loneliness, even if it is painful, we may be surprised to find sources of strength and creativity within ourselves.

Unlike loneliness, solitude is something that we often choose for ourselves. In solitude, we make the time to be with ourselves, to discover who we are, and to renew ourselves. In her beautiful and poetic book *Gift From the Sea,* Anne Morrow Lindbergh (1955/1975) describes her own need to get away by herself to find her center, to simplify her life, and to nourish herself so that she could give to others again. She relates how her busy life, with its many and conflicting demands, fragmented her, so that she felt "the spring is dry, and the well is empty" (p. 47).*

---

*This and all other quotations from this source are from *Gift From the Sea,* by A. M. Lindbergh. Copyright 1955 by Pantheon Books, a division of Random House, Inc.

Through solitude, she found replenishment and became reacquainted with herself:

> WHEN ONE IS A STRANGER TO ONESELF, then one is estranged from others too. If one is out of touch with oneself, then one cannot touch others. . . . Only when one is connected to one's own core is one connected to others. . . . For me, the core, the inner spring, can best be refound through solitude. (pp. 43–44)

If we do not take time for ourselves but instead fill our lives with activities and projects, we run the risk of losing a sense of centeredness. As Lindbergh puts it, "Instead of stilling the center, the axis of the wheel, we add more centrifugal activities to our lives—which tend to throw us off balance" (p. 51). Her own solitude taught her that she must remind herself to be alone each day, even for a few minutes, to keep a sense of herself that would then enable her to give of herself to others. She expressed this thought in words addressed to a seashell she took with her from an island where she had spent some time alone:

> YOU WILL REMIND ME that I must try to be alone for part of each year, even a week or a few days; and for part of each day, even for an hour or for a few minutes, in order to keep my core, my center, my island-quality. You will remind me that unless I keep the island-quality intact somewhere within me, I will have little to give my husband, my children, my friends or the world at large. (p. 57)

Solitude can provide us with the opportunity to examine our lives and gain a sense of perspective. It can give us time to ask significant questions such as "How much have I become a stranger to myself?" and "Have I been listening to myself, or have I been distracted and overstimulated by a busy life?" Moreover, we can use times of solitude to look within ourselves, to renew our sense of ourselves as the center of choice and direction in our lives, and to learn to trust our inner resources instead of allowing circumstances or the expectations of others to determine the path we travel. Some people believe that when they are alone they are lonely. However, if we fundamentally accept our aloneness and recognize that no one can take away all our sense of being alone, we can give ourselves to our projects and our relationships out of our freedom instead of running to them out of our fear.

You may also simply miss the valuable experience of solitude if you allow your life to become too frantic and complicated. Or you may fear that others will think you are odd if you express a need for solitude. Indeed, others may sometimes fail to understand your need and try to get you to join the crowd and have fun. People who are close to you may feel vaguely threatened, as if your need for time alone implied that you have less affection for them. Perhaps their own fears of being left alone will lead them to try to keep you from taking time away from them.

Most of us need to remind ourselves that we can tolerate only so much intensity with others and that ignoring our need for distance can breed resentment. For instance, a mother and father who are constantly with each other and with their children may not be doing a service either to their children or to themselves. Eventually they are likely to resent their "obligations." Unless they take time out, they may be there bodily and yet not be fully present to each other or to their children.

Many of us fail to experience solitude because we allow our lives to become more and more frantic and complicated. Unless we make a conscious effort to be alone, we may find that days and weeks go by without our having the chance to be with ourselves. Moreover, we may fear that we will alienate others if we ask for private time, so we alienate ourselves instead. Perhaps we fear that others will think us odd if we express a need to be alone. Indeed, others may sometimes fail to understand our need for solitude and try to bring us into the crowd or "cheer us up." People who are close to us may feel vaguely threatened, as if our need for time alone somehow reflected on our affection for them. Their own fears of being left alone may lead them to try to keep us from taking time away from them. It is not uncommon to feel uneasy about wanting and taking time alone for ourselves. We may feel a need to make up excuses if we want to decline an invitation to be with others so that we can have some time alone. Claiming what we need and want for ourselves can involve a certain risk; if we fail to take that risk, however, we give up the very thing solitude could provide—a sense of self-direction and being centered.

Taking time to *be* alone gives you the opportunity to think, plan, imagine, and dream—to listen to yourself. If you are comfortable with yourself, you have a good chance of being comfortable with others. By becoming your own best friend, you step into position to become a friend to others.

LEARNING TO CONFRONT THE FEAR OF LONELINESS

There is probably good reason to have some fear of loneliness because there is some evidence that it can influence both our physical health and psychological well-being. People who report being lonely tend to report more depression, use of drugs as an escape, and higher blood pressure (Rice, 1999). Some evidence points to loneliness as being associated with higher risks for heart disease, lessened longevity, and increased risk for recurrent illness (Hafen, Karren, Frandsen, & Smith, 1996). There is probably a difference between those who experience loneliness for a short time or under certain circumstances from those who are chronically lonely and who have few people with whom they can share their lives.

Many people fear being lonely. If we associate the lonely periods in our lives with pain and struggle, we may think of loneliness only as a condition to be avoided as much as possible. Furthermore, we may identify being alone with being lonely and either actively avoid having time by ourselves or fill such time

We can sometimes cope with the fear of loneliness by surrounding ourselves with people and social functions.

Corbis

with distractions and diversions. We may associate being alone with rejection of self and being cut off from others. Paradoxically, out of fear of rejection and loneliness, we may even make ourselves needlessly lonely by refusing to reach out to others or by holding back parts of ourselves in our intimate relationships. At other times, because of our fear of loneliness, we may deceive ourselves by convincing ourselves that we can overcome loneliness only by anchoring our life to another's life. The search for relationships, especially ones in which we think we will be taken care of, is often motivated by the fear of being isolated.

For those of us who want to escape from loneliness, silence can be threatening, because it forces us to reflect and touch deep parts of ourselves. At times we may attempt to escape from facing ourselves by keeping so busy that we leave little time to reflect. Here are some ways we attempt to escape from facing and coping with loneliness:

> We schedule every moment and overstructure our lives, so we have no opportunity to think about ourselves and what we are doing with our lives.

> We strive for perfect control of our environment, so we will not have to cope with the unexpected.

> We surround ourselves with people and become absorbed in social functions in the hope that we will not have to feel alone.

> We try to numb ourselves with television, alcohol, or drugs.

> We immerse ourselves in our "responsibilities."

> We eat compulsively, hoping that doing so will fill our inner emptiness and protect us from the pain of being lonely.

> We spend hours upon hours with the computer.

> We make ourselves slaves to routine, becoming stuck in a narrow and predictable rut and becoming machines that do not feel much of anything.

> We go to night clubs and other centers of activity, trying to lose ourselves in a crowd. By escaping into crowds we hope to avoid coming to terms with deeper layers of our inner world.

Most of us lead a hectic life in a crowded, noisy environment. We are surrounded by entertainment and escapes, which makes it impossible to hear the voice within us. Paradoxically, in the midst of our congested cities and with all the activities available to us, we are often lonely because we are alienated from ourselves. To better understand this paradox, listen to Stella talk about her life and her fears. Stella is a young woman who often fears separateness from others, even though she immerses herself in many relationships and activities. Outsiders tend to envy her "fun-filled" life and wish they were in her place. In a moment of candor, however, she will admit that she feels her life to be empty and that she is in a desperate search for substance.

STELLA'S STORY

I am petrified when I have to spend any time alone in my apartment. I schedule my life so that I spend as little time by myself as possible. I have a long list of phone numbers to call, just in case my panic overwhelms me. My stereo or television is typically blaring so that I am unable to pay attention to what is going on with me. I want so much to fill my inner emptiness. I have a hard time liking myself or thinking I have much value. I look to others for my security, yet I never really find it. In my therapy I am learning to stay with being uncomfortable with myself long enough to face some of my fears.

In some ways Stella illustrates the quiet desperation that is captured in Edward Arlington Robinson's poem "Richard Cory" (1897):

WHENEVER RICHARD CORY WENT DOWN TOWN,
We people on the pavement looked at him:
He was a gentleman from sole to crown,
Clean favored, and imperially slim.
And he was always quietly arrayed,
And he was always human when he talked;
But still he fluttered pulses when he said,

"Good morning," and he glittered when he walked.
And he was rich—yes, richer than a king—
And admirably schooled in every grace:
In fine, we thought that he was everything
To make us wish that we were in his place.
So on we worked and waited for the light,
And went without the meat, and cursed the bread;
And Richard Cory, one calm summer night,
Went home and put a bullet through his head.

There is a loneliness in living in ways that belie the way we present ourselves to the world, as the cases of Stella and Richard Cory demonstrate. Pretending to others to be what we are not, as well as anchoring our lives to others as a way of avoiding facing ourselves, results in our losing a sense of selfhood and feeling alienated.

In our work with clients in therapy groups, we meet people who hide dimensions of themselves from others. Out of their fear of being rejected, they deprive others of getting to know them fully. During the group sessions they reveal themselves in ways that are totally unknown to even the most intimate people in their lives. As they reveal themselves in the context of the group, and generally receive support and reinforcement, they are more willing to show their hidden self to the significant people in their lives. Through this self-disclosure, individuals learn to appreciate facets of themselves that were strangers to them.

We often surround ourselves with people and then try to convince ourselves that we are not lonely. When we are lonely, we crave the companionship of another. Vanzant (1998) says that we tell ourselves that everything would be better if we had another person in our lives. From our perspective, if we want to get back into contact with ourselves, we can begin by looking at the ways we have learned to escape being lonely. We can examine our relationships to determine if we at times use others to fill an inner void. We can ask whether the activities that fill our time actually satisfy us or whether they leave us hungry and discontented. For some of us, being alone may be less lonely than being in a relationship. To truly confront loneliness, we may have to spend more time alone, strengthening our awareness of ourselves as the true center of meaning and direction in our lives.

CREATING OUR OWN LONELINESS THROUGH SHYNESS

Do you ever wonder if you are shy? Some specific characteristics that identify shy individuals are timidity in expressing themselves; being overly sensitive to how others are perceiving and reacting to them; getting embarrassed easily; and experiencing bodily symptoms such as blushing, upset stomach, anxiety, and racing pulse (Weiten & Lloyd, 2000). Shy people are often uncomfortable in social situations, especially if they become the center of attention or if they are expected to be assertive. If you are shy, this does not necessarily have to be a problem for you. In fact, you might decide you like this quality in yourself—and so might many others who know you. Shyness becomes a problem only when you hold yourself back from expressing yourself in ways you would like. You can learn to say and do what you would like when you are with others and still retain your shy nature.

According to Phil Zimbardo (1987), founder of the shyness clinic at Stanford University, shyness is an almost universal experience. In one study 80% of those questioned reported that they had been shy at some point in their lives. Of those, more than 40% considered themselves shy at that time. This means that 4 out of every 10 people you meet, or 84 million Americans, are shy. Shyness exists on a continuum. That is, some people see themselves as chronically shy, whereas others are shy with certain people or in certain situations. It is important to realize that shyness might be a part of your culture. This is why it helps to define "shyness" for yourself. You may be shy in some situations, yet in many situations shyness may not be a part of your personality.

Shyness can lead directly to feelings of loneliness. Zimbardo (1987) believes shyness can be a social and psychological handicap as crippling as many physical handicaps, and he lists these consequences of shyness:

› Shyness prevents people from expressing their views and speaking up for their rights.

› Shyness may make it difficult to think clearly and to communicate effectively.

› Shyness holds people back from meeting new people, making friends, and getting involved in many social activities.

› Shyness often results in feelings such as depression, anxiety, and loneliness.

You may be aware that shyness is a problem for you and that you are creating your own loneliness, at least in part. You may well be asking "What can I do about it?" You can begin by challenging those personal fears that keep you from expressing yourself the way you would like to. It is likely that one reason for your shyness is not having the interpersonal skills that make it possible to express your feelings and thoughts. Put yourself in situations where you will be forced to make contact with people and engage in social activities, even if you find doing this is somewhat scary and uncomfortable.

It helps to understand the context of your shyness, especially to identify those social situations that bring out your shy behavior. Also, it is useful to pinpoint the reasons or combination of factors underlying your shyness. According to Zimbardo (1987, 1994), a constellation of factors explain shyness: being overly sensitive to negative feedback from others, fearing rejection, lacking self-confidence and specific social skills, being frightened of intimacy, and personal handicaps.

A good way to identify those factors that contribute to your shyness is to keep track in your journal of those situations that elicit your shy behavior. It is also helpful to write down the symptoms you experience and what you actually do in such situations. Pay attention to what you tell yourself when you are in difficult situations. For example, your self-talk may be negative, actually setting you up to fail. You may say silently to yourself: "I'm ugly, so who would want anything to do with me?" "I'd better not try something new, because I might look stupid." "I'm afraid of being rejected, so I won't even approach a person I'd like to get to know." "If people really knew what I was like, they wouldn't like what they saw." "Others are constantly evaluating and judging me, and I'm sure I won't measure up to what they expect." These are the very statements that are likely to keep you a prisoner of your shyness and prevent you from making contact with others. You can do a lot yourself to control how your shyness affects you by learning to challenge your self-defeating beliefs and by substituting constructive statements. Learning new ways of thinking about yourself involves self-discipline in pushing yourself to test out your new beliefs by acting in new ways.

People who have difficulty dealing with shyness often withdraw socially. However, withdrawing from social situations generally exacerbates matters and often leads to loneliness. Tracy's experience in coping with shyness illustrates how you can overcome inhibitions and can come out of your shell.

TRACY'S STORY

*W*hen I first began my college education, I was really shy. I would not raise my hand to ask questions in class, I studied by myself, and I did not pursue friendships with my peers. My shyness developed out of a belief that I would look stupid if I asked questions and that my peers would think I was not really smart if they studied with me. If I pursued friendships, I was convinced that people would eventually realize I was not fun or outgoing. I believe my shyness in these early years contributed to my failure at my first college.

When I decided to leave my first college, I made a commitment to myself that I would do what it took to succeed in earning my education at my new school. Part of this commitment was to speak up in class, ask questions, form study groups, and make friends. This was really scary for me, but I knew that not reaching out kept me lonely. I did not want to live that way anymore. I made contact with my teachers and actually became involved in my learning process. As I became involved with my studies and my peers, my self-confidence increased. Along with this came higher grades. I began to believe that I was smart, that I did ask good questions, that others were not judging me, and that others liked who I was, and most important, I liked who I was.

If you are shy, perhaps the best first step to take is to accept this as part of who you are. Then challenge yourself to get involved in activities and to make contact with others. We encourage you to monitor your thoughts, feelings, and actions to become more aware of the effects of shyness in your life. Like Tracy, you can take steps to make contact with others and challenge negative self-talk that is keeping you in your shell.

Take Time to Reflect

1. Do you try to escape from your loneliness? If so, in what ways?

_____

_____

2. Does avoidance of loneliness work for you? If not, what might you do to change?

_____

_____

3. Is shyness a problem for you? In what ways might you be creating your own loneliness with the ways you deal with your shyness?

_____

_____

4. Is time spent alone valuable to you? If so, in what ways?

_____

_____

5. List a few of the major decisions you have made in your life. Did you make these decisions when you were alone or when you were with others?

_____

_____

A journal suggestion: If you find it difficult to be alone, without distractions, for more than a few minutes at a time, try being alone for a little longer than you are generally comfortable with. During this time you might simply let your thoughts wander freely, without hanging on to one line of thinking. In your journal describe what this experience is like for you.

LONELINESS AND OUR LIFE STAGES

How we deal with feelings of loneliness can depend to a great extent on our experiences of loneliness in childhood and adolescence. Later in life we may feel that loneliness has no place or that we can and should be able to avoid it. It is important to reflect on our past experiences, because they are often the basis of our present feelings about loneliness. In addition, we may fear loneliness less if we recognize that it is a natural part of living in every stage of life. There are many areas in which we may experience loneliness. Our differences, such as gender, race, sexual orientation, and language, can result in feelings of loneliness. Once we get beyond viewing loneliness as something that must be overcome at any cost, we may be less concerned about periods when we face loneliness. It helps to recognize that some loneliness is a natural dimension of the human condition.

Loneliness and Childhood

Reliving childhood experiences of loneliness can help you come to grips with present fears about being alone or lonely. Here are some typical memories of lonely periods that people we have worked with in therapy have relived:

> A woman recalls the time her parents were fighting in the bedroom and she heard them screaming and yelling. She was sure that they would divorce, and in many ways she felt responsible. She remembers living in continual fear that she would be deserted.

> A man recalls attempting to give a speech in the sixth grade. He stuttered over certain words, and children in the class began to laugh at him. Afterward he developed extreme self-consciousness in regard to his speech, and he long remembered the hurt he had experienced.

> An African American man recalls how excluded he felt in his all-White elementary school and how the other children would talk to him in derogatory ways. As an adult, he can still cry over these memories.

> A woman recalls the fright she felt as a small child when her uncle made sexual advances toward her. Although she did not really understand what was happening, she remembers the terrible loneliness of feeling that she could not tell her parents for fear of what they would do.

> A man recalls the boyhood loneliness of feeling that he was continually failing at everything he tried. To this day, he resists undertaking a task unless he is sure he can handle it, for fear of rekindling those old feelings of loneliness.

❭ A woman vividly remembers being in the hospital as a small child for an operation. She remembers the loneliness of not knowing what was going on or whether she would be able to leave the hospital. No one talked with her, and she was all alone with her fears.

As we try to relive these experiences, remember that children do not live in a logical, well-ordered world. Our childhood fears may have been greatly exaggerated, and the feeling of fright may remain with us even though we may now think of it as irrational. Unfortunately, being told by adults that we were foolish for having such fears may only have increased our loneliness while doing nothing to lessen the fears themselves.

At this point you may wonder, "Why go back and recall childhood pain and loneliness? Why not just let it be a thing of the past?" It is important that we reexperience some of the pain we felt as children to understand how we may still be affected by this pain now. We can also look at some of the decisions we made during these times of extreme loneliness and ask whether these decisions are still appropriate. Frequently, strategies we adopted as children remain with us into adulthood, when they are no longer appropriate. For instance, suppose that your family moved to a strange city when you were 7 years old and that you had to go to a new school. Kids at the new school laughed at you, and you lived through several months of anguish. You felt desperately alone in the world. During this time you decided to keep your feelings to yourself and build a wall around yourself so others could not hurt you. Although this experience is now long past, you still defend yourself in the same way, because you have not really made a new decision to open up and trust some people. In this way old fears of loneliness might contribute to a real loneliness in the present. If you allow yourself to experience your grief and work it through, emotionally as well as intellectually, you can overcome past pain and create new choices for yourself.

Take Time to Reflect   Take some time to decide whether you are willing to recall and relive a childhood experience of loneliness. If so, try to recapture the experience in as much detail as you can, reliving it in fantasy. Then reflect on the experience, using the following questions as a starting point.

1. Describe in a few words the most intense experience of loneliness you recall having as a child or an adolescent.

_____

_____

2. How do you think the experience affected you then?

_____

_____

3. How do you think the experience may still be affecting you now?

_____

_____

Journal suggestions: Consider elaborating on this exercise in your journal. How did you cope with loneliness as a child? How has this influenced the way you deal with loneliness in your life now? If you could go back and put a new ending on your most intense childhood experience of loneliness, what would it be? You might also think about times in your childhood when you enjoyed being alone. Write some notes to yourself about what these experiences were like for you. Where did you like to spend time alone? What did you enjoy doing by yourself? What positive aspects of these times do you recall?

Loneliness and Adolescence

For many people loneliness and adolescence are practically synonymous. Adolescents often feel that they are all alone in their world, that they are the first ones to have had the feelings they do, and that they are separated from others by some abnormality. Bodily changes and impulses alone are sufficient to bring about a sense of perplexity and loneliness, but there are other stresses to be undergone as well. Adolescents are developing a sense of identity. They strive to be successful yet fear failure. They want to be accepted and liked, but they fear rejection, ridicule, or exclusion by their peers. Most adolescents know the feeling of being lonely in a crowd or among friends. They often have fears of being ostracized. Conformity can bring acceptance, and the price of nonconformity can be steep.

As you recall your adolescent years—and, in particular, the areas of your life that were marked by loneliness—reflect on these questions:

❯ Did I feel included in a social group? Or did I sit on the sidelines, afraid of being included and wishing for it at the same time?

❯ Was there at least one person I felt I could talk to—one who really heard me, so that I didn't feel desperately alone?

Corbis

Adolescents often feel that they are all alone in the world.

> What experience stands out as one of the loneliest times during these years? How did I cope with my loneliness?

> Did I experience a sense of confusion concerning who I was and what I wanted to be as a person? How did I deal with my confusion? Who or what helped me during this time?

> How did I feel about my own worth and value? Did I believe I had anything of value to offer anyone or that anyone would find me worth being with?

> How did my culture affect the way I viewed loneliness? Did I learn that loneliness is a natural condition? Or did I pick up the message that loneliness is a disease to cure?

Ethnic minority adolescents often face cultural isolation. They may face unique challenges in terms of feeling connected to others, knowing who they are, and believing in their abilities. They may buy into stereotypes that contribute to feeling alone and different. Natalie's story shows how a person can find an identity and begin to trust herself.

NATALIE'S STORY

*I*n high school I was told that I was not college material and that "Mexicans are good with their hands." A block that I've had to deal with is the stereotype of Mexican women as being submissive and unable to stand up for themselves—which I've heard all my life from many teachers.

During my senior year in high school, I met Sal, who invited me to a Chicano Youth Leadership Conference. This conference made my outlook about myself change. Up to that point I was a stranger in my own land. I had no cultural identity and no strength to speak up. People there believed in me and told me that I could go to college and be successful. It was the first time that others had more faith in my abilities than I did. Sal became my mentor and challenged me to never underestimate the power I have. He made me feel so proud as a young Chicana and proud of my people. This was my spark to stand up and help the Chicano community.

Can you identify in any way with Natalie's story? Have you ever had difficulty believing in yourself? If so, did this affect your ability to feel connected to others? As you reflect on your adolescence, try to discover some of the ways in which the person you now are is a result of your experiences of loneliness as an adolescent. Do you shrink from competition for fear of failure? In social situations are you afraid of being left out? Do you feel some of the isolation you did then? If so, how do you deal with it? How might you have changed the way you deal with loneliness?

Loneliness and Young Adulthood

In our young-adult years we experiment with ways of being, and we establish lifestyles that may remain with us for many years. You may be struggling with the question of what to do with your life, what intimate relationships you want to establish, and how you will chart your future. Dealing with all the choices that face us at this time of life can be a lonely process. Loneliness can be a result of not having any validation from others.

How you come to terms with your own aloneness can have significant effects on the choices you make—choices that, in turn, may determine the course of your life for years to come. For instance, if you have not learned to listen to yourself and to depend on your own inner resources, you might succumb to the pressure to choose a relationship or a career before you are really prepared to do so, or you might look to your projects or partners for the sense of identity that you ultimately can find only in yourself. Alternatively, you may feel lonely and establish patterns that only increase your loneliness. This last possibility is well illustrated by the case of Saul.

Saul was in his early twenties when he attended college. He claimed that his chief problem was his isolation, yet he rarely reached out to others. His general manner seemed to say "Keep away." It is likely that Saul's negative self-talk made it difficult for him to make contact with others, which increased the chances that others would want to stay away from him. His social withdrawal resulted in him feeling lonely.

One day, as I (Jerry) was walking across the campus, I saw Saul sitting alone in a secluded spot, while many students were congregated on the lawn, enjoying the beautiful spring weather. Here was a chance for him to do something about his separation from others; instead, he chose to seclude himself. He continually told himself that others didn't like him and, sadly, made his prophecy self-fulfilling by his own behavior. He made himself unapproachable and, in many ways, the kind of person people would avoid.

In this time of life we have the chance to decide on ways of being toward ourselves and others as well as on our vocation and future plans. If you feel lonely on the campus, ask yourself what you are doing and can do about your own loneliness. Do you decide in advance that the others want to keep to themselves? Do you assume that there already are well-established cliques to which you cannot belong? Do you expect others to reach out to you, even though you do not initiate contacts yourself? What fears might be holding you back? Where do they seem to come from? Are past experiences of loneliness or rejection determining the choices you make now?

Often we create unnecessary loneliness for ourselves by our own behavior. If we sit back and wait for others to come to us, we give them the power to make us lonely. As we learn to take responsibility for ourselves in young adulthood, one area we can work on is taking responsibility for our own loneliness and creating new choices for ourselves.

Loneliness and Middle Age

Many changes occur during middle age that can result in new feelings of loneliness. Although we may not be free to choose some of the things that occur at this time in our lives, we are free to choose how we relate to these events. Here are some possible changes and crises of middle age:

> Our significant other may grow tired of living with us and decide to leave. If this happens, we must decide how to respond. Will we decide never to

trust anyone again? Will we mourn our loss and, after a period of grieving, actively look for another person to live with?

> Our life may not turn out the way we had planned. We may not enjoy the success we had hoped for, we may feel disenchanted with our work, or we may feel that we passed up many fine opportunities earlier. But the key point is what we can do about our life now. What choices will we make in light of this reality? Will we slip into hopelessness and berate ourselves endlessly about what we could have done and should have done? Will we allow ourselves to stay trapped in meaningless work and empty relationships, or will we look for positive options for change?

> Our children may leave home, and with this change we may experience emptiness and a sense of loss. If so, what will we do about this transition? Will we attempt to hang on? Can we let go and create a new life with new meaning? When our children leave, will we lose our desire to live? Will we look back with regret at all that we could have done differently, or will we choose to look ahead to the kind of life we want to create for ourselves now that we do not have the responsibilities of parenthood?

> Up to this time in our lives, we may have been absorbed in work and family responsibilities. We may have an overwhelming sense of regret over all the time we missed with friends and the time we did not have for recreation, and we may feel a strong desire to change our lives in the direction of integrating leisure time with work.

These are just a few of the changes that many of us confront during midlife. Although we may feel that events are not in our control, we can still choose how we respond to these life situations. For example, Amy and Gary made different decisions about how to deal with their loneliness after divorce, and their attitudes have been central to how they experience their loneliness.

Amy and Gary had been married for more than 20 years before their recent divorce, and they have three children in their teens. Amy is 43; Gary is 41. Here is Gary's story.

GARY'S STORY

I felt resentful at first and believed that somehow we could have stayed together if only Amy had changed her attitude. I live alone in a small apartment and get to see my kids only on weekends. I see my divorce as a personal failure, and I still feel a mixture of guilt and resentment. I hate to come home to an empty apartment with no one to talk to and no one to share my life with. I wonder whether women would find me interesting once they got to know me, and I fear that it's too late to begin a new life with someone else.

For her part, Amy also had many ambivalent feelings about divorcing.

AMY'S STORY

*A*fter the divorce I experienced panic and aloneness as I faced the prospect of rearing my children and managing the home on my own. I wonder whether I can meet my responsibilities and still have time for any social life. I am concerned that men may not be interested in me, especially with my three teenagers.

Even though I'm unsure of myself, I have dated some. At first I felt pressured by my parents to get married again. Yet I'm doing my best to resist this pressure. I'm choosing to remain single for the time being. Although I feel lonely at times, I don't feel trapped.

Experiences like those of Gary and Amy are very common among middle-aged people who find themselves having to cope with feelings of isolation and abandonment after a divorce. Some, like Gary, may feel panic and either retreat from people or quickly run into a new relationship to avoid the pain of separation. If they do not confront their fears and their pain, they may be controlled by their fear of being left alone for the rest of their lives. Others, like Amy, may go through a similar period of loneliness after a divorce yet refuse to be controlled by a fear of living alone. Although they might want a long-term relationship again some day, they avoid rushing impulsively into a new relationship to avoid feelings of pain or loneliness.

Loneliness and the Later Years

Our society emphasizes productivity, youth, beauty, power, and vitality. As we age, we may lose some of our vitality and sense of power or attractiveness. Many people face a real crisis when they reach retirement, for they feel that they are being put out to pasture—that they are not needed anymore and that their lives are really over. Loneliness and hopelessness are experienced by anyone who feels that there is little to look forward to or that he or she has no vital place in society, and such feelings are particularly common among older adults.

The loneliness of the later years can be accentuated by the losses that come with age—loss of sight, hearing, memory, and strength. Older people may lose their jobs, hobbies, friends, and loved ones. A particularly difficult loss is the death of a spouse with whom they have been close for many years. In the face of such losses, a person may ultimately ask what reason remains for living. It may be no coincidence that many old people die soon after their spouses have died or shortly after their retirement.

The loneliness of later years can be accentuated by the losses that come with age.

Joel Gordon

Charles, 65, lost his wife, Betsy, to cancer after a year's battle. During the last few months of Betsy's life, members of the local hospice organization helped Charles care for her at home. Here is an account of Charles's attempt to deal with her death.

CHARLES'S STORY

*B*efore Betsy's death she expressed a desire to talk to me about her impending death. I could not tolerate the reality of her illness and her dying. So, I never talked with her. Even though Betsy has been dead for some time, I still feel guilty for not listening to her and talking. When I look at her chair where she sat, I feel an overwhelming sense of loneliness. At times I feel as though my heart is going to explode. I rarely sleep through the night, and I get up early in the morning and look for tasks to keep me busy. I feel lost and lonely, and it is difficult for me to be in the house where she and I lived together for more than 45 years. Her memories are everywhere. My friends continue to encourage me to talk about my feelings. Although my friends and neighbors are supportive, I'm worried that I'll be a burden for them. I wish that I had died instead of Betsy, for she would have been better able to deal with my being gone than I'm able to cope with her passing.

C. S. Lewis, in *A Grief Observed* (1961), poetically compares grief to a long and winding valley where any bend may reveal a totally new landscape. He writes about his own grief over observing the death of his wife from cancer:

> AND GRIEF STILL FEELS LIKE FEAR. Perhaps, more strictly, like suspense. Or like waiting; just hanging about waiting for something to happen. It gives life a permanently provisional feeling. It doesn't seem worth starting anything. I can't settle down. I yawn, I fidget, I smoke too much. Up until this I always had too little time. Now there is nothing but time. Almost pure time, empty successiveness. (p. 29)

The pangs of aloneness or the feeling that life is futile reflect a drastic loss of meaning rather than an essential part of growing old. Viktor Frankl (1969) has written about the "will to meaning" as a key determinant of a person's desire to live. He notes that many of the inmates in the Nazi concentration camp where he was imprisoned kept themselves alive by looking forward to the prospect of being released and reunited with their families. Many of those who lost hope simply gave up and died, regardless of their age.

At least until recently our society has compounded the elderly person's loss of meaning by grossly neglecting the aged population. Although many elderly are well-taken care of in a convalescent home and are visited by their family members, many others are left alone in an institution with only minimal human contact.

Sometimes, however, older people choose a lonely existence rather than participating in the activities and human relationships that could be open to them. Rudy is an example of an older man who feels basically lost and does not seem able to find a direction that brings him satisfaction. Rudy is 85 years old. His wife died 15 years ago, and he remained in his large house. He reports that he has real difficulty being at home for any length of time. He leaves the house early in the morning in his pickup truck and spends most of his day doing crossword puzzles, except for the time he spends walking a few miles. When he finally returns home late at night, he faces the loneliness he attempted to escape from early in the morning. Although he has occasional contact with extended family at holiday gatherings, he rarely initiates contact with them during the rest of the year. He shies away from people out of his fear of burdening them. What he fails to realize is how much he still has to offer and how much others could benefit from their association with him. His inability to recognize and appreciate what he could offer to others keeps him a prisoner of his loneliness.

We conclude this discussion of the later years—and, in a sense, this entire chapter on loneliness and solitude—by returning to the example of Anne Morrow Lindbergh. In her later years her lifelong courage in facing aloneness enabled her to find new and rich meaning in her life. We were extremely impressed with this woman when we first read her book *Gift From the Sea*, but our respect increased when we read the "Afterword" in the book's 20th anniversary edition (1975). There, she looks back at the time when she originally wrote the book and notes that she was then deeply involved in family life. Since that time her children have left and established their own lives. She describes how a most uncomfortable stage followed her middle years, one that she had not anticipated when she wrote the book. She writes that she went from the "oyster-bed" stage of taking care of a family to the "abandoned-shell" stage of later life. This is how she describes the essence of the "abandoned-shell" stage:

> PLENTY OF SOLITUDE, and a sudden panic at how to fill it, characterized this period. With me, it was not a question of simply filling up the space or the time. I had many activities and even a well-established vocation to pursue. But when a mother is left, the lone hub of a wheel, with no other lives revolving around her, she faces a total reorientation. It takes time to re-find the center of gravity. (p. 134)

In this stage she did make choices to come to terms with herself and create a new role for herself. She points out that all the exploration she did earlier in life paid off when she reached the "abandoned-shell" stage. Here again, earlier choices affect current ones.

Before her husband, Charles, died in 1974, Lindbergh had looked forward to retiring with him on the Hawaiian Island of Maui. His death changed her life abruptly but did not bring it to an end. Its continuity was preserved in part by the presence of her 5 children and 12 grandchildren; moreover, she continued to involve herself in her own writing and in the preparation of her husband's papers for publication. Here is a fine example of a woman who has encountered her share of loneliness and learned to renew herself by actively choosing a positive stance toward life.

Maya Angelou is another person who schedules time for herself so she can retain her center. She lives a very full life, and she finds ways to retain her vitality. She schedules one day a month for herself; nothing is scheduled and her friends know not to call her.

We hope you will welcome your time alone. Once you fully accept it, your aloneness can become the source of your strength and the foundation of your relatedness to others. Think about the examples of Maya Angelou and Anne Morrow Lindbergh and consider how you can make time for yourself to take care of your soul. Taking time to be alone gives you the opportunity to think, plan, imagine, and dream. It allows you to listen to yourself and to become sensitive to what you are experiencing. In solitude you can come to appreciate anew both your separateness from and your relatedness to the important people and projects in your life. Sometimes you may get so busy attending to day-to-day routines that you forget to reflect and provide yourself with spiritual and emotional nourishment. Remember, if you are not a good friend to yourself, it will be difficult to find true friendship in the company of others.

SUMMARY

We have a need to be with others that is best satisfied through many forms of intimate relationships. Yet another essential dimension of the human experience is to be able to creatively function alone. Unless we can enjoy our own company, we will have difficulty finding real joy in being with others. Being with others and being with ourselves are two sides of the same coin.

Some people fail to reach out to others and make significant contact because they are timid in social situations and are relatively unassertive. Many people report that they are troubled by shyness or have had problems with being shy in the past. Shyness can lead to feelings of loneliness, yet shy people can challenge the fears that keep them unassertive. Shyness is not a disorder that needs to be "cured," nor are all aspects of being shy negative. It is important to recognize that certain attitudes and behaviors can create much of the loneliness we sometimes experience.

Each period of life presents unique tasks to be mastered, and loneliness can be best understood from a developmental perspective. Particular circumstances often result in loneliness as we pass through childhood, adolescence, young adulthood, middle age, and the later years. Most of us have experienced loneliness during our childhood and adolescent years, and these experiences can have a significant influence on our present attitudes, behavior, and relationships. It helps to be able to recognize our feelings about events that are associated with each of these turning points.

Experiencing loneliness is part of being human, for ultimately we are alone. We can grow from such experiences if we understand them and use them to renew our sense of ourselves. Moreover, we do not have to remain victimized by early decisions that we made as a result of past loneliness. We do have choices. We can choose to face loneliness and deal with it creatively, or we can choose to try to escape from it. We have some choice concerning whether we will feel lonely or whether we will make connections with others. We can design our activities so that we reject others before they reject us, or we can risk making contact with them.

❯ **Where Can I Go From Here?**

1. Allocate some time each day to be alone and reflect on anything you wish. Note down in your journal the thoughts and feelings that occur to you during your time alone.

2. If you have feelings of loneliness when you think about a certain person who has been or is now significant to you, write a letter to that person expressing all the things you are feeling (you do not have to mail the letter). For instance, tell that person how you miss him or her or write about your sadness, your resentment, or your desire for more closeness.

3. Imagine that you are the person you have written your letter to, and write a reply to yourself. What do you imagine that person would say to you if he or she received your letter? What do you fear (and what do you wish) he or she would say?

4. If you sometimes feel lonely and left out, try some specific experiments for a week or so. For example, if you feel isolated in most of your classes, make it a point to get to class early and initiate contact with a fellow student. If you feel anxious about taking such a step, try doing it in fantasy. What are your fears? What is the worst thing you can imagine might happen? Record your impressions in your journal. If you decide to try reaching out to other people, record in your journal what the experience is like for you.

5. Recall some periods of loneliness in your life. Select important situations in which you experienced loneliness, and spend some time recalling the details of each situation and reflecting on the meaning each of these experiences has had for you. Now you might do two things:

   ❯ Write down your reflections in your journal. How do you think your past experiences of loneliness affect you now?

   ❯ Select a friend or a person you would like to trust more and share this experience of loneliness.

6. Many people rarely make time exclusively for themselves. If you would like to have time to yourself but just have not gotten around to arranging it, consider going to a place you have never been or to the beach, the desert, or the mountains. Reserve a weekend just for yourself; if this seems too much, then spend a day completely alone. The important thing is to remove yourself from your everyday routine and just be with yourself without external distractions.

7. Spend a day or part of a day in a place where you can observe and experience lonely people. You might spend time near a busy downtown intersection, in a park where old people congregate, or in a large shopping center. Pay attention to expressions of loneliness, alienation, and isolation. How do people seem to be dealing with their loneliness? Later, you might discuss your observations in class.

(continued)

> ## Where Can I Go From Here? *(continued)*

8. Imagine yourself living in a typical rest home—without any of your possessions, cut off from your family and friends, and unable to do the things you now do. Reflect on what this experience would be like for you; then write down some of your reactions in your journal.

Resources for Future Study

Web Site Resources

THE SHYNESS HOME PAGE
http://www.shyness.com/

The Shyness Institute offers this Web site as "a gathering of network resources for people seeking information and services for shyness." It is an index of links to articles, associations, and agencies that work with shyness.

InfoTrac College Edition Resources

For additional readings, explore InfoTrac College Edition, our online library.

Go to **http://www.infotrac.college.com/wadsworth**

Hint: Enter the search terms:

> loneliness
> solitude
> shyness
> social isolation
> aloneness

Print Resources

Block, D. (1991). *Listening to your inner voice: Discover the truth within you and let it guide your way.* Center City, MN: Hazelden.

Lindbergh, A. (1975). *Gift from the sea.* New York: Pantheon. (Original work published in 1955)

Moustakas, C. (1961). *Loneliness.* Englewood Cliffs, NJ: Prentice-Hall (Spectrum).

Zimbardo, P. G. (1987). *Shyness.* New York: Jove.

Zimbardo, P. G. (1994). *Shyness.* Reading, MA: Addison-Wesley.

Contemplate death if you
would learn how to live

12

DEATH AND LOSS

> **Where Am I Now?**

Use this scale to respond to these statements:

4 = This statement is true of me *most* of the time.

3 = This statement is true of me *much* of the time.

2 = This statement is true of me *some* of the time.

1 = This statement is true of me *almost none* of the time.

_____ **1.** The fact that I must die makes me take the present moment seriously.

_____ **2.** I do not like funerals, because they make me dwell on a painful subject.

_____ **3.** If I had a terminal illness, I would want to know how much time I had left to live, so I could decide how to spend it.

_____ **4.** Because of the possibility of losing those I love, I do not allow myself to get too close to others.

_____ **5.** If I live with dignity, I will be able to die with dignity.

_____ **6.** One of my greatest fears of death is the fear of the unknown.

_____ **7.** I have had losses in my life that in some ways were like the experience of dying.

_____ **8.** There are some ways in which I am not really alive emotionally.

_____ **9.** I am not especially afraid of dying.

_____ **10.** I fear the deaths of those I love more than I do my own.

In this chapter we invite you to look at your attitudes and beliefs about your own death, the deaths of those you love, and other forms of significant loss. Although the topic of this chapter might seem morbid or depressing, an honest understanding and acceptance of death and loss can lay the groundwork for a rich and meaningful life. If we fully accept that we have only a limited time in which to live, we can make choices that will make the most of the time we have.

We also ask you to consider the notion of death in a broader perspective and to raise such questions as "What parts of me aren't as alive as they might be?" "In what emotional ways am I dead or dying?" and "What will I do with my awareness of the ways in which I'm not fully alive?" Finally, we discuss the importance of fully experiencing grief when you suffer serious losses.

This discussion of death and loss has an important connection with the themes of the previous chapter, loneliness and solitude. When we emotionally accept the reality of our eventual death, we experience our ultimate aloneness. This awareness of our mortality and aloneness helps us realize that our actions do count, that we do have choices concerning how we live our lives, and that we must accept the final responsibility for how well we are living.

Your awareness of death enables you to give meaning to your life. The reality of your finiteness can stimulate you to look at your priorities and to ask what you value most. In this way your willingness to come to terms with your death can teach you how to really live. To run from death is to run from life, for as Gibran (1923) writes, "Life and death are one, even as the river and the sea are one" (p. 71).

This chapter is also a bridge to the next chapter, which deals with meaning and values. Awareness of death is a catalyst for the human search for meaning in life. Our knowledge that we will die can encourage us to ask ourselves whether we are living by values that create a meaningful existence; if not, we have the time and opportunity to change our way of living. On this topic, Morrie Schwartz observes: "Everyone knows they're going to die, but nobody believes it. If we did, we would do things differently" (Albom, 1997, p. 81). Siegel (1989) indicates that death challenges us to seize the moment: "Facing death is often the catalyst that enables people to reach out for what they want" (p. 241). You can see this emphasis on meaning in Norma's response to the question of how she would feel if she found that she had only a short time to live.

NORMA'S STORY

I'm 53 years old, and I have accomplished more in my life than I ever thought possible. So far, my life has been rich and gratifying. I have a husband and four children with whom I generally have a good relationship. Although I know they have a need for me in their lives, they could function well without me. I am not afraid of death, but I would consider death at this time in my life as terribly unfair. There is so much more I want to do. Within me are many untapped talents that I haven't had time to express. Many of my present projects take an enormous amount of time, and although they are mostly satisfying, I've put on hold many other personal and professional aspirations. At times I feel an overwhelming sense of sadness and disappointment over the possibility of running out of time to do those things I was meant to do. Time seems to go by so fast, and I often wish I could stop the clock. It is my hope to live to an old age, yet I do confront myself with the reality that I may not be that fortunate, which provides me with the impetus to want to make changes in my life. The reality of mortality challenges me to reflect on what I would regret not having done if I were to die soon. This reality helps me not to postpone my plans to later, because there may not be a later. The greatest tragedy for me would be, if, on my dying day, I would say that I didn't live my life, rather I lived someone else's life.

Can you relate to any aspect of Norma's account? Are you living *now* the way you want? Do you have goals you have yet to meet? What do you most want to be able to say that you have experienced or accomplished before you die? What are you doing today to have the kind of life you want?

OUR FEARS OF DEATH

We may fear many aspects of death, including leaving behind those we love, losing ourselves, encountering the unknown, coping with the humiliation and indignity of a painful or long dying, and growing distant in the memories of others. For many people it is not so much death itself as the experience of dying that arouses fears. Here, too, it is well to ask what our fears are really about and to face them.

Morrie Schwartz was an elderly professor who was dying. Each Tuesday he met with one of his former students, Mitch, to share his insights about living and dying. Morrie said: "The truth is, once you learn how to die, you learn how to live" (Albom, 1997, p. 82). For Morrie, wasting life is even sadder than dying. Morrie talked about his fears of dying, which included losing more and more of his faculties and becoming increasingly dependent. However, he chose to face his fears and deal with them rather than letting his fears consume him. Even though he knew he was dying, Morrie realized that he had a choice regarding how he would deal with the end of this life: "Am I going to withdraw from the world, like most people do, or am I going to live? I decided I'm going to live—or at least try to live—the way I want, with dignity, with courage, with humor, with composure" (p. 21). One of the lessons we can learn from reading *Tuesdays With*

Morrie is that we do not have to stay away from someone who is dying. Rather than fearing the process, we can learn a lot about living if we allow ourselves to be connected and affected by a person who is dying.

Some people who are dying want to discuss what they are going through, yet loved ones cannot handle such conversations. Although Morrie was quite ready to talk about his death and the meaning of dying and living, Mitch was not ready to hear about death and was uncomfortable discussing this subject for some time. Certainly the life of young Mitch Albom was enriched by his encounters with Morrie in his death process. Albom found new meaning in life, but only by eventually being willing to really listen to Morrie and to talk about what Morrie needed to talk about.

Some people are reluctant to talk about dying with those close to them. Our daughter, Heidi, wrote to a friend's mother who was diagnosed with cancer, yet she did not want those close to her to talk about her condition. It was Heidi's hope that her friend's mother would recognize that she could give those who love her a gift by letting them share her struggle and allowing them to take care of her. Here is some of what she wrote.

HEIDI'S LETTER

*O*ne of my greatest memories with my Gram is sitting at the foot of her big queen chair and me on the little wooden stool. My face lay in her lap and her rose soft hand stroked my cheek. We both cried over the news of her being diagnosed with bladder cancer. We cried and cried and cried, then we laughed and then cried some more. As she would say, we bared our souls and left nothing unsaid. I value that experience and others like it and see its true power. The tears washed over us, and it bathed a fear and helped us both let go and embrace. In the beginning, Gram wanted to hide her diagnosis from others. She didn't want them to worry. But I encouraged her to tell all, which she finally did. What I saw happening was those who were always taken care of by her were given the gift to nurture and take care of such a strong and powerful woman. It is a gift I personally treasure. I still carry the glow of that power.

At this point pause to reflect on your own fears of death, dying, and living. Have you had the opportunity to talk with a dying person? If so, what was this like for you? Do you tend to avoid talking with people who are dying because you are uncomfortable or because you fear death? What expectations seem to arouse the greatest fears in you? How might your fears be affecting how you are choosing to live now? Although it is not necessary to morbidly focus on your death, it is important to deal with your fears of it and to consider what death means to you in terms of *living fully* now.

DEATH AND THE MEANING OF LIFE

Life and death are two facets of the same reality. Learning about death, dying, and bereavement is a pathway to learning about life and living, and the reverse is also true (Corr, Nabe, & Corr, 2000). If we avoid facing the reality of death or of reflecting on death, our capacity for life is also diminished. Acceptance of death does not have to be a morbid topic, for it can revitalize our goals and assist us in finding a deeper purpose for our being.

The existentialists view the acceptance of death as vital to the discovery of meaning and purpose in life. One of our distinguishing characteristics as human beings is our ability to grasp the concept of the future and, thus, the inevitability of death. Our ability to do so gives meaning to our existence, for it makes our every act and moment count.

Rather than living in fear of our mortality, we can view death as a challenge and as an opportunity. Siegel (1989, 1993) maintains that death is not a failure, but failing to live fully is the worst outcome. His writings and lectures are permeated with the assumption that the knowledge of our eventual death is what gives meaning to life. For Siegel (1989), the realization that we will die is a wakeup call to appreciate the urgency and beauty of each day.

> THE GREATEST GIFT OF ALL is that we don't live forever. It makes us face up to the meaning of our existence. It also enables people who never took time for themselves in life to take that time, at last, before they die. (p. 234)

From the Stoics of ancient Greece—who proclaimed "Contemplate death if you would learn how to live"—until modern times, we have been challenged to face our future. Seneca commented that "no man enjoys the true taste of life but he who is willing and ready to quit it." And Saint Augustine said, "It is only in the face of death that man's self is born." A sharply defined example of facing the reality of death, and of giving meaning to life, is provided by those who are terminally ill. Their confrontation with death causes them to do much living in a relatively brief period of time. The pressure of time almost forces them to choose how they will spend their remaining days. Irvin Yalom (1980) found that cancer patients in group therapy had the capacity to view their crisis as an opportunity to instigate change in their lives. Once they discovered that they had cancer, many experienced these inner changes that enabled them to find a powerful focus on life:

> A rearrangement of life's priorities, paying little attention to trivial matters

> A sense of liberation; the ability to choose to do those things they really wanted to do

> An increased sense of living in the moment; no postponement of living until some future time

Michael Siluk/The Picture Cube

Cultural and religious beliefs affect the way people view death.

> A vivid appreciation of the basic facts of life; for example, noticing changes in the seasons and other aspects of nature

> A deeper communication with loved ones than before the crisis

> Fewer interpersonal fears, less concern over security, and more willingness to take risks (p. 35)

We are finite beings, and what we do with our lives counts. We can choose to become all that we are capable of becoming and make a conscious decision to fully affirm life, or we can passively let life slip by us. We can settle for letting events happen to us, or we can actively choose and create the kind of life we want. If we had forever to actualize our potentials, there would be no urgency about doing so. Our time is invaluable precisely because it is limited.

Cultural and religious beliefs affect the way people view death. Some belief systems emphasize making the most of this life, for it is viewed as the only existence. Other belief systems focus on the natural continuity and progression of this temporal life into an afterlife. Just as our beliefs and values affect our fear of death, so do they affect the meaning we attribute to death. Regardless of your philosophical or spiritual views on the meaning of life and death, a wide range of choices is still open to you to maximize the quality of your present life.

Both of our daughters, Heidi and Cindy, were very much a part of their grandmother's final few weeks. Although this was a difficult time, they both learned many invaluable lessons about living from their grandmother, not only at this time when she was dying but also during the many years of her life. Cindy wrote down some of these "lessons my Gram taught me." As you read these life lessons, think about how fully you are living your own life today:

> Look the ones you love deeply in the eyes and without words let them know you love them and that they mean the world to you. Look at them so intensely and with such mindfulness that they feel as if you are the only person in the room with them.

> Say thank you and be grateful. Recognize your blessings, even in the face of despair.

> Say you are sorry when you have hurt or offended someone. It is never too late for an apology.

> Touch the ones you love and invite them to touch you. Touch heals, touch penetrates the soul and fills you up with joy.

> Laugh, smile, and be playful. Do not be too serious for too long. Let laughter enter every relationship you have with every person you know.

> Tell people how much you care about them. If you have a compliment or a kind thought about someone, speak it in the moment; do not wait until it is too late.

> Be forgiving. Do not judge others without trying to understand them. Even if they have done you harm or wronged you, find a way to let it go and to forgive.

> What you give out will come back to you. If you live a life of compassion and love and concern for others, you too will receive these gifts at the end of your days.

> Cry with the ones you love. Be open and share your fears and pain with each other. Hiding these things from each other protects no one. Be courageous in your self-expression and let each one weep or tear when it is necessary.

> Sit patiently with other people's pain. If you share your sorrows, they become less heavy and can easily be transformed into love and peacefulness.

> Take an interest in what other people do. Be genuine and curious in who they are. Ask about the welfare of others.

> Share your wisdom and life lessons without giving advice. Tell stories about your own struggles and accomplishments without being arrogant or self-centered.

❯ Pray and put faith in God. Always know that you are not alone and that you are connected to something beyond yourself. Trust this, ask for strength when you need to, and remember to give thanks as well.

Take Time to Reflect

1. What do you experience when you think about your own death?

_____

_____

2. Do you like the way you are living your life? List some specific things you are not doing now that you would like to be doing.

_____

_____

3. If you had only 6 months left to live, what would you like to be doing during that time?

_____

_____

4. Does the fact that you will die give meaning to your life now? If so, how?

_____

_____

5. In what ways do you think your fears about death and dying might be affecting the choices you make now?

_____

_____

SUICIDE: ULTIMATE CHOICE OR ULTIMATE COP-OUT?

Suicide is one of the leading causes of death in the United States, and it is on the increase. In 1996 suicide was the ninth leading cause of death, accounting for 30,386 deaths. Yet even in the face of these astonishing numbers, we avoid talking about suicide and rely on these common but untrue myths (Marcus, 1996):

> There are no warning signs.
> People who talk about committing suicide will not do it.
> Young people are more likely than old people to kill themselves.
> Once a suicidal crisis has passed, the person is out of danger.
> Suicide is genetic.
> People who are suicidal want to die.

Although it is true that some people do not give any signs that they intend on taking their lives, generally there are warning signs that give some indication that a person is suicidal (Marcus, 1996). Here are some signs that an individual may be in trouble:

> Suicidal thoughts and threats
> Previous suicidal threats or comments
> Preoccupation with death, including talk of feeling hopeless and helpless
> Giving away prized possessions
> Discussing specific methods and a time for killing oneself
> Depression
> Isolation and withdrawal from friends and family
> Extreme changes of behavior and sudden personality changes
> Getting one's life in order
> A sudden appearance of calm or peace after a period during which some of these above-listed characteristics were evident

These signs should be taken seriously, and interventions should be made to help bring about a change in the suicidal person.

Those considering suicide often feel that they are trapped in a dead-end existence and that life is unbearable. They simply do not want to go on in such deadening patterns, and they may feel that the chances of change are slim. Although there are undoubtedly options for living differently, they are unable to see any. Suicidal thoughts can be overwhelming during this time of emotional blindness.

Is suicide an ultimate choice or an ultimate cop-out? This question is complex, with no easy answer. We must each make conscious choices about how fully we are willing to live, realizing that we must pay a price for being alive.

Some people believe suicide is a cop-out, the result of not being willing to struggle or of being too quick to give up without exploring other possibilities. What does your personal experience reveal? At times you may have felt a deep sense of hopelessness, and you may have questioned whether it was worth it to continue living. Have you ever felt really suicidal? If so, what was going on in your life that contributed to your desire to end it? What factor or factors kept you from following through with taking your life? What hidden meanings does suicide have for you?

Taking one's life is a powerful act, and the underlying emotional messages and symbolic meanings are equally powerful:

> A cry for help: "I cried out, but nobody heard me!"

> A form of self-punishment: "I don't deserve to live."

> An act of hostility: "I'll get even with you; see what you made me do."

> An attempt to control and exert power over people: "I will make others suffer for the rest of their lives for having rejected me."

> An attempt to be noticed: "Maybe now people will talk about me and feel sorry for the way they treated me."

> A relief from a terrible state of mind: "Life is too stressful, and I'm fed up."

> An escape from a difficult or impossible situation: "I hate living in an alcoholic family, and death seems like one way to end this situation."

> A relief from hopelessness: "I see no way out of the despair I feel. Ending my life will be better than hating to wake up each morning."

> An end to pain: "I suffer extreme physical pain, which will not end. Suicide will put an end to this nightmare."

Suicide as an Act of Mercy

Can suicide be an act of mercy? Some victims of painful and terminal illnesses have decided when and how to end their lives. Rather than dying with cancer and enduring extreme pain, some people have actually called their families together and then taken some form of poison. In recent years Dr. Jack Kevorkian, the physician from Michigan known as the "suicide doctor," has frequently been the subject of news stories. In 1990 Kevorkian publicly announced his willingness to assist individuals to end their own lives. He offered to provide people with a means for ending their lives when there was no more hope. Kevorkian maintained that he would do what he believed to be right pertaining to self-determination and choices, regardless of opposition from the community. For years Kevorkian provided instructions to individuals who wanted to bring about their deaths, yet he took no active role in that action. In 1998, however, Kevorkian videotaped his own active involvement in bringing about the death of a man in the advanced stages of Lou Gehrig's disease. The videotape showed Kevorkian injecting this man with two chemicals that caused his death. An edited version of this videotape was aired on the CBS *60 Minutes* television program on November 22, 1998. Shortly thereafter Kevorkian was charged with first-degree murder and criminal assisted suicide. A jury ultimately found Kevorkian guilty of second-degree murder and delivery of a controlled substance. On April 13, 1999, Kevorkian was sentenced to 10 to 25 years in prison for murder and 3 to 7 years for delivery of a controlled substance (Corr, Nabe, & Corr, 2000).

Certainly there is a difference between suicide and allowing nature to take its course in cases of extreme illness. Many people are opposed to active measures to end life, yet they also oppose interventions that unnecessarily prolong life by artificial and unusual means. Assisted suicide involves providing lethal means to cause a person's death, with the individual performing the act that ends his or her own life. To date only one state has enacted legislation allowing doctor-assisted suicide for terminally ill patients. This form of rational suicide is sometimes argued to be morally and ethically appropriate when people are in severe pain and there is no hope of recovery (Corr, Nabe, & Corr, 2000).

Take a few minutes to think about how you might respond if you were critically ill and chances were just about nonexistent that you would improve. Might there come a time in your life when there was nothing for you to live for? Imagine yourself in a skilled nursing facility, living in a vegetative state, having lost control of all your bodily functions. You are unable to read, to carry on meaningful conversation, or to go places, and you are partially paralyzed by a series of strokes. Would you want to be kept alive at all costs, or might you want to end your life? Would you feel justified in doing so? What might stop you?

Now apply this line of thought to other situations in life. Is your life yours to do with as you choose? Do you believe it is permissible to commit suicide at *any* period in your life? Suppose you tried various ways of making your life meaningful, but nothing worked and nothing changed. Would you continue to live until natural causes took over? Would you feel justified in ending your own life if your active search had failed to bring you peace?

Reactions to Suicide

The sudden death of a loved one, especially due to suicide, sets the survivors on a grief-stricken journey (Marcus, 1996). When a family member commits suicide, the immediate reaction is generally shock and distress. Soon afterward those left behind experience a range of feelings such as denial, shock, anger, shame, guilt, grief, depression, fear, blame, rejection, and abandonment. When family members are in denial, they may invent reasons that will contribute to their refusal to accept the death as a suicide. Anger is quite common and is often directed toward the deceased: "Why did you shut me out and leave me?" Anger may also be aimed at medical agencies, friends, and other family members. There may be a sense of shame because of religious teachings about suicide. Guilt is often experienced over what the survivors could and should have done to prevent the tragedy. "Maybe if I had been more sensitive and caring," they might feel, "this terrible thing wouldn't have happened." Survivors also may experience fear over the possibility that this act will be repeated by another family member or, perhaps, even by themselves.

Counseling is often very useful in helping survivors deal with their reactions to the suicide of a friend or family member. The nature of the unfinished business, how it is handled, and how the survivor is affected by it all have an impact on the grief process. Typically, those who are left behind experience a deep sense of abandonment, loneliness, and isolation. If family members are willing to seek counseling (either individually or as a family), they can be taught how to express feelings that they might otherwise keep buried inside. Counseling encourages the survivors to talk about the things they may be rehearsing over and over in their heads, and it can help them to talk about their feelings with one another. Counseling can help correct distortions survivors may hold, prepare for their future, learn to let go of regrets and blame, and give expression to their anger. Because of their deep sadness, it may be difficult for family members to become aware of, much less express to one another, the anger that they feel.

FREEDOM IN DYING

The process of dying involves a gradual diminishing of the choices available to us. But even in dying, we can choose how we handle what is happening to us. The following account deals with the dying of Jim Morelock, a student and close friend of mine (Jerry's).*

Jim is 25 years old. He is full of life—witty, bright, honest, and actively questioning. He had just graduated from college as a human services major and seemed to have a bright future when his illness was discovered.

About a year and a half ago, Jim developed a growth on his forehead and underwent surgery to have it removed. At that time, his doctors believed the growth was a rare disorder that was not malignant. Later, more tumors erupted, and more surgery followed. Several months ago, Jim found out that the tumors had spread throughout his body and that, even with cobalt treatment, he would have a short life. Since that time he has steadily grown weaker and has been able to do less and less; yet he has shown remarkable courage in the way he has faced this loss and his dying.

Some time ago Jim came to Idyllwild, California, and took part in the weekend seminar that we had with the reviewers of this book. On this chapter, he

---

*This account is being repeated as it appeared in this book's first edition. Many readers have commented to us about how touched they were as they read about Jim's life and his death, and in this way he seems to have lived on in one important respect.

Courtesy of Betty Jane Morelock

Jim Morelock

commented that although we may not have a choice concerning the losses we suffer in dying, we do retain the ability to choose our attitude toward our death and the way we relate to it.

Jim has taught me a lot during these past few months about this enduring capacity for choice, even in extreme circumstances. Jim has made many critical choices since being told of his illness. He chose to continue taking a course at the university, because he liked the contact with the people there. He worked hard at a boat dock to support himself, until he could no longer manage the physical exertion. He decided to undergo cobalt treatment, even though he knew that it most likely would not result in his cure, because he hoped that it would reduce his pain. It did not, and Jim has suffered much agony during the past few months. He decided not to undergo chemotherapy, primarily because he did not want to prolong his life if he could not really live fully. He made a choice to accept God in his life, which gave him a sense of peace and serenity. Before he became bedridden, he decided to go to Hawaii and enjoy his time in first-class style.

Jim has always had an aversion to hospitals—to most institutions, for that matter—so he chose to remain at home, in more personal surroundings. As long as he was able, he read widely and continued to write in his journal about his thoughts and feelings on living and dying. With his friends, he played his guitar and sang songs that he had written. He maintained an active interest in life and in the things around him, without denying the fact that he was dying.

More than anyone I have known or heard about, Jim has taken care of unfinished business. He made it a point to gather his family and tell them his wishes, he made contact with all his friends and said everything he wanted to say to them, and he asked Marianne to deliver the eulogy at his funeral services. He clearly stated his desire for cremation; he wants to burn those tumors and then have his ashes scattered over the sea—a wish that reflects his love of freedom and movement.

Jim has very little freedom and movement now, for he can do little except lie in his bed and wait for his death to come. To this day he is choosing to die with dignity, and although his body is deteriorating, his spirit is still very much alive. He retains his mental sharpness, his ability to say a lot in a very few words, and his sense of humor. He has allowed himself to grieve over his losses. As he puts it, "I'd sure like to hang around to enjoy all those people that love me!" Realizing that this isn't possible, Jim is saying good-bye to all those who are close to him.

Throughout this ordeal, Jim's mother has been truly exceptional. When she told me how remarkable Jim has been in complaining so rarely despite his constant pain, I reminded her that I'd never heard her complain during her months on duty. I have been continually amazed by her strength and courage, and I have admired her willingness to honor Jim's wishes and accept his beliefs, even though at times they have differed from her own. She has demonstrated her care without smothering him or depriving him of his free spirit and independence. Her acceptance of Jim's dying and her willingness to be fully present to him have given him the opportunity to express openly whatever he feels. Jim has been able to grieve and mourn because she has not cut off this process.

This experience has taught me much about dying and about living. Through him, I have learned that I do not have to do that much for a person who is dying other than to be with him or her by being myself. So often I have felt a sense of helplessness, of not knowing what to say or how much to say, of not knowing what to ask or not to ask, of feeling stuck for words. Jim's imminent death seems such a loss, and it is very difficult for me to accept it. Gradually, however, I have learned not to be so concerned about what to say or to refrain from saying. In fact, in my last visit I said very little, but I feel that we made significant contact with each other. I have also learned to share with him the sadness I feel, but there is simply no easy way to say good-bye to a friend.

Jim is showing me that his style of dying will be no different from his style of living. By his example and by his words, Jim has been a catalyst for me to think about the things I say and do and to evaluate my own life.

Take Time to Reflect

1. If you were close to someone during his or her dying, how did the experience affect your feelings about your life and about your own dying?

_____

_____

2. How would you like to be able to respond if a person who is close to you were dying?

_____

_____

3. If you were dying, what would you most want from the people who are closest to you?

_____

_____

THE STAGES OF DEATH AND LOSS

Death and dying have become topics of widespread discussion among psychologists, psychiatrists, physicians, sociologists, ministers, and researchers. Whereas these topics were once taboo for many people, they are now the focus of seminars, courses, and workshops, and a number of books give evidence of this growing interest.

Dr. Elisabeth Kübler-Ross is a pioneer in the contemporary study of death and dying. In her widely read books *On Death and Dying* (1969) and *Death: The Final Stage of Growth* (1975), she discusses the psychological and sociological aspects of death and the experience of dying. In another book, *AIDS: The Ultimate Challenge*, Kübler-Ross (1993) applies the stages of dying to people with AIDS. Thanks to her efforts, many people have become aware of the almost universal need the dying have to talk about their impending death and to complete their business with the important people in their lives. She has shown how ignorance of the dying process and of the needs of dying people—as well as the fears of those around them—can rob the dying of the opportunity to fully experience their feelings and arrive at a resolution of them.

A greater understanding of dying can help us come to an acceptance of death, as well as be more helpful and present to those who are dying. For this reason, we describe the five stages of dying that Kübler-Ross has delineated, based on her research with terminally ill cancer patients. She emphasizes that these are not neat and compartmentalized stages that every person passes through in an orderly fashion. At times a person may experience a combination of these stages, perhaps skip one or more stages, or go back to an earlier stage he or she has already experienced. In general, however, Kübler-Ross found this sequence: denial, anger, bargaining, depression, and acceptance.

To make this discussion of the stages of dying more concrete, we will examine these stages as they relate to Ann, a 45-year-old cancer patient. Ann was married and the mother of three children in elementary school. Before she discovered that she had terminal cancer, she felt she had much to live for, and she enjoyed life.

Denial

After the initial shock of learning that death will happen soon, denial is a normal first reaction. Most people move on and deal with their impending death in other ways after a short time, but denial may recur at a later time. In Ann's case, her first reaction to being told she had only about a year to live was shock. She refused to believe the diagnosis was correct. Even after obtaining several other medical opinions, she still refused to accept that she was dying. In other words, her initial reaction was one of denial.

Ann's husband also denied her illness and was unwilling to talk to her about it. He felt that talking bluntly might only make her more depressed and lead her to lose all hope. He failed to recognize how important it was for Ann to feel that she could bring up the subject if she wished. On some level Ann knew that she could not talk about her death with her husband.

During the stage of denial, the attitudes of a dying person's family and friends are critical. If these people cannot face the fact that their loved one is dying, they cannot help him or her move toward an acceptance of death. Their own fear will blind them to signs that the dying person wants to talk about his or her death and needs support. In the case of Ann it would not necessarily have been a wise idea to force her to talk, but she could have been greatly helped if those around her had been available and sensitive to her when she stopped denying her death and showed a need to be listened to.

Anger

As Ann began to accept that her time was limited by an incurable disease, her denial was replaced by anger. Over and over she wondered why she—who had so much to live for—had to be afflicted with this dreadful disease. Her anger mounted as she thought of her children and realized that she would not be able to see them grow and develop. During her frequent visits to the hospital for radiation treatments, she directed some of her anger toward doctors "who didn't seem to know what they were doing" and toward the "impersonal" nurses.

It is important that others recognize the need of dying people to express their anger, whether they direct it toward their doctors, the hospital staff, their friends, their children, or God. If this displaced anger is taken personally, any meaningful dialogue with the dying will be cut off. Moreover, people like Ann have reason to be enraged over having to suffer in this way when they have so much to live for. Rather than withdrawing support or taking offense, the people who surround a dying person can help most by allowing the person to fully express the pent-up rage inside. In this way they help the person to ultimately come to terms with his or her death.

Bargaining

Kübler-Ross (1969) sums up the essence of the bargaining stage as follows: "If God has decided to take us from this earth and he did not respond to any angry pleas, he may be more favorable if I ask nicely" (p. 72). Bargaining typically involves a change in behavior or a specific promise in exchange for more time to live. Such bargains are generally made in secret, often with God. Basically, the stage of bargaining is an attempt to postpone the inevitable end.

Ann's ambitions at this stage were to finish her college studies and graduate with her bachelor's degree, which she was close to obtaining. She also hoped to see her oldest daughter begin junior high school in a little over a year. During this time she tried any type of treatment that offered some hope of extending her life.

Depression

Depression occurs when a dying person faces the losses that dying brings and begins to mourn what is already lost and what is still to be lost. In *Tuesdays With Morrie* (Albom, 1997), Morrie was asked if he felt sorry for himself. He replied that in the mornings he often cries as he watches his body wilt away to nothing. "I feel around my body, I move my finger and my hands—whatever I can still move—and I mourn what I've lost. I mourn the slow, insidious way in which I'm dying" (pp. 56–57). He added that he then stops mourning and concentrates on all the good things still in his life.

In Ann's case, bargaining for time eventually ran out and depression began setting in. No possibility of remission of her cancer remained, and she could no longer deny the inevitability of her death. Having been subjected to radiation treatments, chemotherapy, and a series of operations, she was becoming weaker and thinner, and she was able to do less and less. Her primary feelings became a great sense of loss and a fear of the unknown. She wondered about who would take care of her children and about her husband's future. She felt guilty because she was demanding so much attention and time and because the treatment of her illness was depleting the family income. She felt depressed over losing her hair and her beauty.

It would not have been helpful at this stage to try to cheer Ann up or to deny her real situation. Just as it had been important to allow her to fully vent her anger, it was important now to let her talk about her feelings and to make her final plans. Dying people are about to lose everyone they love, and only the freedom to grieve over these losses will enable them to find some peace and serenity in a final acceptance of death.

Acceptance

Kübler-Ross (1969) found that if patients have had enough time and support to work through the previous stages, most of them reach a stage at which they are neither depressed nor angry. Acceptance of death can be reached if they work through the many conflicts and feelings that dying brings:

> ACCEPTANCE SHOULD NOT BE MISTAKEN for a happy stage. It is almost devoid of feelings. It is as if the pain has gone, the struggle is over, and there comes a time for "the final rest before the long journey," as one patient phrased it. (p. 100)

At this stage, the dying person is often tired and weak. Acceptance does not imply submission, defeat, or doing nothing. Instead, acceptance is a form of dealing with reality. It involves a gradual separation from people, life, ties, and roles.

Of course, some people never achieve an acceptance of their death, and some have no desire to. Ann, for example, never truly reached a stage of acceptance. Her final attitude was more one of surrender, a realization that it was futile to fight any longer. Although she still felt unready to die, she did want an end to her suffering. It may be that if those close to her had been more open to her and accepting of her feelings, she would have been able to work through more of her anger and depression.

The Significance of the Stages of Dying

The value of Kübler-Ross's description of the dying process is that the stages describe and summarize in a general way what many patients experience and therefore add to our understanding of dying. But these stages should not be interpreted as a natural progression that is expected in most cases, and it is a mistake to use these stages as the standard by which to judge whether a dying person's behavior is normal or right. Just as people are unique in the way they live, they are unique in the way they die. Sometimes practitioners who work with the terminally ill forget that the stages of dying do not progress neatly, even though they cognitively know this reality. One practitioner told us: "Although I had read Kübler-Ross's book and knew the stages that a dying person was supposed to go through, many of my terminal patients had not read the same book!"

Patients who do not make it to the acceptance stage are sometimes viewed as failures. For example, some nurses get angry at patients who take "backward" steps by going from depression to anger, or they question patients about why they have "stayed so long in the anger stage." People die in a variety of ways and have a variety of feelings during this process: hope, anger, depression, fear, envy, relief, and anticipation. Those who are dying move back and forth from mood to mood. Therefore, these stages should not be used as a method of categorizing, and thus dehumanizing, the dying; they are best used as a frame of reference for helping them.

The Hospice Movement

There is a trend toward more direct involvement of family members in caring for a dying person. An example of this is the hospice program. The term *hospice* was originally used to describe a waiting place for weary travelers during the Middle Ages. Later, hospices were established for children without parents, the incurably ill, and the elderly. In recent years hospice programs have spread rapidly through Europe and North America. They offer care for those who are in the final stages of the journey of life. The services are generally carried out in the dying person's home. More than 90% of all hospice care hours are provided in a patient's home. Much hospice home care takes the place of more expensive and impersonal multiple hospitalizations. Hospice care is aimed at making people as comfortable as possible who are terminally ill or who have no reasonable hope of benefit from cure-oriented intervention (Corr, Nabe, & Corr, 2000). The hospice movement also gives permission to those who are losing a significant person to feel the full range of emotions during the bereavement process. Hospice centers typically offer a variety of counseling services for those who survive the death of a loved one.

According to Kalish (1985), the recent hospice movement has changed the attitude toward a dying person from "There is nothing more that we can do to help" to "We need to do what we can to provide the most humane care." This involves viewing patients and their family members as a unit. Caregivers do not separate the person who is dying from his or her family. Whenever possible, patients are kept at home as long as they wish. Both volunteers and a trained staff provide health care aid, including helping the patient and the family members deal with psychological and social stresses. Hospices aim to provide services that help dying patients experience a sense of self-worth and dignity and to provide support for the family members so that they can prepare for the eventual separation. Although research on these programs is preliminary, hospice patients are more mobile and tend to report less general anxiety and fewer bodily symptoms than those being given traditional care. The spouse is able to spend more time in visiting and caring for the patient (Kalish, 1985).

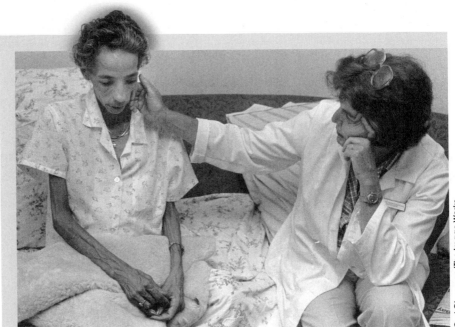

The hospice movement came in response to what many people perceived as the inadequate care for the dying in hospitals.

Carl Glassman/The Image Works

Although a hospice is a humanitarian way of helping people die with dignity, hospice facilities are not always welcomed in the community. For example, in one neighborhood intense objections were raised to a hospice house for people dying of AIDS. Some of the residents had concerns about their property values falling, and others feared bringing people who were afflicted with AIDS into their community.

Sometimes the purpose of hospice is misunderstood, especially in light of the notoriety surrounding physician-assisted suicide. As a family, we were recently confronted with one of the misconceptions regarding the aims of hospice. During the last few weeks of Josephine Corey's (Jerry's mother) life, several family members had decided to request the services of hospice. However, one family member was extremely opposed to this decision because of his mistaken belief that hospice would withhold treatment and by doing so would accelerate her death. He was willing to go to a hospice agency to talk about his concerns, which resulted in a different way of thinking about what hospice could offer. As an entire family, we felt a tremendous amount of support from the hospice staff and also came to realize how much more difficult this situation would have been had we not asked for their help. The various hospice workers were a genuine source of comfort to each of the family members. They also provided the opportunity for Josephine Corey to live out her last few weeks in her own home, which was one of her wishes.

GRIEVING OVER DEATH, SEPARATION, AND OTHER LOSSES

In a way that is similar to the stages of dying, people go through stages of grief in working through death and various other losses. Grief work refers to the exploration of feelings of sorrow, anger, and guilt over the experience of a significant loss. This process is often not an easy or simple one. Some people are never able to accept the death of a child or a spouse. They may get stuck by denying their feelings and by not facing and working through their pain over the loss. At some point in the grief process, people may feel numb or that they are functioning on automatic pilot. Once this numbness wears off, the pain seems to intensify. People who are going through this pain need to learn that they might well get worse before they feel better.

To put to rest unresolved issues and unexpressed feelings, we need to express our anger, regrets, guilts, and frustrations. When we attempt to deny pain, we inevitably wind up being stuck and are unable to express a range of feelings. This unexpressed pain tends to eat away at people both physically and psychologically and prevents them from accepting the reality of the death of a loved one. We are reminded of a woman who reported that she was overcome with emotions and could not stop crying at the funeral of an acquaintance. What surprised her was the way her reaction contrasted with her "strength and composure" over the death of her husband. What she did not realize was that she had not allowed herself to grieve over the loss of her husband and that years later she was having a delayed grief reaction.

Allowing Yourself to Grieve

Grief is a necessary and natural process after a significant loss. However, there are forces in many cultures that make it very difficult for people to experience a complete grief process after they have suffered a loss. For example, in U.S. society there appears to be a cultural norm that fosters an expectation of a "quick cure," and oftentimes others cannot understand why it is taking "such a long time" for a grieving person to "get back to normal." As is the case with any emotion that does not get expressed, unresolved grief lingers in the background and prevents people from letting go of losses and from forming new relationships. Also, unresolved grief is considered a key factor in the onset of a variety of physical illnesses. Siegel (1988, 1989, 1993) cites numerous examples of people who developed cancer after a significant loss through death or divorce.

Most writers on the psychological aspects of death and loss agree that grieving is necessary. A common denominator of all these theories is that there is a general process of moving from a stage of depression to recovery. Although people may successfully work through their feelings pertaining to loss, it can be expected that the loss may always be with them. In successful grieving, however, people are not immobilized by the loss, nor do they close themselves off from other involvements. Another commonality in all these theories is that they recognize that not all people go through the grieving process at the same rate, nor do all people move neatly and predictably from one stage to another.

A chronic state of depression and a restricted range of feelings suffered by some people are often attributed to some unresolved reaction to a significant loss. Such individuals fear that the pain will consume them and that it is better to shut off their feelings. What they fail to realize is that they pay a price for this denial in the long run. This price involves excluding feelings of closeness and joy. At times these people can go on for years without ever expressing emotions over their loss, being convinced that they have adequately dealt with it. Yet they might find themselves being flooded with emotions for which they have no explanation. They may discover that another's loss opens up old wounds that they thought were successfully healed.

My (Marianne's) father died 12 years ago. Although I grieved his death and found support from my friends and family, I find that even years later there are times when I am flooded with emotions of sadness over his loss. Sometimes these emotions take me by surprise, and I do not always know what triggered them. On several occasions when I felt the sadness, I realized afterward that it was a particular anniversary date that had to do with his life and death. My unconscious was more in tune than was my conscious mind. Sometimes people who have lost a loved one expect to complete their grieving in a set time, such as one year. It is important to realize that there is no predictable schedule. Instead, people who are grieving need to experience their sadness and not tell themselves that they should be over this by now.

Most cultures have rituals designed to help people with the grieving process. Examples are the funeral practices of the Irish, the Jewish, the Russians, and others, whereby painful feelings are actually triggered and released. Many cultures have a formal mourning period (usually a year), and in these cultures the mourners are directly involved in the funeral process. In the United States those who suffer from a loss are typically "protected" from any direct involvement in the burial, and people are praised for not displaying overt signs of grief. Many of our rituals make it easy for us to deny our feelings of loss and therefore keep us from coming to terms with the reality of that loss. It has become clear that these practices are not genuinely helpful. Today, more emphasis is being placed on providing ways for people to participate more directly in the dying process of their loved ones (such as the hospice movement) and in the funeral process as well.

If you are experiencing bereavement and are able to express the full range of your thoughts and feelings, you stand a better chance of adjusting to a new environment. Indeed, part of the grief process involves making basic life changes and experiencing new growth. If you have gone through the necessary cycle of bereavement, you will be better equipped to become reinvested with a new purpose and a new reason for living. What major losses have you had, and how have you coped with them? Have you lost a family member, a close friendship, a job that you valued, a spouse through divorce, a material object that had special meaning, a place where you once lived, a pet, or your faith in some person or group? Are there any similarities in how you responded to these different types of loss? Did you successfully work through your feelings about the losses? Or did you allow yourself to express your feelings to someone close to you? In recalling a particular loss, are the feelings still as intense as they were then?

You might experience grief over many types of losses besides a death, such as the breakup of a relationship, the loss of a career, or the children leaving home. In learning to resolve grief, regardless of its source, people need to be able to talk about what they are telling themselves internally and what they are feeling. They typically need to express their feelings over the lack of fairness about their situation. They may eventually face up to the fact that there is no rational reason that will explain their loss.

Stages of Grief Over a Divorce or a Significant Loss

The five stages of dying described by Kübler-Ross can also be applied in understanding other significant losses. To illustrate, we describe a divorce in terms of the five stages. Of course, you can broaden this concept to see whether it applies to separation from your parents, the experience of breaking up with a girlfriend or boyfriend, or the process of seeing your children mature and leave home. The stages can also provide understanding of the process you go through after losing a job and facing the anxieties of unemployment. Although not all people who experience divorce, the breakup of a long-term relationship, or some other loss necessarily go through the stages in the same way, we have found that many people do experience a similar questioning and struggling.

Denial Many people who are divorcing go through a process of denial and self-deception. They may try to convince themselves that their marriage is not all that bad, that nobody is perfect, and that things would be worse if they did separate. Even after the decision is made to divorce, they may feel a sense of disbelief. If it was the other person who initiated the divorce, the remaining partner might ask: "Where did things go wrong? Why is she [he] doing this to me? How can this be happening to me?"

Anger Once people accept the reality that they are divorcing, they frequently experience anger and rage. They may say: "I gave a lot, and now I'm being deserted. I feel as if I've been used and then thrown away." Many people feel cheated and angry over the apparent injustice of what is happening to them. Just as it is very important for dying people to express any anger they feel, it is also important for people who are going through the grief associated with a divorce or other loss to express their anger. If they keep it bottled up inside, it is likely to be turned against them and may take the form of depression, a kind of self-punishment.

Bargaining   Sometimes people hope that a separation will give them the distance they need to reevaluate things and that they will soon get back together again. Although separations sometimes work this way, it is often futile to wish that matters can be worked out. Nevertheless, during the bargaining stage one or both partners may try to make concessions and compromises that they hope will lead to a reconciliation.

Depression   In the aftermath of a decision to divorce, a sense of hopelessness may set in. As the partners realize that a reconciliation is not possible, they may begin to dwell on the emptiness and loss they feel. They may find it very difficult to let go of the future they had envisioned together. They may spend much time ruminating over what their lives might have been like if they had made their relationship work. It is not uncommon for people who divorce to turn their anger away from their spouse and toward themselves. Thus, they may experience much self-blame and self-doubt. They may say to themselves: "Maybe I didn't give our relationship a fair chance. What could I have done differently? I wonder where I went wrong? Why couldn't I do something different to make our relationship work?" Depression can also be the result of the recognition that a real loss has been sustained. It is vitally important that people fully experience and express the grief (and anger) they feel over their loss. Too often people deceive themselves into believing that they are finished with their sadness (or anger) long before they have given vent to their intense feelings. Unresolved grief (and anger) tends to be carried around with a person, blocking the expression of many other feelings. For instance, if grief isn't worked through, it may be extremely difficult for a person to form new relationships, because in some ways he or she is still holding on to the past relationship.

Acceptance   If people allow themselves to mourn their losses, the process of grief work usually leads to a stage of acceptance. In the case of divorce, once the two persons have finished their grieving, new possibilities begin to open up. They can begin to accept that they must make a life for themselves without the other person and that they cannot cling to resentments that will keep them from beginning to establish that life. They can learn from their experience and apply that knowledge to future events.

In summary, these stages are experienced in different ways by each person who faces a significant loss. Some people, for example, express very little anger; others may not go through a bargaining stage. Nevertheless, the value of a model such as this one is that it provides some understanding of how we can learn to cope with the various losses in our lives. Whatever the loss may be and whatever stage of grieving we may be experiencing, it seems to be crucial that we freely express our feelings. Otherwise, we may not be able to achieve acceptance.

BEING "DEAD" PSYCHOLOGICALLY AND SOCIALLY

We find it valuable to broaden the conception of death and dying to include being "dead" in a variety of psychological and social ways. What is dead or dying in us may be something we want to resurrect, or it may be something that should die to make way for new growth.

Sometimes growth requires that we be willing to let go of old and familiar ways of being, and we may need to mourn their loss before we can really move on. You may have experienced a letting go of the security of living with your parents, for example, in exchange for testing your independence by living alone and supporting yourself. In the process you may have lost something that was valuable to you, even if it was incompatible with your further development and growth. The following questions may help you to decide whether you are living as fully as you would like to be.

Are You Caught Up in Deadening Roles?

Our roles and functions can eventually trap us. Instead of fulfilling certain roles while maintaining a separate sense of identity, we may get lost in our roles and in the patterns of thought, feeling, and behavior that go with them. As a result, we may neglect important parts of ourselves, limiting our options of feeling and experiencing. Moreover, we may feel lost when we are unable to play a certain role: a supervisor may not know how to behave when he or she is not in a superior position to others, an instructor may be at loose ends when there are no students to teach, or a parent may find life empty when the children have grown.

Do you feel caught in certain routines and roles? Is today a copy of yesterday? Do you depend on being able to identify with those roles to feel alive and valuable? Have you made the mistake of believing that who you are is expressed by a single role, no matter how much you value that role? Who and what would you be if your roles were stripped away one by one? Are you able to renew yourself by finding innovative ways of being and thinking? At this time in your life you might find that you are so caught up in the student role that you have little time or energy left for other parts of your life. When our roles begin to deaden us, we can ask whether we have taken on a function or identity that others have defined instead of listening to our own inner promptings.

Are You Alive to Your Senses and Your Body?

Your body expresses to a large degree how alive you are. It shows signs of your vitality or reveals your tiredness with life. Use your body as an indication of the degree to which you are affirming life. As you look at your body, ask yourself these questions: "Do I like what I see? Am I taking good care of myself physically,

Corbis

Are you alive to your
senses and your body?

---

or am I indifferent to my own bodily well-being? What am I expressing by my posture? What does my facial expression communicate?"

You can also become deadened to the input from your senses. You may become oblivious to fragrances or eat foods without tasting or savoring them. Perhaps you rarely stop to notice the details of your surroundings. Take time to be alive to your senses. This will help you feel renewed and interested in life. Ask yourself, "What sensations have particularly struck me today? What have I experienced and observed? What sensory surprises have enlivened me?"

Can You Be Spontaneous and Playful?

Can you be playful, fun, curious, explorative, spontaneous, silly? As an adult, it is likely that you take yourself too seriously at times and lose the ability to laugh at yourself. Siegel (1988) emphasizes the value of laughter, play, and humor in healing and staying healthy. Humor shakes us out of our patterned ways and promotes new perspectives. In his therapy groups for cancer patients, Siegel helps them release the child within. Those who cannot play and laugh experience the most difficulty in healing. If you find that you are typically realistic and objective to the point that it is difficult for you to be playful or light, you might ask what inner messages are blocking your ability to let go. Are you inhibited by a fear of being wrong? Are you afraid of being called silly or of meeting with others' disapproval? If you want to, you can begin to challenge the messages that say: "Don't!" "You should!" "You shouldn't!" You can experiment with new behavior and run the risk of seeming silly or of "not acting your age."

Are You Alive to Your Feelings?

We can deaden ourselves to most of our feelings—the joyful ones as well as the painful ones. We can decide that feeling involves the risk of pain and that it is best to think our way through life. In choosing to cut off feelings of depression or sadness, we will most likely cut off feelings of joy. Closing ourselves to our lows usually means closing ourselves to our highs as well.

Because of the ways we sometimes insulate ourselves, we may find it difficult to recognize our flat emotional state. To begin assessing how alive you are emotionally, ask yourself these questions:

> Do I let myself feel my sadness and grieve over a loss?

> Do I try hard to cheer people up when they are sad or depressed, instead of allowing them to experience their feelings?

> Do I let myself cry if I feel like crying?

> Do I ever feel ecstasy and true joy?

> Do I let myself feel close to another person?

> Do I suppress certain emotions? Do I hide my feelings of insecurity, fear, dependence, tenderness, anger, boredom?

> Do I keep myself from showing my feelings out of fear?

Are Your Relationships Alive?

Our relationships with the significant people in our lives have a way of becoming stale and deadening. It is easy to get stuck in habitual and routine ways of being with another person and to lose any sense of surprise and spontaneity. This kind of staleness is particularly common in long-term relationships. Of course, breaking out of predictable patterns in relationships can be fraught with anxiety. We have to decide whether we want security or vitality in our relationships. As you look at the significant relationships in your life, think about how alive both you and the other person in each relationship feel. Do you give each other enough space to grow? Does the relationship energize you, or does it sap you of life? Are you settling into a comfortable, undemanding relationship? If you recognize that you are not getting what you want in your friendships or intimate relationships, ask what you can do to revitalize them. Focus on how you can change yourself rather than getting others to change. You can also consider what specific things you would like to ask from the other person. Simply talking about relationships can do a lot to bring new life into them.

Are You Alive Intellectually?

Children typically display much curiosity about life, yet somehow they lose this interest in figuring out problems as they grow older. By the time we reach adulthood, we can easily become caught up in our activities, devoting little time to considering why we are doing them and whether we even want to be doing them. It is also easy to allow our intellectual potential to shrivel up, either by limiting our exposure or by failing to follow our curiosity.

Take time to reassess the degree to which you keep yourself intellectually active in your classes. In the initial chapter we focused on ways to integrate mental and emotional dimensions of learning. One way of keeping mentally alert is by reflecting on how you can apply whatever you are learning in your classes to your personal development. How might you apply the notion of staying intellectually alive as a student? Have you given up on asking any real and substantive questions that you would like to explore? Have you settled for merely going to classes and collecting the units you need to obtain a degree? Are you indifferent to learning? Are you open to learning new things? Are you changing as a learner?

Are You Alive Spiritually?

There is growing empirical evidence that people's spiritual values and behaviors can promote physical and psychological coping, healing, and well-being (Miller, 1999). This finding has led many health practitioners and those in the counseling profession to conclude that an individual's spiritual values should be viewed as a potential resource in the healing process rather than something to be ignored (Richards, Rector, & Tjeltveit, 1999). Religious beliefs and practices affect many dimensions of human experience, including how to handle guilt feelings, authority, and moral questions, to name a few. To what degree do your spiritual beliefs enhance your life?

As a healer, Bernie Siegel (1988) views spirituality as encompassing the belief in some meaning or order in the universe. From his perspective, there is a loving and intelligent force behind creation. Regardless of what label is used for this force, contact with it allows us the possibility of finding peace and resolving seeming contradictions between the inner world and the outer. Siegel claims that spirituality means accepting what is.

> SPIRITUALITY MEANS THE ABILITY TO FIND PEACE AND HAPPINESS in an imperfect world, and to feel that one's own personality is imperfect but acceptable. From the peaceful state of mind come both creativity and the ability to love unselfishly, which go hand in hand. Acceptance, faith, forgiveness, peace, and love are the traits that define spirituality for me. (p. 178)

How do you define spirituality for yourself? What moral, ethical, or spiritual values do you use to guide your life? Whether you belong to an organized religious group or simply contemplate the beauty of the natural world, you are on a spiritual quest. Take time to reflect on how to make yours a joyous journey.

Take Time to Reflect

1. How alive do you feel psychologically and socially? When do you feel the most alive?

_____

_____

2. When do you feel the least energy and vitality?

_____

_____

3. What specific things would you most like to change about your life so that you could feel more alive? What can you do to make these changes?

_____

_____

HOW WELL ARE YOU LIVING LIFE?

It seems tragic that some people never really take the time to evaluate how well they are living life. Imagine for a moment that you are one of those people who get caught up in the routine of daily existence and never assess the quality of your living. Now assume that you are told that you have only a limited time to live. You begin to look at what you have missed and how you wish things had been different; you begin to experience regrets over the opportunities that you let slip by; you review the significant turning points in your life. You may wish now that you had paused to take stock at many points in your life, instead of waiting until it was too late.

One way to take stock of your life is to imagine your own death, including the details of the funeral and the things people might say about you. Try actually writing down your own eulogy or obituary. This can be a powerful way of summing up how you see your life and how you would like it to be different. In fact, we suggest that you try writing three eulogies for yourself. First, write your actual eulogy—the one you would give at your own funeral, if that were possible. Second, write the eulogy that you fear—one that expresses some of the negative things someone could say of you. Third, write the eulogy that you would hope for—one that expresses the most positive aspects of your life so far. After you have written your three eulogies, write down in your journal what the experience was like for you and what you learned from it. Are there any specific steps you would like to take now to begin living more fully? Reflect on how you might live your life today to bring about your hoped for eulogy. As an additional step, consider sealing your eulogies in an envelope and putting them away for a year or so. Then, at this later date, do the exercise again and compare the two sets of eulogies to see what changes have occurred in your view of your life.

Before he died 25 years ago, Jim Morelock gave me (Jerry) a poster showing a man walking in the forest with two small girls. At the top of the poster were the words "TAKE TIME." Jim knew me well enough to know how I tend to get caught up in so many activities that I sometimes forget to simply take time to really experience and enjoy the simple things in life. You have been challenged to complete the Take Time to Reflect exercises throughout this book. If you have taken the time for yourself, you should have a pretty good idea of what your life is like now. What can you do today to ensure that you will live your life to the fullest?

SUMMARY

In this chapter we have encouraged you to devote some time to reflecting on your eventual death. Doing so can lead you to examine the quality and direction of your life and help you find your own meaning in living. The acceptance of death is closely related to the acceptance of life. Recognizing and accepting the fact of death gives us the impetus to search for our own answers to questions like these: "What is the meaning of my life?" "What do I most want from life?" "How can I create the life I want to live?" In addition, we have encouraged you to assess how fully alive you are right now.

Although terminally ill people show great variability in how they deal with their dying, a general pattern of stages has been identified: denial, anger, bargaining, depression, and acceptance. These same stages can apply to other types of loss, such as separation and divorce. People go through stages of grief in working through their losses. Grieving is necessary if we are to recover from any significant loss. Unless we express and explore feelings of sorrow, anger, and guilt over our losses, we are likely to remain stuck in depression and a feeling of numbness.

If we can honestly confront our fears of death, we can change the quality of our lives and make real changes in our relationships with others and with ourselves. We often live as though we had forever to accomplish what we want. Few of us ever contemplate that this may be the last day we have. The realization that there is an end to life can motivate us to get the most from the time we have. The fact of our finality can also be an impetus to take care of unfinished business. Thus, it is crucial that we live in a manner that will lead to few regrets. The more we fail to deal with immediate realities, the greater the likelihood that we will fear death.

❯ Where Can I Go From Here?

1. For at least a week take a few minutes each day to reflect on when you feel alive and when you feel "dead." Do you notice any trends in your observations? What can you do to feel more alive?

2. If you knew you were going to die within a short time, in what ways would you live your life differently? What might you give up? What might you be doing that you are not doing or experiencing now?

3. Imagine yourself on your deathbed. Write down whom you want to be there, what you want them to say to you, and what you want to say to them. Then write down your reactions to this experience.

4. For about a week write down specific things you see, read, or hear relating to the denial or avoidance of death in our culture.

5. Let yourself reflect on how the death of those you love might affect you. Consider each person separately, and try to imagine how your life today would be different if that person were not in it. Write these impressions in your journal.

(continued)

> **Where Can I Go From Here?** *(continued)*

6. Investigate what type of hospice program, if any, your community has. Who is on the staff? What services does it offer? If you are interested in learning more about hospice services, or to identify a local hospice program, call the Hospice Helpline at (800) 658-8898, or contact the National Hospice Organization, 1901 N. Moore Street, Suite 901, Arlington, VA 22209 (telephone: 703-243-5900).

Resources for Future Study

Web Site Resources

END OF LIFE, EXPLORING DEATH IN AMERICA
http://www.npr.org.programs/death/

National Public Radio (NPR) has aired programs about death and dying in American culture. This Web site offers both printed and audio transcripts of the programs and many bibliographical and organizational resources as well.

SUICIDE . . . READ THIS FIRST
http://www.metanoia.org/suicide/

This site is for those who are dealing with suicidal issues in themselves or others. This site speaks straight to the issue and guides the reader through a thoughtful series of steps to resolve their issues. Suicide and suicidal feelings are dealt with including helpful resources and links for more information.

InfoTrac College Edition Resources

For additional readings, explore InfoTrac College Edition, our online library.

Go to **http://www.infotrac.college.com/wadsworth**

Hint: Enter the search terms:

dying
death AND dying
stages of dying
hospice

bereavement

grief work

suicide

suicide prevention

rational suicide

physician-assisted suicide

Print Resources

Albom, M. (1997). *Tuesdays with Morrie*. New York: Doubleday.

Corr, C. A., Nabe, C. M., & Corr, D. M. (2000). *Death and dying, life and living* (3rd ed.). Belmont, CA: Wadsworth.

Dickenson, D., & Johnson, M. (Eds.). (1993). *Death, dying, and bereavement*. Newbury Park, CA: Sage.

Kübler-Ross, E. (1969). *On death and dying*. New York: Macmillan.

Kübler-Ross, E. (1993). *AIDS: The ultimate challenge*. New York: Macmillan (Collier).

Marcus, E. (1996). *Why suicide? Answers to 200 of the most frequently asked questions about suicide, attempted suicide, and assisted suicide*. San Francisco: HarperCollins.

Siegel, B. (1988). *Love, medicine, and miracles*. New York: Harper & Row (Perennial Library).

Siegel, B. (1989). *Peace, love, and healing. Bodymind communication and the path to self-healing: An exploration*. New York: Harper & Row.

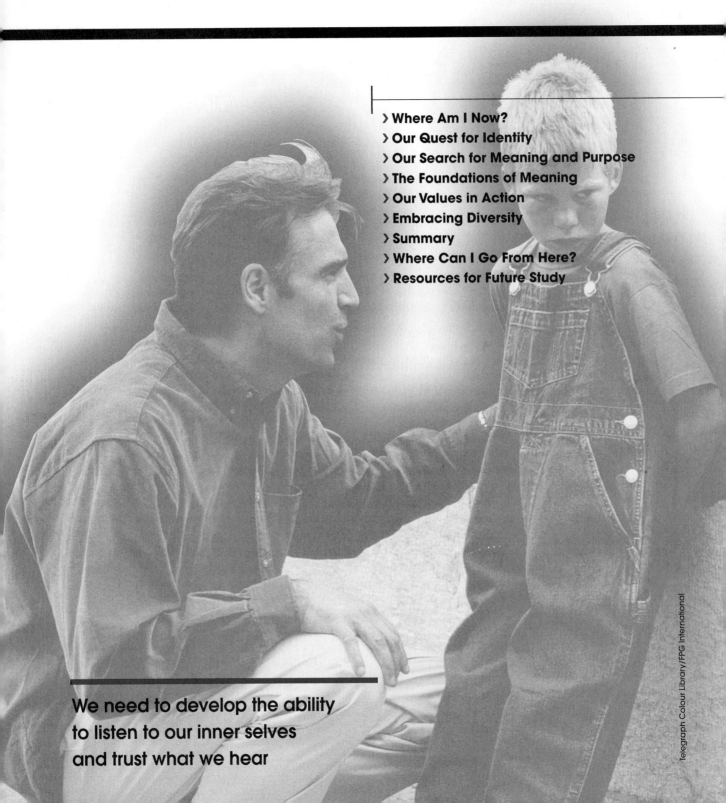

We need to develop the ability
to listen to our inner selves
and trust what we hear

13

MEANING AND VALUES

› Where Am I Now?

Use this scale to respond to these statements:

4 = This statement is true of me *most* of the time.

3 = This statement is true of me *much* of the time.

2 = This statement is true of me *some* of the time.

1 = This statement is true of me *almost none* of the time.

_____ 1. At this time in my life I have a sense of meaning and purpose that gives me direction.

_____ 2. Most of my values are similar to those of my parents.

_____ 3. I have challenged and questioned most of the values I now hold.

_____ 4. Religion is an important source of meaning for me.

_____ 5. I generally live by the values I hold.

_____ 6. My values and my views about life's meaning have undergone much change over the years.

_____ 7. The meaning of my life is based in large part on my ability to have a significant impact on others.

_____ 8. I let others influence my values more than I would like to admit.

_____ 9. I am willing to reflect on my own biases and prejudices, and to challenge them.

_____ 10. I welcome diversity more than being threatened by it.

I n this chapter we encourage you to look critically at the why of your existence, to clarify the sources of your values, and to reflect on questions such as these: "Where have I been, where am I now, and where do I want to go?" "What steps can I take to make the changes I have decided on?" Our quest for meaning involves asking three key existential questions, none of which have easy or absolute answers: "Who am I?" "Where am I going?" "Why?"

"Who am I?" is a question that will be answered differently at different times in our lives. When old identities no longer seem to supply a meaning or give us direction, we have to reinvent ourselves or risk a deadening existence. You must decide whether to let others tell you who you are or take a stand and define yourself anew.

"Where am I going?" questions our plans for a lifetime. What process do we expect to use to attain our goals? Like the previous question, this one demands periodic review as life goals are not set once and for all.

Asking "Why?" and searching for understanding is a human characteristic. We face a rapidly changing world in which old values give way to new ones or to none at all. Part of the quest for meaning requires an active search for meaning, trying to make sense of the world in which we find ourselves.

Many who are fortunate enough to achieve power, fame, success, and material comfort nevertheless experience a sense of emptiness. Although they may not be able to articulate what is lacking in their lives, they know that something is amiss. The astronomical number of pills and drugs humans consume to allay the symptoms of this "existential vacuum"—depression and anxiety—is evidence of our failure to find values that enable us to make sense of our place in the world. In *Habits of the Heart,* Bellah and his colleagues (1985) found among the people they interviewed a growing interest in finding purpose in their lives. Although our achievements as a society are enormous, we seem to be hovering on the very brink of disaster, not only from internal conflict but also from societal incoherence. Bellah and his associates assert that the core problem with our society is that we have put our own good, as individuals and as groups, ahead of the common good.

The need for a sense of meaning is manifested by an increased interest in religion, especially among young people in college. A student told us recently that in her English class of 20 students 4 of them had selected religion as a topic for a composition dealing with a conflict in their lives. Other signs of the search for meaning include the widespread interest in Eastern and other philosophies, the use of meditation, the number of self-help and inspirational books published each year, the experimentation with different lifestyles, and even the college courses in personal growth.

OUR QUEST FOR IDENTITY

Achieving personal identity does not necessarily mean stubbornly clinging to a certain way of thinking or behaving. Instead, it may involve trusting ourselves enough to become open to new possibilities. We need to be continually willing to reexamine our patterns and our priorities, our habits and our relation-ships. Above all, we need to develop the ability to listen to our inner selves and trust what we hear. In this way we can come to understand the core values that shape us.

Values are core beliefs that influence how you act. To make true choices, you must examine the values you accepted when growing up and decide which represent your own self and which you might wish to discard or change. Your values are your own to the extent that you have reflected on them and tailored them to fit the person you are. If your values have been internalized in this way, there is a greater likelihood that these values will influence your behavior.

Sometimes we may decide to go against our cultural upbringing to create an identity that is congruent with our own values. This was true for Jenny, a Vietnamese woman who developed a different set of values from her mother.

JENNY'S STORY

*T*here were many instances when I wanted to be alone or to take time off from work to relax. There would be an attack of accusatory statements indicating that I was selfish, that I was wasting too much time on myself, and that I wasn't devoting enough time to my family obligations. Even the way I spent my money was met with criticism, because I did not save it for a better cause like my family. I spent many hours explaining to my mother about how much it meant to me to buy myself nice things and to spend some of my time enjoying life. In the eyes of my mother and her culture, I was the selfish one. I had to understand this perspective and edit it to my own values.

Pause now and assess how you experience your identity at this time in your life. This Take Time to Reflect exercise may help you do so.

Take Time to Reflect

1. What are some of your key values? To identify a few of your central values, rate the importance of each of these items (4 = extremely important; 3 = important; 2 = somewhat important; 1 = not important).

_____ a relationship with God
_____ loving others and being loved
_____ enjoying an intimate relationship
_____ engaging in recreation

(continued)

_____ family life
_____ security
_____ courage
_____ work and career
_____ laughter and a sense of humor
_____ intelligence and curiosity
_____ being open to new experiences
_____ taking risks in order to change
_____ being of service to others
_____ making a difference in the lives of others
_____ appreciating nature
_____ independence and self-determination
_____ interdependence and cooperation
_____ having control of my life
_____ being financially successful
_____ having solitude and time to reflect
_____ being productive and achieving
_____ being approved of by others
_____ facing challenges
_____ compassion and caring
_____ engaging in competition

Look over the items you rated as "4" (extremely important). If you had to select the top three values in your life, which would they be?

_____

_____

_____

2. How are these three values a part of your everyday life?

_____

_____

3. How often do you experience each of the things you have just listed? What prevents you from doing the things you value as frequently as you would like?

_____

_____

4. What are some specific actions you can take to add meaning to your life?

_____

_____

5. Who are you? Try completing the sentence "I am . . ." 10 different ways by quickly writing down the words or phrases that immediately occur to you.

I am _____

_____

_____

_____

_____

_____

OUR SEARCH FOR MEANING AND PURPOSE

We are the only creatures we know of who can reflect on our existence and, based on this capacity for self-awareness, exercise individual choice in defining our lives. With this freedom, however, comes responsibility and a degree of anxiety. If we truly accept that the meaning of our lives is largely the product of our own choosing—and that the emptiness of our lives is the result of our failure to choose—our anxiety is increased. To avoid this anxiety, we may refuse to examine the values that govern our daily behavior or to accept that we are, to a large degree, what we have chosen to become. Instead, we may make other people or outside institutions responsible for our direction. We pay a steep price for choosing a sense of security over our own freedom—the price of denying our basic humanness.

In *Tuesdays With Morrie* (Albom, 1997) the dying Morrie shared a gem worth reflecting upon: "Learn how to die, and you learn how to live" (p. 83). Morrie makes some perceptive comments that go to the heart of finding purpose and meaning in life:

> SO MANY PEOPLE WALK AROUND with a meaningless life. They seem half-asleep, even when they're busy doing things they think are important. This is because they're chasing the wrong things. The way you get meaning into your life is to devote yourself to loving others, devote yourself to community around you, and devote yourself to creating something that gives you purpose and meaning." (p. 43)

This sage advice is not about making money or stockpiling material items. It is about finding meaning by finding a cause outside of yourself, giving to others, and striving to make the world a better place.

One obstacle in the way of finding meaning is that the world itself may appear meaningless. When we look at the absurdity of the world in which we live, it is easy to give up the struggle or to seek some authoritative source of meaning. Yet creating our own meaning is precisely our challenge as human beings.

Many clients who enter psychotherapy do so because they lack a clear sense of meaning and purpose in life (Yalom, 1980). Yalom states the crisis of meaninglessness in its most basic form: "How does a being who needs meaning find meaning in a universe that has no meaning?" (p. 423). Along with Frankl (1963), Yalom concludes that humans require meaning to survive. To live without meaning and values provokes considerable distress, and in its most severe form may lead to the decision for suicide. We need clear ideals to which we can aspire and guidelines by which we can direct our actions.

Viktor Frankl, a European psychiatrist, dedicated his professional life to the study of meaning in life. The approach to therapy that he developed is known as logotherapy, which means "therapy through meaning" or "healing through meaning." According to Frankl (1963, 1965, 1969, 1978), what distinguishes us as humans is our search for purpose. The striving to find meaning in our lives is a primary motivational force. Humans choose to live and even to die for the sake of their ideals and values. Frankl (1963) notes that "everything can be taken from a man but one thing: the last of the human freedoms—to choose one's attitude in any given set of circumstances, to choose one's own way" (p. 104). Frankl points out the wisdom of Nietzsche's words: "He who has a why to live for can bear with almost any how" (as cited in Frankl, 1963, p. 164). Drawing on his experiences in the death camp at Auschwitz, Frankl asserts that inmates who had a vision of some goal, purpose, or task in life had a much greater chance of surviving than those who had no sense of mission. We are constantly confronted with choices, and the decisions we make or fail to make influence the meaning of our lives.

This relationship between choice and meaning is dramatically illustrated by Holocaust survivors who report that although they did not choose their circumstances they could at least choose their attitude toward their plight. Consider the example of Dr. Edith Eva Eger, a 64-year-old clinical psychologist who practices in La Jolla, California, who was interviewed about her experiences as a survivor of a Nazi concentration camp (see Glionna, 1992). At one point, Eger weighed only 40 pounds, yet she refused to engage in the cannibalism that was taking place. She said, "I chose to eat grass. And I sat on the ground, selecting one blade over the other, telling myself that even under those conditions I still had a choice—which blade of grass I would eat." Although Eger lost her family to the camps and had her back broken by one of the guards, she eventually chose to let go of her hatred. She finally came to the realization that it was her captors who were the imprisoned ones. As she put it: "If I still hated today, I would still be in prison. I would be giving Hitler and Mengele their posthumous victories. If I hated, they would still be in charge, not me." Her example supports the notion that even in the most dire situations it is possible to give a new meaning to such circumstances by our choice of attitudes.

Many of us find meaning by striving to make a difference in the world. We want to know that we have touched the lives of others and that somehow we have contributed to helping others live more fully. Although self-acceptance is a prerequisite for meaningful interpersonal relationships, there is a quest to go beyond self-centered interests. Ultimately, we want to establish connections with others in society, and we want to make a contribution. Bellah and his colleagues (1985) conclude that meaning in life is found through intense relationships with others rather than through an exclusive and narrow pursuit of self-realization. In their interviews, many people expressed a desire to move beyond the isolated self. Healthy relationships are two-sided transactions, characterized by reciprocal giving and taking. Sacrificing yourself, without getting anything in return, is not the way to achieve a meaningful life. We must find a balance in our concern for ourselves and our desire to further the interests of the community.

THE FOUNDATIONS OF MEANING

What Is the Meaning of Life?

In 1988 the editors of *Life* magazine asked a wide spectrum of people from all walks of life the question "What is the meaning of life?" David Friend's (1991) *The Meaning of Life* is the product of 300 thoughtful people. This mosaic of responses offers a variety of approaches to understanding life. As you read, think about the responses that resonate most closely with your own values.

> ❯ "We believe that we are in fact the image of our Creator. Our response must be to live up to that amazing potential—to give God glory by reflecting His beauty and His love. That is why we are here and that is the purpose of our lives" (South African civil rights leader, Archbishop Desmond Tutu, p. 13).

> ❯ "The meaning of life is to live in balance and harmony with every other living thing in creation. We must all strive to understand the interconnectedness of all living things and accept our individual role in the protection and support of other life forms on earth. We must also understand our own insignificance in the totality of things" (Wilma Mankiller, Chief of the Cherokee Nation, p. 13).

> ❯ "It's my belief that the meaning of life changes from day to day, second to second. We're here to learn that we can create a world and that we have a choice in what we create, and that our world, if we choose, can be a heaven or hell" (Thomas E. O'Connor, AIDS activist and lecturer, p. 20).

Heidi Jo Corey

We want to know that we have touched the lives of others and that somehow we have contributed to helping others live more fully.

> "Since age two I've been waltzing up and down with the question of life's meaning. And I am obliged to report that the answer changes from week to week. When I know the answer, I know it absolutely; as soon as I know that I know it, I know that I know nothing. About seventy percent of the time my conclusion is that there is a grand design" (Maya Angelou, writer and actress, p. 20).

> "I believe we as humans have the great challenge of living in harmony with the planet and all its parts. If we achieve that harmony we will have lived up to our fullest potential" (Molly Yard, feminist activist, p. 27).

> "I believe we are here to do good. It is the responsibility of every human being to aspire to do something worthwhile, to make this world a better place than the one he found. Life is a gift, and if we accept it, we must contribute in return. When we fail to contribute, we fail to adequately answer

why we are here" (Armand Hammer, industrialist, physician, and self-made diplomat, p. 29).

> "While we exist as human beings, we are like tourists on holiday. If we play havoc and cause disturbance, our visit is meaningless. If during our short stay—100 years at most—we live peacefully, help others and, at the very least, refrain from harming or upsetting them, our visit is worthwhile" (The Dalai Lama, spiritual leader of Tibetan Buddhism, p. 49).

> "The purpose of human life is to achieve our own spiritual evolution, to get rid of negativity, to establish harmony among our physical, emotional, intellectual and spiritual quadrants, to learn to live in harmony within the family, community, nation, the whole world and all living things, treating all of mankind as brothers and sisters—thus making it finally possible to have peace on earth" (Elisabeth Kübler-Ross, psychiatrist and author, p. 65).

What is the meaning of your life? Can you answer this complex question in a few brief sentences? To help you refine your answer, let's look at some of the dimensions of a philosophy of life.

Developing a Philosophy of Life

A philosophy of life is made up of the fundamental beliefs, attitudes, and values that govern a person's behavior. You may not have thought much about your philosophy of life, but the fact that you have never explicitly defined the components of your philosophy does not mean you are completely without one. All of us operate on the basis of general assumptions about ourselves, others, and the world. The first step in actively developing a philosophy of life is to formulate a clearer picture of your present attitudes and beliefs.

We have all been developing an implicit philosophy of life since we first began, as children, to wonder about life and death, love and hate, joy and fear, and the nature of the universe. If we were fortunate, adults took time to engage in dialogue with us rather than discouraging us from asking questions and deadening our innate curiosity.

During the adolescent years, the process of questioning usually assumes new dimensions. Adolescents who have been encouraged to question and to think for themselves as children begin to get involved in a more advanced set of issues. Many of the adolescents we have encountered in classes and workshops have at one time or another struggled with these questions:

> Are the values I've believed in all these years the values I want to continue to live by?

> Where did I get my values? Are they still valid for me? Are there additional sources from which I can derive new values?

> Is there a God? What is the nature of the hereafter? What is my conception of a God? What does religion mean in my life? What kind of religion do I choose for myself? Does religion have any value for me?

> What do I base my ethical and moral decisions on? Peer group standards? Parental standards? The normative values of my society?

> What explains the inhumanity I see in the world?

> What kind of future do I want? What can I do to help create this kind of future?

A philosophy of life is not something we arrive at once and for all during our adolescent years. Developing our own philosophy of life continues as long as we live. As long as we remain curious and open to new learning, we can revise and rebuild our conceptions of the world. Life may have a particular meaning for us during adolescence, a new meaning during adulthood, and still another meaning as we reach old age. Indeed, if we do not remain open to basic changes in our views of life, we may find it difficult to adjust to changed circumstances. You may find the following suggestions helpful as you go about formulating and reforming your own philosophy:

> Frequently create time to be alone in reflective thought.

> Consider what meaning the fact of your eventual death has for the present moment.

> Make use of significant contacts with others who are willing to challenge your beliefs and the degree to which you live by them.

> Adopt an accepting attitude toward those whose belief systems differ from yours and develop a willingness to test your own beliefs.

All of these suggestions require that you challenge yourself and the beliefs you hold. Keeping track of yourself can provide unexpected rewards.

Take Time to Reflect Complete the following sentences by writing down the first responses that come to mind:

1. My parents have influenced my values by _____

_____

2. Life would hardly be worth living if it weren't for _____

_____

3. One thing that I most want to say about my life at this point is _____

_____

4. If I could change one thing about my life at this point, it would be _____

_____

5. If I had to answer the question "Who am I?" in a sentence, I'd say _____

_____

6. What I like best about me is _____

_____

7. I keep myself alive and vital by _____

_____

8. I am unique in that _____

_____

9. When I think of my future, I _____

_____

10. I feel discouraged about life when _____

_____

11. My friends have influenced my values by _____

_____

12. My beliefs have been influenced by _____

_____

13. I feel most powerful when _____

_____

14. If I don't change, _____

_____

15. I feel good about myself when _____

_____

16. To me, the essence of a meaningful life is _____

_____

17. I suffer from a sense of meaninglessness when _____

_____

Religion and Meaning

Religious faith can be a powerful source of meaning and purpose. Religion helps many people make sense out of the universe and the mystery of our purpose on earth. Like any other potential source of meaning, religious faith seems most authentic and valuable when it enables us to become as fully human as possible. Religion can help us get in touch with our own powers of thinking, feeling, deciding, willing, and acting. For some, religion does not occupy a key place, yet spirituality may be a central force. Reflect on the following questions about your religion or your spirituality to determine whether it is a constructive force in your life:

> Does my religion or spirituality provide me with a set of values that is congruent with the way I live my life?

> Does my religion or spirituality assist me in better understanding the meaning of life and death?

> Does my religion or spirituality allow acceptance for others who see the world differently from me?

> Does my religion or spirituality provide me with a sense of peace and serenity?

> Is my religious faith or value system something I actively choose or passively accept?

> Do my core religious and spiritual values help me live life fully and treat others with respect and concern?

> Does my religion or spirituality help me integrate my experience and make sense of the world?

> Does my religion or spirituality encourage me to exercise my freedom and to assume the responsibility for the direction of my own life?

> Are my religious beliefs or spirituality helping me become more of the person I would like to become?

> Does my religion or spirituality encourage me to question life and keep myself open to new learning?

As you take time for self-examination, how able are you to answer these questions in a way that is meaningful and satisfying to you? If you are honest with yourself, perhaps you will find that you have not critically evaluated the sources of your spiritual and religious beliefs. Although you may hesitate to question your belief system out of a fear of weakening or undermining your faith, the opposite might well be true; demonstrating the courage to question your beliefs and values might strengthen them. Increasing numbers of people seem to be deciding that a religious faith is necessary if they are to find order and purpose in life. Acceptance or rejection of religious faith must come authentically from within ourselves. It is important to remain open to new experiences and learning.

OUR VALUES IN ACTION

Values for Our Daughters

When our daughters Heidi and Cindy were growing up, we hoped they would come to share these important values with us:

> Have a positive and significant impact on the people in their lives

> Be willing to dare and not always choose caution over risk

> Form their own values rather than unquestioningly adopting ours

> Like and respect themselves and feel good about their abilities and talents

> Be open and trusting rather than fearful or suspicious

> Respect and care for others

> Continue to have fun as they grew older

> Be able to express their feelings and always feel free to come to us and share meaningful aspects of their lives

> Remain in touch with their power and refuse to surrender it

> Be independent and have the courage to be different from others if they want to be

> Have an interest in a religion that they freely chose

> Be proud of themselves, yet humble

> Respect the differences in others

> Not compromise their values and principles for material possessions

> Develop a flexible view of the world and be willing to modify their perspective based on new experiences

> Give back to the world by contributing to make it a better place to live

> Make a difference in the lives of others

Our daughters are now independent adults, yet they continue to value time with us and invite us to be involved in their lives. Although their lives are not problem-free, they typically show a willingness to face and deal with their struggles and are succeeding in making significant choices for themselves. If you have children or expect to have children someday, you might pause to think about the values you would like them to develop, as well as the part you will need to play in offering them guidance.

Becoming Aware of How Your Values Operate

Your values influence what you do; your daily behavior is an expression of your basic values. We encourage you to take time to examine the source of your values to determine if they are appropriate for you at this time in your life. Furthermore, it is essential that you be aware of the significant impact your value system has on your relationships with others. In our view, it is not appropriate for you to push your values on others, to assume a judgmental stance toward those who have a different view, or to strive to convert others to adopt your perspective on life. Indeed, if you are secure in your values and basic beliefs, you will not be threatened by those who have a different set of beliefs and values.

In *God's Love Song*, Maier (1991) wonders how anyone can claim to have found the only way, not only for himself or herself but also for everyone else. As a minister, Sam Maier teaches that diversity shared is not only beautiful but also fosters understanding, caring, and the creation of community. He puts this message in a powerful and poetic way:

> IT IS HEARTENING TO FIND COMMUNITIES where the emphasis is placed upon each person having the opportunity to:
>
> ❯ share what is vital and meaningful out of one's own experience;
>
> ❯ listen to what is vital and meaningful to others;
>
> ❯ not expect or demand that anyone else do it exactly the same way as oneself. (p. 3)

Reverend Maier's message is well worth contemplating. Although you might clarify a set of values that seem to work for you, we hope that you will respect the values of others that may be quite different from yours. One set of values is not right and the other wrong. The diversity of cultures, religions, and worldviews provides a tapestry of life that allows us the opportunity to embrace diverse paths toward meaning in life. Whatever your own values are, they can be further clarified and strengthened if you entertain open discussion of various viewpoints and cultivate a nonjudgmental attitude toward diversity. Ask yourself these questions:

❯ Where did I develop my values?

❯ Are my values open to modification?

❯ Have I challenged my values?

❯ Do I insist that the world remain the same now as it was earlier in my life?

❯ Do I feel so deeply committed to any of my values that I am likely to push my friends and family members to accept them?

❯ How would I communicate my values to others without imposing those values?

❯ How do my own values and beliefs affect my behavior?

❯ Am I willing to accept people who hold different values?

❯ Do I avoid judging others even if they think, feel, or act in different ways from me?

Take Time to Reflect

1. At this time, what are some of the principal sources of meaning and purpose in your life?

_____

_____

_____

2. Have there been occasions in your life when you have allowed other people or institutions to make key choices for you? If so, give a couple of examples.

_____

_____

_____

3. What role, if any, has religion or spirituality played in your life?

_____

_____

_____

4. If you were to create a new religion, what virtues and values would you include? What would be the vices and sins?

_____

_____

_____

(continued)

5. What are some of the values you would most like to see your children adopt?

_____

_____

_____

EMBRACING DIVERSITY

One barrier to forming meaningful connections with others is the existence of negative attitudes toward those who are different from us. We sometimes choose to live in an encapsulated world, seeking support from those who think and value as we do. This narrowness prevents us from learning from those who may have a different worldview than our own, and it results in fewer options to participate fully in the human community.

Meaning in life can be found by paying attention to the common ground we all share and by becoming aware of universal themes that unite us in spite of our differences. In the early chapters of this book, we emphasized that a meaningful life is not lived alone but is the result of connectedness to others in love, work, and community. It is through acceptance and understanding of others that we are able to discover the deepest meaning in life. If we live in isolation, we are walling ourselves off from the possibilities of engaging in social interest.

In this section we invite you to explore the costs to us all of prejudice and discrimination—which grow out of fear and ignorance. We encourage you to reflect on a philosophy of life that embraces understanding and acceptance of diverse worldviews. We ask you to consider attitudes and behaviors you are willing to change so you can demonstrate acceptance and respect for others, whether they are like or unlike you.

What Can You Do to Better the World?

Some claim that the world is getting worse and that humanity is doomed. Even if you do not accept this premise, you might find some evidence for the need for bettering humanity. But where can we start to make it better? Bettering humanity may seem like an overwhelming task, but it is less staggering if we start with ourselves. It is easier to blame others for the ills of the world than to accept that

Joel Gordon

If we live in isolation, we are walling ourselves off from the possibilities of engaging in social interest.

we might be contributing to this malady. It is well to ask ourselves, "What am I doing, even in the smallest way, that contributes to the problems in our society? And what can I do to become part of the solution to these problems?"

Prejudice, discrimination, hatred, and intolerance, especially toward those who are different from us, are all paths toward an empty existence. Prejudice, a preconceived notion or opinion about someone, can be overt or covert. People can be obvious and blatant about their particular prejudices, or they can hide them. Prejudice is a very subtle thing, and it may occur outside of conscious awareness. Ridley (1995) reminds us that unintentional racism can be even more harmful than intentional racism. At least with blatant racists people know where they stand, whereas subtle forms of racism are often difficult to pinpoint.

Becoming aware of our own subtle prejudice and unintentional racism is the first step toward change. Laughing at or being impatient with someone who has an accent, telling or laughing at racial jokes, speaking in generalities about a whole group of people as though they are all the same, and assuming that our culture is superior to any other are all signs of prejudice founded on racist attitudes. If you want to become more accepting of others, reflect on some of the ways you have acquired your beliefs about particular groups of people and begin to question the source of those beliefs.

Prejudice has negative consequences. For the victims, it results in acts of discrimination that keep them from participating fully in the mainstream of society. People often feel intimidated by differences, whether these are differences in skin color, lifestyle, or values embraced. At the root of prejudice is fear, low self-esteem, ignorance, and feelings of inferiority. Prejudice is a defense mechanism that protects individuals from facing undesirable aspects of themselves by projecting them onto others. Treating others in a demeaning way may give these people an illusion of superiority.

Breaking Down the Walls That Separate Us

Language difficulties and value differences can make intercultural communication challenging. Awareness of these obstacles is the first step toward increasing communication and breaking down the walls that separate people. Whenever you are in a multicultural exchange, keep in mind that the more you know about other cultures the better you are likely to communicate. Do not judge or harshly criticize yourself if you realize that you lack the ability to transcend your differences. Give yourself credit for being open enough to recognize your limitations, for this is the beginning of being able to change.

Unity and diversity are related concepts, not polar opposites. It is not that diversity is good and right and homogeneity is bad and wrong. Both sameness and difference are part of the rainbow. Vontress, Johnson, and Epp (1999) take the position that it is important to recognize that people are more alike than they are different. As humans we share some common ground that enables us to understand one another despite our differences. Concerns about loving, living, relating, and dying are human problems that transcend culture. Vontress and his colleagues reject the tendency to stereotype people according to the ethnic, racial, or cultural groups into which they were born. Instead, they recognize that each of us is unique and that we share important concerns about life. The challenge is to move beyond the stereotypes and prejudices that set people apart and strive to understand each individual in his or her subjective world.

Building Connections by Reaching Out to Others

Living in a multicultural society, we are a people with many diverse backgrounds. It is a challenge to learn to embrace and appreciate diversity rather than be threatened by it. Unless we are able to accept this challenge, we remain isolated and separate from one another. Here are some ideas about how you can break down the barriers that keep you separate from other people:

> Acknowledge and understand your own biases and prejudices.
> Challenge your prejudices by looking for data that do not support your preconceived biases.

❭ Challenge your fears and anxieties about talking about racial or cultural differences.

❭ Look for similarities and universal themes that unite you with others who differ from you in certain ways.

❭ Avoid judging differences; view diversity as a strength.

❭ Be respectful of those who differ from you.

❭ Attempt to learn about cultures that differ from your own.

❭ Talk about yourself and your experience with people who differ from you. Try to keep it simple and not global.

❭ Be open and flexible.

❭ Be willing to test, adapt, and change your perceptions.

The more you know about your own culture, the more you will be able to understand the cultures of others. And the more you know about diverse cultures, the better able you will be to connect with them in a positive way. One living example of welcoming diversity is found in Glide Memorial Church in San Francisco. The pastor of this church, the Reverend Cecil Williams, along with the executive director of the church, Janet Mirikitani, are committed to welcoming diverse people into their spiritual community, a community that truly embraces love and acceptance. Reverend Williams (1992) works to empower individuals who are recovering and provides assistance to troubled communities. The pastor does not see his congregation as a melting pot where all people are blended together. Instead, Glide Memorial Church is more akin to a salad bowl filled with different leaves. Reverend Williams does far more than preach about love to a packed congregation on Sunday; he is actively engaged in spreading the meaning of love. He demonstrates ways to find meaning and purpose in life through acts of love. Through the efforts of Glide, hundreds of homeless are fed each day, substance abusers are given hope of a new kind of life, and society's outcasts are welcomed into a loving community. By giving people unconditional love and acceptance, Reverend Williams and his people bring out the best in those they encounter.

We challenge you to reflect on ways you can augment the meaning of your life by making connections with others and striving to make a significant difference. You can change the world in small ways by touching the lives of others through your acts of kindness and generosity. The purpose of your life can take on expanded dimensions if you are interested in making the world a better place for all of us. This process of making a difference in the human community begins with seeing ways that diversity can enhance life.

The *Quick Discrimination Index* can help you assess your attitudes toward cultural diversity. Even if you think you are free of prejudice toward others, you may discover some subtle biases. Once you are aware of them, you can begin working toward tolerance and acceptance.

The Quick Discrimination Index

We hope you will take and score this social-attitude survey, which is designed to assess sensitivity, awareness, and receptivity to cultural diversity and gender equity. This is a self-assessment inventory, and it is essential that you strive to respond to each item as honestly as possible. This inventory is not designed to assess how you should think about cultural diversity and gender equity issues; rather, its aim is to assess subtle racial and gender bias. You can use this inventory to become more aware of your attitudes and beliefs pertaining to these issues.

DIRECTIONS: Remember there are no right or wrong answers. Please circle the appropriate number to the right.

	Strongly disagree	Disagree	Not sure	Agree	Strongly agree
1. I do think it is more appropriate for the mother of a newborn baby, rather than the father, to stay home with the baby (not work) during the first year.	1	2	3	4	5
2. It is as easy for women to succeed in business as it is for men.	1	2	3	4	5
3. I really think affirmative-action programs on college campuses constitute reverse discrimination.	1	2	3	4	5
4. I feel I could develop an intimate relationship with someone from a different race.	1	2	3	4	5
5. All Americans should learn to speak two languages.	1	2	3	4	5
6. It upsets (or angers) me that a woman has never been president of the United States.	1	2	3	4	5
7. Generally speaking, men work harder than women.	1	2	3	4	5
8. My friendship network is very racially mixed.	1	2	3	4	5
9. I am against affirmative-action programs in business.	1	2	3	4	5
10. Generally, men seem less concerned with building relationships than women.	1	2	3	4	5
11. I would feel OK about my son or daughter dating someone from a different race.	1	2	3	4	5
12. It upsets (or angers) me that a racial minority person has never been president of the United States.	1	2	3	4	5
13. In the past few years, too much attention has been directed toward multicultural or minority issues in education.	1	2	3	4	5
14. I think feminist perspectives should be an integral part of the higher education curriculum.	1	2	3	4	5
15. Most of my close friends are from my own racial group.	1	2	3	4	5
16. I feel somewhat more secure that a man rather than a woman is currently president of the United States.	1	2	3	4	5

The Quick Discrimination Index (continued)

	Strongly disagree	Disagree	Not sure	Agree	Strongly agree
17. I think that it is (or would be) important for my children to attend schools that are racially mixed.	1	2	3	4	5
18. In the past few years too much attention has been directed toward multicultural or minority issues in business.	1	2	3	4	5
19. Overall, I think racial minorities in America complain too much about racial discrimination.	1	2	3	4	5
20. I feel (or would feel) very comfortable having a woman as my primary physician.	1	2	3	4	5
21. I think the president of the United States should make a concerted effort to appoint more women and racial minorities to the country's Supreme Court.	1	2	3	4	5
22. I think white people's racism toward racial-minority groups still constitutes a major problem in America.	1	2	3	4	5
23. I think the school system, from elementary school through college, should encourage minority and immigrant children to learn and fully adopt traditional American values.	1	2	3	4	5
24. If I were to adopt a child, I would be happy to adopt a child of any race.	1	2	3	4	5
25. I think there is as much female physical violence toward men as there is male physical violence toward women.	1	2	3	4	5
26. I think the school system, from elementary school through college, should promote values representative of diverse cultures.	1	2	3	4	5
27. I believe that reading the autobiography of Malcolm X would be of value.	1	2	3	4	5
28. I would enjoy living in a neighborhood consisting of a racially diverse population (Asians, blacks, Latinos, whites).	1	2	3	4	5
29. I think it is better if people marry within their own race.	1	2	3	4	5
30. Women make too big a deal out of sexual-harassment issues in the workplace.	1	2	3	4	5

The total score measures overall sensitivity, awareness, and receptivity to cultural diversity and gender equality. Of the 30 items on the QDI, 15 are worded and scored in a positive direction (high scores indicate high sensitivity to multicultural/gender issues), and 15 are worded and scored in a negative direction (where low scores are indicative of high sensitivity). Naturally, when tallying the total score response, these latter 15 items need to be *reverse-scored*. Reverse scoring simply means that if a respondent circles a "1" they should get five points; a "2" four points, a "3" three points, a "4" two points, and a "5" one point.

The following QDI items need to be *reverse-scored*: 1, 2, 3, 7, 9, 10, 13, 15, 16, 18, 19, 23, 25, 29, 30.

Score range = 30 to 150, with high scores indicating more awareness, sensitivity, and receptivity to racial diversity and gender equality.

Take Time to Reflect

1. To what extent are you threatened by people who think and believe differently from you? Do you tend to be drawn to human diversity, or do you tend to shy away from those with a different worldview?

_____

_____

_____

2. What value do you place on diversity as part of your philosophy of life?

_____

_____

_____

3. What steps are you willing to take to move in the direction of challenging your prejudices or restricted ways of thinking?

_____

_____

_____

4. What one action can you take to make a significant, even though small, difference in society? To what extent do you believe you are able to influence others?

_____

_____

_____

SUMMARY

Seeking meaning and purpose in life is an important part of being human. Meaning is not automatically bestowed on you; it is the result of your active thinking and choosing. We have encouraged you to recognize your own values and to ask both how you acquired them and whether you can affirm them for yourself out of your own experience and reflection. This task of examining your values and purposes continues throughout your lifetime.

If you are secure about your value system, you will also be flexible and open to new life experiences. At various times in your life you may look at the world somewhat differently, which will indicate a need to modify some of your values. This is not to say that you will change your values without giving the matter considerable thought. Being secure about your values also implies that you do not need to impose them on other people. We hope you will be able to respect the values of others that may differ from your own. You can learn to accept other people who have a different worldview from yours without necessarily approving of all of their behavior. If you are clear about the meaning in your own life, and if you have developed a philosophy of life that provides you with purpose and direction, you will be more able to interact with others who might embrace different value systems. Being able to talk openly with these people can be a useful avenue for your own personal growth.

In this chapter we have focused on the central role of values as a basis for meaning in life. In addition to finding meaning through projects that afford opportunities for personal growth, we have seen that meaning and purpose extend to the broader framework of forming linkages with others in the human community. Accepting others by respecting their right to hold values that may differ from yours is a fundamental dimension of a philosophy of life based on tolerance. Prejudice, based on fear and ignorance, is often a barrier that separates us from others instead of uniting us. We hope you will welcome diversity as a bridge to link yourself with others who differ from you. It may be overwhelming to think of solving the global problems of prejudice and discrimination, but you can begin in smaller but still significant ways by changing yourself. Once you recognize the barriers within yourself that prevent you from understanding and accepting others, you can take steps to challenge these barriers.

❯ Where Can I Go From Here?

1. Ask a few close friends what gives their lives meaning. How have they found their identities? What projects give them a sense of purpose? How do they think their lives would be different without this source of meaning?

(continued)

> ## Where Can I Go From Here? *(continued)*

2. Make a list of what you consider to be the major accomplishments in your life. What did you actually do to bring about these accomplishments? What kinds of future accomplishments would enhance the meaning of your life?

3. Writing a paper that describes your philosophy of life can help you integrate your thoughts and reflections about yourself. Ideally, this paper will represent a critical analysis of who you are now and the factors that have been most influential in contributing to that person. If you attempted to write at least a part of your philosophy of life as you began this book, you have a basis for comparison if you now revise your philosophy of life.

   The following outline for your paper is very comprehensive, and writing such a paper can be a major project in a course. As you review the outline, select one or two major topics and use them as a focus for your paper. Feel free to use or omit any part of the outline, and modify it in any way that will help you to write a paper that is personally significant. You might also consider adding poetry, excerpts from other writers, and pictures or works of art. If you take this project seriously, it will help you clarify your goals for the future and the means to obtain them.

   a. Who are you now? What influences have contributed to the person you are now? In addressing this question consider factors such as influences during childhood and influences during adolescence.

   b. How are love and intimacy factors in your life? Consider some of the following elements as you develop your answer:
      > Your need for love
      > Your fear of love
      > The meaning of love for you
      > Dating experiences and their effect on you
      > Your view of gender roles
      > Expectations of others and their influence on your gender role
      > Attitudes toward the opposite sex
      > Meaning of sexuality in your life
      > Your values concerning love and sex

   c. What place do intimate relationship and family life occupy in your life?
      > The value you place on marriage
      > How children fit in your life
      > The meaning of intimacy for you

> ## Where Can I Go From Here? *(continued)*

> - The kind of intimate relationships you want
> - Areas of struggle for you in relating to others
> - Your views of marriage
> - Your values concerning family life
> - How social expectations have influenced your views
> - Gender roles in intimate relationships

d. What are your thoughts about death and meaning?
> - Your view of an afterlife
> - Religious views and your view of death
> - The way death affects you
> - Sources of meaning in your life
> - The things you most value in your life
> - Your struggles in finding meaning and purpose
> - Religion and the meaning of life
> - Critical turning points in finding meaning
> - Influential people in your life

e. Whom do you want to become? In addressing this question consider some of the following:
> - How you see yourself now (strengths and weaknesses)
> - How others perceive you now
> - What makes you unique
> - Your relationships with others
> - Present struggles

f. How would you describe your future with others? (Consider the kind of relationships you want and what you need to do to achieve them.)

g. What are your future plans for yourself?
> - How you would like to be 10 years from now
> - What you need to do to achieve your goals
> - What you can do now
> - Your values for the future
> - Choices you see as being open to you now

Resources for Future Study

Web Site Resource

WEB OF CULTURE
http://www.webofculture.com/home/home.html

Although this site is intended for businesses, it includes a wide range of issues and approaches to increase cross-cultural understanding. It features extensive worldwide information on subjects such as capitals, currency, gestures, headlines, and languages.

InfoTrac College Edition Resources

For additional readings, explore InfoTrac College Edition, our online library.

Go to **http://www.infotrac.college.com/wadsworth**

Hint: Enter the search terms:

meaning in life
personal meaning
philosophy of life
religious faith
value systems
human diversity
prejudice
racism

Print Resources

Albom, M. (1997). *Tuesdays with Morrie.* New York: Doubleday.

Bellah, R. N., Madsen, R., Sullivan, W. M., Swidler, A., & Tipton, S. M. (1985). *Habits of the heart: Individualism and commitment in American life.* New York: Harper & Row (Perennial Library).

Burke, M. T., & Miranti, J. G. (1992). *Ethical and spiritual values in counseling.* Alexandria, VA: American Counseling Association.

Dalai Lama. (1999). *Ethics for a new millennium.* New York: Riverhead Books.

Dalai Lama, & Cutler, H. C. (1998). *The art of happiness: A handbook for living.* New York: Riverhead Books.

Frankl, V. (1963). *Man's search for meaning.* New York: Washington Square Press.

Frankl, V. (1965). *The doctor and the soul.* New York: Bantam Books.

Frankl, V. (1969). *The will to meaning: Foundation and applications of logotherapy.* New York: New American Library.

Frankl, V. (1978). *The unheard cry for meaning.* New York: Bantam.

Joy, W. B. (1979). *Joy's way: A map for the transformational journey.* Los Angeles, CA: Jeremy P. Tarcher.

Joy, W. B. (1990). *Avalanche: Heretical reflections on the dark and the light.* New York: Ballantine.

Katz, J. (1999). *Running to the mountain: A journey of faith and change.* New York: Villard.

Ridley, C. R. (1995). *Overcoming unintentional racism in counseling and psychotherapy.* Thousand Oaks, CA: Sage.

Seligman, M. E. P. (1993). *What you can change and what you can't.* New York: Fawcett Columbine.

Vontress, C. E., Johnson, J. A., & Epp, L. R. (1999). *Cross-cultural counseling: A casebook.* Alexandria, VA: American Counseling Association.

Williams, C. (1992). *No hiding place: Empowerment and recovery for our troubled communities.* San Francisco: Harper.

Williamson, M. (2000). *Healing the soul of America: Reclaiming our voices as spiritual citizens.* New York: Touchstone.

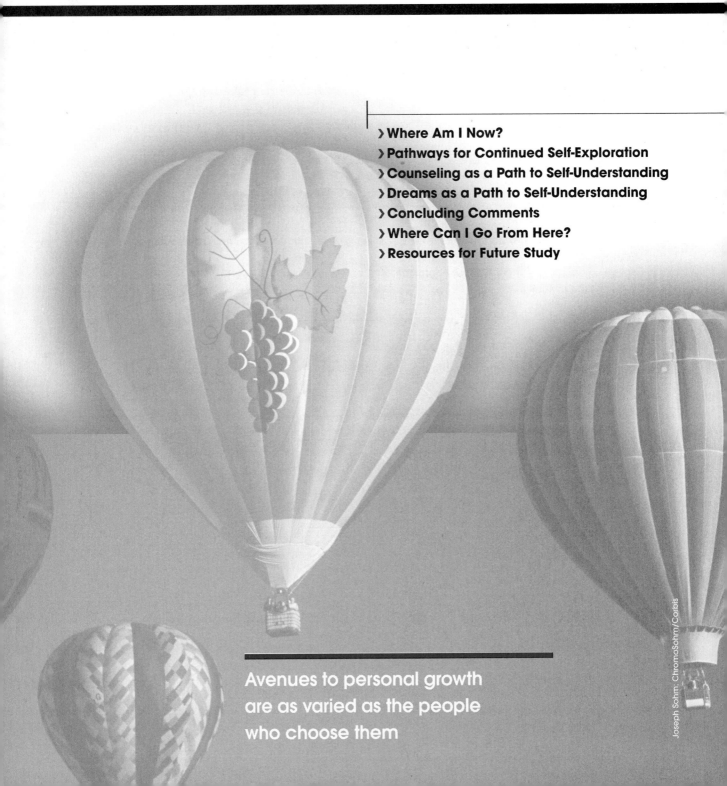

Avenues to personal growth
are as varied as the people
who choose them

14

PATHWAYS TO PERSONAL GROWTH

Use this scale to respond to these statements:

4 = This statement is true of me *most* of the time.

3 = This statement is true of me *much* of the time.

2 = This statement is true of me *some* of the time.

1 = This statement is true of me *almost none* of the time.

_____ 1. I am motivated to keep up with regular journal writing.

_____ 2. I would like to begin meditation practices.

_____ 3. I intend to incorporate relaxation methods into my daily life.

_____ 4. Now that I have read this book, I see that I have more choices available to me than I realized.

_____ 5. Personal growth is a journey rather than a fixed destination.

_____ 6. I really intend to do what it takes to continue the self-exploration I have begun through this course and book.

_____ 7. If I had a personal problem I could not resolve by myself, I would seek professional assistance.

_____ 8. I dream a lot and am able to remember many of my dreams.

_____ 9. I see dreaming as a way to understand myself and to remain psychologically healthy.

_____ 10. I intend to develop an action plan as a way to begin the changes I most want to make in my life.

Throughout this book you have been invited to discover new choices you might like to make. In this relatively brief chapter, we invite you to review what you learned from reading the book and to determine where you will go from here. Will you stop here, or will this be a commencement—a new beginning in the best sense? If you have invested yourself in the process of questioning your life, now is a good time to make a commitment to yourself (and maybe to someone else) to actively put to use what you have been learning about yourself.

You can deliberately choose experiences that will help you become the person you choose to be. As you consider what experiences for continued personal growth you are likely to choose at this time, be aware that as you change you can expect that what brings meaning to your life will also change. The projects you were deeply absorbed in at an earlier time in your life may hold little meaning for you today. And where and how you discover meaning today may not be the pattern for some future period.

Often, we make resolutions about what we would like to be doing in our lives or about experiences we want to share with others, and then we fail to carry them out. Is this true of you? Are there activities you value yet rarely get around to doing? When you stop to think about it, how would you really like to be spending your time? What changes are you willing to make today, this week, this month, this year? We encourage you to reflect on the previous chapters and identify some of the areas that most stood out for you.

Growth can occur in small ways, and there are many things you can do on your own (or with friends or family) to continue your personal development. A few of the resources available to you for continued personal growth are outlined in the pages that follow. Different resources may fit your needs at different stages of your personal growth. We invite you to investigate any of these avenues that you feel are appropriate for you at this time.

PATHWAYS FOR CONTINUED SELF-EXPLORATION

Develop a Reading Program

One excellent way to motivate yourself to explore life is by reading good books, including selected self-help books. We caution you to beware of those self-help books that offer quick solutions, that promise a prescription for eternal happiness, or that give you steps to follow to find guaranteed success. The References and Suggested Readings section at the end of this book includes a variety of self-help books that should give you a fine start on developing a personal reading program. Many students and clients tell us how meaningful selected books have been for them in putting into perspective some of the themes they have struggled with, and we encourage you to take advantage of this resource. Is reading a project you are willing to commit yourself to doing? What are some areas that

Todd Gipstein/Corbis

Growth can occur in small ways, and there are many things you can do on your own to continue your personal development.

you are most interested in reading about? What are a few books that you might select? Would it be helpful to create a schedule to make reading a priority?

Continue Your Writing Program

Along with setting up a reading and reflection program for yourself, another way to build on the gains you have made up to this point is to continue the practice of journal writing. If you have begun a process of personal writing in this book or in a separate notebook, maintain this practice. Even devoting a short period a few times each week to reflecting on how your life is going and then recording some of your thoughts and feelings is useful in providing you with an awareness of patterns in your behavior. You can learn to observe what you are feeling, thinking, and doing; then you have a basis for determining the degree to which you are successfully changing old patterns that were not working for you. Have you been regularly making use of journal writing as a part of this course? Will you commit to continuing this practice?

Contemplate Self-Directed Behavior Change

Now that you have finished this book, you have probably identified a few specific areas where you could do further work. If you decide that you are frequently tense and that you do not generally react well to stress, for example, construct a self-change program that includes practicing relaxation methods and breathing exercises. Identify some target areas for personal change and set realistic goals. Then develop some specific techniques for carrying out your goals, and practice the behaviors that will help you make those changes. What kind of self-change program are you most interested in launching? When might you begin?

Practice Ongoing Self-Assessment

Throughout this book you have been challenged to assess the ways that you think, feel, and act on a variety of topics. Review your responses to the Where Am I Now? sections for each chapter and assess your written responses to the Take Time to Reflect exercises. Taking time to consolidate your thoughts will enhance your learning and provide you with some signposts for future changes. Did you find any persistent themes in your review of these chapter exercises? What one thing would you like to begin changing today?

Take Advantage of Support Groups

Most colleges and community mental health centers offer a variety of self-help groups that are facilitated by a person who has coped or is coping with a particular life issue. A good support group will help you see that you are not alone in your struggle. The experience can also provide you with alternatives that you may not be considering. Other examples of support groups include those that deal with rape or incest, consciousness-raising groups for women and for men, groups for reentry students, groups for people concerned about gay and lesbian issues, and medical self-help groups. As is the case with self-help books, you are advised to proceed with some caution in joining a support group. Is this the right group for you at this time in your life?

COUNSELING AS A PATH TO SELF-UNDERSTANDING

We hope you will remain open to the idea of seeking counseling for yourself at critical transition periods in your life or times when you feel particularly challenged with life events or choices to be made. Reading this book and participating in this kind of class may have raised personal issues that you were unaware of before. To wrestle with choices about life is supremely human, and taking this course has probably shown you that you are not alone with your struggles. We encourage you to trust yourself to make your own choices, but even a few counseling sessions at the right time can assist you in clarifying your options and can provide you with the impetus to formulate action plans leading to change.

In our view, it is essential to attend to both your physical and your psychological health, because psychological pain often affects physical well-being.

When you find that you cannot give yourself the help you need or get needed assistance from your friends and family, you may want to seek out a professional counselor. When people are physically ill, they generally seek a physician's help. Yet when people are "psychologically ill," they often hesitate to ask for help. Counseling does not necessarily involve a major revamping of your personality. Instead of getting a major overhaul, you might need only a minor tune-up! Many people refuse to take their car to a mechanic unless it breaks down because they do not want to take the time for preventive maintenance. Some will avoid a trip to the dentist until they are in excruciating pain with a toothache. Likewise, many people wait until they are unable to function at home, at work, or at school before they reach out for professional counseling. Your road to personal growth will be smoother if you opt for a few tune-ups along the way.

You do not have to be in a crisis to benefit from either individual or group counseling. Counselors can help their clients move ahead when they feel stuck in some aspect of living. If you can identify with any of these statements, you might consider seeking counseling:

> I feel out of control of my life.
> I am unhappy with where I am heading.
> I feel stuck in terms of making constructive choices.
> I am the victim of a crime or some form of abuse.
> I have no purpose or direction in life.
> I am experiencing chronic depression.
> I am in an unsatisfying relationship.
> I am struggling with addictive behaviors.
> I am alienated from myself and others.
> I am experiencing a spiritual crisis.
> I am experiencing a significant loss.
> I am having problems related to work or school.
> I am under chronic stress or have stress-related ailments.
> I am the victim of discrimination and oppression.
> I am divorcing or ending a significant relationship.
> I feel that I am using only a fraction of my potential.

Counselors are mentors who guide you in making use of your inner resources. Good counselors do not attempt to solve your problems for you. Instead, they teach you how to cope with your problems more effectively. In many respects counselors are psychological educators, teaching you how to get the most from living, how to create more joy in your life, how to use your own strengths, and how to become the person you want to be.

A counselor's function is to teach you how to eventually become your own therapist. Counselors do not change your beliefs through brainwashing; rather, they assist you in examining how your thinking affects the way you feel and act. A counselor will help you identify specific beliefs that may be getting in the way of your living effectively. You will learn how to critically evaluate your values, beliefs, thoughts, and assumptions. Counseling can teach you how to substitute constructive thinking for self-destructive thinking. If you find it hard to identify and express feelings such as joy, anger, fear, or guilt, counseling can help you learn to do so. If your present behavior prevents you from getting where you want to go, counselors can help you explore alternative ways of acting.

Therapeutic work can be difficult for you *and* for the counselor. Self-honesty is not easy. Confronting and dealing with your problems takes courage. By simply going in for counseling, you have taken the first step in the healing process. Recognizing the need for help is itself significant in moving forward. Self-exploration requires discipline, patience, and persistence. There may be times when progress seems slow, for counseling does not work wonders. Indeed, at times you may feel worse before you get better because old wounds are brought to the surface and explored.

Selecting the counselor who is right for you is of the utmost importance. Just as it is important to go to a physician you trust, it is critical that you find a counselor whom you can trust. Ask questions about the counselor's training and background before you make a commitment to work with that person. In fact, ethical therapists feel a responsibility to inform their clients about the way counseling works. Another good way to find an effective therapist is to ask others who have been in counseling. A personal referral to a specific person can be useful. However you select a counselor, do some research and make a thoughtful decision. Counseling is a highly personal matter, and you stand a greater chance of doing the hard work self-learning demands if you trust your counselor.

Remember, counseling is a process of self-discovery aimed at empowerment. Counseling is not an end in itself but a tool that can enable you to effectively cope with future blocks you are likely to encounter. If your counseling is successful, you will learn far more than merely how to solve a specific problem. You will acquire skills you can use to confront new problems and challenges as they arise. Ultimately, you will be better equipped to make your own choices about how you want to live.

DREAMS AS A PATH TO SELF-UNDERSTANDING

Why is it important for us to teach ourselves to dream? In his splendid book, *Teach Yourself to Dream,* Fontana (1997) tells us that "dreams are our chance to eavesdrop on a conversation between our unconscious and conscious minds, offering us opportunities to understand ourselves better and achieve greater inner harmony" (p. 8). We can learn how to reveal the special meaning of our dreams, how to make our dreams more vivid, and how to use our dreams for guidance in times of personal difficulty. Many of the messages we receive in dreams are associated with concerns, anxieties, and hopes of daily life:

> IN A BROAD SENSE, dreams often relate to what might be, rather than what actually is. A dream could thus suggest that you might wish to enlarge your horizons, or to explore new avenues and opportunities. Sometimes dreams seem to warn us of dangers, or to caution us to think more carefully about a particular course of action. The one clear message is that dreams are far too important to be ignored. (p. 23)

Dreams can reveal significant clues to events that have meaning for us. If we train ourselves to recall our dreams—and this can indeed be learned—and discipline ourselves to explore their meanings, we can get a good sense of our struggles, wants, goals, purposes, conflicts, and interests. Dreams can shed a powerful light on our past, present, and future dynamics and on our attempt to construct meaning. Dreaming helps us deal with stress, work through loss and grief, resolve anger, and bring closure to painful life situations.

If you learn to recall your dreams and to pay attention to the wisdom of your unconscious, dreams can be healing. Many people forget their dreams because they do not value them as being important enough to remember (Fontana, 1997). In Western culture most of us are brought up to believe dreams serve no real purpose and that they should not be taken seriously. Fontana suggests that we would do well to reassess our negative attitudes about dreaming and change them. He advises that we tell ourselves that our dreams are helpful, that we remember them, and that we welcome what our dreams can teach us about becoming more fulfilled and effective human beings.

As much as we believe in the healing capacity of dreams, we have some concerns in writing about this topic. Indeed, a little knowledge can be a dangerous thing. Sometimes people attempt to analyze their dreams (and the dreams of their friends and family members) without a full understanding of the complexity of dream interpretation. We caution you to avoid analyzing and interpreting dreams of others unless you have the necessary education and training in dream work.

One of the best ways to keep track of your dreams is to record them in your journal. Sharing a dream with someone you trust can be self-revealing and helpful. If you journal around themes in your dreams, you may begin to see more parallels between your sleeping and waking life.

Until recently, I (Jerry) rarely had dreams that I could remember. But a few years ago I attended a conference focused on exploring dreams. I began to record whatever fragments of dreams I could recall, and interestingly, during this conference I started to recall some vivid and rich dreams. I have made it a practice to record in my journal any dreams upon awakening, along with my impressions and reactions to the dreams. It helps me to share my dreams with

Marianne or other friends; especially useful is comparing impressions others have of my dreams.

All the images in my dreams are manifestations of some dimension within me. In Gestalt fashion, I typically allow myself to reflect on the ways the people in my dreams represent parts of myself. "Becoming the various images" in the dream is one way for me to bring unconscious themes forward. I am finding that my dreams have a pattern and that they are shorthand ways of understanding conflicts in my life, decisions to be made at crossroads, and themes that recur from time to time. Even a short segment of a dream often contains layers of messages that make sense when I look at what is going on in my waking state.

Exploring the Meaning of Dreams

People have been fascinated with dreams and have regarded them as significant since ancient times. But dreams have been the subject of scientific investigation only since the mid-19th century. Dreams are not mysterious; they are avenues to self-understanding.

Fritz Perls, the father of Gestalt therapy, discovered some ingenious methods to assist people in better understanding themselves. He suggested that we become friends with our dreams. According to Perls (1970), the dream is the most spontaneous expression of the existence of the human being; it is a piece of art that individuals chisel out of their lives. It represents an unfinished situation, but it is more than an incomplete situation, an unfulfilled wish, or a prophecy. Every dream contains an existential message about oneself and one's current struggle. Gestalt therapy aims at bringing a dream to life by having the dreamer relive it as though it were happening now. This includes making a list of all the details of the dream, remembering each person, event, and mood in it, and then becoming each of these parts by acting and inventing dialogue. Perls saw dreams as "the royal road to integration." By avoiding analysis and interpretation and focusing instead on becoming and experiencing the dream in all its aspects, the dreamer gets closer to the existential message of the dream.

Rainwater (1979) offers some useful guidelines for dreamers to follow in exploring their dreams:

> Be the landscape or the environment.

> Become all the people in the dream. Are any of them significant people?

> Be any object that links and joins, such as telephone lines and highways.

> Identify with any mysterious objects, such as an unopened letter or an unread book.

> Assume the identity of any powerful force, such as a tidal wave.

> Become any two contrasting objects, such as a younger person and an older person.

❭ Be anything that is missing in the dream. If you do not remember your dreams, then speak to your missing dreams.

❭ Be alert for any numbers that appear in the dream; become these numbers and explore associations with them.

When you wake from a dream, is your feeling state one of fear, joy, sadness, frustration, surprise, or anger? Identifying the feeling tone may be the key to finding the meaning of the dream (Rainwater, 1979). As you play out the various parts of your dream, pay attention to what you say and look for patterns. By identifying your feeling tone and the themes that emerge, you will get a clearer sense of what your dreams are telling you.

Dreams are full of symbols. Gestalt therapists contribute to dream work by emphasizing the individual meaning of symbols. The person assigns meaning to his or her own dream. For example, an unopened letter could represent a person who is clinging to secrets. An unread book might symbolize an individual's fear of not being noticed or of being insignificant. A Gestalt therapist might ask the person, "What is the first thing that comes to you when you think about an unopened letter?" One person replies, "I want to hide. I don't want anyone to know me." Another individual says, "I wish somebody would open me up." To understand the personal meaning of a dream, a therapist often asks, "What might be going on in your life now where what you just said would make sense?" In Gestalt therapy no established meaning fits everyone; rather, meaning is deciphered by each individual.

Dreams are a rich source of meaning. If you listen closely to them, they will prompt you to look at ways in which you may want to change your life. I (Marianne) recently had a dream that challenged me to examine the way I was living. The dream occurred during a time when I was feeling personally and professionally overextended. I was giving out more than I was taking for myself. Here is my dream, which occurred while I was in Germany.

> MY MOTHER HAS COOKED me a very special meal, and I am looking forward to eating it. There are many people there. By the time I go to get my food, everyone else has eaten the meal and none is left for me! I am very angry, resentful, and hurt that there is no more food.

The meaning of this dream was obvious to me. The overriding message was that I was not taking care of myself or nurturing myself. I was consciously aware that I was working hard and not relaxing enough, but the dream made me confront my choices.

If you listen to your dreams, you will learn something more about yourself. You can use this knowledge to make better choices and to live your life more fully. Dreams are the link between our inner and outer lives, and dreams give us a unique opportunity to listen to and learn from our inner wisdom. If you are interested in doing further reading about dreams, we highly recommend Fontana's (1997) book, *Teach Yourself to Dream.*

Dare to Dream

Dreams can reveal significant aspects of our past and present struggles. As a gateway to the unconscious, dreaming can also inform us of our future strivings. To better design a personal vision for your future, we encourage you to dream when you are awake as well as when you are asleep. Don Quixote dared "to dream the impossible dream." We encourage you to follow a similar path. The greatest hindrance to your growth may be a failure to allow yourself to imagine all the possibilities open to you. You may have restricted your vision of what you might become by not allowing yourself to formulate a vision or pursue your dreams. If you reflect thoughtfully on the messages in your dreams, a range of choices will unfold for you. We have met many people who continue to surprise themselves with what they have in their lives. At one time they would not have imagined such possibilities—even in their wildest dreams—but their dreams became reality for them. Too many of us restrict our vision of the possible by not allowing ourselves the luxury of reflecting on an impossible dream. Dare to dream, and then have the courage to follow your passions.

CONCLUDING COMMENTS

If you have become more aware of personal issues than you were when you began the course, and if you are eager to continue on the path of self-examination and reflection, you have already taken the first steps down the path of self-actualization. Sometimes people expect dramatic transformations and feel disappointed if they do not make major changes in their lives. Remember that it is not the big changes that are necessarily significant; rather, it is your willingness to take small steps that will lead to continued growth. Only you can change your own ways of thinking, feeling, and doing. Look for subtle ways of increasing your personal freedom.

The knowledge and skills that you have gained from both the course and the book can be applied to virtually all of your future experiences. Recognize that there is no one right path for you to follow. You will encounter many paths and make critical decisions at various transition points in your life. Remain open to considering new paths.

At this point you probably have a clearer vision of the personal goals that you most want to pursue. Make plans to accomplish these new goals, but avoid overwhelming yourself with too many things to do lest you become discouraged. Personal change is an ongoing process that really does not come to an end until you do. We sincerely wish you well in your commitment to take the steps necessary, no matter how small, in your journey to becoming the person you were meant to be. Remember that even a journey of a thousand miles begins with the first step—so start walking!

❯ Where Can I Go From Here?

1. If you have trouble remembering your dreams, before you go to sleep (for about a month) tell yourself "I will have a dream tonight, and I will remember it." Keep a paper and a pen near your bed, and jot down even brief dream fragments you may recall when you wake up. If you do not recall dreaming, at least write that down. This practice may increase your ability to remember your dreams.

2. If you are aware of dreaming fairly regularly, develop the practice of writing your dreams in your journal as soon as possible upon awakening. Look at the pattern of your dreams; become aware of the kinds of dreams you are having and what they might mean to you. Simply reading your descriptions of your dreams can be of value to you.

3. Make a list of all the reasons you would not want to seek out a counselor when you are in psychological pain or coping with a problem that hampers your personal effectiveness. Apply this same list to answer the question why you would not seek out a physician when you are in physical pain. Review this list to determine your attitudes regarding psychological health and physical health.

4. What have been the highlights of this course and book? What changes in yourself have you noticed? What have you learned that you can take with you wherever you go?

5. If you have invested yourself in this book and in this course, you have acquired a set of skills that you can continue to use, one being the art of self-assessment. Respond to each of the following questions in your journal. Do not check off the question until you feel you have responded as fully as you can.

    a. Have you felt good about the kind of student you have been this term? If the rest of your college career will be much like this term, what will that be like for you?

    b. Go back to the discussion of becoming an active learner in Chapter 1. To what degree have you become more involved and active as a student and a learner?

    c. What kind of student are you? How far have you progressed since you began this book? What are some of the most significant steps you have taken?

    d. You were invited to become a coauthor of this book by writing in it and personalizing the material. Take time to reread some of what you wrote in the Take Time to Reflect sections and in your journal. What patterns do you see in your thoughts?

    e. Describe the student and person you would like to be one year from today. Consider these questions as you imagine different directions:

       ❯ If you had right now what you wanted in your life, what would that be?

       ❯ If you were the kind of student today that you would like to be, how would you be?

       ❯ What might be getting in your way of being the kind of person and student that you would like to be?

       ❯ What are a few specific actions you need to take if you want to accomplish new goals?

       ❯ What will help you to stick with a plan aimed at becoming more of the person and student you want to become?

Resources for Future Study

Web Site Resources

AMERICAN ASSOCIATION OF MARRIAGE AND FAMILY THERAPY
http://www.aamft.org/

This site is maintained by the American Association of Marriage and Family Therapy (AAMFT). It explains how professional therapy can help couples and families experiencing difficulty. The site also offers links to important family and marriage-related resources including their "Find a Therapist" service.

MENTAL HEALTH NET
http://www.mentalhelp.net/

This is an excellent site that explores all aspects of mental health. Many psychological disorders and treatments are discussed along with professional issues. There are links to more than 8,000 mental health resources.

THE STUDENT COUNSELING VIRTUAL PAMPHLET COLLECTION
http://uhs.bsd.uchicago.edu/scrs/vpc/virtulets.html

This resource provides links to useful online information for a range of personal concerns of college students, many of which are discussed in this book.

THE ALBERT ELLIS INSTITUTE
http://www.rebt.org/

This site describes rational emotive behavior therapy (REBT). The site also offers facts about the Institute, questions and answers about REBT, a forum for asking Dr. Ellis questions directly, resources for self-help, therapist referrals, workshop schedules, professional services and products, and a complete selection of all of the Institute's publications and products.

HOW TO FIND HELP WITH LIFE'S PROBLEMS (APA BROCHURE)
http://helping.apa.org/brochure/index.html

This site, designed by the American Psychological Association, gives suggestions about seeking out different types of therapy for different types of problems. The site also answers questions about therapy, insurance, confidentiality, finding a therapist, and choosing one who is right for you.

THE EFFECTIVENESS OF PSYCHOTHERAPY: THE *CONSUMER REPORTS* STUDY
http://www.apa.org/journals/seligman.html

This article is by Martin E. P. Seligman and discusses the *Consumer Reports* (1995, November) study on the effectiveness of psychotherapy.

Dr. Ivan's Depression Central
http://www.psycom.net/depression.central.html

This site by psychiatrist Ivan K. Goldberg, M.D., provides very extensive coverage of mood disorders and treatments and links to other sites about mood and other disorders.

 InfoTrac College Edition Resources

For additional readings, explore InfoTrac College Edition, our online library.

Go to **http://www.infotrac.college.com/wadsworth**

Hint: Enter the search terms:

> support group
> dreams
> dream work
> dream AND therapy
> dream AND couns
> dream AND psych

Print Resources

Fontana, D. (1997). *Teach yourself to dream: A practical guide.* San Francisco: Chronicle Books.

Hwang, P. O. (2000). *Other-esteem: Meaningful life in a multicultural society.* Philadelphia, PA: Accelerated Development (Taylor & Francis).

Miller, T. (1995). *How to want what you have: Discovering the magic and grandeur of ordinary existence.* New York: Avon.

Moulton, P., & Harper, L. (1999). *Outside looking in: When someone you love is in therapy.* Brandon, VT: Safer Society Press.

Seligman, M. E. P. (1990). *Learned optimism: How to change your mind and your life.* New York: Pocket Books.

Seligman, M. E. P. (1993). *What you can change and what you can't.* New York: Fawcett Columbine.

Stone, H., & Stone, S. (1993). *Embracing your inner critic: Turning self-criticism into a creative asset.* San Francisco: Harper.

Vanzant, I. (1998). *One day my soul just opened up.* New York: Simon & Schuster (Fireside).

References and Suggested Readings*

ADLER, A. (1958). *What life should mean to you.* New York: Capricorn.

ADLER, A. (1964). *Social interest: A challenge to mankind.* New York: Capricorn.

ADLER, A. (1969). *The practice and theory of individual psychology.* Paterson, NJ: Littlefield.

ADLER, S. (2000, April 22). Going to extremes: Beer guzzlers, teetotalers on rise at college [on-line]. Available: *http://abcnews.com/sections/living/DailyNews/drinking000314.html.*

ALBOM, M. (1997). *Tuesdays with Morrie.* New York: Doubleday.

*AMADA, G. (1995). *A guide to psychotherapy.* New York: Ballantine.

AMERICAN ASSOCIATION FOR WORLD HEALTH. (1994). *AIDS and families* [Booklet]. Washington, DC: Author.

ARNETT, J. J. (2000). Emerging adulthood: A theory of development from the late teens through the twenties. *American Psychologist, 55*(5), 469–480.

ARONSON, E. (2000, May 28). *The social psychology of self-persuasion.* Keynote address at the Evolution of Psychotherapy Conference, Anaheim, CA.

*BASOW, S. A. (1992). *Gender: Stereotypes and roles* (3rd ed.). Pacific Grove, CA: Brooks/Cole.

BASS, E., & DAVIS, L. (1994). *The courage to heal: A guide for women survivors of child sexual abuse* (3rd ed.). New York: Harper (Perennial).

BATESON, M. C. (1990). *Composing a life.* New York: Plume.

BEISSER, A. R. (1970). The paradoxical theory of change. In J. Fagan & I. L. Shepherd (Eds.), *Gestalt therapy now* (pp. 77–80). New York: Harper & Row (Colophon).

*BELLAH, R. N., MADSEN, R., SULLIVAN, W. M., SWIDLER, A., & TIPTON, S. M. (1985). *Habits of the heart: Individualism and commitment in American life.* New York: Harper & Row (Perennial).

*BENSON, H. (1976). *The relaxation response.* New York: Avon.

BENSON, H. (1984). *Beyond the relaxation response.* New York: Berkeley Books.

BENSON, H. (2000, May 25). *Timeless healing: The power and biology of belief.* Keynote address at the Evolution of Psychotherapy Conference, Anaheim, CA.

BERNE, E. (1975). *What do you say after you say hello?* New York: Bantam.

*BLACK, C. (1987). *It will never happen to me.* New York: Ballantine.

BLOCK, D. (1991). *Listening to your inner voice: Discover the truth within you and let it guide your way.* Center City, MN: Hazelden.

*BLOOMFIELD, H. H., WITH FELDER, L. (1983). *Making peace with your parents.* New York: Ballantine.

*BLOOMFIELD, H. H., WITH FELDER, L. (1985). *Making peace with yourself: Transforming your weaknesses into strengths.* New York: Ballantine.

*BLY, R. (1990). *Iron John: A book about men.* New York: Random House (Vintage).

*BOLLES, R. N. (1999). *What color is your parachute? A practical manual for job hunters and career changers.* Berkeley, CA: Ten Speed Press.

BORYSENKO, J. (1996). *A woman's book of life: The biology, psychology and spirituality of the feminine life cycle.* New York: Riverhead.

BORYSENKO, J., WITH ROTHSTEIN, L. (1988). *Minding the body, mending the mind.* New York: Bantam.

*BURKE, M. T., & MIRANTI, J. G. (1992). *Ethical and spiritual values in counseling.* Alexandria, VA: American Counseling Association.

*BURNS, D. D. (1981). *Feeling good: The new mood therapy.* New York: New American Library (Signet).

*BURNS, D. D. (1985). *Intimate connections.* New York: New American Library (Signet).

*BUSCAGLIA, L. (1972). *Love.* Thorofare, NJ: Charles B. Slack.

BUSCAGLIA, L. (1992). *Born for love: Reflections on loving.* New York: Fawcett (Columbine).

*CAMERON, J. (1992). *The artist's way: A spiritual path to higher creativity.* New York: G. P. Putnam's Sons.

CARDUCCI, B. J. (1999). *Shyness: A bold new approach: The latest scientific findings, plus practical steps for finding your comfort zone.* New York: HarperCollins.

---

*An asterisk before an entry indicates a source that we highly recommend as supplementary reading.

*CARNEY, C. G., & WELLS, C. F. (1999). *Working well, living well: Discover the career within you* (5th ed.). Pacific Grove, CA: Brooks/Cole.

*CARR, J. B. (1988). *Crisis in intimacy: When expectations don't meet reality.* Pacific Grove, CA: Brooks/Cole.

CARTER, B., & McGOLDRICK, M. (EDS.). (1999). *The expanded family life cycle: Individual, family, and social perspectives* (3rd ed.). Boston: Allyn & Bacon.

*CASEY, K., & VANCEBURG, M. (1985). *The promise of a new day: A book of daily meditations.* New York: Harper/Hazelden.

CENTERS FOR DISEASE CONTROL AND PREVENTION. (1993a). *Facts about condoms and their use in preventing HIV infection and other STD's.* Atlanta: Author.

CENTERS FOR DISEASE CONTROL AND PREVENTION. (1993b). *National AIDS Clearinghouse.* Atlanta: Author.

CENTERS FOR DISEASE CONTROL AND PREVENTION. (1994a). *HIV/AIDS Surveillance Report, 6*(1), 1.

CENTERS FOR DISEASE CONTROL AND PREVENTION. (1994b). *Surgeon general's report to the American public on HIV infection and AIDS.* Rockville, MD: Author.

CENTERS FOR DISEASE CONTROL AND PREVENTION. (1994c). *Voluntary HIV counseling and testing: Facts, issues, and answers.* Rockville, MD: Author.

CENTERS FOR DISEASE CONTROL AND PREVENTION. (1999a). *Condoms and their use in preventing HIV infection and other STDs.* Rockville, MD: Author.

CENTERS FOR DISEASE CONTROL AND PREVENTION. (1999b). *HIV and its transmission.* Rockville, MD: Author.

CHAPMAN, A. B. (1993). Black men do feel about love. In M. Golden (Ed.) *Wild women don't wear no blues: Black women writers on love, men and sex.* New York: Doubleday.

*CHARLESWORTH, E. A., & NATHAN, R. G. (1984). *Stress management: A comprehensive guide to wellness.* New York: Ballantine.

CHOUDHURY, B. (1978). *Bikram's beginning yoga class.* New York: Jeremy P. Tarcher (Putnam).

COCHRAN, S. V., & RABINOWITZ, F. E. (1996). Men, loss, and psychotherapy. *Psychotherapy, 33*(4), 593–600.

COREY, G., COREY, C., & COREY, H. (1997). *Living and learning.* Belmont, CA: Wadsworth.

*CORR, C. A., NABE, C. M., & CORR, D. M. (2000). *Death and dying, life and living* (3rd ed.). Belmont, CA: Wadsworth.

COURTNEY-CLARKE, M. (1999). *Maya Angelou: The Poetry of Living.* New York: Clarkson Potter.

*COVEY, S. R. (1990). *The seven habits of highly effective people.* New York: Simon & Schuster (Fireside).

CROOKS, R., & BAUR, K. (1996). *Our sexuality* (6th ed.). Pacific Grove, CA: Brooks/Cole.

*DALAI LAMA, & CUTLER, H. C. (1998). *The art of happiness: A handbook for living.* New York: Riverhead.

*DALAI LAMA. (1999). *Ethics for the new millennium.* New York: Riverhead.

DASS, R. (1978). *Journey of awakening: A meditator's guidebook.* New York: Bantam.

DAWSON, G. (2000). *Life is so good.* New York: Random House Value.

DEETS, H. B. (2000, January/February). The graying of the world: Crisis or opportunity? *Modern Maturity,* p. 82.

DELANY, S. L., WITH HEARTH, A. H. (1997). *On my own at 107: Reflections on life without Bessie.* San Francisco: HarperCollins.

DELANY, S. L., DELANY, A. E., & HEARTH, A. H. (1993). *Having our say: The Delany sisters' first 100 years.* New York: Dell (Delta).

DICKENSON, D., & JOHNSON, M. (EDS.). (1993). *Death, dying, and bereavement.* Newbury Park, CA: Sage.

DONATELLE, R., SNOW-HARTER, C., & WILCOX, A. (1995). *Wellness: Choices for health and fitness.* Redwood City, CA: Benjamin/Cummings.

*DWORKIN, S. H., & GUTIERREZ, F. J. (EDS.). (1992). *Counseling gay men and lesbians: Journey to the end of the rainbow.* Alexandria, VA: American Counseling Association.

*EASWARAN, E. (1991). *Meditation.* Tomales, CA: Nilgiri Press.

EDELMAN, M. W. (1992). *The measure of our success: A letter to my children and yours.* Boston: Beacon Press.

EDLIN, G., GOLANTY, E., & BROWN, K. (2000). *Essentials for health and wellness* (2nd ed.). Sudbury, MA: Jones & Bartlett.

*ELKIND, D. (1984). *All grown up and no place to go.* Reading, MA: Addison-Wesley.

*ELLIS, A. (1988). *How to stubbornly refuse to make yourself miserable about anything—Yes, anything!* Secaucus, NJ: Lyle Stuart.

*ELLIS, A. (1999). *How to make yourself happy and remarkably less disturbable.* Atascadero, CA: Impact.

*ELLIS, A., & HARPER, R. A. (1997). *A guide to rational living* (3rd ed.). North Hollywood, CA: Wilshire.

ERIKSON, E. (1963). *Childhood and society* (2nd ed.). New York: Norton.

ERIKSON, E. (1968). *Identity: Youth and crisis.* New York: Norton.

ERIKSON, E. (1982). *The life cycle completed.* New York: Norton.

FALUDI, S. (1991). *Backlash: The undeclared war against American women.* New York: Crown.

FEUERSTEIN, G., & BODIAN, S. (EDS.). (1993). *Living yoga: A comprehensive guide for daily life.* New York: Jeremy P. Tarcher (Putnam).

FIELD, F. M. (1998). Massage therapy effects. *American Psychologist, 53*(12), 1270–1281.

FINKLEHOR, D. (1984). *Child sexual abuse: New theory and research.* New York: Free Press.

*FONTANA, D. (1997). *Teach yourself to dream: A practical guide.* San Francisco: Chronicle Books.

*FONTANA, D. (1999). *Learn to meditate: A practical guide to self-discovery and fulfillment.* San Francisco: Chronicle Books.

*FORWARD, S., & BUCK, C. S. (1988). *Betrayal of innocence: Incest and its devastation.* New York: Penguin.

FORWARD, S., & TORRES, J. (1987). *Men who hate women and the women who love them.* New York: Bantam.

*FRANKL, V. (1963). *Man's search for meaning.* New York: Washington Square Press.

*FRANKL, V. (1965). *The doctor and the soul.* New York: Bantam.

*FRANKL, V. (1969). *The will to meaning: Foundation and applications of logotherapy.* New York: New American Library.

*FRANKL, V. (1978). *The unheard cry for meaning.* New York: Bantam.

FRIEND, D. (1991). *The meaning of life.* Boston: Little, Brown, & Company.

*FROMM, E. (1956). *The art of loving.* New York: Harper & Row (Colophon). (Paperback edition, 1974)

GARDNER, H. (1983). *Frames of mind: The theory of multiple intelligences.* New York: Basic Books.

*GEORGE, M. (1998). *Learn to relax: A practical guide to easing tension and conquering stress.* San Francisco: Chronicle Books.

GERSON, K. (1987). What do women want from men? Men's influence or women's work and family choices. In M. S. Kimmel (Ed.), *Changing men: New directions in research on men and masculinity.* Newbury Park, CA: Sage.

*GIBRAN, K. (1923). *The prophet.* New York: Knopf.

*GLASSER, W. (1998). *Choice theory: A new psychology of personal freedom.* New York: Harper & Row.

GLIONNA, J. M. (1992, January 12). Dance of life. *Los Angeles Times.*

GOLDBERG, H. (1976). *The hazards of being male.* New York: New American Library.

GOLDBERG, H. (1979). *The new male: From self-destruction to self-care.* New York: New American Library (Signet).

GOLDBERG, H. (1983). *The new male–female relationship.* New York: New American Library.

*GOLDBERG, H. (1987). *The inner male: Overcoming roadblocks to intimacy.* New York: New American Library (Signet).

*GOLEMAN, D. (1995). *Emotional intelligence.* New York: Bantam.

GOOD, M., & GOOD, P. (1979). *20 most asked questions about the Amish and Mennonites.* Lancaster, PA: Good Books.

*GOTTMAN, J. M., & SILVER, N. (1999). *The seven principles for making marriage work.* New York: Three Rivers Press.

GOULD, R. L. (1978). *Transformations: Growth and change in adult life.* New York: Simon & Schuster (Touchstone).

GOULDING, M., & GOULDING, R. (1979). *Changing lives through redecision therapy.* New York: Brunner/Mazel.

GOULDING, R., & GOULDING, M. (1978). *The power is in the patient.* San Francisco: TA Press.

GRAY, J. (1992). *Men are from Mars: Women are from Venus.* New York: HarperCollins.

GUNARATANA, J. (1991). *Mindfulness in plain English.* Boston: Wisdom Publications.

HAFEN, B. Q., KARREN, K. J., FRANDSEN, K. J., & SMITH, N. L. (1996). *Mind/body health.* Boston: Allyn & Bacon.

HALES, D. (2001). *An invitation to health* (9th ed.). Belmont, CA: Wadsworth/Thomson Learning.

HAMACHEK, D. E. (1988). Evaluating self-concept and ego development within Erikson's psychosocial framework: A formulation. *Journal of Counseling and Development, 66,* 354–360.

HAMACHEK, D. (1990). Evaluating self-concept and ego status in Erikson's last three psychosocial stages. *Journal of Counseling and Development, 68*(6), 677–683.

*HANH, T. N. (1991). *Peace is every step: The path of mindfulness in everyday life.* New York: Bantam.

*HANH, T. N. (1997). *Teachings on love.* Berkeley, CA: Parallax Press.

HARLOW, H. F., & HARLOW, M. K. (1966). Learning to love. *American Scientist, 54,* 244–272.

HARRIS, A. S. (1996). *Living with paradox: An introduction to Jungian psychology.* Pacific Grove, CA: Brooks/Cole.

HARRIS, I. M. (1995). *Messages men hear: Constructing masculinities.* Bristol, PA: Taylor & Francis.

HENDRICK, S. (1995). *Close relationships: What couple therapists can learn.* Pacific Grove, CA: Brooks/Cole.

HERMAN, J. (1981). *Father-daughter incest.* Cambridge, MA: Harvard University Press.

HERR, E. L., & CRAMER, S. H. (1988). *Career guidance and counseling through the life span* (3rd ed.). Boston: Scott, Foresman.

*HIRSHMANN, J. R., & MUNTER, C. H. (1995). *When women stop hating their bodies: Freeing yourself from food and weight obsession.* New York: Fawcett (Columbine).

HIV/AIDS TREATMENT INFORMATION SERVICE. (1999). *HIV and its treatment: What you should know* [Pamphlet]. Rockville, MD: Author.

HODGE, M. (1967). *Your fear of love.* Garden City, NY: Doubleday.

HOLLAND, J. L. (1994). *Self-directed search (form R).* Odessa, FL: Psychological Assessment Resources, Inc.

HOLLAND, J. L. (1997). *Making vocational choices: A theory of vocational personalities and work environments* (3rd ed.). Odessa, FL: Psychological Assessment Resources, Inc.

HOLMES, T. H., & RAHE, R. H. (1967). The social readjustment rating scale. *Journal of Psychosomatic Research, 11,* 213–218.

*HWANG, P. O. (2000). *Other-esteem: Meaningful life in a multicultural society.* Philadelphia, PA: Accelerated Development (Taylor & Francis).

*JAMPOLSKY, G. G. (1981). *Love is letting go of fear.* New York: Bantam.

*JAMPOLSKY, G. G. (1999). *Forgiveness: The greatest healer of all.* Hillsboro, OR: Beyond Words.

JOHNSON, E. M. (1992). *What you can do to avoid AIDS.* New York: Times Books.

JONES, L. (1996). *HIV/AIDS: What to do about it.* Pacific Grove, CA: Brooks/Cole.

JORDAN, J. V., KAPLAN, A. G., MILLER, J. B., STIVER, I. P., & SURREY, J. L. (1991). *Women's growth through connection: Writings from the Stone Center.* New York: Guilford.

JOURARD, S. (1971). *The transparent self: Self-disclosure and well-being* (rev. ed.). New York: Van Nostrand Reinhold.

*JOY, W. B. (1979). *Joy's way: A map for the transformational journey.* Los Angeles, CA: Jeremy P. Tarcher.

JOY, W. B. (1990). *Avalanche: Heretical reflections on the dark and the light.* New York: Ballantine.

JUDY, R., & D'AMICO, C. (1997). *Workforce 2020: Work and workers in the 21st century.* Indianapolis, IN: Hudson Institute.

*JULIA, M. (2000). *Constructing gender: Multicultural perspectives in working with women.* Pacific Grove, CA: Brooks/Cole.

JUNG, C. G. (1961). *Memories, dreams, reflections.* New York: Vintage Books.

JUSTICE, B., & JUSTICE, R. (1979). *The broken taboo: Sex in the family.* New York: Human Sciences Press.

KABAT-ZINN, J. (1990). *Full catastrophe living.* New York: Delacorte.

*KALISH, R. A. (1985). *Death, grief, and caring relationships* (2nd ed.). Pacific Grove, CA: Brooks/Cole.

*KATZ, J. (1999). *Running to the mountain: A journey of faith and change.* New York: Villard.

*KEEN, S. (1991). *Fire in the belly: On being a man.* New York: Bantam.

*KEYS, R. (1991). *Timelock: How life got so hectic and what you can do about it.* New York: HarperCollins.

KILMARTIN, C. T. (1994). *The new masculine self.* New York: Macmillan.

KIMMEL, M. (1996). *Manhood in America: A cultural history.* New York: The Free Press.

*KING, B. M. (1999). *Human sexuality today* (3rd ed.). Upper Saddle River, NJ: Prentice-Hall.

KINOSIAN, J. (2000, May–June). Right place, write time. *Modern Maturity.*

KOBASA, S. C. (1979a). Personality and resistance to illness. *American Journal of Community Psychology, 7,* 413–423.

KOBASA, S. C. (1979b). Stressful life events, personality and health: An inquiry into hardiness. *Journal of Personality and Social Psychology, 37,* 1–11.

KOBASA, S. C. (1984, September). How much stress can you survive? *American Health,* 64–67.

KOBASA, S. C., MADDI, S. R., & KAHN, S. (1982). Hardiness and health: A prospective study. *Journal of Personality and Social Psychology, 42*(1), 168–177.

*KÜBLER-ROSS, E. (1969). *On death and dying.* New York: Macmillan.

KÜBLER-ROSS, E. (1975). *Death: The final stage of growth.* Englewood Cliffs, NJ: Prentice-Hall (Spectrum).

KÜBLER-ROSS, E. (1981). *Living with death and dying.* New York: Macmillan.

KÜBLER-ROSS, E. (1993). *AIDS: The ultimate challenge.* New York: Collier Books (Macmillan).

*LERNER, H. G. (1985). *The dance of anger: A woman's guide to changing the patterns of intimate relationships.* New York: Harper & Row (Perennial).

LERNER, H. G. (1989). *The dance of intimacy: A woman's guide to courageous acts of change in key relationships.* New York: Harper & Row (Perennial).

LERNER, H. G. (1993). *The dance of deception: Pretending and truth-telling in women's lives.* New York: Harper & Row (Perennial).

LERNER, J. (1998). *The mother dance: How children change your life.* New York: HarperCollins.

LEVANT, R. F. (1996). The new psychology of men. *Professional Psychology: Research and Practice, 27*(3), 259–265.

LEVANT, R. F., & POLLACK, W. S. (EDS.). (1995). *The new psychology of men.* New York: Basic Books.

*LEVINSON, D. J. (1978). *The seasons of man's life.* New York: Knopf.

LEVINSON, D. J., WITH LEVINSON, J. D. (1996). *The seasons of woman's life.* New York: Ballantine Books.

LEWIS, C. S. (1961). *A grief observed.* New York: Seabury.

*LINDBERGH, A. (1975). *Gift from the sea.* New York: Pantheon. (Original work published in 1955)

*LOCK, R. D. (2000a). *Job search: Career planning guide, Book 2* (4th ed.). Pacific Grove, CA: Brooks/Cole.

LOCK, R. D. (2000b). *Student activities for taking charge of your career direction and job search: Career planning guide, Book 3* (3rd ed.). Pacific Grove, CA: Brooks/Cole.

*LOCK, R. D. (2000c). *Taking charge of your career direction: Career planning guide, Book 1* (4th ed.). Pacific Grove, CA: Brooks/Cole.

*LOTT, B. (1994). *Women's lives: Themes and variations in gender learning* (2nd ed.). Pacific Grove, CA: Brooks/Cole.

MADDI, S. R., & KOBASA, C. S. (1984). *The hardy executive: Health under stress.* Homewood, IL: Dow Jones-Irwin.

MAHALIK, J. R. (1999a). Incorporating a gender role strain perspective in assessing and treating men's cognitive distortions. *Professional Psychology: Research and Practice, 30*(4), 333–340.

MAHALIK, J. R. (1999b). Interpersonal psychotherapy with men who experience gender role conflict. *Professional Psychology: Research and Practice, 30*(1), 5–13.

*MAIER, S. (1991). *God's love song.* Corvallis, OR: Postal Instant Press.

MALTZ, W. (1991). *The sexual healing journey: A guide for women and men survivors of sexual abuse.* New York: HarperCollins.

MALTZ, W., & HOLMAN, B. (1987). *Incest and sexuality: A guide to understanding and healing.* Lexington, MA: D. C. Heath.

*MARCUS, E. (1996). *Why suicide? Answers to 200 of the most frequently asked questions about suicide, attempted suicide, and assisted suicide.* San Francisco: HarperCollins.

MASLACH, C. (1982). *Burnout: The cost of caring.* Englewood Cliffs, NJ: Prentice-Hall (Spectrum).

MASLOW, A. (1968). *Toward a psychology of being.* New York: Van Nostrand Reinhold.

MASLOW, A. (1970). *Motivation and personality* (2nd ed.). New York: Harper & Row.

MASLOW, A. (1971). *The farther reaches of human nature.* New York: Viking.

*McGOLDRICK, M. (1999). Women and the family life cycle. In B. Carter & M. McGoldrick (Eds.) *The expanded family life cycle: Individual, family, and social perspectives* (3rd ed., pp. 106–123). Boston: Allyn & Bacon.

*McGOLDRICK, M., & CARTER, B. (1999). Self in context: The individual life cycle in systemic perspective. In B. Carter & M. McGoldrick (Eds.) *The expanded family life cycle: Individual, family, and social perspectives* (3rd ed., pp. 27–46). Boston: Allyn & Bacon.

MEISELMAN, K. C. (1978). *Incest: A psychological study of causes and effects with treatment recommendations.* San Francisco, CA: Jossey-Bass.

MEISELMAN, K. C. (1990). *Resolving the trauma of incest: Reintegration therapy with survivors.* San Francisco, CA: Jossey-Bass.

*MILLER, J. B., & STIVER, I. P. (1997). *The healing connection: How women form relationships in therapy and in life.* Boston: Beacon Press.

MILLER, T. (1995). *How to want what you have: Discovering the magic and grandeur of ordinary existence.* New York: Avon.

MILLER, W. R. (ED.). (1999). *Integrating spirituality into treatment: Resources for practitioners.* Washington, DC: American Psychological Association.

MILLER, W. R., & THORESEN, C. E. (1999). Spirituality and health. In W. R. Miller (Ed.), *Integrating spirituality into treatment: Resources for practitioners* (pp. 3–18). Washington, DC: American Psychological Association.

*MOORE, T. (1994). *Care of the soul: A guide for cultivating depth and sacredness in everyday life.* New York: Harper (Perennial).

MORNELL, P. (1979). *Passive men, wild women.* New York: Ballantine.

MORRIS, M. (1984). *If I should die before I wake.* New York: Dell.

MOULTON, P., & HARPER, L. (1999). *Outside looking in: When someone you love is in therapy.* Brandon, VT: Safer Society Press.

*MOUSTAKAS, C. (1961). *Loneliness.* Englewood Cliffs, NJ: Prentice-Hall (Spectrum).

NAISBITT, J., & ABURDENE, P. (1991). *Megatrends 2000.* New York: Avon.

*NAPIER, A. Y. (1990). *The fragile bond: In search of an equal, intimate and enduring marriage.* New York: Harper & Row (Perennial).

OUELLETTE, S. C. (1993). Inquiries into hardiness. In L. Goldberger & S. Breznitz (Eds.), *Handbook of stress: Theoretical and clinical aspects* (2nd ed.). New York: Free Press.

*PECK, M. S. (1978). *The road less traveled: A new psychology of love, traditional values and spiritual growth.* New York: Simon & Schuster (Touchstone).

*PECK, M. S. (1987). *The different drum: Community making and peace.* New York: Simon & Schuster (Touchstone).

PECK, M. S. (1993a). *Further along the road less traveled: The unending journey toward spiritual growth.* New York: Simon & Schuster.

PECK, M. S. (1993b). *A world waiting to be born: Civility rediscovered.* New York: Bantam.

*PERLS, F. S. (1969). *Gestalt therapy verbatim.* New York: Bantam.

PERLS, F. S. (1970). Four lectures. In J. Fagan & I. L. Shepherd (Eds.), *Gestalt therapy now* (pp. 14–38). New York: Harper & Row (Colophon).

PLECK, J. (1995). The gender role paradigm: An update. In R. Levant & W. Pollack (Eds.), *A new psychology of men.* New York: Basic Books.

*POLLACK, W. (1998). *Real boys.* New York: Henry Holt.

*RABINOWITZ, F. E., & COCHRAN, S. V. (1994). *Man alive: A primer of men's issues.* Pacific Grove, CA: Brooks/Cole.

*RAINWATER, J. (1979). *You're in charge! A guide to becoming your own therapist.* Los Angeles: Guild of Tutors Press.

RANDAHL, G. J. (1991). A typological analysis of the relations between measured vocational interests and abilities. *Journal of Vocational Behavior, 38,* 333–350.

*REAL, T. (1998). *I don't want to talk about it: Overcoming the secret legacy of male depression.* New York: Simon & Schuster (Fireside).

*RICE, P. L. (1999). *Stress and health* (3rd ed.). Pacific Grove, CA: Brooks/Cole.

RICHARDS, P. S., RECTOR, J. M., & TJELTVEIT, A. C. (1999). Values, spirituality, and psychotherapy. In W. R. Miller (Ed.), *Integrating spirituality into treatment:*

Resources for practitioners (pp. 133–160). Washington, DC: American Psychological Association.

RIDLEY, C. R. (1995). *Overcoming unintentional racism in counseling and psychotherapy.* Thousand Oaks, CA: Sage.

*RINPOCHE, S. (1994). *Meditation.* San Francisco: Harper.

ROBINSON, E. A. (1943). *The children of the night.* New York: Scribner's.

ROBINSON, F. P. (1970). *Effective study* (4th ed.). New York: Harper & Row.

ROGERS, C. R. (1961). *On becoming a person: A therapist's view of psychotherapy.* Boston: Houghton Mifflin.

ROGERS, C. R. (1980). *A way of being.* Boston: Houghton Mifflin.

ROSEN, E. J. (1999). Men in transition: The "new man." In B. Carter & M. McGoldrick (Eds.) *The expanded family life cycle: Individual, family, and social perspectives* (3rd ed., pp. 124–140). Boston: Allyn & Bacon.

RUSH, F. (1980). *The best kept secret: Sexual abuse of children.* Englewood Cliffs, NJ: Prentice-Hall.

*SCHNARCH, D. (1997). *Passionate marriage.* New York: Henry Holt & Co.

SCHNITZER, E. (1977). *Looking in.* Idyllwild, CA: Strawberry Valley Press.

SCHULTZ, D., & SCHULTZ, S. E. (2001). *Theories of personality* (7th ed.). Pacific Grove, CA: Brooks/Cole.

*SCHWARTZ, M. (1996). *Morrie: In his own words.* New York: Dell (Delta Book).

SELIGMAN, M. E. P. (1990). *Learned optimism: How to change your mind and your life.* New York: Pocket Books.

*SELIGMAN, M. E. P. (1993). *What you can change and what you can't.* New York: Fawcett (Columbine).

SHARF, R. S. (1993). *Occupational information overview.* Pacific Grove, CA: Brooks/Cole.

SHARF, R. S. (2000). *Life's choices: Problems and solutions.* Pacific Grove, CA: Brooks/Cole.

SHEEHY, G. (1976). *Passages: Predictable crises of adult life.* New York: Dutton.

SHEEHY, G. (1981). *Pathfinders.* New York: Morrow.

SHEEHY, G. (1992). *The silent passage.* New York: Random House.

*SHEEHY, G. (1995). *New passages: Mapping your life across time.* New York: Random House.

*SIEGEL, B. (1988). *Love, medicine, and miracles.* New York: Harper & Row (Perennial).

*SIEGEL, B. (1989). *Peace, love, and healing. Bodymind communication and the path to self-healing: An exploration.* New York: Harper & Row.

SIEGEL, B. (1993). *How to live between office visits: A guide to life, love, and health.* New York: HarperCollins.

*SIZER, F., & WHITNEY, E. (2000). *Nutrition: Concepts and controversies* (8th edition). Belmont, CA: Wadsworth.

STEINER, C. (1975). *Scripts people live: Transactional analysis of life scripts.* New York: Bantam.

*STONE, H., & STONE, S. (1993). *Embracing your inner critic: Turning self-criticism into a creative asset.* San Francisco: Harper.

SUMMIT ON SPIRITUALITY. (1995, December). *Counseling Today,* p. 30.

*TANNEN, D. (1987). *That's not what I meant: How conversational style makes or breaks relationships.* New York: Ballantine.

*TANNEN, D. (1991). *You just don't understand: Women and men in conversation.* New York: Ballantine.

*TAVRIS, C. (1989). *Anger: The misunderstood emotion.* New York: Simon & Schuster (Touchstone).

*TAVRIS, C. (1992). *The mismeasure of women.* New York: Simon & Schuster (Touchstone).

*TERKEL, S. (1975). *Working.* New York: Avon.

TRACY, V. M. (1993). *The impact of childhood sexual abuse on women's sexuality.* Unpublished doctoral dissertation. La Jolla University: San Diego, CA.

*TRAVIS, J. W., & RYAN, R. S. (1994). *Wellness workbook* (3rd ed.). Berkeley, CA: Ten Speed Press.

TUTU, D. M. (1999). *No future without forgiveness.* New York: Doubleday.

U.S. DEPARTMENT OF HEALTH AND HUMAN SERVICES. (1987, Spring). *Facts about AIDS* [Pamphlet]. Washington, DC: U.S. Government Printing Office.

U.S. DEPARTMENT OF HEALTH AND HUMAN SERVICES. (1988a). *Understanding AIDS* [Pamphlet]. Washington, DC: U.S. Government Printing Office.

U.S. DEPARTMENT OF HEALTH AND HUMAN SERVICES. (1988b). *Women, sex, and AIDS* [Pamphlet]. Washington, DC: U.S. Government Printing Office.

U.S. DEPARTMENT OF HEALTH AND HUMAN SERVICES. (1989). *Many teens are saying no* [Pamphlet]. Washington, DC: U.S. Government Printing Office.

U.S. DEPARTMENT OF HEALTH AND HUMAN SERVICES. (1991a). *AIDS and you* [Pamphlet]. Washington, DC: U.S. Government Printing Office.

U.S. DEPARTMENT OF HEALTH AND HUMAN SERVICES. (1991b). *Caring for someone with AIDS* [Pamphlet]. Washington, DC: U.S. Government Printing Office.

U.S. DEPARTMENT OF HEALTH AND HUMAN SERVICES. (1991c). *HIV infection and AIDS: Are you at risk?* [Pamphlet]. Washington, DC: U.S. Government Printing Office.

U.S. DEPARTMENT OF HEALTH AND HUMAN SERVICES. (1991d). *How you won't get AIDS* [Pamphlet]. Washington, DC: U.S. Government Printing Office.

U.S. DEPARTMENT OF HEALTH AND HUMAN SERVICES. (1991e). *Voluntary HIV counseling and testing: Facts, issues, and answers* [Pamphlet]. Washington, DC: U.S. Government Printing Office.

U.S. DEPARTMENT OF HEALTH AND HUMAN SERVICES. (1999). *Integrating cultural, observational, and epidemiological approaches in the prevention of drug abuse and*

HIV/AIDS. Washington, DC: U.S. Government Printing Office.

U.S. DEPARTMENT OF LABOR. (1979). *Guide for occupational exploration*. Washington, DC: U.S. Government Printing Office.

U.S. DEPARTMENT OF LABOR. (1991). *Dictionary of occupational titles* (4th ed., revised). Washington, DC: U.S. Government Printing Office.

U.S. DEPARTMENT OF LABOR. (1998). *Occupational outlook handbook, 1998–1999*. Washington, DC: U.S. Government Printing Office.

VANDERBILT, H. (1992, February). Incest: A four-part chilling report. *Lear's, 4*(12), 49–77.

*VANZANT, I. (1998). *One day my soul just opened up*. New York: Simon & Schuster (Fireside).

VERGEER, G. E. (1995). Therapeutic applications of humor. *Directions in Mental Health Counseling, 5*(3), 4–11.

*VONTRESS, C. E., JOHNSON, J. A., & EPP, L. R. (1999). *Cross-cultural counseling: A casebook*. Alexandria, VA: American Counseling Association.

*WEBB, D. (1996). *Divorce and separation recovery*. Portsmouth, NH: Randall.

*WEBB, D. (2000). *50 ways to love your leaver: Getting on with your life after the breakup*. Atascadero, CA: Impact.

*WEENOLSEN, P. (1996). *The art of dying: How to leave this world with dignity and grace, at peace with yourself and your loved ones*. New York: St. Martin's Press.

*WEIL, A. (2000). *Eating well for optimum health: The essential guide to food, diet, and nutrition*. New York: Knopf.

*WEITEN, W., & LLOYD, M. A. (2000). *Psychology applied to modern life: Adjustment at the turn of the century* (6th ed.). Belmont, CA: Wadsworth.

*WILLIAMS, B., & KNIGHT, S. M. (1994). *Healthy for life: Wellness and the art of living*. Pacific Grove, CA: Brooks/Cole.

*WILLIAMS, C. (1992). *No hiding place: Empowerment and recovery for our troubled communities*. San Francisco: Harper.

WITKIN, G. (1994). *The male stress syndrome: How to survive stress in the '90s* (2nd ed.). New York: Newmarket.

WYLIE, M. S. (2000). Soul therapy. *Family Therapy Networker, 24*(1), 26–37, 60–61.

*YALOM, I. D. (1980). *Existential psychotherapy*. New York: Basic Books.

*ZIMBARDO, P. G. (1987). *Shyness*. New York: Jove.

ZIMBARDO, P. G. (1994). *Shyness*. Reading, MA: Addison-Wesley.

Index